MARCEL PROUST
A BIOGRAPHY

MARCEL PROUST

A BIOGRAPHY
Volume One

BY
GEORGE D. PAINTER

Le tombeau d'Albertine est près de mon berceau
MARCELINE DESBORDES-VALMORE

RANDOM HOUSE
NEW YORK

Library of Congress Cataloging in Publication Data
Painter, George Duncan, 1914-
Marcel Proust: a biography
Reprint of the ed. published by Chatto & Windus, London.
1. Proust, Marcel, 1871-1922—Biography.
2. Novelists, French—20th century—Biography.
PQ2631.R63Z78958 1978   843'.9'12 [B]   77-090263
ISBN 0-394-50040-7 (v. 1)
ISBN 0-394-50041-5 (v. 2)

Manufactured in the United States of America

2 3 4 5 6 7 8 9   9 8 7 6 5 4 3 2   2 4 6 8 9 7 5 3

First Edition

For

HENRY REED

CONTENTS

ACKNOWLEDGMENT

The author and publishers wish to express their grateful appreciation to the owners of copyright in the illustrations, in particular to Monsieur Pierre Cailler of Geneva, publisher of *Marcel Proust. Documents iconographiques*, by Georges Cattaui, from which nos. 2, 5-7, 9-12, 14, 16 and 18 are taken, and to Monsieur P. Gagey of Illiers for nos. 3-4 from his *Illiers, le Combray de Marcel Proust.*

LIST OF PLATES

PREFACE

BELIEVING that the published sources are now adequate in quantity and quality, but that the subject has never yet been treated with anything approaching scholarly method, I have endeavoured to write a definitive biography of Proust: a complete, exact and detailed narrative of his life, that is, based on every known or discoverable primary source, and on primary sources only. The mass of material is vast, complex and scattered. I have tried to winnow it, to extract all that is relevant, to place it in its organic and significant order, to preserve the main thread of the story through necessary digressions, and to serve the needs of both the general reader and the Proustian scholar. There seems to be no good reason why an interesting subject should be made boring in the name of scholarship, or why the most scrupulous accuracy should not be achievable without draining the life-blood from a living theme. Fortunately the quality of life was already abundant in the sources. I have invented nothing whatever; and even when I give the words of a conversation, or describe the state of the weather or a facial expression at a particular moment, I do so from evidence that seems reliable. I think I may claim that something like nine-tenths of the narrative here given is new to Proustian biography, or conversely that previous biographers have used only about one-tenth of the discoverable sources.

This is not intended as a controversial work: my purpose is to discover facts and elicit their meaning, and the larger part of this book is devoted to the plain narrative of Proust's life. But I must explain that my uncustomary approach to *A la Recherche du Temps Perdu*, my belief that Proust's novel cannot be fully understood without a knowledge of his life, is necessitated by the facts, and is not due to mere ignorance of the accepted clichés. It has become one of the dogmas of Proustian criticism that his novel can and must be treated as a closed system, containing in itself all the elements necessary for its understanding. To take two examples from many dozens, Monsieur X is praised for having 'emptied his mind'—did he have to empty it of so very much?— 'of all Proustian matter extraneous to the novel which he has set himself to examine'; "I do not propose," says Professor Y, "in this study, which is an attempt to interpret Proust's great novel, to discuss the external facts of his life.'' But they like to have it both ways. They use, and so does Professor Z, unproven biographical axioms for critical purposes: they argue (again to take one instance of many) from the supposed total homosexuality of the author, that the women loved by the Narrator are disguises of men loved by Proust, that they must therefore be psychologically unconvincing, and that Proust has falsified the whole drama of human love. I have not tried to deny Proust's homosexuality—on the contrary, I shall give the first full account of it based on evidence. But readers who have felt all along that Proust's picture of heterosexual love is valid and founded on personal experience will be glad to find their instinct justified. Here, then, is one among very many unrealised biographical facts about Proust the critical bearing of which is fundamental and indispensable. In general, however, there is no aspect of Proust or his work—his style, philosophy, character, morality, his attitude to music, painting, Ruskin, snobism and so on—which can be studied without an accurate and detailed knowledge of his life, or which has so far escaped distortion for lack of such knowledge.

This first volume is the place for analysis of the autobiographical material used by Proust in his novel: a discussion of his methods of synthesis will appear in the second volume, when the period at which he wrote it is reached. But it may be appropriate here to remark in advance on some of the further ways in which Proust's biography is significant for our understanding of *A la Recherche*. I hope those who judge this aspect of my work will consider whether the facts are true, rather than whether the critical approach demanded by the facts happens to be fashionable at the present moment.

I shall show that it is possible to identify and reconstruct from ample evidence the sources in Proust's real life for all major, and many minor characters, events and places in his novel. By discovering which aspects of his originals he chose or rejected, how he combined many models into each new figure, and most of all how he altered material reality to make it conform more closely to symbolic reality, we can observe the workings of his imagination at the very moment of creation. The 'closed system' Proustians have been egoistically contented to know of Proust's

novel only what it means to themselves. It is surely relevant to
learn what the novel meant to the author, to understand the
special significance which, because they were part of his life and
being, every character and episode had for Proust and still retains
in its substance. What do they know of *A la Recherche* who only
A la Recherche know?

A still more important consequence follows from the study of
Proust's novel in the light of his biography. *A la Recherche* turns
out to be not only based entirely on his own experiences: it is
intended to be the symbolic story of his life, and occupies a place
unique among great novels in that it is not, properly speaking, a
fiction, but a creative autobiography. Proust believed, justifiably,
that his life had the shape and meaning of a great work of art: it
was his task to select, telescope and transmute the facts so that
their universal significance should be revealed; and this revelation
of the relationship between his own life and his unborn novel is
one of the chief meanings of Time Regained. But though he
invented nothing, he altered everything. His places and people are
composite in space and time, constructed from various sources
and from widely separate periods of his life. His purpose in so
doing was not to falsify reality, but, on the contrary, to induce it
to reveal the truths it so successfully hides in this world. Behind
the diversity of the originals is an underlying unity, the quality
which, he felt, they had in common, the Platonic ideal of which
they were the obscure earthly symbols. He fused each group of
particular cases into a complex, universal whole, and so dis-
engaged the truth about the poetry of places, or love and jealousy,
or the nature of duchesses, and, most of all, the meaning of the
mystery of his own life. In my belief the facts demonstrated in the
present biography compel us to take an entirely new view of
Proust's novel. "A man's life of any worth is a continual allegory,"
said Keats: *A la Recherche* is the allegory of Proust's life, a work
not of fiction but of imagination interpreting reality.

It would be absurd to suppose that Proust's greatness is in any
degree lessened by his reliance on reality. His work is an illustration of Wordsworth's distinction between Fancy and Imagination
—between the art which invents what has never existed and the
art which discovers the inner meanings of what exists. We may
or may not feel that Imagination is superior to Fancy; but we
cannot possibly maintain that it is inferior. Proust was perhaps

deficient in or indifferent to Fancy; but he was among the greatest masters of Imagination. It would be equally absurd to pretend that *A la Recherche* is a mere *roman à clef*—a novel, that is, which is a literal narrative of real events in which only the names are changed. As Proust himself explained to a friend, "there are no keys to the people in my novel; or rather, there are eight or ten keys to each character".

I do not apologise for the abundance of detail in this biography, not only because it is the function of a definitive biography to be complete, but because it was from the mass of such detail that Proust's novel was created. Dates of day, month and year (chronology, too, has to be regained) are given for every datable incident. I have tried to bring his friends and acquaintances to life as they were when he knew them, by describing their appearance, characters and subsequent careers, and by telling the social anecdotes which he revelled in and used in his novel. Sometimes it has been possible to discuss the synthesis of a Proustian character in one place, but usually the ingredients can only be mentioned as they occur in the chronological course of his life: collective references will be found, however, in the Index. Here, too, I have aimed at completeness: if Bergotte or Saint-Loup, for instance, have half a dozen or more originals, each contributing something of his own, I hope the reader would not wish me to conceal it. Often even the sources of the proper names are important, because they had some special significance in Proust's life, as indeed they have in his novel, of which two major sections are called Names of Places and Names of People. My enquiries into the sexual inversion, or Jewish, plebeian or noble birth of persons whom Proust knew, are necessitated by the nature of the case, and do not correspond to any prejudices or predilections on my own part.

It has been necessary to interrupt the main narrative with four long digressions: on the topography of Illiers, on Proust's hosts, hostesses and acquaintances in society, on the Dreyfus Affair, and on Proust's study of Ruskin; but these are subjects of funda-mental importance in his life and novel, they could be treated in no other way, and I believe the digressions will be found not un-interesting in themselves. Sometimes the evidence on essential matters is unusually complex and intractable: my discussions of the order of composition and relationship to Proust's life of the stories in *Les Plaisirs et les Jours* and *Jean Santeuil,* and of a few points elsewhere, could not be made easy reading. But these passages are only a few pages of the whole, I have done my best to make them lucid and concise, and I can only ask the reader to take the occasional rough with the smooth.

To avoid needless repetition—and also, I confess, to avoid laying all my cards on the table before the game is finished—I have postponed giving a full bibliography of the sources used, together with detailed references for each statement, till the second and final volume, which will appear in six years' time. Occasionally, however, and usually in order to correct some predecessor's misstatement, I have given my sources in a foot-note. I share the general reader's dislike of footnotes; but some-times I have reluctantly relegated to the bottom of the page some discussion of a point of detail which would have interrupted the main narrative; and it seemed imperative to give references (to the standard *Pléïade* edition of the original text in three volumes) on each occasion when Proust introduced material from his life in particular passages of his novel. All translations from the French are my own.

I had already made my researches into the dating of Proust's letters and the originals of his characters before the appearance of those two monumental works, Professor Philip Kolb's *La Correspondance de Marcel Proust* (1949) and Antoine Adam's *Le Roman de Proust et le problème des clefs* (*Revue des Sciences humaines,* jan.-mars 1952, pp. 49-90). I have added to, re-examined and sometimes differed from their conclusions; but my debt to them, though limited, is great, and I acknowledge it with admiration and gratitude. In Chapters 2 and 3, along with other sources including my own visit to Illiers in September 1950, I have consulted P. L. Larcher's exquisite *Le Parfum de Combray* (1945). My chapter on Ruskin is independent of Jean Autret's *L'Influence de Ruskin sur la vie, les idées et l'œuvre de Marcel Proust* (1955), but I have made some use of his views on the extent of Proust's first-hand knowledge of Ruskin, Turner and Giotto. In Chapter 12 I have had the benefit of Professor Kolb's description of the original manuscript of *Jean Santeuil,* thanks to the kindness of Mr Miron Grindea, editor of *Adam,* who showed me the advance proofs of Professor Kolb's article in the special Proust number of his magazine.

I have dedicated this first volume to Henry Reed, my friend of more than thirty years, with whom I first read Proust in our schooldays. I have also remembered, after a gulf of twenty-two years, R. B. and her far-reaching question to me: "Who was Swann?"

GEORGE D. PAINTER

London,
May, 1959

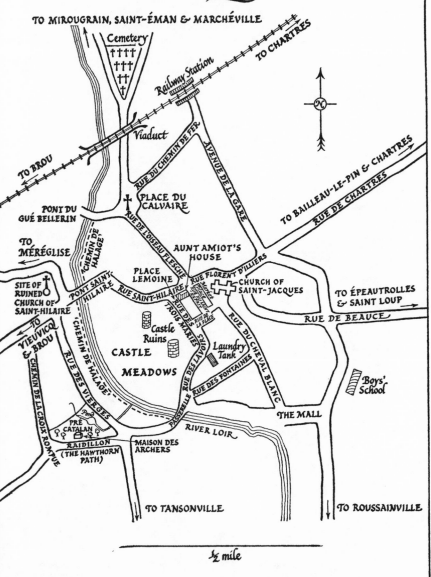

Plan of Illiers

TO MIROUGRAIN, SAINT-ÉMAN & MARCHÉVILLE

Cemetery

Railway Station

TO CHARTRES

N

Viaduct

TO BROU

RUE DU CHEMIN DE FER

AVENUE DE LA GARE

TO BAILLEAU-LE-PIN & CHARTRES

RUE DE CHARTRES

PONT DU GUÉ BELLERIN

PLACE DU CALVAIRE

CHEMIN DE HALAGE

RUE DE L'OISEAU FLESCHE

TO MÉRÉGLISE

AUNT AMIOT'S HOUSE

PLACE LEMOINE

RUE FLORENT D'ILLIERS

CHURCH OF SAINT-JACQUES

TO ÉPEAUTROLLES & SAINT LOUP

SITE OF RUINED CHURCH OF SAINT-HILAIRE

PONT SAINT-HILAIRE

RUE SAINT-HILAIRE

RUE DES TROIS MARIES

RUE DE LA PLACE

RUE DE BEAUCE

TO VIEUVICQ & BROU

CHEMIN DE HALAGE

Castle Ruins

CASTLE MEADOWS

RUE DES LAVOIRS

Laundry Tank

RUE DU CHEVAL BLANC

Boys' School

RUE DES VIERGES

CHEMIN DE LA CROIX ROMPUE

PASSERELLE

RUE DES FONTAINES

THE MALL

Pont

PRÉ CATALAN

RAIDILLON (THE HAWTHORN PATH)

MAISON DES ARCHERS

RIVER LOIR

TO TANSONVILLE

TO ROUSSAINVILLE

½ mile

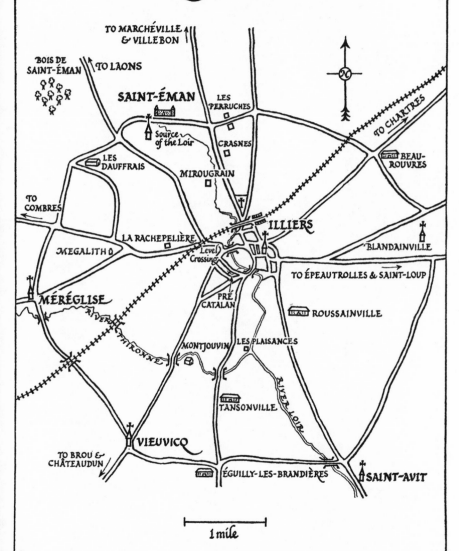

The Country Round Illiers

TO MARCHÉVILLE & VILLEBON

BOIS DE SAINT-ÉMAN

TO LAONS

SAINT-ÉMAN

LES PERRUCHES

TO CHARTRES

Source of the Loir

CRASNES

LES DAUFFRAIS

BEAU-ROUVRES

MIROUGRAIN

TO COMBRES

LA RACHEPELIÈRE

ILLIERS

MEGALITH

Level Crossing

BLANDAINVILLE

MÉRÉGLISE

PRÉ CATALAN

TO ÉPEAUTROLLES & SAINT-LOUP

RIVER THIRONNE

MONTJOUVIN

LES PLAISANCES

ROUSSAINVILLE

RIVER LOIR

TANSONVILLE

VIEUVICQ

TO BROU & CHÂTEAUDUN

ÉGUILLY-LES-BRANDIÈRES

SAINT-AVIT

1 mile

Chapter 1

THE GARDEN OF AUTEUIL

THE doorway of the house where Louis Proust was born, in the Rue du Cheval Blanc at Illiers, is a single stone arch of exactly the same form as the double arch in the romanesque side-porch of the nearby church. It would be wrong to infer that there is something ecclesiastical about the houses of the people of Illiers; the truth is rather that there is something domestic about the church of Saint-Jacques. But the Prousts tended to have a vague connection with the church. When Louis Proust married Virginie Torcheux, about 1827, he moved to 11 Place du Marché, opposite Saint-Jacques, and sold spices, thread, sugar, wooden shoes and tallow-candles to his fellow-citizens; but in the room behind the shop he made wax-candles for all the worshippers in the parish, and dreamed of the day when his son would be a priest. His first child was a girl, Élisabeth, born 16 August 1828. His son Adrien was born on 18 March 1834, and in due course won a scholarship to the high school at Chartres, where he took his baccalaureate in letters and science. Towards the end of his life Adrien Proust made light of the honours with which his profession and his country had loaded him, and boasted of a distinction which somehow meant far more: "My name is in the roll of honour of the Collège de Chartres," he said. But, like his son Marcel after him, he could not fulfil his father's ambition; he decided that his vocation for the priesthood was insufficient and, without losing his Catholic faith, became a convert to science. In July 1853, two years before the death of Louis Proust, he passed the necessary certificate of aptitude for physical sciences and went to Paris to become a doctor. No Proust had ever left Illiers before him; it was a turning-point in a chain of events which led, deviously and inevitably, to *A la Recherche du Temps Perdu*.

The heroic age of French medicine was just beginning; the learned but hitherto Molièresque profession of healing was being transformed into an experimental, and therefore an exact, science, and the conquest of disease and the exploration of the mind already seemed possible. Among Adrien Proust's near contemporaries were men great in their day but now forgotten—Chauffard, Parrot, Vulpian—and others who are still remembered: Potain,[1] whom even Mme Verdurin thought second only to Dr Cottard as a diagnostician, and Charcot, the psychiatrist who taught Freud. One of his fellow-students sounds oddly familiar, and need only be spelt with a double 't' to become recognisable: his name was Cotard.

Adrien Proust took his doctorate of medicine on 29 December 1862 with a thesis on 'idiopathic pneumothorax'. He became *chef de clinique* at the Charité hospital in 1863, and on 14 March 1866 was admitted with special mention in the *concours d'agrégation*, the state examination for licence to teach in university schools of medicine. In the same year the third of the four great cholera epidemics of the nineteenth century reached France. Even in the largest and worst-hit towns only twenty in every thousand fell ill; but of every thousand sufferers, five hundred died. Dr Proust distinguished himself by his untiring devotion to duty and disregard of danger, and saw his patients die of a disease which could not be cured or prevented in the individual. In the career of every great specialist there is a moment of inspiration, inextricably compounded of desire to save the world and of personal ambition, in which his life-work is revealed to him. Dr Proust decided to prevent cholera in the mass by keeping it out of Europe; he took over from his masters Tardieu and Fauvel the principle of the *cordon sanitaire*, and invented the slogans which would make it intelligible and interesting to politicians. "The question of international hygiene passes and surpasses political frontiers," he announced, and "Egypt is Europe's barrier against cholera": M. de Norpois himself could not have put it more aptly. In 1869 the Minister of Agriculture and Commerce sent him to Persia, via St Petersburg and Astrakhan, to discover the routes by which previous epidemics had entered Russia. He travelled on horseback through appalling heat, and was received with special regard at Teheran by the Shah, who presented him with a magnificent Persian carpet, and by the Grand Vizier Ali Pasha at Constantinople. In August 1870, a few days before the disaster of Sedan, he received the red ribbon of the Légion d'Honneur from the

[1] *Pléiade*, I, 188

Empress Eugénie, and on 3 September, the day before the fall of the Second Empire, he married Jeanne Weil.

Mlle Weil was a beautiful and intelligent Jewess, aged twenty-one, fifteen years younger than Dr Proust. Her father, Nathé Weil, then aged fifty-four, was a wealthy stockbroker, whose family originally came from Metz in Lorraine; he became a surly old gentleman with a kind heart, on whom his grandson was to model M. Sandré in *Jean Santeuil*. Her mother, whose maiden name was Adèle Berncastel, then aged forty-five, was as gentle and self-sacrificing as Nathé Weil was independent and un-gracious; next only to abnegation and her family Mme Nathé loved music and literature, especially the literature of the *grand siècle*, and above all the letters of Mme de Sévigné, in whom she recognised a motherly love like her own for her daughter. She handed on all her own qualities to Jeanne, including perhaps a preference for a husband who would be her own opposite, with whom her wifely devotion and her love of art would be safe, precisely because he had no special need for them. So Dr Proust was to advance towards fame in his profession, secured from the rear by his wife's loving admiration and her perfect management of his home: it was to be, for both, an extremely happy marriage.

Within a few weeks of her wedding Mme Proust was pregnant, and the times were hard for a young expectant mother. The victorious German army began the siege of Paris on 19 September, and for more than four months the city was cut off from the outside world. Meat, bread, fruit and milk became scarce, and though her parents were rich and her husband a doctor, it is unlikely that Mme Proust had the food she needed for herself and her unborn child. In the country round Illiers the Germans were campaigning against the Army of the Loire, and Dr Proust had no news of his widowed mother. In October they sacked Châteaudun, fifteen miles to the south, and occupied Chartres, fifteen miles to the north-east. Towards the end of December he sent a letter by balloon-post to a friend at Tours, a wholesale draper named Esnault: 'Has she left Illiers? Is she with you? Is she well? Such are the questions which I beg you to answer by pigeon-post and to add all the information you may have about any of my family.' From the address of this letter it seems that he and his wife were living at 8 Rue Roy, a little street running into the Boulevard Haussmann. They were never to move more than a few hundred yards from this point, and when nearly fifty years later their son Marcel was at last uprooted from the district sacred to his parents, it was the death of him.

After the hungry winter of the siege came the German entry into Paris and the troubled spring of the Commune. In May the Government forces of Citizen Thiers returned to the city, the 'Bloody Week' of street-fighting followed, and one morning as Dr Proust was walking to his work at the Charité he was narrowly missed by a stray bullet. His young wife was so over-come by the shock that it was thought advisable for them to move to the house of her uncle Louis Weil at 96 Rue La Fontaine, Auteuil, and here on 10 July 1871 Marcel Proust was born.

At first he was thought too weak to live, and long afterwards he liked to attribute his lifelong ill-health to his mother's priva-tions and anxiety during the siege and the Commune. Perhaps, from the beginning, she agreed with him, and felt responsible for history's injury to her unborn child; for she tried to redeem her guilt with exaggerated care. He grew to believe, resentfully, that she loved him best when he was ill and he tried to win her love by being ill. Meanwhile, however, he was soon well enough to enter the Catholic Church of his father. Mme Proust kept her Jewish faith out of devotion to her parents; but Marcel was duly christened at Saint-Louis d'Antin, the local church of their home in Paris. In after-life he would point with some pride to the certificate of his christening, and to the later certificate of confirm-ation, signed by the Archbishop of Paris himself. Yet he was always conscious of belonging, thanks to his mother, to two great proscribed nations, who once lived in neighbouring regions, till the wrath of God scattered them over the face of the earth; for her blood made him a tribesman of Abraham, her over-anxious love a native of the Cities of the Plain.

Their Paris home for nearly thirty years was a large apartment at 9 Boulevard Malesherbes. The boulevard is lined with chestnut-trees and commands a pleasant vista from the rear of the Madeleine to the domed church of Saint-Augustin, built the year before Proust's birth. 'One of the ugliest districts in Paris,' he called it in *Du Côté de chez Swann*; but even so, the 'violet belfry' of Saint-Augustin seen over the rooftops seemed to him 'to give this view of Paris the character of certain views of Rome by Piranesi'.[1] On

---

[1] *Pléiade*, I, 66

the ground floor was the tailor's shop of M. Eppler; next door was another, that of Sandt and Laborde (it was a family joke to call them 'Sandford and Merton'); and one of these no doubt suggested Jupien's shop in the lodger's wing of the Duchesse de Guermantes's mansion. The handsome double doors remain as they were in the 1870s, surmounted by a carved stone shield, framed in oak-leaves and bearing the number Nine. The house has seven storeys, each with its iron balustrade running the whole length of the façade. From the second-floor balcony Marcel was to watch the fitful appearances of the sunlight, augury of the afternoon's weather which would release him, if all went well, to play with the original of Gilberte Swann in the Champs-Élysées. On the opposite corner the Morriss column still stands, to which every morning he would run to study the theatre-bills, announcing 'the glittering white plume of *The Queen's Diamond Necklace* or the smooth, mysterious satin of *The Black Domino*'.[1] But these memories come from the 1880s; the important events of the '70s took place elsewhere, and only four incidents of this decade belong to 9 Boulevard Malesherbes.

The first was the birth on 24 May 1873, when Marcel was not yet two years old, of his brother Robert. Robert took after his father: he retained all through his life Dr Proust's narrow mouth, with the thick, pursed, kindly, Holbeinesque lips, which were to be seen only by rare glimpses beneath Marcel's moustache. The son who pleases and obeys is loved, no doubt, neither more nor less than the son who rouses anxiety and admiration; Robert was the son who obeyed. He became almost as eminent a surgeon as his father had been a physician and hygienist; he, too, was to be a Professor in the Faculty of Medicine and belong to the Légion d'Honneur. But perhaps one may see in Marcel as well as in Robert something of the surgeon who dissects in order to heal. Robert was to write a textbook on *The Surgery of the Female Genital Organs*; and it is a subject not entirely foreign to the Marcel who described the naked Albertine asleep. The relationship between the brothers was always affectionate, never intimate. There is an early photograph of Marcel, aged six, and Robert, aged four; Marcel, with bobbed hair in a fringe and a timid smile, wears a grey serge frock buttoning down the front, and lays his

[1] I, 73

arm protectively round his brother's neck; and Robert, in a frilly
white skirt, nestles against Marcel with a self-confident expression.
Witnesses have recorded that Marcel kept his protective attitude
towards Robert until the end of his life: 'it made one realise the
full force of the term "brotherly love",' wrote Lucien Daudet.
Marcel had no good reason for jealousy; his mother, though no
doubt she loved them both equally, knew that he needed her love
more than the easy-going Robert; Marcel was always her 'little
wolf', *mon petit loup*, and Robert was only *mon autre loup*. But
the shock of his brother's birth may have helped to make Marcel's
love for his mother so tyrannical and exorbitant; and he managed
to draw her into a kind of amiable conspiracy against his rival. In
the letters between Marcel and his mother Robert is a kind of
private joke: he has nicknames, such as Dick, or His Majesty, and
needs to be saved from the consequences of his rashness or sloth.
If anyone was jealous, Marcel decided, it must be Robert. In an
early draft of his novel he introduced Robert in his high chair,
complaining, with a piercing scream, that "Marcel has had more
chocolate blancmange than me!"[1] In *A la Recherche*, although no
doubt his reasons were mainly aesthetic, he preferred to abolish
Robert entirely.

The other three incidents may seem trivial, but are somehow
characteristic, and two were thought sufficiently important by
Proust to be introduced into *Jean Santeuil*. One New Year's Day
Marcel and Robert were enlisted to help in the distribution of New
Year gifts—a ceremony held particularly sacred in the Proust
family, and often alluded to in *A la Recherche*.[2] Mme Proust gave
Marcel a five-franc piece to take to her cousin's cook, but on the
way he saw a little bootblack, scarcely older than himself, looking
so cold and unhappy that he could not resist giving him the five-
franc piece. Mme Proust was furious, and punished him: he still
remembered the incident vividly forty years later, when he told
it to his housekeeper Céleste. All through his life he was to invite
the anger of his parents—even after they were dead—by the
extravagance of his generosity, and to purchase with pity and
money the love of the poor and unhappy. Then again, there was a
period in his early childhood when he was fascinated by the moon,
and begged to be given books on astronomy for his presents. One
winter afternoon, when Mme Proust was entertaining her friends

[1] *Contre Sainte-Beuve*, 296   [2] E.g. I, 52, 77, 486

in the drawing-room, she asked him to show them his 'books about the moon'. Marcel returned and proudly displayed not only the astronomy books, but also a little illustrated grammar, in which there was a picture of the moon with a nose and a funny face; for it seemed to him that this too, quite as much as the others, was 'a book about the moon'.[1] He was at the age—which he was so fortunate as never to outgrow—'when the world has not yet become something completely known and real, when it seems that an unfamiliar place in the real world might well give access to the world of the unreal'. One day his mother took him with her to the Deligny cold baths near the Pont de la Concorde; he was left in the waiting-room while she put on her bathing-costume, and then he was admitted to 'a vast liquid cavern', where the other bathing ladies and their cubicles receded to a seemingly endless distance. He felt he had come to the waters under the earth, 'the entrance to the polar seas'; and when his mother walked towards him, wearing a streaming rubber cap, and throwing kisses, he 'would not have been surprised to hear that he was the son of a water-goddess'.[2]

But the important events of the 1870s did not belong to the too familiar 'home' at 9 Boulevard Malesherbes. That island of bourgeois furniture in the desert of grey houses, however beloved, was too much the scene of a normal state of life to become a Paradise, which is a state of exception. Proust's Edens were the gardens of Auteuil and Illiers, which later became the gardens of Combray. He saw them only at holiday-times, and afterwards forfeited them eternally through the original sin of asthma; but if he had never lost them, they would never have become Paradise.

Auteuil, then as now, was a residential suburb between the western borders of Paris and the Bois de Boulogne; but then it still retained something of the country hamlet, now lost for ever, in which Molière and Boileau had their villas. In the months before Mme Proust moved there to have her baby, Auteuil had been twice bombarded, first by the Prussians, next, far more terribly, by the Government army from Versailles. On 24 May 1871 Edmond de Goncourt crossed Paris, still under shell-fire, with his faithful servant Pélagie, to find his house in the Boulevard Montmorency riddled with bullets, the doors on the second

---

[1] *Jean Santeuil*, vol. 1, 196   [2] *Jean Santeuil*, vol. 1, 193-4.
The incident is also used in *Albertine Disparue* (*Pléiade*, III, 653).

floor blown to splinters by 'quite a little shell, one of the last to
be fired', a crater in the middle of his lawn 'in which one could
bury an elephant'. That night he watched, through the shattered
branches of his garden trees, 'Paris in flames, looking like a
Neapolitan gouache, on a sheet of black paper, of Vesuvius in
eruption'. It was no doubt at this very time, when Paris was
dangerous and Auteuil for the first time safe, that Mme Proust
moved to the green suburban haven of 96 Rue La Fontaine.

It was a large house, 'about as tasteless as it possibly could be',
in a big garden with formal gravel paths and flower-beds, and
lawns, and trees which had grown too tall for the garden, and an
ill-omened fountain, into whose shallow waters Marcel once fell
when he was a child. One hot summer day in the early 1890s his
second-cousin Valentine Thomson came to tea in the charge of
her Aunt Laure.[1] Valentine was the daughter of Mme Proust's
cousin Henriette Peigné-Crémieux, who married the politician
Gaston Thomson, the Navy Minister of 1905-08; she was then a
little girl and Marcel was in his early twenties. Marcel did the
honours of the garden with a solemn and sacramental air: the
flower-beds and the over-tall trees, both bad for his asthma, most
of all the dreadful fountain, had become part of the mythology of
his life. As he spoke of the fountain, Mme Proust joined in, and
so did Aunt Laure; their faces, the amused child noticed, were
serious, almost awed; for if the accident of the fountain had been
important when it happened, it was surely still more important
now, when the infant Marcel was submerged not only in its
sinister waters, but in fifteen years of family history. Then he took
the little girl indoors, and the ceremony proceeded. Each piece
of 'grim, frumpy, solid furniture, smothered with frills of silk,
dark and uninviting like a roomful of ancient, overdressed maiden
aunts', had to be shown and explained, 'as if he were introducing
me to dear friends'. So he was: he searched through life in vain
for friends who would match the unending loyalty, the instant
comprehension of his great-uncle's sideboards.

During the springs and summers of twenty-five years, whenever the family needed a holiday and Dr Proust was unable to
leave Paris, they would move to Auteuil. Every morning the
Doctor took the Auteuil-Madeleine omnibus, just opposite the

[1] Aunt Laure was Mme Proust's distant cousin Mme Charles Nathan, née
Laure Rodrigues-Ely. See Proust, Mme, 36, note 2, 221.

house, and in less than an hour would be at his work in the Hôtel-Dieu or the Charité hospital. He was ritually preceded by his man-servant, running with dramatic gestures to stop the bus, pleading with the driver to be patient, while behind him his master waved a last au revoir to the children. These morning departures became a family joke, a traditional story useful for the entertainment of visitors. As for arriving, 'I can't express the pleasure I felt,' Proust wrote long afterwards, 'when after walking down the Rue La Fontaine in the hot sun and the scent of the lime-trees, I went upstairs to my room. There, in the twilight, coloured mother-of-pearl by the glazed reflection of the Empire-blue satin curtains (very inappropriate to their rural surroundings), the unctuous air of the warm morning had just finished varnishing and isolating the honest smells of the soap and the wardrobe with its mirror-glass doors.' In the pantry there was cider, 'which we drank from tumblers whose glass was so thick that one felt tempted to bite them'. And in the dining-room 'the air was transparent and congealed, like an immaterial agate veined with the scent of the cherries already piled high in the fruit dishes'. He was fascinated by the little cut-glass prisms on which the knives and forks were propped—'an exceedingly vulgar middle-class fashion, but I liked it. Their iridescence did more than add mystery to the odour of gruyère cheese and apricots. In the half light of the dining-room these rainbow knife-rests threw peacock-feather patterns on the walls, which seemed to me as miraculous as the stained-glass windows in Rheims Cathedral.'[1]

In that room with the Empire-blue curtains, and the garden with the over-tall chestnuts, when he was only seven years old, the most important event in Proust's life happened. It told him that love is doomed and happiness does not exist. He spent his life, in his friendships, his love-affairs and relations with society, in trying to disprove it, and only succeeded in perpetually reproducing it; till in his great novel he went back beyond it, to the time outside Time where it had not yet happened, and therefore could never happen. One summer evening at Auteuil Marcel's mother was helping to entertain a medical colleague of Dr Proust, and could not come up to his bedroom to give him his usual good-night kiss. The anguished child watched the group in the moonlit garden, as they talked and sipped their after-dinner

[1] *De David à Degas*, p. viii. Also mentioned in *A la Recherche*, III, 168.

unconscious purpose of regaining his mother's love, and of
punishing her at the same time for withholding it, that he fell ill.

During another visit to Auteuil, when Marcel was nine years
old, the family took a walk in the nearby Bois de Boulogne with
some friends. On the way back he was seized by a fit of suffocation, and seemed on the point of dying before the eyes of his
terrified father. His lifelong disease of asthma had begun.
Medically speaking, his malady was involuntary and genuine; but
asthma, we are told, is often closely linked to unconscious con-
flicts and desires, and for Proust it was to be, though a dread
master, a faithful servant. In his attacks of asthma the same causes
were at work as in his childhood fits of hysterical weeping; his
unconscious mind was asking for his father's pity and his mother's
love; and his breathlessness reproduced, perhaps, the moment of
suffocation which comes equally from tears or from sexual
pleasure. He sinned through his lungs, and in the end his lungs
were to kill him. Other great writers, Flaubert and Dostoevsky,
suffered from epilepsy, which stood in an inseparable and partly
causal relation to their art. Asthma was Proust's epilepsy. In early
years it was the mark of his difference from others, his appeal for
love, his refuge from duties which were foreign to his still unconscious purpose; and in later life it helped him to withdraw
from the world and to produce a work 'de si longue haleine'.
Meanwhile, however, he was only a little boy choking and
writhing in the scented air under the green leaves, in the deadly
garden of spring.

Chapter 2

THE GARDEN OF ILLIERS

MARCEL'S grandfather at Illiers had died long ago, on 2 October 1855, when the future Dr Proust was still a young medical student in Paris: Louis Proust was never to know that his son would be successful and famous, any more than Dr Proust in his turn could know that his own beloved but disappointing child would be anything more than an idler in society and a dilettante in literature. Virginie Proust, the grandmother, kept the family grocer's shop at 11 Place du Marché, for eleven years more, until her son passed his *agrégation* in 1866 and became able to help in her support with his earnings. Then she retired to live in an apartment over a shop, only a few doors away, at No. 6; and there, in her front room with its esparto carpet and calico curtains, she sat by the window looking at the market-place below and the church opposite—against its walls at that time were the shops of the local hatter, the barber and the clockmaker—for twenty-three years. The church clock threw its hours and quarters down to the fortunate widow, as she watched the cobbled square which to the natives of Illiers is the hub of the universe. Her time was lost, so easily it passed, but never wasted. Even on ordinary days there was always someone passing, and on Friday market-day and Sunday mass-day everybody was passing; Friday and Sunday were never far away, and Easter or high summer, when her son brought his family from Paris, always came soon.

Her daughter Élisabeth had married in May 1847 a prosperous tradesman of Illiers, Jules Amiot. He kept a draper's shop at No. 14 in the market-place, and his dwelling-house was at No. 4 in the Rue du Saint-Esprit, which runs parallel with the market-place a few yards to the south-west, and is now called, after Proust's father, Rue du Docteur Proust. It was with Marcel's Aunt and Uncle Amiot that the family stayed when they visited Illiers.

They took the train from Paris via Chartres on the day before

Good Friday; and when they left the great cathedral on its grey plateau they travelled south-west for fifteen miles through the endless flat land of the Beauce. As they drew near to Illiers they watched through the carriage window for the first sight of the spire of Saint-Jacques; for 'Combray at a distance, seen from the train when we arrived there in the week before Easter, was nothing but a church that epitomised the town'.[1] It was the signal for Dr Proust to say: "Fold your rugs up, we shall be there in a minute"; and they hastily collected their luggage for leaving the train, which waited, as it still waits, only two minutes at Illiers, and then 'ran on over the viaduct, leaving behind it the frontiers of Christendom whose extreme limit, to me, was marked by Combray'.[2] After crossing the railway-line they walked down the Avenue de la Gare under the still leafless lime-trees, turned right into the Rue de Chartres, left across the market-place into the Rue de la Place; and there, on the opposite side of the Rue du Saint-Esprit, was the house of Aunt Amiot. The frozen travellers warmed themselves by the dining-room fire, while Uncle Jules tapped the barometer in hope that the fine weather would return, and Mme Proust ordered Marcel's hot-water bottle ("Not just hot, boiling") and his pillows ("So that he can't lie down even if he wants to, four if you have them, they can't be too high"). That night the child would wake with a beating heart, as the two booming notes with which Saint-Jacques chimes the quarters trembled on the dark air; to-morrow or the next day, to him as to the good people of Illiers who slept around him, habit would have made them inaudible.

His bed was screened by high white curtains, and covered in the daytime with flowered quilts, embroidered counterpanes and cambric pillowcases which he had to remove and drape over a chair, 'where they consented to spend the night', before he could go to bed. On a bedside table stood a blue glass tumbler and sugar-basin, with a water-jug to match, which his aunt always told Ernestine to empty on the day after his arrival, 'because the child might spill it'. On the mantelpiece was a clock muttering under a glass bell, so heavy that whenever the clock ran down they had to send for the clockmaker to wind it again; on the armchairs were little white antimacassars crocheted with roses, 'not without thorns', since they stuck to him whenever he sat down; and the

[1] I, 48   [2] I, 114

window had three sets of impracticable curtains, which it was impossible to draw all at once. The whole room was full of objects 'which obviously hadn't been put there in the hope that they would be of use to anyone'; but their very uselessness gave them an individuality, a mysterious life of their own. On the wall hung an engraving of Prince Eugene, looking handsome and fierce in his military cloak. This picture Marcel innocently took to be unique, and was amazed one day to find its twin hanging in a railway refreshment-room, where it served to advertise a brand of biscuits; his uncle, he realised, must have received it, one among many, 'as a free gift from the munificent manufacturer'. A photograph of Botticelli's Primavera would have been much more in accordance with William Morris's precepts for interior decoration, as he afterwards confessed; 'but if I ever saw Prince Eugene again, I think he would have more to tell me than the Primavera'. The contents of his bedroom at Illiers had a quality more precious to him than beauty: they were raw material for his imagination. In the 1890s he was to go through a period of 'good taste'; afterwards, however, to the end of his life, he filled his rooms with hideous but sacred objects which spoke to him of his dead parents, his childhood, time lost. He had come into the world not to collect beauty ready-made, but to create it.

Marcel would spend the morning in his uncle's garden on the far side of the Loir or on walks with the family. When possible he would return before twelve-o'clock lunch to read in the dining-room by the fire, of which his uncle would soon be exclaiming: "That's what I like to see! I can do with a bit of a fire—it was pretty cold in the kitchen-garden at six o'clock this morning, I can tell you! And to think that it's nearly Easter!" Meanwhile the china plates on the wall refrained from interrupting the reading child; the sound of the pump in the garden only made him look up for a moment; but soon the servant came in to lay the table, the walkers returned from Méréglise, the letter-writers came downstairs. "Now then, put your book away, it's lunch-time," said Dr Proust, and they sat down to the delicious fowl which Ernestine, with cries of "Filthy beast", had yesterday murdered in the yard. Her cooking was exquisite, but Aunt Élisabeth's judgment was even more so. Sometimes she would only nibble at a dish, and then everyone knew that the verdict she refrained from giving must be unfavourable. The look of unshakeable and well-considered disapproval in her gentle eyes would send her husband into a rage; he would beg her ironically for her opinion, press her with questions, lose his temper; but she would rather have been burned at the stake than reveal her knowledge that there wasn't quite enough sugar in the pudding. After lunch the glass retort would be brought in, in which Jules Amiot insisted on making the coffee himself; it was 'like an instrument in a chemist's laboratory, except that it smelt good'; and later in the season Uncle Jules would mix the strawberries with cream cheese, of which Marcel was inordinately fond, stopping, 'with the experience of a colourist and the divination of a gourmand', when the mixture had reached exactly the right shade of pink.

It was only in the earlier years at Illiers that Aunt Élisabeth considered herself well enough to come down to meals, or indeed to take meals at all. She refused, step by step, to leave Illiers, her house, her room, and finally her bed; she existed, it seemed, solely on Vichy water, pepsin, lime-tea and the famous madeleines—a plump but diminutive sponge-cake in the form of a scallop-shell, which is still to be found in Illiers, partly, no doubt, because Proustian tourists have been found to welcome it with a mysterious enthusiasm.[1] Like her nephew after her, Aunt Élisabeth became an imaginary invalid, a voluntary prisoner in her bedroom, and died at last of a malady in which no one but the sufferer had ever quite believed. In the end, too late, she was operated upon by Dr Maunoury, the glory of the whole country-side and brother of the general who helped to save Paris in 1914; and everyone agreed at last that she had really been ill, for she died. It is an ironic fact that Marcel's hereditary neurasthenia, his tendency to an illness which was at once hypochondriac and genuine, was transmitted to him not by his sensitive over-loving mother, who nevertheless did so much to perpetuate his weakness, but from his euphoric, extravert father's side of the family.

Gradually Aunt Élisabeth had discouraged all her friends from calling, for they either annoyed her by believing that she was

---

[1] The scallop-shaped madeleine cake has been known in Illiers from time immemorial. Illiers was one of the halting-places on the mediaeval pilgrimage route from Paris to the shrine of St James the Apostle at Compostella in Spain. The church took its name from St James, and the madeleine-cake its shape from the shell worn by the pilgrims in their hats. Proust alludes to this in the madeleine incident (I, 45).

Adèle Weil
Proust's grandmother

Portrait of Dr Adrien Proust
by Jules Lecomte du Nouy, 1885

Saint-Jacques
from the banks
of the Loir

Aunt Amiot's house
at Illiers

perfectly well, and only needed 'a brisk walk in the sunshine or a good red beefsteak', or distressed her by thinking she was really as ill as she said she was. Only two visitors were still welcome; one of them was the parish priest, Abbé, afterwards Canon Joseph Marquis, who took Marcel through his first steps in Latin and taught him the names of all the flowers in his garden. But even he exhausted the poor lady with his passion for the etymology of place-names, which so enthralled her nephew, or infuriated her by recommending the view from the tower of Saint-Jacques—as if she could ever climb those ninety-seven steps! In *Du Côté de chez Swann* he is said 'to be thinking of writing a book on the parish of Combray'[1]; and towards the end of his life, in 1907, he did indeed publish the result of his labours, in a large and learned volume called, simply, *Illiers*, which traces the history of the little town from prehistoric times to the building in the 1880s of the new boys' school.[2] But Aunt Élisabeth's most welcome visitor, who never tired her like the curé, who always pleased her by believing that she was ill and did not frighten her by thinking she might die, was the person who in *A la Recherche* is called Eulalie. She lived as servant-companion with the widowed Virginie Proust in the Place du Marché, and came every Sunday afternoon, in her nun-like black mantle and white coif, with news of the morning's mass and the week's gossip; and she left, to the intense disapproval of the jealous Ernestine, with a small gold coin discreetly palmed and pocketed.

Ernestine Gallou, Aunt Élisabeth's housekeeper, must have been still a young woman in Marcel's childhood, for in the early 1930s she was still alive, 'a little old lady, bowed and dwarfed with age, with a pale wrinkled face and fine grey eyes'. She could do nothing against the hated 'Eulalie', but in everything else she was the tyrant of the household. Her devotion to her mistress was profound, but years of familiarity had worn away her deference. The visitors from Paris, however, had never lost their prestige, and to them she was as obliging as she was severe to poor Aunt

---

[1] I, 103

[2] It is often supposed that the name of the curé at Combray (who in fact remains nameless) is Abbé Perdreau; but Abbé Perdreau, who is only mentioned once (I, 57), when Aunt Léonie sees his niece from her window, is a different person. A namesake of his was curé of Saint-Jacques at Illiers from 1777 to 1792.

Élisabeth, and never forgot that coffee and hot-water bottles should always be 'not just hot, but boiling'. "It's amazing how intelligent that girl is, and how well she understands things," Mme Proust would say. But she kept to herself the management of the other servants and all direct communication with her employers; if she was all smiles in the dining-room, in the kitchen she was merciless and treacherous to her unhappy inferiors. The other servants never stayed long; some left at the end of the first month, and only the bravest and most industrious could endure for as long as a year. Marcel observed her cruelty to the kitchen-maid with indignation and pity, which were tempered not only by his appreciation of her cooking, but by a secret complicity: it was the child's first sight of sadism, of the nerve of evil which runs, whether we are conscious of it or not, through all mankind, including ourselves, and which had been planted in him, once and for all, by his anger against his mother. Ernestine's talk was full of old words and turns of speech, which later he met again in Molière or Saint-Simon; her face had qualities of nobility and courage, credulity and cunning, which he recognised in the sculptures of Chartres or the porch of the imaginary Saint-André-des-Champs near Combray. She became for him a symbol of a bygone France, 'a mediaeval peasant who had survived to cook for us in the nineteenth century',[1] with a pedigree as ancient as that of any Guermantes. She was the first of a long line of family servants who together merged into Françoise; and her mistress, almost without modification, became Aunt Léonie.

The door of Ernestine's kitchen, 'a miniature temple of Venus overflowing with the offerings of the milkman and the green-grocer', opened on a little garden which was more like a court-yard, since most of it was paved, though space was found for a tiny lawn, a flower-bed of pansies and a chestnut-tree. There was no room here for Marcel's grandmother Weil to walk in the wind and rain, as she did in his novel, while her wicked relatives indoors tempted her husband to drink a glass of brandy; indeed, it is unlikely that she ever visited Illiers, and the scene of these events was certainly Uncle Louis Weil's more spacious garden at Auteuil. But here at Illiers, too, the family would sit with their liqueurs after dinner, on the cane garden-chairs at the iron garden-table; there was a family friend who would call, like

[1] I, 151

Swann, at this time in the evening; and for Marcel 'the drama of going to bed' and the anxious ceremony of his good-night kiss were enacted at Illiers as at Auteuil. Projecting from Ernestine's back-kitchen into the garden was a single-storeyed building, with windows of tinted glass, the cubby-hole of Uncle Jules and the studio of his son André, who painted. Jules Amiot had lived in Algeria as a young man, and his sanctum was adorned with native mats on the stone floor, with carved coconuts and photographs of palm-trees and mosques. After lunch, when the others took a siesta, and Dr Proust remarked, "It's strange, I don't feel well if I don't have a nap in the daytime," Uncle Jules would say, "I'd sooner walk ten miles than lie down now, it would give me a fever," and retire to his room, where he was supposed to be engaged in some important work. But when Marcel came to call him for the afternoon walk he would not reply at first, and then would answer in a startled voice, and come out rubbing his eyes; for the sleep he maligned had overtaken him on his wickerwork chaise-longue, by his hookah, as he arranged his photograph album or meditated on his fabulous youth.

The garden door opened into the Place Lemoine, where the Rue Saint-Hilaire, which continues the Rue de Chartres down to the river and the Pont Saint-Hilaire, meets the Rue des Trois Maries. It had a narrow grille through which one can still peep into the stone-flagged garden, and over it hung the famous jangling bell, which sounded automatically whenever one of the family came in 'without ringing'. Its interminable clanging could be heard in Mme Larcher's front room across the Place Lemoine, and she would always say to her visitors: "There goes Jules Amiot's doorbell"; it could never be mistaken for the 'double tinkle, timid, oval and gilded' of the visitors' bell. In his novel Proust brought the Auteuil garden and with it Swann to Combray, but he kept the garden gate of Illiers and the two bells, which took their place among the most potent symbols of Time Lost.

Past Aunt Amiot's front door ran the Rue du Saint-Esprit, 'monotonous and grey, with its three gritstone steps before nearly every door, like a furrow cut by a sculptor of gothic images in the very stone in which he has carved a crib or a calvary'. Next door to the right lived M. Pipereau, who gave his name to Dr Piperaud in Proust's novel; and next door to the left, on the street corner, was Legué's grocery, which Ernestine patronised when she had no time to go as far as Mme Damoiseau's in the Rue de la Place. In the hot summer afternoons, when Marcel was reading in the darkness of his shuttered bedroom, his sense of the brilliance of the sunlight outside would come from the din of M. Legué's hammer, which 'seemed to scatter a distant shower of scarlet stars', as he broke up old packing-cases in his yard. In the novel Legué is called Camus; but there was indeed a grocer called Camus elsewhere in Illiers, and nowadays one of his descendants and namesakes keeps the grocery at Méréglise. Opposite, at No.3, was the shop of M. Desvaux, the gunsmith, who embarrassed Marcel whenever he went to his bedroom window by waving amicably from his doorstep, where he would stand smoking his pipe and chatting with the passers-by. At No. 1, on the corner opposite Legué's, lived Mme Goupil, daughter of Dr Galopin, after whom the former Rue de l'Oiseau Flésché, which continues the Rue du Saint-Esprit in the direction of the railway, is now called Rue du Docteur Galopin. She appears in the novel under her own name, when Aunt Léonie sees her going to church, wearing her new silk gown made in Châteaudun, and without an umbrella, although a black cloud is looming behind the church tower.[1] Her father is introduced as Dr Percepied, in whose carriage Marcel has the revelation of the three spires of Martinville le-Sec; but here Proust is playing one of his favourite tricks with names, for at Illiers Percepied was really the name of the postman, while at Combray Galopin is the pastrycook from whom Mme Goupil buys a tart, and who owns the new dog, 'as clever as a Christian', whose appearance so startles Aunt Léonie.[2] Mme Goupil, who was on visiting terms with the Amiots, was a lady of majestic demeanour and imperturbable dignity: "I don't think she'd turn a hair if the church-spire fell on her head," a medical friend of Dr Proust was heard to remark. She had married a wealthy property-owner of Illiers, and in the novel it is at her wedding, under the alias of Dr Percepied's daughter, that the Narrator has his first sight of the Duchesse de Guermantes in the chapel of Gilbert the Bad. Her waxen and hieratic face was said to have inspired the figure of St Lucy, her patron saint, in the stained-glass window by the pulpit in the church.

In the Rue de la Place, which leads from the Rue du Saint-Esprit to the market-place, was a grocery kept by Mme

[1] I, 101   [2] I, 58

Damoiseau, the 'épicerie Borange' of Combray, which was also the telephone-exchange and the only bookshop in Illiers. On either side of the door, 'more mysterious and teeming with ideas than the porch of a cathedral', 'a mosaic of books and magazines'[1] still hangs. Friday, in our time, is still market-day; the cobblestones are strewn with straw, cauliflowers, hobnailed boots, ironmongery and carpets, and everyone in Illiers is there as stallholder or purchaser. When a visitor passes, however unobtrusive his appearance, all pause to stare in amazed hostility, with something of the emotion felt by Aunt Léonie when she saw from her window 'a dog she didn't know'. But later in the day, when he dares to show his face again, all is well and their glances are friendly; he has been identified as a *proustien anglais* who is staying at the Hôtel de l'Image, and he is no longer a strange dog.

The church of Saint-Jacques is half surrounded by the wide market-place, half built-in by ancient houses; and even the market-place side shows the traces, like shadows in time, of shops built by mediaeval squatters and pulled down since Proust's days. To the English visitor, accustomed to the little English parish-church, Saint-Jacques seems enormous; the roof of the nave, with the ugly modern clock whose Rhinegold chime is nevertheless so antique and beautiful, has an endless steep slope which recalls the churches of Holland. The spire rises on a square, buttressed tower with a turret at the side; it is in two tiers, resembling a large squat extinguisher on top of which has been placed a tall thin extinguisher; and above is a long mast with a weather-cock at the summit. No wonder that the spire comes into view at every side-street, at every road leading out of Illiers, and soars at an immense height, always with three or four jackdaws circling or alighting, over rooftops one would have thought steep enough to hide it. The asymmetry and oddity of the spire gives it the humble yet majestic air which made Aunt Amiot say: "If it played the piano, I'm sure it would play with real feeling"; and each new angle from which it is seen, 'like a solid surprised at an unknown moment of its revolution', seems intended by the unknown architect to be the best viewpoint of all.

The church of Saint-Jacques at Illiers is less ancient than Saint-Hilaire at Combray: it was built in the late eleventh century, restored in the fifteenth century by Florent d'Illiers, who left only

[1] I, 84

the romanesque doorway and a portion of wall from the older church, and has no Merovingian crypt, no golden cross presented by King Dagobert, no tomb of Sigebert's little daughter. Most of the interior, indeed, is of the nineteenth century, for it was 'restored' by Abbé Louis Carré and by his successor, the good Canon Marquis, who was determined, despite his passion for history and etymology, that his church should be absolutely modern.[1] Proust did not libel him when he made him say to Aunt Léonie: "I admit there are a few things in my church that are well worth a visit, but there are others that are getting very old."[2] The glass is modern, there is no stonework to be seen except the Canon's new altar, and the floor, once paved with the tombs of abbots and marquises of Illiers, is now covered with marble tiles. Nevertheless, this is not the vulgar, rootless nineteenth century of English church restoration, but one in which old traditions of magnificence and good taste were still alive. The panelling which conceals the walls is painted a faded purplish brown, adorned with golden lozenges, crosses and crowns; and though the purple is sombre, the vivid colour of the rest is dazzling and sumptuous to English Protestant eyes. In Proust's time some of the original stained glass still remained; but all is gone now, blown to pieces, along with the refugees from Belgium and the North herded in the market-place, by the exuberant Italian air-raids of June 1940; and the windows are still glassless, covered with the canvas and boarding so familiar in English churches since that year. Under the tower is a side-chapel sacred not to Gilbert the Bad, but to the Virgin. It is this chapel of the Virgin which was decorated with pink and white hawthorn in the 'month of Mary', and in which at Combray the Duchesse de Guermantes sat, 'in the intermittent, hot sunshine of a windy and rainy day', at the wedding of Dr Percepied's daughter.[3] The pews of the local nobility, the Goussencourts of Saint-Éman (which is Guermantes), and the squires of Tansonville, Éguilly-les-Brandières and Beaurouvre, were in fact in this chapel of the Virgin, and Marcel must often have seen the châtelaine of Saint-Éman sitting there at Sunday

[1] Abbé Carré (1850-72) provided the purple panelling and the Florent d'Illiers window in the choir. The further restoration was the work of Canon Marquis, who proudly declared: "in my opinion the correct principle of restoration is to harmonise the furnishings with the original style of the church".

[2] I, 103   [3] I, 174-8

mass, the first avatar of the Duchesse. Even the presence of
Gilbert the Bad is not far to seek. The arms of the marquises of
Illiers (or, six annulets azure, three, two and one) appear on the
seventeenth-century roofbeams; it was their first ancestor,
Geoffroy d'Illiers, builder of the castle of Illiers, who suggested
the desperate life and horrible end of Gilbert the Bad; and Basin,
the second Lord of Illiers, a contemporary of William the
Conqueror, gave his name to Gilbert's descendant, Basin, Duc de
Guermantes. The most celebrated member of the family was
Florent d'Illiers, who fought beside Joan of Arc (whose statue is
in the market-place outside the church-porch) as lieutenant of the
Bastard Dunois, and was buried in Saint-Jacques; he appears
along with Christ, Saint Jacques, Saint Hilaire and Miles d'Illiers,
Bishop of Chartres, in a window over the choir. From a female
cousin of Florent descended the poet Ronsard, and by the
Chantemesle branch the Marquises of Illiers were connected with
the Balzacs.[1] Throughout the seventeenth century they employed
the Prousts as their stewards and stood as godparents to their
children. The Lords of Illiers could not trace their descent as far
back as the Duchesse de Guermantes's ancestress Geneviève de
Brabant, wife of the eighth-century Count Palatine Siegfried,
whose wrongful accusation of adultery by the infamous Golo was
part of the repertoire of the magic lantern in Marcel's bedroom;
but they helped to create the Guermantes's, to ensure that Marcel,
in his childhood at Illiers, should see the French nobility as living
symbols of a mediaeval past, miraculous survivors of a glowing
window in a gothic church and the nursery-tales flashed in green
and scarlet on his bedroom wall.

Marcel's uncle made up for the minuteness of his back-garden
by possessing two other gardens. In the Rue des Lavoirs, which
continues the Rue des Trois Maries on the way to the River Loir,
and is so called from the stagnant oblong tank, surrounded by a
lean-to shelter, where the laundry of Illiers is washed, he had a
vegetable-garden; and at the far side of the river, on the edge of
open fields, was his pleasure-garden, the Pré Catelan, which he
proudly named after the famous enclosure in the Bois de Boulogne
at Paris.

As they walked down the Rue des Lavoirs to the Pré Catelan,

[1] Cf. II, 1053, for the probable emotions of M. de Charlus if he had learnt
that the Guermantes's were related to the Balzacs.

carrying their trowels and fishing-lines, Marcel and Robert passed
on their right one of the two ruined towers of the castle of Illiers,
built in 1019 by the wicked Geoffroy d'Illiers, Vicomte de
Châteaudun, during his quarrel with Fulbert, Bishop of Chartres.
The other tower, a hundred yards further along the meadows
stretching between the town and the river, had an unhallowed
significance for Marcel: it could be seen from the lavatory window
at the top of the house, as he sat in the little room scented by a
festoon of iris-roots from the banks of the garden-pond. Here,
since it was the only place in the house where he was allowed to
lock himself in, he would retire whenever he needed privacy to
read, weep, or make his first experiments in the pleasures of sex—
experiments which were not without their heroic side, since he
was not sure at first that their rending delight would not be the
death of him. In the morning he would vow not to give way to
temptation; but after lunch, when he was replete with Ernestine's
chicken, the idea would return, 'sending a mounting, delicious
wave of blood to his heart', and he would climb again to his grotto
of pleasure, where only the branches of flowering currant and the
castle tower could see him. In his novel he transferred the under-
ground chamber of the first tower to this second, and brought the
ruined keep to the market-town of Roussainville-le-Pin, on the
Méséglise Way, and surrounded it with woods; but the real
Roussainville is a tiny hamlet a mile south of Illiers, without ruins,
woods or market, a whole quarter of the compass away from
Méréglise; and the suffix le-Pin comes from Bailleau-le-Pin, a
village six miles north-east of Illiers on the road to Chartres.
Perhaps the naughty boys and girls of the town, led by 'Théodore'
(who was Victor, the errand-boy at Legué's grocery, choirboy at
Saint-Jacques, and brother of Jules Amiot's gardener Ménard),
played in these ruins at Illiers as at Combray, and Marcel with
them; or perhaps it was only the thought of his forbidden
pleasures in the lavatory that made Roussainville in the rain seem
to be 'chastised like a village in the Old Testament by God the
Father'.[1]

After the laundry-tank (on the left), the kitchen-garden, the
castle ruins and a field of grazing cows (on the right), the Rue des
Lavoirs ends in a wooden footbridge over the Loir, variously
known as the Pont-Vieux, the Passerelle or the Grand' Planche,

[1] I, 152

and associated in the novel with Legrandin. There is a tradition at Illiers that in the days when this bridge was only a single plank and had no railings, the village drunkard would totter over it, crying "Lord, lord, let me across and I'll give up the drink"; but when he reached the other side he would begin to dance and sing, and shout "Now I can go on drinking!" On the far side of the bridge is a path leading upstream along the Loir, called at Combray the tow-path (*chemin de halage*); but it can never have been used for towing at Illiers, since a line of trees grows between it and the river, and the Loir here is too shallow for barges. A little further on the walled lane from the footbridge leads into the Rue des Vierges, which runs to the right towards the Pont Saint-Hilaire, while a turning left goes to Tansonville, two miles away to the south. But Tansonville gave no more than its name and its château to Swann's park, the original of which lies directly before us, on the opposite side of the Rue des Vierges: it is none other than Jules Amiot's pleasure-garden, the Pré Catelan.

Up the left-hand side of the Pré Catelan climbs a narrow lane, separated from the garden by a hedge of pink and white hawthorns. To Marcel the pink hawthorns seemed twice as beautiful as the white: similarly, he reflected, the pink iced biscuits at Mme Damoiseau's grocery were twice as expensive as the white. The hawthorns reminded him, too, of the colour of his favourite strawberries crushed with cream-cheese; and they seemed not only edible but holy; for just as they made the altar of Saint-Jacques look like a hedge in bloom in the month of Mary, so here in the *petit sentier* the hawthorn chapels took on something of the religious sanctity of the church. Their scent was not yet fatal to him, and once, when he was ill, his mother brought him branches of his beloved pink flower and laid them on his bed, a present from Ménard the gardener. Through the gaps in the hedge he could look down to the lawns and ornamental water; and perhaps once he saw there some little girl with reddish hair, freckles and a sly look, a first appearance of Gilberte. The Amiots and Prousts were often joined for picnics in the Pré Catelan by friends and their children; and all we know of Proust's method of fusing people from different periods of his life into single characters for his novel suggests that there was someone at Illiers who became the Gilberte of Combray.

Uncle Jules had laid out the flat lower part of his garden near the Rue des Vierges with lawns, gravel paths, dwarf palms, geranium-beds and an ornamental water, not a lake as in Swann's park, but a broadening, still hardly too wide for leaping, of a brook running into the Loir. This winding pond, now almost silted up, had a rustic bridge, water-lilies, swans and carp, so many that the children were allowed to fish for them—hence the fishing-line with its bobbing cork which the Narrator sees in the water by Gilberte[1]—and its banks were bordered with forget-me-nots and the blue and yellow irises whose roots scented the room at the top of the house. Along the paths were curious, turreted dove-cotes of variegated brick, modelled on the Arab pigeon-houses which Uncle Jules had seen in Algeria. Somewhere in this region Marcel and Robert planted a poplar sapling, for which Robert searched in vain more than fifty years later, among the other trees near the great catalpa, a fortnight before his death in 1935. The spire of Saint-Jacques, nearly half a mile away, shows through the trees, as it did at Tansonville.[2] There is a sound of gently falling water from a weir in the Loir near by.

Above the lawns was a steep hill covered with a dense copse of hazels, known as the Bois Pilou, where Marcel and Robert played at hide-and-seek, and sometimes frightened themselves into believing they were really lost. Near the left-hand side of the garden, separated by the hawthorn hedge from the *petit sentier*, a path with stone steps climbed the slope, a favourite haunt, nowadays at least, of long, fat, steel-grey slow-worms. Half-way up Uncle Jules had built an octagonal summer-house in red brick, the Maison des Archers. Its foundations were an artificial grotto, and the first floor was a furnished rest-room where Marcel could lie reading *Le Capitaine Fracasse* on a pink divan. Still further up the slope was a concrete tank which supplied water for the hose-pipes and fountains below. It was filled by a pump worked by horses, who every few days would plod round a circular track, one at each end of a rotating beam with the pump in the middle. When the horses were not working, only the shadow of the beam would turn with the sun: "You see, it's a kind of sundial," Uncle Jules told Marcel. At the bottom of the tank, when the water was low, Marcel could see a dim entanglement of pipes, green with water-weeds; a newt slept clinging to the sides, until he startled it and it leapt into the water. From the path by the tank, over the hawthorns of the *raidillon* to the left, meadows could be seen which were visible from nowhere else; and they seemed to Marcel a mysterious country set in the middle of the real world, like the underworld of water in which he had seen his mother bathing. A few yards further up the path, the park ended in a little plateau containing an immemorial asparagus-bed, beside which grew the strawberries of which his uncle was so proud. "They are *exquisite*," Mme Proust would earnestly say; and "Yes, they *are* good," Uncle Jules would reply modestly, "they are real wood-strawberries." On the far side of the asparagus-bed the end of the garden was marked by a white gate, past which the landscape dramatically changed into mile upon mile of rolling plain: here was the Méréglise way.

There is no direct path to Méréglise here, however; the haw-thorn path turns sharply right at the white gate, and runs down-hill through land which then was green cornfields scattered with scarlet poppies, and now is allotment-gardens, into the main road from Illiers to Brou, here called Chemin de la Croix Rompue. This leads back to the outskirts of Illiers, and crosses the opposite end of the Rue des Vierges near the site of the church of Saint-Hilaire, demolished in the French Revolution, which gave its name to the church at Combray. Jules Amiot rescued carved stone from its ruins for the front gate of his Pré Catelan in the Rue des Vierges. Here a road to the left leads to Méréglise, and on the right is the Loir with its only road-bridge, the Pont Saint-Hilaire, over which it is delightful to lean and watch the trailing green water-weeds and the motionless trout. Here the Rue Saint-Hilaire leads from the bridge past the Place Lemoine and the Rue du Saint-Esprit to the market-place.

Sometimes, when the family walked back from picnic-tea in the Pré Catelan in the red twilight after sunset, Dr Proust would take them a longer way round. From the town-side of the Pont Saint-Hilaire another 'towing-path' leads up the Loir to a foot-bridge called the Pont du Gué Bellerin. Here is the triangular Place du Calvaire, with its cross and image of the Crucified, which in *Du Côté de chez Swann* becomes 'the Mall'. A road to Saint-Éman runs north under the railway viaduct and past the cemetery, where at Combray Dr Percepied once met the music-teacher Vinteuil; and the Rue de l'Oiseau-Flésché, named after an inn where the mediaeval archers of Illiers met to shoot at a bird tied to a pole, leads to the right towards the Rue du Saint-Esprit.[1] But the parents and the blissfully weary children would press forward along the Rue du Chemin de Fer into the Avenue de la Gare. As they looked back, the cross was silhouetted against the water of the Loir near the Gué Bellerin, lit crimson by the western sky, but in the Avenue de la Gare, which contains, as at Combray, 'the most attractive villas in the town', the moon was already shining. In every garden (for this is almost the only street at Illiers where the houses have front gardens) 'the moonlight, as in the paintings of Hubert Robert, scattered its broken staircases of white marble, its fountains, its iron gates left half-open'. Marcel was dragging his feet and dropping with sleep, and 'the scent of the lime-trees seemed like a reward which could only be won at the expense of great fatigue, and wasn't worth the effort'. At last Dr Proust would stop and say: "Where are we now?" No one knew; but the kind, bearded father would point with a laugh to their back-garden gate in the Place Lemoine, and Mme Proust, whose respect for her husband reached its peak when she considered his interest in meteorology or his sense of direction, would murmur: "My dear, you are amazing!"

[1] The Rue de l'Oiseau and its inn are among the Narrator's most persistent memories of Combray. Cf. I, 48, 55, 166; II, 531; III, 624, 856, 955

Chapter 3

THE TWO WAYS

TO the child Marcel the two favourite walks of the family seemed to be in diametrically opposite directions, so that no two points in the world could be so utterly separated as their never-reached destinations. Whether they left the house by the front door or by the garden-gate, they would turn one way for Méréglise and the other way for Saint-Éman. To Méréglise, since the Rue Saint-Hilaire, though a short-cut, was less interesting, they would go by the Rue des Lavoirs and the *passerelle*, up the hawthorn path beside the Pré Catelan, and along the Chemin de la Croix-Rompue to the Méréglise turning by the site of Saint-Hilaire. In his novel Proust called Méréglise 'Méséglise', for euphony; and as the way there went by the Pré Catelan, which he had transformed into Swann's park, he was able to say with truth that it was also Swann's Way.

A few yards from the Pont Saint-Hilaire the Méréglise way climbs a slope: behind, the spire of Saint-Jacques rises to its full height, and sends its last chime to the departing wanderer; but in front, past the level-crossing of the railway on its way to Brou, is the landscape of rolling plain already seen from the top of the hawthorn path, pierced by the spires of village churches and barred by dark woods on the far horizon. The air here has a limpid, milky quality which in England one breathes only in the West Country; and a warm wind, 'the tutelary genius of Combray', is always blowing. To the Narrator this wind seems to bring a message from Gilberte at Laon,[1] as well it might: for though Proust intended to lead his reader astray to the cathedral-town of Laon in Seine-et-Marne, 150 miles from Illiers, he was thinking privately of Laons at the northern end of Eure-et-Loire, near the birthplace of the husband of Mme Goupil; and the road to Laons may be seen from here. Can a daughter of Mme Goupil, or the niece with whom Aunt Léonie sees her walking, have been the first original of Gilberte?

[1] I, 145

Along the right-hand grass verge of the road, past a pre-historic standing-stone, is an endless line of apple-trees, surrounded in September by the red rings of fallen apples, and all summer through by the circles of their shade: 'It was on the Méséglise Way,' says the Narrator, 'that I first noticed the round shadow which apple-trees cast on the sunlit ground.'[1] Later in life Proust would drug himself for a week with veronal and cafeine, in order to get up in the daytime and visit his favourite trees in bloom on the outskirts of Paris; but he rode in a taxi hermetically sealed to cut off their deadly scent, which in his childhood he had loved with impunity.

Méréglise itself, however, far from being an important town large enough to send the Duc de Guermantes to represent it in the Chamber of Deputies, is a small hamlet of about forty houses, a little church, and two or three shops, including nowadays the grocery of M. Camus. Its gardens are coloured with russet dahlias shedding their petals through wire netting, and with pink laundry hanging up to dry. The Proustian magic somehow stops short of this insignificant village; as in *Du Côté de chez Swann*, the way to Méréglise is more important than Méréglise itself. 'Of Méséglise,' says the Narrator, 'I never knew anything but the Way.'[2] But the church of Méréglise, at least, has its part to play in the most remarkable of all the manifestations of the Méséglise Way.

The church of Saint-Jacques, which seemed lost for ever behind the hill between the Pont Saint-Hilaire and the level-crossing, has been in view again all along the road to Méréglise, but never for long in the same place. The road winds imperceptibly, and the spires and towers of Vieuvicq, Méréglise, Saint-Éman and Marchéville, in a kind of ritual dance, change their places incessantly in relation to Saint-Jacques and one another. It is the phenomenon of the moving spires which the Narrator sees in Dr Percepied's carriage, though there it takes place at the centre, and here round the circumference of a circle. Along the rough track of flint and sand which leads north-east to Saint-Éman and Marchéville just before the standing-stone, the illusion is even more bewildering; and this is the very route taken by Dr Percepied on his way to his patient at 'Martinville-le-Sec'. It was more than twenty years later that Proust saw the enchantment repeated, this time in the centripetal form which it takes in his novel, by the spires of Caen; but then, as we shall see, it was in the country near 'Balbec', after the deaths of his parents, and in a motor-car driven by the young chauffeur who was one of the originals of Albertine.

The Méréglise way, Dr Proust always said, was the finest view of a plain he had ever seen, while the Saint-Éman way was the very type of a river-landscape. The shortest route to Saint-Éman was by the Rue de l'Oiseau-Fléché to the Place du Calvaire and the cemetery, after which the path leads all the way by the banks of the Loir; but if they wished to see as much as possible of the river they could go first by the Rue des Lavoirs to the *passerelle*, and along the two 'towing-paths' to the Place du Calvaire again; and this, though the first half of it belongs to the Méréglise way, is the route Proust describes in his novel. But the Loir above Illiers soon becomes only a narrow though charming brook. For the river-scenery of the Guermantes Way he described the country downstream from the *passerelle*, with its motionless anglers, and water-lilies, and rowing-boats, and introduced the Pré Catelan a second time: this time it is the 'property thrown open to the public by its owner, who had made a hobby of aquatic gardening'.[1] A mile below Illiers, near Tansonville, the Thironne, which comes from beyond Méréglise and gave part of its name to the Vivonne of Combray, flows into the Loir. Where the two rivers meet is a garden called Les Plaisances, to which he obliquely refers in his description of the Guermantes Way: beside the water, he says, is 'une maison dite de plaisance', where a young woman, disappointed in love, has come 'in the popular phrase, to bury herself'; and he sees her standing pensively framed in her window, and looking up as the family passes.[2] Half a mile further up the Thironne is a water-mill, whose white front wreathed in climbing plants is reflected in a millpond covered with water-lilies, and whose name sends a shudder through Proust's readers: it is Montjouvin. The mysterious young woman really existed in the country round Illiers, though she lived neither at Montjouvin nor Les Plaisances, but at Mirougrain. In the novel her dwelling-place is a fusion of all three, while the girl herself has become two separate characters, one of whom is far more important than the forsaken maiden, who never reappears: she is none other than

[1] I, 169   [2] I, 170, 171

Mlle Vinteuil. This complex of topography and persons befits the complex of forbidden love which it embodies; for it is at 'Montjouvain', and through Vinteuil's daughter, that the innocent Combray is linked with the Cities of the Plain.

At Combray Mirougrain is a farm belonging to Aunt Léonie; it is one of her favourite daydreams that one day her house will be burned down with all the family in it, and that she will have time to escape at her leisure and go to spend the summer 'in her pretty farmhouse at Mirougrain, where there was a waterfall'.[1] At Illiers Mirougrain is a country-house called Le Rocher de Mirougrain, a mile up the Loir in the direction of Saint-Éman. The Loir broadens here into a still pool, crossed at one end by a wooden footbridge; on the far side is a steep slope, from which one can look down on the house; and, just as at Mlle Vinteuil's 'Montjouvain', there is a pond below the house, and a red-tiled gardener's hut by the pond. No one will ever know whether in real life Marcel hid in the bushes on the slope to spy on the lonely young lady of the house; but it is not unlikely that he did, and local gossip suggested that he might see something he ought not to see.

Her name was Juliette Joinville d'Artois, and in 1880, when Marcel was nine, she was in her early twenties. Her melancholy love of the past had taken a form which would horrify a modern archaeologist: she had collected prehistoric dolmens from the surrounding countryside, fortunately overlooking the one near Méréglise, and built with them a monstrous edifice in her garden, which she proudly called 'my temple'. 'In this fair-haired, frail, twenty-year-old child,' she remarks of herself in a volume called *A Journey through My Heart*, published in 1887, 'I see a soul longing to kill its body, a body doing all it can to bring rest to its weary soul. And in the colossal, awe-inspiring, defensive mass of my temple I see a savage desire to create a place of refuge, a shelter against further misfortunes.' Her only companion was a deaf-mute man-servant, whose presence gave rise to strange rumours in Illiers: she had chosen him, she said, from love of silence, and from desire to learn and teach the deaf-and-dumb language; but was it not rather, as scandal suggested, because he would be unable to tell what he saw at Mirougrain? Nothing more is known to-day of the morals, seventy years ago, of poor Mlle

[1] I, 116

Joinville d'Artois. She lived in a lonely house and was a subject
for scandal: for the other qualities of Mlle Vinteuil, her homosexuality so closely united to her sadism, Proust had only to look
in himself. We shall find him, many years later, inviting the
partners of his pleasure to desecrate the images of his dead
parents, as part of the ritual of his enjoyment; for the form of
sadism which in Mlle Vinteuil seems hardly to deserve the name
(since she cannot really hurt her dead father by encouraging her
friend to spit on his photograph) was to him the most real,
horrifying and irresistible.

In his novel Proust called Vinteuil's Mirougrain 'Montjouvain', and situated it on the Méséglise Way; whereas, since
Mirougrain is in fact on the river in the direction of Saint-Éman,
it would seem to belong of right to the Guermantes Way. But
there are several links which made this change of place and name
natural to his imagination. The road to Laons, which begins on
the way to Méréglise, runs past Mirougrain; both Mirougrain and
Montjouvin are on a river and by a pond; and in the eighteenth
century the château of Montjouvin, of which nothing now
remains but its water-mill, was owned by a certain Jean-Jacques
Jouvet de Mirougrain. When Dr Percepied met Vinteuil by the
cemetery, where he had gone to weep over his wife's grave, the
unhappy music-teacher was a long way from Montjouvain, but
little more than half a mile from Mirougrain.

Saint-Éman can be reached from Mirougrain either by following the road to Laons, or along the path by the bank of the Loir,
or by the road which leads from the Place du Calvaire at Illiers
past the cemetery. Half a mile beyond Mirougrain is the farm on
the right of the road, 'at some distance from two other farms
which were themselves close together', which seems to the
Narrator one of the chief symbols of the Guermantes Way; for on
their way back it is only half an hour from home, where dinner
will be later than usual, as is the rule when they have walked
towards Guermantes; he will be sent to bed immediately after the
soup course, and his mother, 'kept at table just as though there
had been company to dinner', will not come upstairs to give him
his good-night kiss.[1] The isolated farm is called Crasne, and the
two other farms are the hamlet of Les Perruches. At Les Perruches
a turning left soon reaches Saint-Éman.

[1] I, 182-3

At Saint-Éman is the château of the Goussencourts, with its towers in the shape which the French call pepper-pots. For the vast woods which surround the country home of the Duchesse de Guermantes, however, Proust was thinking of the forests which half encircle Illiers on the edge of the highlands of the Perche a few miles further west; and one of these is called the Bois de Saint-Éman. At Saint-Éman, too, is one of the sources of the Loir, which the Narrator first sees long after his childhood at Combray, on his walk to Guermantes with Gilberte after her marriage to Saint-Loup, near the verge of Time Regained. This fabulous place, 'as extra-terrestrial as the gate of Hell', is in fact, as he is so disappointed to find, 'nothing but a kind of laundry-tank in which bubbles rise to the surface'.[1] But the most surprising sight at Saint-Éman is a signpost which reads: 'Méréglise, 3 kilometres.' Not content with their trick with the church spires, the winding roads of the Méréglise way have succeeded in bringing Méréglise nearer to Saint-Éman than either village is to Illiers. Gilberte was quite serious when she said: "If you like we can go to Guermantes by Méséglise, it is the nicest walk"; and when she says: "If we took the road to the left and then turned to the right, we should be at Guermantes in less than a quarter of an hour", she is thinking of the track by the megalith, which is on the left coming from Méréglise, and turns right, half-way to Saint-Éman, at a hamlet called Les Dauffraies; though she is exaggerating the shortness of the walk, which at any comfortable walking-speed would take at least three-quarters of an hour. The 'perfect and profound valley, carpeted with moonlight', in which they stop for a moment, 'like two insects about to plunge into the blue calix of a flower',[2] is the narrow ravine formed by the Loir a little below Saint-Éman.

We have seen the streets and church of Illiers, the hawthorn path and the garden pond, and have taken the two ways which, after all, can so easily be made one. It is at first sight surprising that the real landscape of Illiers should resemble so closely the created, mythical and universal landscape of Combray; and certainly in no other section of *A la Recherche du Temps Perdu* did the literal truth need so little alteration in order to make it coincide with the ideal truth. Partly this is because Proust saw Illiers in childhood, when the visual object, which later serves

[1] III, 693   [2] III, 692-3

only to mask immaterial truth, is still able to reveal it: for to the child's eye object and symbol are one and the same. Partly, too, it is because he wrote of Combray after many years, when memory had already performed its task of rejecting the inessential. Perhaps there is even some danger of exaggerating the objectivity of the presence in the Illiers landscape of the symbols Proust saw there: they are undoubtedly real outside this world, but in this world may they not be illusions? Perhaps, as the Baron de Charlus said of Combray, Illiers is only 'a little town like so many others',[1] and if Proust had spent his childhood holidays in one of those many other little towns, he would have extracted the same truths from different symbols. And yet, at Illiers, the church and grey streets and gardens of Combray are there for all to see; the village spires perform their strange movement, the two ways of rolling plain and narrow river lead for ever in opposite directions, and nevertheless meet. In the real topography of Illiers the mysterious significance of the symbolical landscape of Combray was already latent. However, the differences between Illiers and Combray are real and important; by observing them we may detect Proust in the act of adjusting the truth of Illiers to make it conform still more closely to the truth of Combray.

It was necessary first of all to set Combray free, to divert the reader's attention and his own imagination from the real Illiers. He planted clues which suggest that Combray is in Normandy or Champagne; he invented new streets, the Rue Sainte-Hildegarde, Rue de la Eretonnerie, Rue de Saintrailles, and changed the position of old ones, so that the Rue du Saint-Esprit moves to the back of Aunt Léonie's house, and the Mall, which at Illiers is on the southern edge of the town, is to the north by the Place du Calvaire. Saint-Jacques takes the name of the demolished Saint-Hilaire. There is no equivalent near Illiers of the large town of Thiberzy, whither Françoise had to go before dawn to fetch the midwife for the kitchen-maid (although Combray, like Illiers, is large enough to support a midwife of its own). There is no village called Champieu on the Méréglise way, nor any church of Saint-André-des-Champs, in the sculptured figures of whose porch the Narrator could see Françoise and her philosophy, Théodore the grocer's boy, and the peasant girl sheltering from the rain, whom he longed in vain to meet alone. The original of

[1] III, 795

Saint-André has been variously identified as Notre-Dame-de-Champdé at Châteaudun, or Saint-Loup-de-Naud, or a little church in the Rue de la Maladrerie at Illiers; but Proust was no doubt thinking primarily of the porches of Chartres, and next of the concentrated essence of the gothic churches he visited in the early 1900s. 'In order to describe a single church, one needs to have seen a great many,'[1] he says in *Le Temps Retrouvé*; and even the church of Saint-Hilaire at Combray has paving from Lisieux and Dives, and stained glass from Évreux, Pont-Audemer and the Saint-Chapelle in Paris. He took the name of Combray from Combres, a village a few miles past Méréglise; but it suggests the Combourg of Chateaubriand's boyhood in Brittany, the Cambrai in Flanders of which his friend Bertrand de Fénelon's famous ancestor was bishop; and there is an actual Combray in Normandy near Lisieux. He generalised Illiers so that it should become universal, the paradise of innocent vision from which every human being is expelled at the end of his childhood. He shifted the known landscape of Illiers to give it the kaleidoscopic quality of a dream—the kind of dream in which, going a little past the furthest point reached in childhood walks on the outskirts of an inland industrial birthplace, we find ourselves in sight of Paris or the sea.

The most far-reaching adjustments occurred, however, not in the topography but in the people of Combray. Proust wished to make Combray a symbol of the family; and so that all the family should be there, he imported his maternal grandparents and Uncle Louis Weil (who, as Uncle Adolphe, takes possession of Jules Amiot's den in the garden), although it is probable that they never visited Illiers. Grandfather Weil, indeed, was notorious for never having spent a night away from Paris in all his eighty years, except during the siege of 1870, when he took his wife to Étampes for safety. Whether the great-aunt (who teases Swann for living near the Halle aux Vins) and Aunts Flora and Céline (who thank him so obscurely for the present of Asti) ever existed, remains unknown. Perhaps they too belonged to Paris and his mother's side of the family; though in *Journées de Lecture* the great-aunt seems identical with Aunt Élisabeth Amiot before she became bed-ridden. Jules Amiot disappears from the novel: since his garden had been made over to Swann, his function as 'the

[1] III, 907

gardening, early-rising uncle' had lapsed; and it is one of Aunt
Léonie's most terrible nightmares that 'her poor Octave', who is
long dead, should turn out to be still alive and insist on her taking
a walk every day.[1]

It was necessary also that Combray and its chapter should be
the whole novel in miniature, and contain the germs of all its
themes and events. For the rest of the novel the Narrator follows
up the ways on which he first set foot at Combray: however far
he seems to be leaving it behind, he is really circling back, and
Time Regained is also Combray regained. Characters who belong
chiefly, as did their originals in real life exclusively, to Paris,
appear also in Combray. Sometimes, as in the case of Swann, the
Duchesse de Guermantes or Gilberte, their connection with
Combray is aided by the existence at Illiers of persons in whom
Proust afterwards saw analogies with the corresponding person in
Paris: in each place there was a family friend, an unapproachable
noblewoman, a little girl he loved. Sometimes he was helped by
coincidences of history and geography: he named the Narrator's
friend, Robert de Saint-Loup-en-Bray, from Saint-Loup-de-Naud
in Seine-et-Marne, whose church he visited with a group of young
noblemen who collectively suggested his hero; but there is also a
village of Saint-Loup eight miles east of Illiers. He made Saint-
Loup marry Gilberte partly because one of the originals of Saint-
Loup in real life married one of the originals of Gilberte; but the
name was already linked with Tansonville, where the château
was occupied in 1710 by a certain Robert de Durcet after his
marriage with Claire de Saint-Loup. As for the suffix en-Bray, no
doubt it comes from Bourg-en-Bray near Saint-Loup-de-Naud;
but there is a River Braye which flows into the Loir some fifty
miles downstream from Illiers.

Sometimes characters seen at Combray, such as Charlus,
Odette or Legrandin, have originals with no possible association
with Illiers. Perhaps this is true of Vinteuil: Illiers was large
enough to possess a music-teacher, but there is no published
record of his existence. Legrandin can be identified with a person
who resembled him in every way, except that he had no link with
Illiers and was a doctor instead of an engineer. Dr Henri Cazalis
(1840-1909) was a professional friend of Dr Proust; but he was
also, under the pseudonym of Jean Lahor, a symbolist poet of

[1] I, 110

minor reputation and merit and an intimate friend of Mallarmé
and Francis Jammes; and he was noted for social climbing.

Illiers was more, even, than an earthly paradise lost, a symbol
of innocence, childhood, natural beauty and family affection for
loved ones since aged or dead. It gave Proust not only the first
chapter of his novel, but the philosophy of the whole: for it was
here that he had his first intimations of unconscious memory. At
first, as recorded in *Jean Santeuil*, the memory was preconscious
rather than unconscious, roused by the repetition of some sight
or feeling of the previous year, forgotten during the intervening
winter in Paris, but remembered instantly and without obstruc-
tion on his return to Illiers. He would see cordon apple-trees in
flower in the orchards of the Rue des Lavoirs, and recollect seeing
them a year ago; or at home in Paris he would hear buzzing flies
in his room, and they would call to mind his bedroom in the Rue
du Saint-Esprit, and the dazzling noise of M. Legué breaking up
his packing-cases next door. Memories of this kind only became
truly unconscious when they had been driven deeper by the
passage of years, by long periods in which they had no opportunity of recurring, and by changes in his personality. Then the
memory was mysterious, and not even recognisable at first as
memory; only prolonged effort could bring its source to consciousness, and the struggle was rewarded not only by the joy
and release of success, but by the intrinsic value of what was
discovered: a fragment of the past miraculously preserved in
eternity, a moment of time regained. Unconscious memory was
linked with other feelings of inexplicable delight in which
memory had no part, such as the ecstasies he owed to the moving
spires, or the 'little phrase' in what became the Vinteuil Sonata.
They revealed the existence, somewhere deep within him, of a
region in which beauty was real and eternal, uncontaminated by
disappointment, sin and death. Later in life these feelings became
more important than anything else in the world, more valuable
than the false enchantments of love or society: they were sign-
posts, marked with an unexpectedly short distance, to the only
true reality. If he could find his way back to their lost country,
his life would be justified and his sins forgiven.

But Illiers, like Time, had to be lost before it could be regained.
The break seems to have come when he was thirteen, after the
summer which was long known as 'the summer of Augustin

Class Five, in which he made his first appearance
et roll of honour on 31 December 1884. Thanks
he seems to have gone up after only one term into
which he is again found on the roll of honour on
385; but he stuck there for two years, reaching the
once more on 28 February 1887. As he joined the
in the following October, he must have spent only
rm in Class Two; or perhaps, in the expression of
boy slang, he 'jumped' it altogether. No doubt this
ress was caused by his ill-health: his school friend
us speaks of his prolonged absences, which often
from writing his end-of-term compositions. More-
a pupil full of fantasy, an elusive apprentice of
d daydreams, inspired more by his delight in
ing and feeling than by any ambition to shine on
n *Jean Santeuil* the father's colleagues predict a
r at school for a boy who already knows Victor
fred de Musset by heart; but Jean is punished for in-
ottom for French composition, and finishes his first
a single prize. Instead of writing the brief, correct
are expected of him, he covers page after page,
y his own facility and by 'the infinite and delicious
nspired by the burning of Joan of Arc or the speech
ble de Bourbon'; and the composition he has written
enthusiasm is greeted by the laughter of the whole
uses himself of vanity and a desire to be admired,
nsiders he has inherited from his father's 'inoffensive
and he cannot bear to think that the boy next to
rich, well-born and plays with real agate marbles,
n ignorant of his social successes. One morning, when
eep in Hannibal's crossing of the Alps, he leans over
s: "Do you know, I've had dinner with the head-
What's that you said?" the startled rich boy exclaims
aster calls them out, and asks what they were talking
ean feels ready to die of embarrassment and pride as
ion mumbles: "Santeuil was saying he'd been to
the Head."[1] At last Jean's angry father sends him as
o the terrible Lycée Henri-Quatre; and though Dr
er punished Marcel in this way, he may well have

[1] *Jean Santeuil*, vol. I, 114-17

Thierry'. In the Pré Catelan, where in previous years he had lain
in the hazel-copse by the asparagus-bed reading Dickens, George
Eliot, or Gautier's *Le Capitaine Fracasse*, he was now captivated
by *La Conquête de l'Angleterre par les Normands*, and *Récits des
Temps Mérovingiens*. After the obligatory game of hide-and-seek,
and the picnic tea, during which his book must be left unopened
on the grass by the pool, Marcel would escape to read in a horn-
beam-tree at the top of the garden; and the voices of the family
calling him in vain had as little power to disturb him as the distant
chimes of the church clock, 'which seemed to peal from somewhere behind the blue sky'. But it was decided that Illiers was bad
for his health. The Loir, Dr Proust declared, was a menace to the
whole town; and his friends the hawthorns and the apple-trees
in flower had turned against him, and punished his love with the
agonies of asthma. Only sea or mountain air could cure him, and
in future his holidays were spent with his grandmother on the
coast of Normandy or with his mother at inland health-resorts.
Perhaps his education also made the former impromptu visits to
Illiers impossible; for he had now left his preparatory school for
the Lycée Condorcet, and had outgrown the arithmetic lessons of
the village optician, and Canon Marquis's tuition in Latin and the
names of flowers. He saw Illiers again in rare visits, which
continued till he was past thirty. But the spell was broken, and
Illiers now resembled only the Combray of the sojourn at Tansonville with Gilberte de Saint-Loup: the Loir was 'a meagre, ugly
stream', and the Méréglise and Saint-Éman ways had lost, or had
not yet acquired, their meaning.

As he grew older, his memories of Illiers became ever more
vivid and more vague, like the landscape of a dream. Geography
changed, space was altered by time. In what street was the house
of Aunt Élisabeth, at which end of Illiers was the Mall? The back-
garden widened and stretched, and along its gravel paths his dead
grandmother strode up and down in the rain; the family visitor
had the melancholy, ironical face of Charles Haas. He built a
country house in the Pré Catelan for Swann and Gilberte, and
brought a Lesbian girl to Le Rocher de Mirougrain.

Chapter 4

THE GARDEN OF THE CHAMPS-ÉLYSÉES

MARCEL'S face was changing: it moved indeed in several directions and on several planes, as if uncertain of its destination. Would it take after his father, or his mother, or be a new individual—and if the last, should it be hysterical, cheerful, or gravely melancholy? There are four surviving photographs of the period between his tenth and twelfth years. In the first he is with Robert, who quietly hugs his brother's arm in an attitude which had hardly altered since the photograph in which Marcel was five and both were in frocks; but Marcel's face has a frozen frenzy which recalls the young Rimbaud, a timidity masked by arrogance and anger. It is about the time of his first attack of asthma in the Bois de Boulogne: is this the nervous face of the young asthmatic, jealous of his brother (for a child can be both fond and envious of his rival) and wooing his mother with fits of weeping rage—or, since the other photographs are so very different, is it only a normal boy trying to keep still for the photographer? Both brothers wear wide Eton collars over their shoulders, Lavallière cravats, and knee-breeches which leave an expanse of thin bare leg above their white socks and high buttoned boots. Their hair has been meticulously curled; perhaps this is the photograph of which he was thinking in *Du Côté de chez Swann*, when the Narrator tears out his curl-papers and spoils his velvet jacket and new hat embracing the hawthorns at Tansonville. Or perhaps it is the next, though now his hair is straight and worn in a fringe, for here are the new hat and the velvet jacket; and this, whether or not it is the Combray photograph, is certainly the one Céleste Albaret found when rummaging in the Narrator's drawer at Balbec: "He tried to make us think they always dressed him quite simply. And there, with his little cane, he's nothing but furs and laces, such as no prince ever wore!"[1] She might well think of a prince, for the morocco frame is covered with golden fleur-de-lis; he sits on the photographer's balustrade, the new hat beside him

[1] II, 848

and the toy riding-cane on hi
gence in his face, as if he me
le-Sec. It is one of the most
childhood, and the next two
anticlimax. Both were taken o
arm in arm again; they are in
has a look of positively chirpy
1882, the year in which he ent

For the past year or two he
the Cours Pape-Carpentier, w
Jacques Bizet, son of the com
1875 soon after the disastrou
custom for the little boys to be
so perhaps Marcel may have s
intelligent mother, daughter
Halévy, and future hostess of
he would begin to frequent h
friend for life; but now she
society.

His parents chose the Lycé
was so near home: the school e
few yards north from the Bo
minutes' walk from 9 Bouleva
coincidence, no choice could
like the grim schools of the I
Quatre, Saint-Louis, or Stani
learning, Condorcet was co
culture. The beginning of le
marked, it is true, by the traditi
as Marcel's schoolfriend Rob
invite us rather than order u
mostly minor literary figures
force knowledge into their pu
them in the love and practice
reaches of the school, in the c
the boys were allowed by th
Giraud, to choose their own t

There is a little documentary
days, during the period of fiv
1882 to the beginning of *rhétor*

years to
in the C
to this su
Class Th
14 Febru
roll of h
rhétoriqu
the sum
French s
irregular
Robert
prevente
over, 'he
meditatio
reading,
prize-day
brilliant
Hugo an
attention
year with
essays w
intoxicate
melancho
of the Co
with tear
class. He
which he
self-conce
him, who
might re
the class
and whis
master!"
aloud; the
about; an
his comp
dinner wi
a boarde
Proust ne

threatened it. Marcel's parents, like Jean's, decided at last that his failures were due not to ill-health, nor to idleness, but to 'lack of will-power'. They repeated the accusation so often that Marcel half believed it, and made it one of the characteristics of the heroes of both his novels; and his critics have believed it after him.

Perhaps Marcel's prolonged stay in Class Three was caused not by ill-health, still less by *manque de volonté*, but by the sorrows of love. His little playmate at Illiers was already lost in the past; but in the summer of 1886, when he was not quite fifteen,[1] he was seized by a passion for her counterpart in Paris which long after-wards, only a few years before his death, he still thought of as 'one of the two great loves of my life'. Her name was Marie de Benardaky, and he met her in the Champs-Élysées, where he used to play every afternoon after school (which ended at three o'clock), and on the Thursday half-holiday, with a group of schoolfellows from Condorcet and a little band of girls. The boys were later to have distinguished careers, if Robert Dreyfus, who was one of them, is to be believed: 'In our little group,' he says, 'which met so harmoniously near the roundabouts, there were future scholars, philosophers, industrialists, doctors, engineers, economists, politicians, barristers, generals, and an ambassador.' The ambassador was Maurice Herbette, the politician Paul Bénazet, and the philosopher was Léon Brunschwicg, editor of Pascal, who is said to have had much in common with Bloch in Proust's novel. There were also two who became minor poets, Louis de la Salle and Jean de Tinan. Among the girls were Antoinette and Lucie Faure, daughters of the deputy from Le Havre, who ten years later became President of the Republic, and Gabrielle Schwartz.

Lucie Faure was five years older than Marcel, while her sister Antoinette was his senior by only a year. His friendship with

---

[1] The earliest stage of his acquaintance with Mlle de Benardaky is dated by a letter to Antoinette Faure written on 15 July 1886. The date is fixed by his description of the famous review of the army at Longchamp by General Boulanger on 14 July 1886, which he saw, he says, 'yesterday'. 'I go to the Champs-Élysées nearly every day,' he writes; 'Blanche is still very sweet, with her angelic face so teasing and so resigned. Marie Benardaki [*sic*] is very pretty and more exuberant than ever. She *fought* Blanche with her fists the other day, and Blanche had to give in!' Cf. *Bulletin de la Société des Amis de Marcel Proust*, no. 7 (1957), 271-5, where the letter is wrongly assigned to 1887.

Antoinette was at its height about eighteen months before the present period, and was a milder prefiguration of his love for Marie de Benardaky: in a photograph taken in the Parc Monceau, Mlle Faure, with a plumed hat and carrying an umbrella, is about fourteen, and Marcel, in a striped straw hat, is only thirteen. The Comtesse de Martel, otherwise the novelist Gyp, saw him playing with Antoinette in the Champs-Élysées, and was amused to meet the little boy a few days later buying the complete works of Molière and Lamartine in Calmann Lévy's bookshop in the Rue de Grammont[1]; where recognising her as a friend of Antoinette he greeted her with a pallid but charming smile. When Gyp next had tea with Mme Faure she asked who he was. "He's Dr Proust's son, I've known his mother for years," replied that lady, "he's amazingly intelligent, but unfortunately rather frail, and he's a great friend of Antoinette's." Marcel used to recite his favourite poems to Antoinette, and then ask timidly, "Did you like that?"; and in return she taught him how to make caramels. She could always make him obey her with a glance of her grey eyes, with their extraordinarily long lashes: "have you ever noticed Antoinette's eyelashes, madame?" he asked Gyp earnestly.

Marie de Benardaky and her younger sister Nelly were daughters of a Polish nobleman, Nicolas de Benardaky, who is said to have gained his wealth as a tea-merchant. He had once been master of ceremonies at the court of the Tsar, and was still entitled to be called 'Your Excellency'. M. de Benardaky lived at 65 Rue de Chaillot, which runs into the Avenue Marceau a quarter of a mile to the west of the Champs-Élysées; for these elysian lawns were the joint playground of the noble children of the west end of Paris and the bourgeois children of the centre. He had a reputation for arrogance, while his wife, whose maiden name was Lebrock, was said to care for nothing but champagne and love. She was statuesque and beautiful, and was remembered for her appearance at a fancy-dress ball as a Valkyrie, complete with spear. Her daughter Marie had long black hair and a rosy, laughing face; she can have had little outward resemblance to the red-haired, freckled and sullen Gilberte. As Proust remembered her long afterwards, she was fifteen when he fell in love with her, and

[1] The shop of Calmann Lévy, who later published *Les Plaisirs et les Jours*, was a favourite resort of Charles Haas, original of Swann, and of Anatole France, original of Bergotte.

perhaps he was right; for although according to Gotha she was born at Pavlovsk on 12 July 1874, and would therefore only have been twelve, Gotha is known to be less fallible on the ages of princes than on those of princesses, particularly when these belonged before their marriage only to the minor nobility.[1]

Except for the hooting torrent of automobiles which rushes past their gravel bank towards the Arc de Triomphe, the Champs-Élysées to-day are much the same as they were seventy years ago. The lawns by the Alcazar d'Été and the Théâtre des Ambassadeurs, on which Marcel played prisoner's base, are now railed off; but the laurel shrubberies of his games of hide-and-seek are still there, and the nymph of the fountain still arranges her long stony tresses. In the novel she is holding out a baby, and after the snowfall an icicle hangs from her hand, 'which seemed to explain her gesture'[2]; but in the real Champs-Élysées she is childless, and in order to make his joke, Proust had to present her with one of the three putti, carrying wheat, grapes and doves, who form the centre-piece of another fountain further up, by the Théâtre Marigny. The only surviving roundabout has been banished to this part of the park since Marcel's time. Near by is a cedar, bearing a notice which reads 'Probable age in 1950, 90 years': here, too, is something which saw Marcel at play with 'Gilberte', and could perhaps tell us whether their wrestling match in the shrubbery ever occurred, or whether, as he affirmed long afterwards, 'there was never anything in the least improper in my relations with her'. The wooden booths, lettered A to H, where ginger-bread, barley-sugar, toy drums and windmills were sold, still line the avenue under the chestnut-trees; and there is the public lavatory in which the Narrator's grandmother had her stroke, a dignified edifice of cast-iron painted green. Perhaps the Marquise, its guardian and hostess, was a real figure, and perhaps in real life Marcel was plunged into an ecstasy of unconscious memory when the musty odour of her 'salon' reminded him of Jules Amiot's den in the back-garden at Illiers. But the story of the Marquise's exclusiveness, her pride in 'choosing her society', is also told in *Jean Santeuil* of Mme Laudet, at whose farm, Les Aigneaux, the people of Étreuilles are served with refreshments on Sundays: "I only receive people I like," she says.[3]

---

[1] The *Almanach de Gotha* for 1900 even dates her birth as 1876.
[2] I, 398, 405   [3] *Jean Santeuil*, vol. 1, 23ᶜ

In the happy fields of the Champs-Élysées, the third of the gardens of his childhood, Marcel held court among his young friends. Leaving prisoner's base to those who preferred it, he would stroll along the gravel-walk by the Alcazar d'Été talking of Sarah Bernhardt and Mounet-Sully, and repeating the verses of his favourite poets. He already possessed his amazing verbal memory for poetry, and Musset, Hugo, Racine, Lamartine and Baudelaire were among his repertoire. The day of the symbolists had not yet arrived, though he knew the work of Verlaine; and his chief enthusiasm among living poets was Leconte de Lisle, greatest of the Parnassians, from whose prose translations of the Iliad and Odyssey the Homeric argot of Bloch is derived. 'He charmed his little companions,' says Robert Dreyfus, 'and he also rather baffled us. But most astonished of all were the grown-ups, who were unanimous in their rapture at the refinements of his courtesy, the complications of his good intentions. I see him now, very handsome and very sensitive to cold, smothered in jerseys and mufflers, rushing to meet our mothers or grandmothers, bowing at their approach and always finding the right words to touch their hearts, whether he broached subjects usually reserved for his elders, or merely enquired after their health.' The novelist Gyp saw him one day (though this was in the Parc Monceau) pinched and shivering with cold, clutching a hot roast potato in each of his frozen hands. In those days it was customary for Parisian ladies to stop on their way to the Opéra to buy roast potatoes, which they would keep in their muffs as a substitute for central heating during the performance; so this conduct was less eccentric than it might now seem. When he left he would present the potatoes to the chair-woman, by way of a tip: she grew to expect them, and would have been hurt if he had forgotten.

Soon, however, he would see Marie and Nelly de Benardaky hurrying through the trees ahead of the violet plume on the hat of their governess; he abandoned his recitation of Leconte de Lisle, or his talk of Sarah Bernhardt, and ran to join their game of prisoner's base. He would always try to be on Marie's side and to arrange for her to win; and once when he hesitated out of polite-ness and made as if to join her sister, the good-natured Nelly laughed and said "No, you're on Marie's side, it makes you so happy." Marie gave a mocking but indulgent smile, and he felt that his love, since it was thus publicly admitted, must surely be returned. On rainy days he would stand by the window at home, gazing in despair at the streaming balcony and the glistening Boulevard Malesherbes; till a pale ray of sunlight shone on the railings and cast a filigree shadow on the grey stone-work, which gradually brightened, like a crescendo in music, to 'the fixed and unalterable gold of a fine day'. He hurried to the Champs-Élysées, and there was Marie already, greeting him with the familiar "Let's start playing at once, you're on my side."

In December came the snow, levelling the boulevard with the pavements and deadening the noise of the traffic. "There won't be anyone at the Champs-Élysées," said Mme Proust, "and if that's why you're looking at the sky, you can be sure Mlle de Benardaky won't come—they won't let her spoil her fine dresses just for that." Suppressing a desire to strike his unfeeling mother, Marcel replied: "No, I know she won't be there," and went, not so much in order to see Marie, as to view the white ruin of his hopes. The deserted lawns were deep in snow, and icicles hung from the naked protuberances of the cherubs on the fountain; but there, after all, was Marie advancing in front of her governess, with glowing cheeks and a fur toque over her long black hair. One by one their other friends arrived. Soon they were sliding on the glazed gravel paths, and throwing snowballs; and as he recalled with irony long afterwards, when Marie hurled down his neck the snowballs which he himself had given her, he felt it was a sign of predilection on her part, almost a declaration of their love, and that all their company knew it.

Every evening before he went to sleep he would say to himself "I shall see her to-morrow"; and if he woke in the small hours he would fall asleep again with the thought: "It's already to-day!" As he lay in bed he promised himself that to-morrow he would make a decisive step in his love, or at least memorise the elusive details of Marie's face; but when to-morrow came the afternoon would pass in the insignificant ritual of prisoner's base, and her face would have changed. 'He measured his pleasure in seeing her by the immensity of his desire to see her,' he wrote afterwards in *Jean Santeuil*, 'and by his grief at seeing her go; for he enjoyed her actual presence very little.'[1] Sometimes in the Champs-Élysées he felt that the little girl he saw was somehow a different person from the little girl he loved: such are the characteristic

[1] *Jean Santeuil*, vol. I, 89

symptoms of romantic love, which loves not a person but an
ideal, a personified desire, a projection of one's self.

In February he was kept away from the Champs-Élysées by a
bout of influenza; but his agony at the thought that Marie would
be enjoying prisoner's base without him was happily relieved by
the news that she was ill too. When he was convalescent a letter
came from her asking him in her mother's name to tea, 'at five
o'clock, on any day you wish'. He entered the house he had
thought inaccessible for ever, outside which he had stood and
stared on afternoons when Marie had stayed away from the
Champs-Élysées, and whose number in the Rue de Chaillot,
together with the name of that poetic street, had echoed in his
thoughts with 'a painful and deleterious enchantment'. The staircase was dark, and in the profound obscurity of the vestibule it
was impossible to tell whether the dim figure standing by a gothic
sideboard was some footman waiting for his mistress to end her
visit, or the master of the house himself. In the drawing-room the
paintings on the ceiling, the coloured glass in the windows, the
lap-dog and the tea-table seemed not only part of the beauty and
mystery of his beloved and her mother, but also evidence of a
social superiority of which Marie must never become aware. He
tried in vain to persuade his parents to change their furniture and
their habits; and then, reflecting that Marie would in all prob-
ability never visit them and learn the humiliating truth, he assured
her next time that in his home as in hers there were loose-covers
on the chairs, and chocolate was never served at tea-time. The
awe-inspiring concierge bowed affably before him, her parents
changed from 'implacable deities' into a lady and gentleman who
urged him to come often, to 'teach Marie all about literature', and
assured him that he had a good influence upon her. His parents,
however, were not altogether content with this new acquaintance.
Certainly, it was only proper that M. and Mme de Benardaky
should admire the intelligence of Marcel; but they were out of his
class, and perhaps not very favourable representatives of their
own. "Mme de Benardaky has reached such a high position in
society," said the witty Mlle de Malakoff, "that the only person
you see in her house who isn't out of the top drawer is herself."
Even Marcel himself, now or later, came to look critically on
Marie's parents: there is a distinct resemblance between Odette
Swann and her *louche* salon in *A l'Ombre*, and Mme de Benardaky

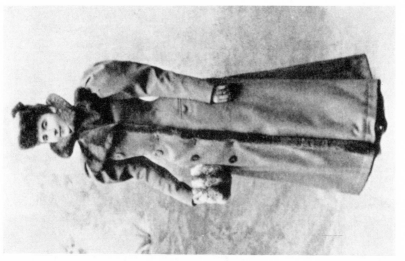

Marie de Benardaky

Proust in the Parc Monceau with Antoinette Faure

Portrait of Proust by Jacques Émile Blanche, 1892

Mme Laure Hayman

and the company she kept. There were to be at least two other ladies who contributed to the character of Odette; but the one who kept mixed company (Mme Hayman) was unmarried, and the one who was married (Mme Straus) had a salon of extreme distinction and was notoriously faithful to her husband.

In the spring of 1887 he ceased to see Marie. In *Jean Santeuil* it is because his parents, alarmed at the unhappiness and emotional instability caused by his passion, forbid their meetings, while in *A l'Ombre* the Narrator, convinced at last that his friend does not return his love, decides for himself never to see her again. Perhaps both versions were true in real life; but for a time in his despair Marcel wished to commit suicide, to throw himself from the balcony of 9 Boulevard Malesherbes—the former barometer of his hopes—on the pavement below; and when he recovered, his life was irretrievably changed. His first attempt to love and be loved by someone other than his mother—to escape, that is, from incest—had failed. Ability to love a person of the opposite sex, and of one's own age, is the only valid escape from the prison of the family; and that way was now barred. If he were to risk loving another young girl his suffering, his humiliation and his mother's displeasure would only be repeated. No doubt he was doomed even before he met Marie de Benardaky—if not by some ante-natal predisposition, then by tensions whose work was done for ever in his early childhood—to lifelong homosexuality. Perhaps, too, as not infrequently happens in the puberty of a future homo-sexual, his unconscious mind had deliberately made a hetero-sexual choice which was certain to fail, in order to set itself free for its true desire. In every homosexual, perhaps, there is a heterosexual double, uppermost at first, who must be imprisoned and made powerless before his stronger brother can come to life. Marcel had tried to be 'normal': if he had failed, it was Marie's fault for rejecting him; and his mother had wished it, and was therefore partly to blame. He was absolved. But Marie had also taught him to believe, perhaps rightly, that love, outside the family, is the only feeling which can never be returned.

During most of his life he continued to be intermittently fascinated by young girls. They inspired him with a mingled attraction and repulsion, desire and fear, and a whole little band of them invaded his novel; but there was safety in numbers. Once and only once, after his mother's death, when he was at the beginning of middle age, he thought for a time of marrying one, but decided to write his novel instead. Almost to the end of his life he continued, now and then, to fall in love with women; but somehow his choice always happened to be a respectable married lady, twenty years older than himself, or a high-class, equally safe and unattainable cocotte; or if he loved an unmarried woman of his own age or younger, then she was usually the fiancée or mistress of a friend. The married ladies or the cocotte, Freudians would say, were mother-images; and they would rightly add that a preference for women already bespoken to male friends is a typical symptom of homosexuality. These were substitutes for his mother, those were substitutes for his friends. But there was a rejected part of himself, forever prevented by stronger forces from coming to power, for which the young girls were also substitutes for Marie de Benardaky; and when he migrated to the Cities of the Plain he took with him a prisoner crushed beneath the weight of Time and Habit, a buried heterosexual boy who continued to cry unappeased for a little girl lost.

Chapter 5

BALBEC AND CONDORCET

AN inventory of the contents and condition of the fourteen-year-old Marcel's mind, in the period shortly before his meeting with Marie de Benardaky, has been preserved in a leaf of a confession-book belonging to Antoinette Faure, one of his playmates in the Champs-Élysées. The book was an import from Victorian England to anglomaniac Paris, and the twenty-five questions are printed in English—perhaps Marcel had already learned enough of the language from his mother to understand them, or perhaps Antoinette translated for him. He writes in a fluent, uninhibited hand, with precocious self-expression and wit; and words such as 'intelligence', 'naturalness', 'beauty', 'the land of the ideal' occur and recur, showing that he was accustomed to submit all questions to these touchstones. His 'favourite occupations' are 'reading, revery, poetry, the theatre'. His 'ideal of happiness' is 'to live near all the people I love, with the beauties of nature, plenty of books and music, and a French theatre near by'. His 'pet aversion' is 'people who have no feeling for goodness, and do not know the pleasures of affection'—perhaps he is thinking of Dr Proust. All this is nothing extraordinary, and no doubt others of Mlle Faure's young friends, those future politicians, generals and society hostesses, made no less idealistic entries. But Marcel's originality lay in the strength of will which would enable him to pursue his vision of goodness and beauty, deepened but unchanged, in later life, when others convince themselves that the quest is unimportant, or that life has given them what they sought. He would see that the Ideal is not to be found in the world of space and time, and press on to seek it elsewhere; and at this point the object of the search would become not happiness, but salvation.

His cultural tastes, however, remain immature. His 'favourite prose authors' are still George Sand and Augustin Thierry, for he is faithful to the memories of the night when his mother read *François le Champi* at his bedside, and the summer of Augustin

Thierry at Illiers. His favourite poet is Alfred de Musset, whom Bloch tolerated only because he had written 'one absolutely meaningless line'.[1] Among painters he mentions only the execrable Meissonier, who became the idol of the French bourgeoisie by painting pictures of fat red cardinals at supper, and among musicians only Mozart (a great composer, but Proust was by nature a Wagnerian) and Gounod, a Meissonier of music. But the confession-album continues its inquisition, and two entries reveal something of the cross-currents with which the boy is striving. 'What is your idea of the depths of misery?' he is asked, and replies 'to be separated from Mother'. 'For what fault have you most indulgence?' it persists, and he answers: 'for the private life of geniuses'. He was never to feel indulgence for his own vices, never to separate sin from guilt; but here it is as if he had some premonition that the time, thirty years ahead, when he would descend to the lowest pits of Sodom, where love and cruelty are imitated for hire, would coincide with—and perhaps be indispensable to—the moment of revelation and victory.

Illiers, with its lilacs and hawthorns, was now a forbidden country. Only the air of sea or mountains was safe for his asthma, and he spent his holidays with his mother or grandmother on the Normandy coast, at Dieppe, Tréport, Trouville or Cabourg, or at Salies-de-Béarn in the Pyrenees. It is regrettable that so little information concerning these seaside holidays of his 'teens has survived, for he seems to have distilled from the summers of the 1880s many aspects of the first visit to Balbec in *A l'Ombre*. With the sole exception of *Un Amour de Swann* (in which it is probable that little came from his personal experience), there is no episode in his novel where the materials for comparison with his real life are so scanty. Evidence is not lacking, however, for the two salient features of the Narrator's first holiday at Balbec, his relations with his grandmother and the presence of the little band. In a letter to his mother from Cabourg on 9 September 1891, two summers after the death of Mme Nathé Weil, Proust wrote of 'those sea-side holidays when grandmother and I, lost in one another, walked battling with the wind and talking'. And in an early prose piece he described 'some little girls I once watched at play by the sea'. One was running with shuffling steps, pretending to be a princess in a carriage, while another was chasing her to return a

[1] I, 90

muff which she had left behind, and shouting at the top of her voice: "Madame! Your Royal Highness has forgotten her muff! The Princess has forgotten her muff! Your muff, Princess!" And the first little girl thanked her with a smile, and took the muff with a dignified absence of surprise.[1] Perhaps these little girls may seem too childish to represent Albertine and her friends, who were, nevertheless, young enough to play at diabolo and ferret. But the idea of the little band is here, as well as in the Champs-Élysées; and we shall find Proust at play later with at least two more groups of young girls, one in Paris in 1891, the other at Cabourg in the late 1900s. In a conversation with André Gide, which we shall meet in its place many years later, he used expressions which have been taken to mean that the original little band was composed of boys; but in fact his words to Gide are only a general statement that in the heterosexual parts of his novel he used 'the feelings of tenderness and charm supplied by his homosexual memories'. We shall find that the female characters loved or desired by the Narrator invariably began, at least, as girls or women to whom Proust himself was attracted in real life: he never merely transposed them from boys or men, though he sometimes reinforced them with elements from his homosexual life.

In 1887, during the summer after his winter's love for Marie de Benardaky, Marcel visited the health-resort of Salies-de-Béarn with his mother. With them at the Hôtel de la Paix was Mme Proust's best friend, the beautiful wife of Anatole Catusse, later senator for the district of Tarn-et-Garonne. The two ladies shared a taste for music, a similar turn of wit, and that love of amiable gossip, of discussing the actions and motives of acquaintances and strangers, which is so valuable an example in the mother of a great novelist. In the conversation and singing of Mme Catusse Marcel found some consolation for 'the boredom which Salies inspires in one who hasn't enough "double muscles" (as Tartarin would say) to walk in the cool shade of the countryside near by, and find there the grain of poetry which is indispensable to one's existence, but is not to be found in the hotel terrace, with its silly chatter and tobacco smoke, where we spend all our time'. One day Mme Catusse promised to sing for him 'a little song if I begin her portrait in words, a big one if I finish it, and as many songs as I like if it is full-length'. His friends were calling him to join their

[1] *Chroniques*, 135

game of croquet in the hotel garden; but instead he sat down at the desk of Mlle Biraben, the proprietress, to write about Mme Catusse to his grandmother in Paris. The embarrassed boy describes the young woman's eyes, complexion, hair and figure for a reward ('the divine melodies of Massenet and Gounod') and in a manner ('it's frightfully difficult to rival Alfred de Musset') which recall the confession-album of the previous year. But the banalities of gallantry are mixed with the more interesting clichés of his new love for the Homeric translations of Leconte de Lisle; and as he swears 'by Artemis the white goddess and Pluto of the burning eyes', the voice of Bloch is heard. Perhaps his ardour is almost genuine, and he has already turned from the love of young girls to the pursuit of a mother-substitute; but soon he curses 'the genii hostile to the peace of mankind who have forced me to write such nonsense about someone I really like and who has been so kind to me'; and seeing the absurdity of the situation, he ends with a cheerful 'Good-morning, Grandmama, and how do you do?'

In the first half of 1887, cured of his first love, and of the no less detrimental habits of loitering on the way home from the Lycée Condorcet, spoiling his dinner by devouring rich cakes at a pâtisserie, and chatting for hours with the concierge, Marcel had begun to work hard at school. He was rewarded in July by a second prize for history and geography, a third for Latin and a fourth for 'general excellence'. His worst subject was mathematics; and when Robert, in his efforts to help his elder brother, entreated him: "Really, Marcel, you must at least *try* to understand," Marcel would reply: "Impossible!" A letter to his mother of 24 September, after his return from Salies-de-Béarn, shows him reading Loti, visiting the Louvre, and walking in the Bois de Boulogne, where his Great-Uncle Louis meets him in the Avenue des Acacias with his carriage. He is experimenting with his health: he has had 'transparent nights, with the conscious feeling that I am asleep, but am on the point of waking up', a sensation well known to the Narrator of *A la Recherche*; and then, one morning, he utters a cry of surprise on waking, because he has slept calmly and his mouth tastes fresh. The day before he had driven in the Bois in a closed carriage; and he draws the not very hygienic conclusion that he had better try to stop his open-air walks there. Perhaps it was in this summer that he accompanied Mme Catusse

in the horse-omnibus from Auteuil to the Madeleine. He felt he
ought to make polite conversation, and thought he was succeed-
ing, until his mother's friend asked: "Are you going to talk like
this all the way?"; 'after which cold shower', as he reminded her
long afterwards, 'no further sound was heard but the rumbling
of the bus on the cobbles of the Rue La Fontaine'.

In October he began his year of *rhétorique* at Condorcet, the
first half of the two years' course leading to the baccalaureate—a
year which Marcel airily described as 'a circular tour from Homer
to André Chénier by way of Petronius'. The class was shared by
rude M. Cucheval, polite M. Dauphiné—'It's really amusing to
let oneself be guided by two such different minds,' he reported a
year later to Robert Dreyfus—and the witty Maxime Gaucher.
M. Cucheval was forthright, uncompromising, 'a real savage of a
schoolmaster', and yet, 'however much you're Cuchevalised, it
does you no harm. Don't think him a fool, just because he makes
silly jokes, and is too much of a barbarian to enjoy exquisite
combinations of syllables or verbal contours. He's a relief from
those idiots who round off all their periods—a thing he can't and
won't do. He's absolutely delightful, the ideal of a good teacher,
and the very reverse of boring.'

Maxime Gaucher, who was literary critic on the *Revue Bleue*,
and whom Marcel calls 'an infinitely free and charming intelligence', was the first to realise his pupil's exceptional talent. Week
after week he made Marcel read his compositions aloud to the
class, praising them, criticising them, and suddenly overcome by
helpless laughter at some audacity of style. One of these pieces
has survived, an essay on Corneille and Racine which shows
remarkable maturity of thought and language. Proust is already
writing his seamless, interwoven prose with sentences a hundred
words long and virgin of paragraphs; and when he made Gisèle
write her famous letter from Sophocles among the shades to
Racine, beginning 'My dear friend', he may have been thinking
of the subject of this essay, but hardly of its matter or style, in
which there is nothing of which to be ashamed. Once he was even
asked to read his latest composition to a visiting inspector from
the Sorbonne, Eugène Manuel, a mediocre poet who put up for
the Académie Française whenever there was a vacancy, but always
in vain. The outraged inspector heard him to the end, and turning
to M. Gaucher asked, "Haven't you anyone, even at the bottom

of your class, who can write French more clearly and correctly?";
only to receive the cutting and punning reply: "Sir, none of my
pupils is taught to write French like a Manual." M. Cucheval,
however, that 'ideal of a good teacher', did not at first return his
pupil's regard. Before the end of the October term 'a dozen silly
fools were writing decadent prose, M. Cucheval said I'd divided
the class into factions, and was a poisoner of young minds, and
some people even thought I was a poseur!' Marcel's essays were
greeted by storms of booing and applause—'if it hadn't been for
Gaucher they'd have massacred me'. After a few months M.
Cucheval began to come round; but just before the final examination he was heard to remark: "He'll get through, because he's only
a joker, but it'll be his fault if another fifteen of them are
ploughed."

In the summer of 1888, alas, Maxime Gaucher fell ill, and died
on 24 July. His place was taken till the end of term by M. Dupré,
who was 'affectionate, kind, and full of delicacy, but a bore'. He
knew the works of Leconte de Lisle, it was true, but 'what's the
use of hearing modern writers talked about by someone who likes
them with far too many reservations? It makes you tap your feet
and grind your teeth.' The other master in *rhétorique*, the cold,
thin and ceremonious M. Dauphiné, likewise admired Leconte de
Lisle, but thought him 'cuwious' and was puzzled by 'his taste for
the stwange and exotic'. M. Dauphiné lisped, and when his pupils
misbehaved would say "Monsieur Halévy and Monsieur Bizet,
I must ask you to withdwaw." These two, the son and nephew
of Bizet's widow, were particularly unruly, perhaps because
the innocent and blue-spectacled M. Martin, the school
superintendent, had told them: "With famous names like yours,
you know, you'll never be expelled."

There is a photograph of the class of M. Cucheval, a huge
pyramid of fifty boys, most of whom are older than Marcel. He is
an alert, asthenic child of sixteen, with narrow chest, sloping
shoulders, and collar turned up to keep out the draught. M.
Cucheval has the heavy dignity of a St Bernard dog with a beard.
Marcel is motionless, caught half-way between the little prince of
Illiers and the dandy of the 1890s; but soon the pyramid will col-
lapse, M. Cucheval will bark, the boy in the front row will put on
his bowler hat, and time will begin to pass. In the July examina-
tions of 1888 Marcel won first prize for French composition and

third prize for Latin and Greek. Was the other half of M. Cucheval's prophecy fulfilled, and did this success mean the failure of fifteen imitators?

Early in September his mother took Robert to Salies-de-Béarn, while Marcel stayed at Auteuil. He missed little, for the weather at Salies was unbearably hot; but during the first day of parting he wept, and was lectured by Great-Uncle Louis, who said his grief was 'sheer egotism'. 'This little psychological discovery caused him such pure joy of pride and self-satisfaction that he gave me a merciless sermon'. His grandfather was less severe and only called him a 'silly boy', while his grandmother shook her head with a smile and said: "It would take more than this to prove that you really love your mother!" But next morning he went to the Bois de Boulogne and laughed aloud with joy; the sun was out, the air was still cool, and he felt an unaccustomed pleasure in breathing and walking, just as in the long-lost summer of Augustin Thierry at Illiers. He sat on the grass by the smaller lake, reading *Le Mariage de Loti* and watching the violet shadow on the water, till the returning sunlight sparkled on lake and leaves. At lunch he behaved particularly well, and instead of the usual furious glares from his grandfather, there came only a mild rebuke ("You shouldn't *rub* so!") when he wiped away a few last tears with his handkerchief.

The servants, Victoire and Angélique, as he wrote to his mother, were convinced that he had a 'little friend' who would soon console him for her absence—and the servants were right. During this September he was interested in a pretty Viennese girl whom he had met at the Perrin dancing-school in the Rue de la Victoire, not far from Condorcet. The cynicism with which he wrote of her to Robert Dreyfus was no doubt assumed, but it does not suggest any profound feeling or enjoyment: 'I've had an extremely uncomplicated affair which ended very boringly in the inevitable way, and has given birth to an absorbing liaison that threatens to last at least a year, to the greater profit of café concerts and places of that kind to which one takes that kind of person.' Perhaps the 'platonic passion for a celebrated cocotte', which he mentions in the same letter, struck a little deeper. Her name was Léonie Closmesnil, and he watched her every afternoon driving along the Avenue des Acacias in the Bois, and alighting to walk in the Tir aux Pigeons, with her characteristic lingering step, and long skirts sweeping the gravel.[1] He tried to analyse her fascination, in which one may recognise the Freudian identification of the courtesan with the mother, in purely aesthetic terms: the rounded lines of her neck and shoulders were those of an Etruscan vase, the corner of her mouth was that of a Luini or Botticelli Virgin; the pink of her dress was more exquisite than the September sky above the Bois at six in the evening, and the blue of her hat-band reminded him of deep, still water. He wrote to her to inform her of his admiration, and she wrote back; then he sent a photograph, and she gave him several of herself, which he kept till the end of his life, in his album crammed with the images of women and men he had loved or liked, of picnics and house-parties, the records of his wasted time. For one moment of his novel she became Odette, whom Swann, too, was to compare to a Botticelli: Proust revealed to a friend that when Odette walks by the Tir aux Pigeons, 'letting the long train of her mauve skirt trail behind her', and the onlooking gentleman says to his friend: "I was in bed with her on the day MacMahon resigned",[2] she is Léonie Closmesnil.

He was already trying, tied to the cord which led so deeply and painfully to the bottom of his heart that it would always pull him back, to escape from the family. Perhaps he would never have wished or dared to devote his September to the pretty girl and the beautiful cocotte if his mother had been at home. But she had left him for a holiday with his young brother, for whom she was trying to find a riding-companion—perhaps young Eiffel ('his father built the Tower, you know!') would do? So Marcel good-humouredly sent on 'His Majesty's' new hunting-horn, which seemed much too big, more like a trumpet to be blown on Judgment Day: "It looks very funny and I can't think what it's for," said Victoire. Perhaps it was in this month that he ventured still further into the forbidden country of normal love, and retreated still more disenchanted. A schoolfellow persuaded him to visit a brothel, an incident which he recalled in his novel, when Bloch informs the Narrator to his amazement that 'women never ask for anything better than to make love', and by taking him to a house

---

[1] She wore a white lock of hair, intentionally bleached, on her forehead, and was known as 'the Butcheress', because her first lover had been a butcher. Odette, too, appears in the Bois 'with a single grey lock in her hair, now turned yellow' (I, 419).   [2] I, 420, 421

of ill fame performs a service which bears 'the same useful relation to love as that of handbooks on mediaeval towns to travel'.[1]But the experience was horrible; the proprietress had the face of a murderess, and when he left, he afterwards told his comrades (who thought the remark exquisitely absurd), "I felt as if I had left part of my moral being behind me."

In October 1888 he began his year of *philosophie* under Marie-Alphonse Darlu, 'the great philosopher', as he wrote in the preface to *Les Plaisirs et les Jours*, 'whose inspired words, more sure of survival than many a book, brought thought to birth in me and so many others'. Darlu was a bearded and spectacled little man with an energetic and highly coloured face; Anatole France said condescendingly of him that he 'had a pretty brain', little knowing that Darlu, with equal condescension, said the same of Anatole France. He had a strong southern accent, so that philosophy to him was 'phi-loh-soh-phy' and stupidity 'stoo-pi-di-ty'. On the desk in front of him he would place his top-hat, and take it as a concrete example for any abstruse doctrine he was expounding: as Fernand Gregh said, 'he brought the whole of philosophy, like a conjuror, out of that hat'. Marcel always remembered his explanation of the theories of Leibnitz: "Suppose my hat is a monad; well, I drop my handkerchief into the hat . . ."—but what the handkerchief represented we are not told. He would startle his pupils into thinking for themselves by a policy of severe sarcasm. Once, a year after Marcel's time, he announced that a certain composition came first, and then crushed the unhappy pupil with the words, perhaps a little too exalted for a schoolboy: "All the same, these are the fantasies of a sick brain, *aegri somnia*, a philosophy fit for Sganarelle!" Darlu's destructive and constructive criticism did more for Marcel than the delighted appreciation of Maxime Gaucher; and he surprised the boy by complaining not, like M. Cucheval, of the incoherence or eccentricity of his essays, but of their tendency to banality and loose metaphor—"all these bad habits you've picked up from magazines and reviews". "How can you write a phrase like 'the red conflagration of the sunset'? That sort of colouring is only fit for some little newspaper in the provinces, no, I won't say even that, in the colonies!" For when

---

[1] I, 575, 576. In *Jean Santeuil* (vol. 1, 130) he even gives the address of the brothel in the Rue Boudreau, which may well be correct, since that street was on his way home from Condorcet.

a writer tries to startle, he is likely only to utter a cliché. He will only be profoundly original when he seeks painfully for a universal truth; and this will be most universal when it is most personal. Darlu's influence on Marcel was crucial, and may be traced even into *A la Recherche du Temps Perdu*, not only in certain features of the character of Bergotte, but in the very core of the novel. This influence went beyond the mere adoption of his apparently contradictory doctrines, such as the importance of scientific discovery ("How agreeable it would be, to be a really intelligent scientist and get to the bottom of these things," Darlu would say) or the 'unreality of the sensible world'. Marcel learned that it is not sufficient for a great work of art to be poetic or moral: it must also be metaphysical; and the deepest theme of *A la Recherche* is the revelation of a purely metaphysical truth. He was no longer satisfied with vague sensations, but felt it his duty to discover and express their meaning; and if the Narrator refuses to rest content with his mysterious delight in the spires of Martinville or the taste of the madeleine, and persists in obstinate questioning till he conquers their secret, it is partly thanks to the teaching of Darlu. No doubt, however, Darlu only gave his pupil qualities which he possessed already, waiting for liberation; and the Socratic master would modestly conclude with: "But I'm not here to give you all this advice, my job is to teach you philosophy."

Meanwhile, not satisfied with writing 'decadent prose' for their homework, the pupils of Condorcet had been raising a crop of handwritten schoolboy magazines. In the words of a doggerel poem which appeared in one of them in 1890:

> '*Excuse me, sir, have we had showers?*
> *What are these fresh, poetic flowers? . . .*
> *Let me explain, it's nothing new:*
> *The whole class writes, their master is Darlu.*'

The editors were Daniel Halévy and Jacques Bizet, though Marcel often appeared as contributor or member of the editorial board. The earliest was *Lundi*, 'an artistic and literary review', which began in 1887 and had a white cover with an elegant pen-and-ink drawing of two cupids allegorically supporting a folio volume open at Verlaine's line 'The eclectic triumph of the Beautiful'. In the spring of 1888 came the *Revue de Seconde* ('*Class Two Review*'), organ of the audacious new school of subtilitism, of which Halévy, aged fifteen, proclaimed himself the founder and leader. It died in March, at the thirteenth number; but from its ashes sprang the *Revue Verte*, written on the green paper, prescribed for the sake of his pupils' eyes and his own, by the master of Class Two, Eugène Lintilhac. Nothing of it survives but Mr Secretary Marcel's written, semi-humorous protest against Halévy's request, seconded by Bizet, for permission to copy certain articles for the good of posterity. The *Revue Verte*, he argues, 'unlike the so-called public press', is published not for financial gain nor in a large number of copies (this is no exaggeration, for there was never more than one copy, free of charge), but 'for the amusement of an extremely limited and select group'. These 'fleeting reflections of the mobility of imaginations at play' must be 'protected against the criticism of readers for whom they were never scribbled'; otherwise 'Mr Secretary will be under the regretful necessity of refusing his participation in a review so widely different from that in which he hitherto thought of collaborating.' But Daniel Halévy consoled himself in the 1920s for the early death of the *Revue Verte* by launching the famous *Cahiers Verts*, no. 68 of which was the *Souvenirs sur Marcel Proust* of their schoolfellow Robert Dreyfus.

The most important of these little magazines was the last, the *Revue Lilas*, named after the colour of the little twopenny exercise books, bought at the stationer's in the Passage du Havre near Condorcet, in which it was written. There is a persistent rumour that Marcel's essay on the spires of Martinville appeared in it; and though there is no actual evidence for this, it is just possible that the rumour may be based on reliable oral tradition, perhaps deriving from Daniel Halévy himself. But one of Marcel's contributions survives, dedicated 'to my dear friend Jacques Bizet', and headed 'for the *Revue Lilas*, to be destroyed after publication'. He imagines himself in his bedroom at the age of fifteen, oppressed by 'the horror of usual things', the banality of his lighted lamp, the noise of crockery in the next room, the dark violet sky with its gleaming stains of moonlight and stars. Then he is seventeen, it is the present, and everything is transformed: the Boulevard Malesherbes below his window, with 'the blue moonbeams dripping from the chestnut-trees', and the 'fresh, chill breathing of all these sleeping things', becomes a nightscene as exquisite as the moonlit garden of Combray, and 'usual things' are no longer horrible. 'I have made them sacred, and Nature too, because I could not conquer them. I have clothed them with my soul, with the inner splendour of images. I live in a sanctuary surrounded by a pageant. I am the centre of things, and each of them brings for my enjoyment sensations or sentiments that are magnificent or melancholy. I have glorious visions before my eyes.' This little sketch of the return of beauty and significance to things made sterile by habit touches one of the capital themes of Proust's art: it is already Time Regained in miniature.

His school friendships, however, gave him less satisfaction than his writing. 'There was something about him which we found unpleasant,' Daniel Halévy recalled many years after Proust's death; 'his kindnesses and tender attentions seemed mere mannerisms and poses, and we took occasion to tell him so to his face. Poor, unhappy boy, we were beastly to him.' In a minor episode of *Jean Santeuil* there are three boys whose intelligence the hero admires: they jostle him in the playground, and when he writes them 'such a beautiful, sincere and eloquent letter that tears came into his eyes as he wrote', only mock him the more. 'Jean did not understand that his craving for sympathy, his morbid and over-refined sensibility, which made him overflow with affection at the least show of kindness, were mistaken for hypocrisy, and only shocked and irritated these young people, in whom the indifference of their colder nature was accentuated by the heartlessness of youth.' So he takes his vengeance, in this novel of revenges, by making Jean meet one of them two years later, and find that he is silly after all.[1] But if Marcel suffered much in his schooldays from physical bullying, there would be other hints of it. At Condorcet, as in most French schools, violence was as unknown as other organised games; there was no worship of the strong and stupid, and intellectual prowess was respected and encouraged, even by the masters. His suffering came from his need to repeat with his fellow-creatures, in friendship as in love, the relationship he had known with his mother, the only one that could satisfy him, the only one that was impossible. A former schoolfellow told Jacques Émile Blanche, long afterwards, of his terror when he saw Marcel coming towards him, to take his hand and declare his need of 'a tyrannical and total affection'. And the bewildered little Halévy, two years his junior, saw him 'with his huge oriental eyes,

---

[1] *Jean Santeuil*, vol. 1, 325-7

his big white collar and flying cravat, as a sort of disturbed and disturbing archangel'. At first Halévy responded to Marcel's advances, then avoided him in alarm, only to bewilder him a month later with a shy 'good-morning'. And his cousin Bizet was just as bad: 'why did he say he was my friend, and then drop me completely? What do they want?—to get rid of me, annoy me, mystify me, or what? And I thought they were so nice!'

In the little, artificial world of childhood and school, love and friendship had disappointed him; but in the great real world outside, into which he would soon be released, perhaps love and friendship would be great and real also. Moreover, he had begun to see a third and last mirage of happiness from human relationships, in the realm of high society where those relationships might, it seemed, be considered and enjoyed as a work of art. In the autumn of 1888 he took his first tentative steps towards the Guermantes Way.

He might, if he wished, have found his admission through the ready-made connections of his father; for Dr Proust knew politicians such as Félix Faure, diplomats such as Camille Barrère and Gabriel Hanotaux, society physicians such as Dr Samuel Pozzi. Marcel met Dr Pozzi at dinner with his parents when he was only fifteen, and always remembered that his first 'dinner in town', no doubt a year or two later, had been with Pozzi in the Place Vendôme. But such an entry would have been too slow, humble and tainted, rather as if his Narrator had been reduced to meeting the Duchesse through the combined good offices of Mme Bontemps's husband, M. de Norpois and Dr Cottard. The high society of Paris was never as exclusive as it is symbolically represented in *A la Recherche*. Political, scientific or literary eminence, even mere intelligence or charm, were valid passports to the salons, and society was a career open to the talents. But Marcel wanted the *haut monde* to be more exclusive than it actually was, both to enhance its glamour and to increase his merit in arriving there; and for both these reasons, again, he wished to arrive suddenly and miraculously, and to be instantly accepted. This second wish was granted to him in real life, as to the Narrator in his novel; for Marcel was to discover that in this life all our desires are fulfilled, on the condition that they do not bring the happiness we expected from them.

The key to the Guermantes Way was absurdly simple: indeed,

its very obviousness may not only have answered his ambition, but have helped to create it. Two of his schoolfellows, Jacques Baignères and Jacques Bizet, happened to be sons of two of the chief mistresses of salons in the layer of society immediately below the nobility, where the upper bourgeoisie and the Faubourg Saint-Germain met on common ground. Jacques Baignères was the son of the prominent hostess Mme Laure Baignères, though not, if rumour was correct, of her husband. A visitor unaware of her intimate association with the Orleanist leader M. de Rémusat once asked: "Which does your son most resemble, yourself or M. Baignères?"; and she imperturbably replied "Jacques is just like his father." Jacques Bizet's widowed mother a few years earlier had married Émile Straus, a wealthy Jewish lawyer, after a long and ardent courtship: when asked why she had become his wife, she answered "Because it was the only way I could get him to leave me in peace." But Jacques Bizet remembered his mother saying: "Listen, my child, if I were to marry again, whom would you like best for a step-father?" "Émile," he replied without hesitation, and she kissed him, for she too preferred Émile Straus. Already, in the December of 1888, Marcel was inviting Mme Straus and Jacques Bizet to share his box with the other Jacques for the first night of Edmond de Goncourt's *Germinie Lacerteux* at the Odéon on the 15th; and to persuade her he added a characteristic piece of double-edged flattery: "I've found some lines in Vigny which even you ought to like, for they seem to have been written for your glorification—he must have foreseen you!"

When the news that Marcel was meeting academicians and showing 'an undue partiality for dukes' reached Condorcet, his schoolfellows felt he had betrayed the high ideals of the *Revue Lilas*. They mocked him to his face, but succeeded only in hurting his feelings, not in changing them, or in understanding that the power which drove him to the Guermantes Way was not snobism but genius. The legend that Proust was a society-writer and a snob had begun, and would be replaced by the truth of his greatness only in the last three years of his life, thirty years later. So his last year of school closes in umbrage and obscurity. In the baccalaureate exam he took a first prize for French composition; he began to choose beautiful cravats; and suddenly he was no longer a schoolboy, but a young man of eighteen with a moustache. He was abandoned by and tired of Bloch: it was time to find Saint-Loup.

Chapter 6

BERGOTTE AND DONCIÈRES

PROUST could never remember who had first taken him to the salon of Mme Arman de Caillavet. It was some time in the summer of 1889, and she greeted him with the remark she always served out for newcomers: "You'll find instruction as well as amusement here, it's just like a school prize-book." Then she introduced him to Anatole France, and he found to his disappointment that the writer whom he had imagined as 'a sweet singer with snowy locks' was a little man aged forty-five, of half-clerical, half-military appearance, with 'a red nose like a snail-shell and a pointed black beard'. From that moment of contrast between imagination and reality the character of Bergotte was to be born.

His hostess lived at 12 Avenue Hoche. Her maiden name was Léontine Lippmann, she had married the wealthy Albert Arman in 1868, and at this stage in her progress she was called simply Mme Arman. A few years later her husband added to the family surname the name of a vine-growing château on his country estate of Capian, and she was known as Mme Arman de Caillavet; and then the Arman was suppressed altogether and she became Mme de Caillavet, which sounded best of all. But she always professed that this self-ennobling of Albert's was absurd, and insisted to the end of her life on signing herself 'L. Arman Caillavet', accepting the 'Caillavet', it is true, but rejecting the 'de'.

In 1889 she was forty-two, still unaged and good-looking, loaded with pearls, with a small, intelligent head and short waved hair, and blue eyes which, although a little too prominent, had kept their air of mystery. Something of her imperious manner entered into Mme Verdurin. Mme Arman hurried to greet the proud and timid daughter of the dramatist Bjoernson with cries of "A Norwegian! What luck, what a recruit for my salon! You're just the number I need!" But whenever Mme Arman called on this desirable Viking, the servant always announced: "Madame regrets that she cannot receive Madame. She is in the middle of washing her hair." "Will this woman never finish washing her hair?" complained Mme Arman, but in vain.

Like Mme Verdurin, she felt herself persecuted by *les ennuyeux*. Strangely enough, however, these bores were not people whom she despaired of luring to her salon, but those she was anxious to expel from it; just as, at the age of three, she had tried to throw her baby brother out of the window, saying "He bores me." If the nobility were never to be seen at her receptions, it was chiefly because she didn't want them there, for her only ambition was to attract writers and politicians. In Proust's novel the Baron de Charlus visits Mme Verdurin partly as an act of enormous grace, partly for ends of his own; but in real life Comte Robert de Montesquiou, one of the chief originals of Charlus, was reduced to pleading for Mme Arman's favour, and cadged her invitations with little success. The letters in which he expresses his thwarted admiration and injured feelings, all in vain, are positively heart-rending. When he succeeded at last in enticing her and France to his mansion to meet his cousin, Comtesse Greffulhe, on whom Proust modelled several aspects of both the Duchesse and the Princesse de Guermantes, it was the culmination of seventeen years of hitherto fruitless intrigue. Mme Arman was perhaps an intellectual snob, but she was not a social one. Montesquiou was both: in wooing her it was France and her other pet lions he was after.

Her husband was noted for his sudden, alarming and often untimely appearances, and was therefore said to resemble a jack-in-a-box. M. Arman had a wart on his nose, the trailing ends of his cravat had been compared to the sails of a windmill, and his manner was humorously truculent; 'but he was a very good fellow,' writes Fernand Gregh, 'and there was more in him than people said'. Whenever he saw a new face among his wife's guests, he would pop up and say, "I am not Anatole France"; or he would introduce himself with, "I am the Master—I mean, of the house," and shout, "Monsieur France, here's another admirer for you!" He wrote the yachting column in *Le Figaro* under the preposterous pseudonym of Jip Topsail. He delighted in teasing France, who once helped him in his column with a few beauties of description which the editor carefully deleted. "Ha ha!" bellowed M. Arman, who had a strong southern accent, "you may be a great writer and an academician, but they couldn't find room for your blue skies and white clouds and sails like birds' wings!" "You know everything about the art of writing, M. Arman," France began with careful irony; but Mme Arman broke in with: "Hold your tongue, Albert, you're always saying something stupid." Clearly M. Arman shared several traits with that other great yachtsman, the bluff, teasing, hen-pecked M. Verdurin. Mme Arman had captured France in 1886 from a rival hostess, Mme Aubernon de Nerville. For some years after their first meeting in 1876 the two ladies had been great friends, and Mme Aubernon, when complimented on her charming companion, would say complacently, "Yes, I invented her myself." But Mme Arman decided to set up her own salon, and their rupture was the late nineteenth-century equivalent of the quarrel between the ageing Mme du Deffand and the young Julie de Lespinasse. Along with France, she stole the younger Dumas, the dramatist, Professor Brochard of the Sorbonne, the critic Jules Lemaître and the playwright Pailleron. The others continued to frequent both salons, but France never returned to Mme Aubernon's. "Is it true," she taxed him, "that you tell everybody you'll never come to my house again because my dinners bore you?" "I may have said so, madam," replied the embarrassed France, "but I never meant it to be repeated."

For a few years Mme Arman was forced to tolerate the occasional visits of the great man's wife. At first Mme France was an exquisite blonde who was sometimes mistaken for France's daughter; but she put on weight, her teeth became repulsively irregular, and in her domineering presence France trembled and stammered more than ever. Then he ceased to speak to her or to notice her presence. One day in June 1892 she invaded his study, where he was writing his fortnightly article for the *Universel*, and called him by a word which he considered 'gross, unseemly and basely insulting'—some say the word was '*cocu*'. A little later she heard the street-door close, and ran to the window: France was already receding along the Rue Chalgrin, carrying his inkwell, pen and unfinished article on a tray; he still wore his slippers and skull-cap, and the cord of his dressing-gown trailed on the pavement behind him. On 2 August 1893 they were divorced. No doubt the fault was not entirely on France's side; but Proust might well write of Bergotte that he was said to have 'behaved cruelly to his wife'.[1] Henceforth France ate and spent his days at Mme

Arman's. They made love every morning at his bachelor home, and then walked to Avenue Hoche for lunch. At tea-time he would enter the drawing-room and say, "I happened to be passing your house, and couldn't resist the pleasure of laying my delighted homage at your feet"; but everybody knew he had been writing in the library all afternoon. In Proust's novel this anecdote is told of M. de Norpois and Mme de Villeparisis.[1]

Anatole France was timid, lazy and unambitious; but Mme Arman, seized with the desire to create a great writer, made him self-confident, industrious and famous. Did she make him great? At least there is something in the faded prose of France, a joy, an irony, a craftsmanship, which has enabled him, alone of the secondary novelists of the French 1890s, to survive a little to-day. In his novel Proust gave the guardianship of Bergotte, so like Mme Arman's of France, not to Mme Verdurin but to Odette, Swann's wife. Bergotte spends every day at Mme Swann's, 'on exhibition', and her salon is built round him. She whispers to an influential guest: "I'll speak to him, and he'll write an article for you"; it is rumoured that she collaborates in his works; and the Narrator tells us that 'between the elegance of Mme Swann's salon and one whole aspect of the work of Bergotte there are relationships so close that each, for the old men of to-day, can become alternately a commentary on the other.'[2] In all this Proust is thinking of Mme Arman and France. He took the name of Bergotte from M. Bergeret, the hero of France's tetralogy *L'Histoire Contemporaine*; but it is also a near-anagram of Bourget, a novelist whom he met, as we shall see, in association with yet another original of Odette Swann. To people of Proust's generation the name could not fail to suggest also the philosopher Bergson, particularly to Proust himself, who was Bergson's cousin by marriage; but although the influence of Bergson's philosophy upon Proust's novel was considerable, there is little more of Bergson in Bergotte. There is, however, something of Renan, whom Proust visited on 17 January 1889, taking with him the old Grecian's *Vie de Jésus*; and after a long conversation, of which afterwards he had little to relate, he returned with the volume signed by the author.[3] The snail-shell nose is Renan's,

---

[1] II, 221   [2] II, 743-5

[3] 'For Marcel Proust,' wrote Renan, who died in 1892, 'whom I ask to keep an affectionate memory of me when I am no longer in this world.'

for the nose of Anatole France was quite different, being long, thin and a little to one side; and Bergotte's famous invocation to the Korai on the Acropolis was suggested by Renan's *Prière sur l'Acropole*. Bergotte's early essay on Racine, which Gilberte gives to the Narrator in a white packet tied with mauve ribbons, was a contribution by France, which was also printed separately, to an edition of Racine's works published in 1874.[1] Conversely, when M. de Norpois remarks that Bergotte has 'the subtlety of a deliquescent mandarin', Proust has in mind Lemaître's comparison of France to 'an extraordinarily learned and subtle mandarin'.

Was the influence of France upon Proust comparable to that of Bergotte on the Narrator? Many of France's themes—the unreality of the phenomenal world, the poetic nature of the past in which the only true reality is hidden, the impossibility of knowing another person, the continual process of change in the self, feelings and memory, his pessimism—are to be found in *A la Recherche*. The influence of his style is there long outgrown, but it is perceptible not only in Proust's early stories, written in the 1890s and collected in *Les Plaisirs et les Jours*, for which France wrote the preface, but even in *Jean Santeuil*. When the Narrator of *A la Recherche* speaks of 'a book I began to write', and of finding 'the equivalent in Bergotte of certain of my own phrases, whose quality was insufficient to determine me to continue it',[2] Proust is thinking of his unfinished *Jean Santeuil*; though no doubt the process was really in the reverse direction, and he had already found in France's novels the passages which he unconsciously reproduced in *Jean Santeuil*.

To the Narrator, however, the work of Bergotte was a discovery which was one of the foretastes of Time Regained, and gave him 'a joy that I felt I was experiencing in a deeper, vaster, more unified region of myself, from which all obstacles and separations seemed to have been removed'.[3] As we shall see, the only writer from whom Proust was to be granted a similar revelation—and that only a partial and temporary one, since the true revelation was to come from himself—was Ruskin, whom he

[1] But the reference in Bergotte's essay to the 'plastic nobility' and 'Delphic symbol' of Berma's acting in *Phèdre* comes from a critique by Jules Lemaître on Sarah Bernhardt's appearance in Racine's play at the Théâtre de la Renaissance in November 1893.

[2] I, 96

[3] I, 94

discovered ten years later. It is true that for a year or two France, along with Loti, was his favourite contemporary novelist. He never ceased to respect him, and he never replaced him with another, for when he outgrew France he turned to the masters of the past, to Balzac, Stendhal or Flaubert, or to the Russians, Tolstoy or Dostoevsky, or to English novelists, George Eliot and Hardy; and last of all to himself, for since Bergotte did not exist he was compelled, as a last resort, to become him. France was the only living novelist (except Barrès, who also contributed a little to Bergotte) whom he met and enthusiastically admired in early youth, and in gratitude he built the character of Bergotte, an apotheosis of France, around him. But he had to invent the greatness of Bergotte, in whose work, the magic of which is so subtly conveyed but so rarely demonstrated by quotation, there is something higher than France or any other French novelist of his time.

'On entering the drawing-room of Mme Arman,' wrote one of her guests, 'one had the impression of being in a railway-station, of which Anatole France was the stationmaster.' Mme Arman sat to the right of the fireplace, while France leaned against the mantelpiece, gesturing, stammering, hunting for the right word, but always holding forth. 'His conversation was that of a superior but crashing bore,' thought Henri de Regnier, who was however fond of talking himself; but to Fernand Gregh it seemed 'literally enchanting with its mixture of irony and kindness, wit and grace, naturalness and erudition, fantasy and good sense'. Towards Proust he adopted the paternal tone of Bergotte. "How do you manage to know so many things, Monsieur France?" asked Proust, and France replied: "It's quite simple, my dear Marcel. When I was your age I wasn't good-looking and popular like you. So instead of going into society I stayed at home and did nothing but read." No doubt he also uttered Bergotte's famous remark, that the pleasures of the mind would compensate for Marcel's ill-health. 'I would not exchange the painful pleasures of the intelligence for all the gay frivolities and empty experiences of the ordinary man,' he wrote in *Le Temps* of 9 November 1891. But when he said to Proust at Mme Arman's "You, Marcel, who love so much the things of the intelligence," his young friend interrupted: "I don't love the things of the intelligence at all; I only love life and movement."

Perhaps, however, the chief immediate influence upon his life which Proust encountered at this time in Mme Arman's salon was that of a person who was not there, her son Gaston. It can hardly be a coincidence that the military service of Gaston Arman, whom so far he had never met,[1] was immediately followed by that of Proust. Every Wednesday at Mme Arman's (for her day was the same as Mme Verdurin's) he would hear the latest news of Gaston in the army: his life in barracks at Versailles, the practical jokes for which he was so frequently confined to those barracks, the horrors and heroism of his route-marches and billeting in barns in the country of the Loire. He would see the photograph of Gaston on leave, standing in the sunlight on the balcony of 12 Avenue Hoche, fierce and resplendent in his artillery-man's uniform, the image of a rather portly Saint-Loup. Proust heard, admired and envied: why should he not do the same? He joined the army of his own free will, for with his father's influence he could easily have obtained exemption on the grounds of ill-health; and exemptions were also freely granted to those taking a university education. But it is true that unless he was either to spend three long years in military service or evade it altogether, the time was now or never.

The period of compulsory military service since 1872 had been five years, but for volunteers only one year. In practice, for more than half the total number of recruits, the full period of five years was not insisted upon, since it would have meant an intolerable strain upon finance and manpower.[2] Nevertheless, the only way in which one could be sure of serving only one year was to have parents rich enough to pay 1,500 francs (£60) for one's uniform and maintenance, to have been educated up to baccalaureate or equivalent standard, and to volunteer. Such volunteers served in

[1] So he said, more than thirty years later. But it seems certain that Gaston Arman was at Condorcet a year above Proust, for in her letters to her son, though she never names his school, Mme Arman mentions Élie Halévy, Léon Brunschwicg and Jacques Baignères as his schoolfellows. Proust must have known him there, but perhaps only by sight. Cf. also the entry for Gaston de Caillavet in *Qui êtes-vous?*, 1910-11.

[2] The class of each year was about 240,000 men: if each had served his full time the army, including 100,000 officers, N.C.O.s and long-service men, would have numbered 1,300,000 men. In fact, exemptions were numerous, many others were sent on indefinite leave after one year, and only about 500,000 were under arms at a time.

the ranks, but were treated as a kind of officer-cadet. If their
training was satisfactory, they would pass out as sub-officers[1] in
the reserve. They would then have to serve occasional periods of
a month's training, and would gradually be promoted to
lieutenant, captain or even higher rank. But on 15 July 1889 a
law was passed limiting military service to three years and
abolishing the *volontariat*. Proust seized the opportunity to
volunteer before the new law became effective on 1 November,
and on 15 November he was called to the colours in the 76th
Infantry at Orleans. The following year of the discipline and love
of comrades which to certain neurotics are so welcome was one
of the happiest of his life.[2]

His way was smoothed by his status as a volunteer. Army
officers regarded the young noblemen and sons of the upper
bourgeoisie who made up the ranks of the *volontariat* as men of
their own class and as future colleagues; and whether officially or
not the volunteers were allowed to have batmen to take care of
their uniform and equipment. His commanding officer, Colonel
Arvers—'my excellent colonel'—was of a paternal and kindly
disposition, and Trooper Proust had been recommended to his
special care through the political contacts of Dr Proust. Colonel
Arvers went so far as to grant him exemption, no doubt on
medical grounds, from early morning parade and from jumping
ditches when at riding-exercise. Another of his officers was
Captain Walewski, a grandson of Napoleon by his amour with
Marie Walewska. He was respected by his men not only for his
glorious descent and personal resemblance to the great Emperor,
but for his courtesy and kindness in command. He is an evident
original of the Prince de Borodino at Doncières.[3] There was also

[1] The *sous-officier* was a senior N.C.O. of rank ranging from sergeant to
sergeant-major.
[2] His army pay-book gives his height as five feet six inches (1·68 metres)
on 11 November 1889. He may well have grown a little further by his
twenty-first year. He was therefore of middle height, which explains why
some of his friends have described him as tall, others as short. His hair and
eyes, in the army's opinion, are 'chestnut' (*'châtains'*). A surviving lock of his
hair, clipped from his dead body in November 1922, is very dark brown,
almost black, with only a very few grey hairs.
[3] Count Walewski's mother had been a mistress of Napoleon III.
Similarly, the Narrator remarks, 'the second Princesse de Borodino was
thought to have bestowed her favours upon Napoleon III', and accounts by
this for Borodino's facial resemblance to both Emperors (II, 129).

a Captain Saivrin, a friend of friends of Mme Proust, from whom she sometimes had indirect news of her 'little wolf'. In immediate command over Proust was Lieutenant de Cholet, a handsome young officer with black moustaches, who presented him at the end of his year with a signed photograph 'to Marcel Proust, volunteer cadet (*conditionnel*), from one of his torturers'. It was Cholet who once, like Saint-Loup,[1] hurt his feelings by saluting him coldly, pretending not to recognise him, in the street.

In theory the volunteers were strictly forbidden to take lodgings in town; but in practice they would hire a private room —Proust's was at Mme Renvoyzé's in the Rue des Bons Enfants near the cathedral—where they would dine and drink champagne or punch in the evening, while late-comers shaved and changed into their best uniforms in the adjoining dressing-rooms. When an officer met them on the stairs he would smile, seeming to cast a wistful eye on the champagne visible through the open door; and to make his good-will perfectly clear, he might even condescend to ask one of them for a light. "You ought to have asked him in, he'd have been quite welcome," someone would say afterwards, 'with the jesting air', as Proust wrote in *Jean Santeuil*, 'of a bourgeois saying to a friend who has just seen the Tsar of Russia drive past: "You should have brought him along to dinner, you could have told him I'd be delighted."'[2] A few yards from the Rue des Bons Enfants and the nearby much-restored cathedral, traditionally known as 'the ugliest in France', were the church and street of Saint-Euverte, after which Proust named in his novel the hostess who was the Baron de Charlus's pet aversion, and at whose reception Swann heard the Vinteuil Sonata. On the bank of the Loire two miles above the town is the Château de Saint-Loup.

In February an introduction from Dr Proust brought an invitation to dinner from the Prefect of the Loire, M. Boegner, to Proust and another gentleman-ranker named Mayrargues. Young Robert de Billy, a volunteer in the 30th Artillery stationed at Orleans, was also there, with his gaiters and buttons brilliantly polished, his white gloves newly washed, and the handle of his sabre resting in the regulation position in the crook of his arm.

[1] II, 138
[2] *Jean Santeuil*, vol. 2, 291

Mayrargues seemed smart enough, he thought, but the other
guest had a greatcoat several times too large; 'his deportment and
manner of speaking did not conform with the military ideal; he
had enormous questioning eyes, and his flow of conversation was
amiable and easy.' At first Proust's Condorcet ways did not
please a youth who had recently left the formidable Lycée Saint
Louis: the fellow talked of nothing but the delights of metaphysics, and the genius of a schoolmaster named Darlu. But soon
they became fast friends, and compared this first encounter to the
meeting of Bouvard and Pécuchet in Flaubert. Billy had had a
strict French Protestant education: 'I owe it in great part to
Marcel,' he says, 'if I knew the joy of thinking otherwise than in
accordance with fixed principles.'

Incredible as it may seem, in view of his later ill-health and
physical inactivity, Proust enjoyed his life in the army. 'It's
curious,' he wrote to a friend fifteen years later, 'that you should
have regarded the army as a prison, I as a paradise.' He swam,
rode, fenced and marched, and rejoiced to be called '*mon vieux*' by
the common soldiers his companions: he experienced, for one
whole year, the delightful illusion of being normal and accepted.
There was a new poetry in the grey autumnal landscape, in the
daily scenes of life in the barrack-room, which he likened to the
genre paintings of the Dutch School. 'The rural character of the
places,' he wrote in *Les Plaisirs et les Jours*, 'the simplicity of
some of my peasant-comrades, whose bodies were more beautiful
and agile, their minds more original, their character more natural
than those of the young men I had known before or knew later,
the calm of a life in which occupations are more regulated and
the imagination less trammelled than in any other, in which
pleasure is the more constantly with us because we have no time
to run about looking for it and so miss it altogether, all these
things concur to make this period of my life a series of little
pictures full of happy reality and a charm on which time has since
shed its delicious sadness and its poetry.'[1] Orleans, with its
cobbled streets, warm inns and misty views of the nearby
countryside, became Doncières; and because he first came
there in autumn, and overlaid Saint-Loup's garrison-town
with later visits to Fontainebleau (1896), Versailles (1906
and 1908) and Lisieux (1907) which happened at the same

[1] *Les Plaisirs et les Jours*, 216

melancholy time of year, Doncières is a place where it is always autumn.[1]

Meanwhile his mother wrote to him, and he to her, every day. Her correspondence is full of gossip about home, as letters to a soldier in exile should be, but tantalisingly void of information about the addressee; and only one letter from Orleans of Trooper Proust, and that to his father, has survived. She describes Robert ('Proustovitch') unmercifully massaging his father's lumbago, and Dr Proust roaring, "You're hurting me like blazes! God in Heaven, how you're hurting me!" and then adding, "Why are you stopping? Get on with it, boy!" Or she asks the servant to prepare a fish dinner one Friday, when Catholic friends are coming, and remarks, 'Angélique will think I'm going to be converted!' She sends on a message from Anatole France, 'Tell Marcel I'm very fond of him'; and Lucie Faure, his playmate in the Champs-Élysées, says, 'Tell him the same from me.' Or she offers a little good advice; his father wishes him to cut down his intake of cream-cheese, so—'Think of a number, then halve it', or, most practical of all (had he been punished for neglecting to polish them?), 'Gaiters, gaiters, gaiters, gaiters!' She visited him regularly, and so occasionally did Robert Proust, Horace Finaly, with whom he had stayed at Ostend the previous August, and other friends.

His father's mother, Louis Proust's widow, had died at Illiers on 19 March 1889; but on 2 January 1890 came a more terrible loss, the death of his maternal grandmother, Mme Nathé Weil.

[1] Does Doncières also contain memories of a time when Proust was no longer a soldier himself, but the guest of a soldier? In 1893-94 his friends Louis de la Salle and Daniel Halévy served their year at Fontainebleau, while Pierre Lavallée was at Chartres; in 1894-95 Robert Proust was at Rheims with Fernand Gregh, Robert Dreyfus and other old friends; and in 1895 a pianist friend, Édouard Risler, who may perhaps have suggested the piano-playing Marquis de Poitiers in *Jean Santeuil*, served at Chartres. There is no direct evidence for such a visit, but there are plenty of months unaccounted for in the 1890s in which it might have occurred; and in *Jean Santeuil*, at least, the hero experiences army life both as a soldier and as a visiting onlooker. The name Doncières comes from a character in *Connaís-toi*, a play by Paul Hervieu, whom Proust knew well, produced at the Comédie Française in 1909. Doncières is a junction on the line between Balbec and Paris, and its first syllable recalls the junction-town of Mézidon, sixteen miles south of Cabourg, where the branch-line from Cabourg joins the main line from Paris to Cherbourg.

At our last glimpse of the poor lady, a fortnight before, she is on a milk diet, and refusing even that, 'unless you can make it not taste of milk'. In memory of her beloved mother Mme Proust began to read and quote Mme de Sévigné, just as the Narrator's mother does in *Sodome et Gomorrhe*. ' "I know another mother who counts as nothing for herself, who has transmitted herself entirely to her children," ' she wrote—'Isn't that just like your grandmother? Only she wouldn't have *said* it!' Proust wept for his loss and his mother's grief, but was told: 'Think of her, by all means, and cherish her as I do: but don't let yourself go, and spend days in tears, because it's only bad for your nerves, and she wouldn't wish it. No, the more you think of her, the more it is your duty to be as she would like you to be, and act as she would like you to act.' But the last days of the grandmother in *Le Côté de Guermantes* are drawn chiefly, as will be seen, from the last illness of Mme Proust herself fifteen years later.

Almost every week-end Proust was able to come home on leave to Paris, which was less than two hours from Orleans by rail. On one of his first leaves he visited Mme Arman, and there at last met the famous Gaston, whose military service had just ended. 'Gaston was so charming to me that our friendship began immediately.' In the barrack-room Proust talked of nothing else and so impressed his batman and the corporal that they sent Gaston an address of homage for New Year's Day. Throughout that year Proust was to be seen at Sunday tea-time in Mme Arman's salon, buried in his uniform and the enormous cushions of one of her best armchairs. The weary head of the soldier lay back, drooping to one shoulder; his face was serious, his large brown eyes were melancholy; and then at the least pretext he would burst into his nervous but infectious laugh, and the pale face was lit up by his white teeth. At six o'clock Mme Arman would stuff him with cakes and sandwiches, and load him with more to take away—"You may need them in the train"; and then he would make the round of the drawing-room to say good-bye, embarrassed by the parcels and his képi, bustled from behind by Gaston. When at last Gaston tore him from the final benediction of Anatole France and pushed him downstairs, their cab had been waiting for more than half an hour. In the Rue du Faubourg Saint-Honoré there was a pastry-cook whose clock was always slow—they were reassured; but in the Rue Royale a restaurant

clock was always fast, and they were plunged into despair. At the
Gare d'Orléans Gaston hurried after his friend as far as the platform, chased by the angry cabman—they had promised him
double, and now he was afraid of being bilked altogether. Then
Gaston returned alone, having missed dinner in the cause of
friendship.

One afternoon at Mme Arman's Proust was introduced to
Gaston's fiancée, Mlle Jeanne Pouquet, and immediately began to
compliment her effusively on her beauty. Blushing and frightened,
the young girl walked away, only to be asked: "Are you turning
your back on me because you're afraid I won't notice your lovely
hair?" She complained to Gaston—"I think your friend Proust is
horrid." "Not at all, he's delightful. Besides, even before he spoke
to you, he told me you were simply charming!" Meanwhile
Proust had been busy with Jeanne's mother, who now came up
and said: "Young Monsieur Proust has quite made a conquest of
me, and I've asked him to come and see us on his next leave."
"Then I shall arrange to be out," replied the infuriated girl. But
Proust, fascinated equally by her magnificent plaits of dark hair
and by the fact that she already belonged to his friend, had fallen
in love. 'Gilberte's plaits seemed to me a matchless work of art,'
he wrote long afterwards; 'for a section of them, however infinitely small, what celestial herbal would I not have chosen as a
reliquary!'[1]

Soon it was Gaston's turn to be angry. Proust had invited
Jeanne and her mother ('or if she can't come, your governess or a
maid will do just as well for a chaperone') to stay at Orleans, 'to
visit the churches and museums and go hunting'. He would book
rooms at the best hotel, and knew a tapestry-man and an antique-
dealer who would make their apartment really comfortable:
'there's nothing extraordinary about that, is there?' He had
discovered that she had cousins near Orleans, whose father, Louis
Darblay, was an enthusiastic huntsman. Suddenly Proust
developed a longing to ride to hounds, and intrigued for an
introduction to M. Merle, their kennel-master. He found a
château to let near Orleans, 'quite a small one': they must come
and stay with him there, Gaston too, and all their friends. "But
if the château is so small, how can we all come?"—and they never
came. Next he tried to obtain her photograph, and Gaston was

[1] I, 503

furious again. Reduced to more indirect means, he proposed that all the girls of their set should exchange photographs with all the young men; and to set an example he arrived at Mme Pouquet's weekly dance with a packet of photographs of himself, which he proceeded to distribute. Their mothers hurried up with loud cries of horror, and all was to begin again. He began to scrape acquaintance with her most distant relatives; and a chorus of uncles, aunts and cousins, charmed by his assiduity, began to sing his praises. Perhaps they would invite him to their country-houses, perhaps there would be photograph-albums there, and then—"I shan't stick at theft," he said. He won the photograph only twenty years later, when Jeanne had ceased to resemble it, but even then he was still receiving New Year cards from the same obscure aunts in Périgord. 'To obtain Gilberte's photograph I committed acts of baseness which did not get me what I wanted, but involved me for the rest of my life with some extremely boring people.'[1]

In the summer of his army year he was given clerical work at divisional headquarters; 'but the Chief of Staff, not without reason, was exasperated by my handwriting, and threw me out'. On a sunny day, against the leafy trellis of a garden wall, he was photographed four times: no doubt these are the photographs he handed round at Mme Pouquet's dance. In one he is marking time in his greatcoat and képi, with an ingratiating smile, doing his best to look like a soldier in the chorus of some comic opera by Offenbach; in the second he wears a heavy sweater with collar and carries a riding-stock; in the third, inscribed 'to the one and only Gaston', he is pensively reading, and has slyly contrived to make the greatcoat look like a monk's habit, the book like a breviary.

That August Dr Proust was sent to investigate an outbreak of cholera in Spain, which recalls the Spanish tour of the Narrator's father with M. de Norpois in *A l'Ombre*.[2] He returned, still hot and dusty, announcing that 'travel is a delightful thing, because you're so glad to go, and so glad to come back'. It was a month of photographs: to compensate for one in which the photographer had made her grimace, Mme Proust sent her son another in which she had an air of inspiration. 'I look like Goethe,' she wittily wrote, 'gazing up at a fourth-floor window and saying "I am in

[1] I, 503   [2] I, 701

love with one who is far above me.'" In September Proust spent a short leave with her at Cabourg, and immediately on his return to Orleans wrote to his father, who was staying at Aix-les-Bains at the country-house of Dr Cazalis. On his way to the station at Cabourg a group of housemaids, stirred by his soldier's uniform, had blown kisses, much to the horror of his mother's friends. 'So the maids of Orleans whom I had abandoned had their revenge, and I am punished—if M. Cazalis will allow me to quote one of his finest lines—"for scorning the rosebuds of their naked breasts".'[1]

For the last few months of his military service Proust was placed in the instruction-squad, with a view to promotion to the rank of *sous-officier*. 'I am having great difficulty in fixing my attention and learning by heart,' he told his father; and his final position was sixty-third in a squad of sixty-four. 'Because of my wretched health, I was such a mediocre soldier that I remained a mere private[2],' he wrote thirty years later. As a last incongruous episode of his life in the army, he begged Colonel Arvers to be allowed to stay on for a few months; alas, it could not be arranged. He was free to continue his climb into society and his wooing of Jeanne Pouquet; but his release seemed more like an expulsion from yet another paradise. Now he must try to satisfy not a fatherly colonel, but an actual father, who demanded that he should face the claims of adult life and adopt a bread-winning career.

[1] At Aix Dr Proust had met Maupassant: 'I hope you liked him,' writes his son; 'I've only met him twice, but he must know more or less who I am.' This is interesting, since the novelist C., who is the putative author of *Jean Santeuil*, so closely resembles Maupassant in appearance and habits. In *A la Recherche*, C.'s function is taken over by Elstir; and it will be seen later how an incident at Beg-Meil in 1895 caused the novelist to be changed into a painter. Proust's meetings with Maupassant were no doubt in the salon of Mme Straus, which Maupassant frequented in the late 1880s. For a time Maupassant was unsuccessfully in love with his hostess, and he made her one of the heroines in his last novel, *Fort comme la Mort*.

[2] As Proust was in an infantry regiment, he was not strictly speaking a 'trooper'; but the nickname was given him by his family, no doubt because his training included riding exercises.

Chapter 7

THE STUDENT IN SOCIETY

ON 20 November 1890, soon after his unwilling release from the army, Proust enrolled as a student in the Faculté de Droit at the Sorbonne. By way of having two strings to his bow he also joined the École des Sciences Politiques: at the end of his three years as a student, he thought, he would at least have the choice between two equally uninviting careers, the law and the diplomatic service. Among his fellow-students were Robert de Billy, Gabriel Trarieux, who became a symbolist poet, and Jean Boissonnas, a future ambassador. He listened with respect to the lectures of the distinguished historians, Anatole Leroy-Beaulieu and Albert Sorel, and of the philosophers Paul Desjardins and Henri Bergson. Bergson became his cousin-in-law when he married a niece of Mme Proust, Mlle Neuburger, in 1891. For the platitudes of Comte Albert Vandal, however, he felt only amused contempt: the object of his course, it seemed, was to teach the budding diplomat to think and speak like M. de Norpois. One morning Vandal was explaining the origin of the Russo-Turkish war of 1877. A Serb had been killed by a Turkish soldier when trying to draw water from a forbidden well: "Gentlemen," said Vandal, "from that well came a conflagration which set fire to the whole of Eastern Europe." Proust suddenly began to write in his hitherto virgin notebook, and Billy looking over read the following doggerel:

'For exquisite Vandal's Attic salt
Who cares a damn? Not Gabriel,
Robert, or Jean, or even Marcel,
Though he is serious to a fault.'

Vandal had a nervous trick of suddenly closing one eye, so that people thought he must be winking at them: a weakness shared by Dr Cottard, who made Swann fear they might have met on the stairs in a brothel, while Charlus suspected him of making immoral advances.[1] But as the four young men strolled back from

[1] I, 202; II, 919

the Left Bank they talked of more important subjects, of metaphysics and the symbolist movement and the Russian novel and
Ibsen. In these conversations, Billy remembered, Proust made
cunning use of the Socratic method of questioning, which he had
learned from Darlu, and so induced his friends to utter truths
which they were unaware of knowing.

Meanwhile he never missed the 'dancing-lesson' which Mme
Pouquet held every week, at ten in the evening, in her house at
62 Rue de Miromesnil. In fact there was neither dancing-master
nor lesson; but their hostess felt it was important not to call it
a soirée, as none of the girls there was old enough to 'come out'.
He arrived when everyone was leaving, for he only wanted to see
Jeanne, and persuade the willing Gaston to stay; and then they
talked with Jeanne and her mother, until M. Pouquet appeared,
in an affable rage, and asked "Are you going to bed to-day or
to-morrow?" "But, Papa, it's past midnight, so we're certain to
go to bed to-day," said Jeanne. M. Pouquet showed the wooers
the door with "Now then, young fellows, it's time you were
leaving," and old Louis, the alcoholic butler, would grumble:
"Monsieur ought to turn them out earlier; he doesn't realise that
these young people can stay in bed till nine, but we servants have
to be up with the sun." Proust was delighted with Louis's conversation, and gave him stupendous tips; but the old man would
say: "He's a nice lad enough, only he doesn't know his place. He's
always hanging round Mlle Jeanne, and Madame doesn't notice
anything—but M. Gaston can see what's going on." When
Proust was invited to tea he would arrive early for a talk with
Fifine, the chamber-maid, whom he admired because she refused
to steal one of the coveted photographs of Jeanne for him. When
the ladies arrived home they were told: "Monsieur Marcel's been
here for hours." "Why, where is he?" "In the linen-room with
Fifine!"

That winter Gaston, who was to become one of the most
popular writers of light comedy of his generation, devised a little
revue to be performed by their friends. Jeanne appeared as
Cleopatra and as a concierge; and a photograph survives of her
in the latter role, wearing a loud gown and a huge feathered
bonnet, round-faced, thick-lipped and eager in a pathetic moment
of time lost. Proust was given the important role of prompter,
but at the dress rehearsal he was overcome by enthusiasm at the

costumes which he now saw for the first time and the talent of his friends. He interrupted every line with uncontrollable laughter and cries of "Bravo!" At the end of the rehearsal the indignant cast rounded upon him and took back the prompt-book. That night he wrote an extremely bad poem, 'On a Young Lady who this evening played Cleopatra, to the present trouble and future damnation of a young man who happened to be present', containing the lines:

> *'You have dethroned the Queen of Nile, for you*
> *Are both the artist and the work of art.'*

Soon afterwards Gaston wrote for Jeanne a one-act play called *Colombine*. They asked Proust to be Pierrot: "You're just right for the part, you're so pale and your eyes are so big!"; but he refused to act on the stage a character which he was already playing in real life.

In the summer of 1891 he frequented with Gaston and Jeanne a tennis-court in the Boulevard Bineau at Neuilly. Instead of playing he sat under the trees with the girls in a group which the others scornfully called 'gossips' corner' and 'the Court of Love'. He was made responsible for the refreshments, and arrived carrying a huge cardboard box of cakes; and when everyone was hot with playing he was sent to a near-by café and returned groaning and panting with a basket of beer and lemonade. Sometimes a tennis ball hurtled among the glasses and girls of the Court of Love, and he would cry with justified indignation, "You did that on purpose." He was photographed kneeling and strumming on a tennis-racket for a guitar at the feet of Jeanne standing on a chair, while Gabrielle Schwartz, Gabriel Trarieux and the Daireaux and Dancognée girls struck attitudes around them. His emotions among this little band later became associated with Gilberte in the Champs-Élysées and the budding grove of girls at Balbec. In 1912, when he was about to publish in *Le Figaro* an early version of his love for Gilberte, he wrote to Jeanne: 'You will find amalgamated in it something of my feelings when I wasn't sure whether you would be at the tennis-court. But what's the use of recalling things which you took the absurd and unkind course of pretending never to notice!'

After two years his relationship with Jeanne had become static and thoroughly explored, and therefore uninteresting. Jeanne was

flattered and amused, but untouched by his love, and he ceased
to love her. In May 1893, by which time he had pursued four more
women and begun at last to love young men, she married Gaston.
Proust was asked to be best man, but declined; he refused even
to go to dinner in their new home, writing: "How could you
invite me, Madame? If you didn't understand that I couldn't come,
you will be equally unable to understand my reasons for declining!" It is rumoured that Gaston de Caillavet, like Robert de
Saint-Loup, was not altogether a faithful husband, though his
wife, unlike Gilberte, was thought too naïve to notice it. Once,
it is said, when he went out for the first time after an illness,
Jeanne asked him where he had spent the day. "I went to the Bois
de Boulogne, my dear." "But it's been raining all day! What ever
did you do there?" "Oh, I just sat on a seat." "Really, dear, do
you think that was wise?" For Proust this marriage of the first
friend and the first love of his early manhood was buried ever
deeper beneath the weight of later events in which it had no part;
until seventeen years later, when *A la Recherche* was already
begun, he met the beautiful daughter of Gaston and Jeanne—as
his Narrator met the daughter of Saint-Loup and Gilberte at the
Princesse de Guermantes's final party—and realised its ideal
significance. In real life the marriage was no miraculous reconciliation of two worlds: husband and wife were both from the
same layer of the upper bourgeoisie, and it was Gaston who,
through his mother, was half Jewish. But in his novel it became
the symbol of the meeting of the two ways of Illiers and Combray,
and the incarnation of that meeting in the person of Mlle de Saint-
Loup.

In September 1891 Proust visited Cabourg, where he was overcome by memories of his boyhood holidays there with his dead
grandmother, and wrote to his mother on the 9th the letter
already quoted: 'How different it is from those seaside holidays
when Grandmother and I, lost in one another, walked battling
with the wind and talking.' These weeks correspond to the
Narrator's delayed grief during the early part of his second visit
to Balbec. Towards the end of the month he moved to Trouville
for a stay at Mme Charlotte Baignères's villa Les Frémonts, high
on a hill over the Channel, the original as we shall see later of
La Raspelière with its 'three views'. On the promenade he was
impressed by a rouged, middle-aged, great lady, whose sinuous

figure seemed to coil about her parasol like a snake round a rod, and whose reticule was carried by a little negro page in red satin. She was the Princesse de Sagan, and he made her Mme de Villeparisis's friend the Princesse de Luxembourg. Soon, in a gown of a bygone, Second Empire elegance, the Princesse toiled up the hill to Les Frémonts from her Villa Persane with her great friend the Marquise de Galliffet, who was a first cousin of Mme Baignères. Both ladies were daughters of Second Empire financiers (the Princesse was a Seillière, the Marquise a Laffitte), separated from their husbands, and continuing in their middle fifties to lead lives of assiduous gallantry. We shall meet them again three chapters later, but may note meanwhile that another original of the Princesse de Luxembourg was Princesse Alice of Monaco, and that in *A la Recherche* the Luxembourgs as a family correspond to the royal house of Monaco.

Another visitor to Les Frémonts was the painter Jacques Émile Blanche, who came over from his parents' summer villa at Dieppe, where his friends among the English colony included Sickert, Beardsley, Whistler, Conder and Wilde. Blanche was ten years older than Proust, and had left Condorcet, where he had studied English under Mallarmé and philosophy under Victor Brochard (the chief original of Brichot), two years before Proust's arrival. They had likewise failed to meet at Auteuil, although the famous private lunatic asylum kept by Dr Antoine Blanche was only a few yards from Louis Weil's villa; and their paths had first crossed earlier in 1891 at the salons of Mme Straus, Princesse Mathilde and Mme Baignères. Blanche's parents were wealthy—"We have a hundred thousand francs a year, not counting our dear lunatics," his mother would say complacently. He was a burly, heavy-featured young man, sharp-tongued and vindictive, a talented and delightful painter, and destined later to be an almost equally brilliant writer; his work in both fields has lived. On 1 October at Les Frémonts, during the hour before dinner, he made a pencil sketch for the well-known portrait of Proust which he painted in his studio at Auteuil during the mornings of the following spring, and exhibited in the Salon des Artistes Français of 1892. After the sittings they would lunch with Dr Blanche, who from professional habit, and long familiarity with madmen of genius— Maupassant at this time was one of his inmates—would cry: "Now, Jacques, you must try not to upset him—pay no attention, my dear boy, keep absolutely calm, Jacques doesn't mean a word he's saying—just sip a glass of cold water and count up to a hundred!" Proust showed his naïve satisfaction with the painting in *Jean Santeuil*, in the description of his hero's portrait by 'Le Gandare': 'a radiant young man still posing before the whole of Paris . . . with eyes like fresh almonds . . . and features cool and luminous as a spring morning, a beauty not so much thoughtful as gently pensive'.[1] But the romantic and elegant young man-about-town of the oil portrait is Proust's ephemeral vision of himself on the Guermantes Way, at the Princesse de Wagram's ball; and Blanche showed keener divination in the pencil sketch of a hunched, unkempt youth, with a glare of terrifying intensity, in the hour before dinner at Les Frémonts. Proust saw a great deal of Blanche during 1892 at the salons of the hostesses named above and of Laure Hayman (Odette) and Mme Aubernon (Mme Verdurin); and he was presented with a photograph of his ugly companion inscribed: 'to his great friend Proust, '92'. Possibly Elstir as 'Monsieur Tiche' at Mme Verdurin's represents Blanche at Mme Baignères's. Their estrangement in 1893 was caused partly by Blanche's contempt for Proust's social ambitions, partly by Montesquiou, who had put Blanche on his black list; and it was prolonged some years later by their different views during the Dreyfus Affair, in which Blanche took the anti-Dreyfusist side.[2]

Towards the winter of 1891 Proust had already found a new subject of interest, and was not displeased to notice that Jeanne Pouquet was a little jealous, and that Gaston was jealous of her jealousy. His old great-uncle Louis Weil was the lover of a famous cocotte, to whom he had introduced his delighted great-nephew three years before, in the autumn of his last year at school. Proust now renewed the acquaintance, and turned from Gilberte to Odette.

Laure Hayman was a descendant of the English painter Francis Hayman (1708-76), who taught Gainsborough and was one of the founders of the Royal Academy. She was born in 1851 on a

[1] *Jean Santeuil*, vol. 3, 296-7. The rest of the passage corresponds accurately to the Blanche portrait, except that Jean wears a rose in his buttonhole, whereas Proust sported an orchid spray. In the name 'Le Gandare' Proust alludes to the society portraitist La Gandara.

[2] It is significant that all Blanche's published reminiscences of Proust relate either to the years 1891-92 or to the period after their reconciliation twenty years later, shortly before the war.

ranch in the Andes; her father, an engineer, died when she was still a child, and her mother, after trying in vain to live by giving piano-lessons, brought her up as a courtesan. Her lovers were quite as distinguished as the Grand Duke who supplied the cigarettes of Uncle Adolphe's lady in pink. They included the Duc d'Orléans, the King of Greece, Karageorgevitch, pretender to the Serbian throne, said to be the only man she really loved, Prince Karl Egon von Fürstenberg, the financier Raphael Bischoffsheim, and Michael Herbert, a secretary at the English embassy in Paris.[1] Albert Flament[2] called her 'the educator of dukes', and her lessons included not only the art of love but the correct use of language. Vicomte Charles de la Rochefoucauld wrote to her from Biarritz, with unconscious derangement of epithets: 'We're having torrential heat here,' to which she replied by return of post: 'The rain here has been positively torrid.' "He's got blue blood, all right," she would remark, "I can't even teach him to spell—and as for his French. . . !" Like Odette she lived in a little house in the Rue La Pérouse, with a back-entrance on the Rue Dumont d'Urville.

When Proust first met her, in the autumn of 1888, she was thirty-seven and he was seventeen: she was now just forty. She was plump but wasp-waisted,[3] and wore an extremely low décolletée with festoons of pearls dangling, three a side, from what little of her bosom was hidden from view. Her hair was ash-blonde, tied with a pink ribbon; her eyes were black, and when she was excited tended to open too wide—"I have almond eyes, but in the wrong direction," she would say with a laugh. She owned a large collection of china, and added Proust to it, calling him 'my little porcelain psychologist'. He replied by

---

[1] Michael Herbert, brother of Lord Pembroke and Lady Lonsdale, was astonished to find that he was not asked to contribute to her expenses, which were looked after by M. Bischoffsheim. "An English girl wouldn't have been satisfied with a banker," he declared admiringly.

[2] He saw her riding in the Bois, still beautiful, on the morning of 3 April 1899, and recorded the fact in his diary, adding: 'A handsome woman looks still more graceful on horseback.'

[3] As a photograph of this period shows. In a later photograph she is painfully haggard and thin, while the festoons of pearls have increased to five a side. But in earlier photographs she is exceedingly pretty and fluffy, though quite un-mysterious and not in the least like Botticelli's fresco of Jethro's daughter, to which Swann compared Odette.

comparing the what-not on which she kept her Saxe figurines to an altar: "we live in the century of Laure Hayman, and its reigning dynasty is Saxe," he said; and afterwards he made Odette collect Saxe, and say of any object whose appearance she liked: "How pretty that is, it's just like the flowers on a piece of Saxe." He was attracted not only by Mme Hayman's beauty but by her salon, which was full of dukes, club-men, writers and future academicians. One of these was Paul Bourget, who had described her in his short story *Gladys Harvey*: 'Gladys has something of the courtesan of the eighteenth century, and not too much of the ferociously calculating harlot of our brutal and positivist age.' In December 1888 she had given Proust, who now showed it to the horrified Jeanne Pouquet, a copy of *Gladys Harvey* bound in flower-embroidered silk from one of her petticoats, and inscribed 'You mustn't like everything in Gladys Harvey!'; and then she wrote of him to Bourget, enclosing the schoolboy's enthusiastic letter of thanks. 'Judging by his letter, your "little Marcel" must be simply delightful,' replied Bourget, and continued in the vein of Bergotte: 'but he must never allow his love of literature to die out. He will cease to like my books because he likes them too much; but may he never fall out of love with the beauty of art which he seeks in my unworthy self! And, though this advice coming via the lips of a Delilah may seem ironic, tell him to work and develop all that lies hidden in his already so admirable intelligence.' So Proust, while still a schoolboy, had been introduced by an original of Odette to an original of Bergotte.

Unlike Odette, Mme Hayman seems to have been an intelligent, sensible, witty and cultured woman. She was never supposed to have ruined anyone, and her lovers may have felt that she gave value for money. Her affection for Louis Weil was sincere, and whereas Odette as mistress of Uncle Adolphe was barred by the family, Laure Hayman was accepted by the Prousts. She was on visiting terms with Dr Proust, and would give him news of his son's activities; so that whenever Dr Adrien said with an air of impenetrable mystery, "You've been seen at . . .", or "They tell me you have . . .", Proust would know that Mme Hayman had called. Once, with the best intentions, she succeeded in thoroughly upsetting both father and son, by warning Dr Proust of Marcel's extravagance. The young man's allowance could be nothing like that of a Grand Duke; yet he insisted on loading her with her favourite chrysanthemums and giving her lunch at the most expensive restaurants. Jacques Émile Blanche hints that Proust's affair with Mme Hayman was not merely platonic: it was all a very long time ago, but Blanche, who was a friend of both at this time, was perhaps in a position to know. It would not have been the first nor the last time that Proust's relations with women were physical; and it may be significant that in *Jean Santeuil* it is the hero himself who undergoes with Mme Françoise S. the love-affair which in *A la Recherche* was transferred to Swann and Odette.

But admission to Mme Hayman's drawing-room was no passport to society, for although dukes were there they were never accompanied by their duchesses. Even Mme de Caillavet's salon was a mere picture-frame for Anatole France. It is time to visit in turn the four other salons in which at this period, in 1891 and 1892, Proust began to move towards the Guermantes Way.

Jeanne Pouquet was not the only beloved whom Proust tried to make jealous by confiding the open secrets of his intimacy with Mme Hayman. The flowers that deluged his great-uncle's mistress had already fallen, in the winter and spring after he left the army, on Mme Straus: once he succeeded in bringing them even to her bedside, where she sat, 'beautiful as an angel with a slight indisposition,' and scolded him for his extravagance. But now, he cuttingly explained, she mustn't think he loved her less because the flowers had stopped. His daily walks with Mme Hayman and the lunches that follow are so expensive that (except a franc's worth of poppies for Mme Lemaire) he can't afford to buy any! Mme Straus had rebuked him for his passion and dismissed him: now, in November 1891, she announced that they were friends as before. "You are unique, as in everything else, in the art of making hearts vibrate till they break," he sighed, and explained that his love for her was now only platonic: however, "one should always show *great indulgence* for platonic love." Gradually she began to appreciate the intelligence of her little Cherubino; and Proust, in turn, freed from the unholy attraction of this beautiful lady—for she resembled his mother in age, wit and Jewish birth, and was the mother and aunt of his schoolfriends Bizet and Halévy—became her friend for life. He began again to frequent her salon, which was growing ever more brilliant: the way into the Faubourg Saint-Germain was opening before him.

The social ascent of Fromental Halévy's daughter and Bizet's widow had been extraordinary, almost impossible; though she never forgot her middle-class musical origins, and once, when asked by a great lady whether she was fond of music, replied: "They played a great deal of it in my first family." Her portrait by Delaunay, white and appealing in widow's black, had created a sensation in the Salon of 1878: Degas found his way to the house in the Rue de Douai where she lived in retirement with her uncle Léon Halévy, and begged to be allowed to see her combing her hair. Then, as we have seen, Émile Straus, the favourite lawyer (and, it was said, the illegitimate half-brother) of the three Barons Rothschild, Alphonse, Edmond and Gustave, insisted on marrying her. He came up to town every morning with Joseph Reinach, who used to say: "I could always relax on the train with Émile—he did all the talking, it was Geneviève, Geneviève all the way." "You *must* see Geneviève," Straus told the Rothschilds, and soon all society was saying "We must see Geneviève." Long lines of carriages drew up in the Rue de Douai, and followed after their marriage in 1886 to their apartment in the Boulevard Haussmann, at the corner of the Avenue de Messine, opposite the statue of Shakespeare. Jacques Bizet, now a medical student, found it convenient to open a ground-floor window at dead of night and disappear along the boulevard on business best known to himself. In the morning, M. Straus would rise early to wait for him on the stairs, to the amusement of his indulgent mother: "Émile has such a sense of theatre," she said. Whether or not Jacques's escapades were connected with his friend, M. Straus decided first that Proust had a bad influence on his step-son, next that, on the whole, he had not. He made a call of reconciliation at 9 Boulevard Malesherbes, and amid the bronzes, potted palms, plush and mahogany of the drawing-room, looking for something to be polite about, noticed a little drawing by Henri Monnier. It was a present to Dr Proust from a grateful patient, Caran d'Ache, the caricaturist. "Charming, charming," murmured M. Straus.

Émile Straus was a slim little man with grey hair and a smile of extreme but amiable irony. His eyes, owing to a disability acquired in the Franco-Prussian war, were always half-closed. Like Swann he devoted his life and his enormous wealth to the clothing and social career of his wife: his friends recognised him immediately when they read the scene in *A l'Ombre* where Swann peeps benevolently through the curtains at Odette's guests.[1] There is, indeed, a distinct likeness between his photographs and those of Charles Haas, the chief original of Swann. Both are dressed with the same exquisite, imperceptible elegance; their features are whimsical and Jewish; but M. Straus lacks the melancholy, puzzled look of M. Haas. Sometimes, however, when he asked his guests "Have you heard Geneviève's latest?" he resembled for a moment the Duc de Guermantes saying the same of his wife Oriane; and he would go on to explain, like the Duke, that his wife's intelligence was admirable not so much for its wit as for its sound common sense. He was an exceedingly but quite unjustifiably jealous husband.

Mme Straus's wit is important, for Proust made it his chief model for the celebrated 'Guermantes wit'. Some of her sayings are repeated as chestnuts to this day, though their authorship is forgotten. It was she who said: "I was just about to say the same myself," when her former music-teacher Gounod remarked at a performance of Massenet's *Hérodiade* that the passage they had just heard was "perfectly octagonal"; or "I'd no idea you had any," when the dramatist Pailleron, after reviling her friend Louis Ganderax for a hostile article in the *Revue des Deux Mondes*, said: "And now you can have your revenge on *my* friends." When it was rumoured that the lady novelist Marcelle Tinayre was to be given the cross of the Légion d'Honneur, she commented: "A woman's breast was never meant to be honoured." Of a gentleman who pursued her with unwarranted optimism, she said: "Poor Achille, it would be so much less trouble to make him happy than it is to make him unhappy." Of her florist, who had the same name as the general who shouted "*Merde*" when invited to surrender at the Battle of Waterloo—so that the word was ever afterwards known euphemistically as '*le mot de Cambronne*'—she remarked, "She is so nicely spoken that she calls herself Cambronne." The Duchesse de Guermantes, then Princesse des Laumes, makes a similar joke on the name of Mme de Cambremer at Mme de Saint-Euverte's party.[2] When she uttered, or urged by her husband repeated her 'latest', her face was that of the Duchesse inviting and sharing the hearer's amusement. It was Mme Straus who once put on black shoes instead of red when dressing for a fancy-dress ball, and like the Duchesse was compelled by her angry husband to change them; but it was in no such circumstances of cruelty and selfishness: Proust ran upstairs to fetch the red shoes, and all was well.

Mme Straus's beauty was wholly different from that of the Duchesse or Odette or any others of their originals. It resided in the sincerity of her expression, the fervour of her eyes ('like black stars', said Abel Hermant) and the elegance of her dress. The poetry of her little hats tied under the chin, her tubular skirts, her slim folded parasols, survives unfaded to this day in her photographs of the 1890s. Her features had lost the fresh youth of Delaunay's painting: they were gipsy-like, heavy, thick-lipped, but still fascinating. A nervous tic made her open her eyes wide and then suddenly screw them up, or protrude her lower lip, or bend her head abruptly to her left shoulder: Mme Albert Gillou compared her face to 'a sky disordered by summer lightning'.

In the huge rotunda drawing-room of the Boulevard Haussmann the walls were hung with eighteenth-century paintings by Nattier and Latour, side by side with Monets and the Delaunay portrait of the hostess—"Don't you agree that it's lovelier than the Mona Lisa?" Proust would ask his fellow-guests, as he leaned adoringly over her chair or sat on a cushion at her feet. Her salon consisted partly of writers and artists, partly of the Faubourg Saint-Germain. But it was neither literary, since she refused to talk literature, nor social, for the Faubourg was in the minority and came only as personal friends of the hostess. It was composed of persons whom she invited for the sake of their intelligence, and who came for the sake of hers. Henri Meilhac, who collaborated as Offenbach's librettist with her cousin Ludovic Halévy (Daniel's father), was almost one of the family: Proust refers several times to the 'Meilhac and Halévy style' of the Duchesse de Guermantes's wit.[1] Meilhac arrived with trailing laces, being too fat to tie his shoes, and exchanged epigrams with Forain, whom she had met through his master Degas. In his youth Forain had sheltered Rimbaud in his studio, until that atrocious young man left after defecating in his host's morning milk by way of farewell. He was now as famous for his savage wit as for his art. Among the men of letters were the dramatists Hervieu and Porto-Riche, the novelist Bourget, and the bearded, spectacled Louis Ganderax, the literary editor of the *Revue de Paris*. He was feared by his

[1] I, 334; II, 207, 495-6; III, 1009

contributors for the ruthlessness of his proof-corrections, "pursuing hiatuses," said Anatole France, "into the very interior of words"; and Jules Renard pretended that when frogs croaked in lily-ponds they were only repeating: "Ganderax! Ganderax!" One of her humbler friends was a gentle and melancholy musician named Ernest Guiraud, who once uttered a remark which in *A la Recherche* is made to the Narrator's grandmother.[1] Mme Straus had good-naturedly asked him to bring his illegitimate daughter to call on her. "Does she take after her mother?" she asked, and the naïve father replied: "I don't know, I never saw her dear mother without her hat on."

Among her nobler guests was Prince Auguste d'Arenberg, who appears in Odette's salon as the Prince d'Agrigente: Mme Straus had intrigued with her friends among the republican politicians to have him appointed president of the administrative council of the Suez Canal. Comte Othenin d'Haussonville would be there, absent-mindedly twirling his monocle and following a train of thought usually connected with his ancestress Madame de Staël, whose life he was exhuming from the archives at Coppet. Others included Princesse Mathilde, Louis de Turenne, and several English friends, Lord Lytton, the English ambassador, Lady de Grey, later Marchioness of Ripon, and Reggie Lister. But the three who most concern Proust and his novel were the Comtesse de Chevigné, Comtesse Greffulhe and Charles Haas. The first became the Duchesse de Guermantes, the second contributed to both the Duchesse and the Princesse de Guermantes, and the last was Charles Swann himself. At that time, however, Proust could only admire the two ladies from afar: to be invited with a great lady, he found, was not the same as being invited by her. But Haas, with whom he was never to become personally intimate, but who meant so much to his novel and his life, must be examined immediately.

Charles Haas was, as he himself used ironically to say, "the only Jew ever to be accepted by Parisian society without being immensely rich." He was, however, far from poor, for his father, a stockbroker, had left him a comfortable fortune. His gallantry in the Franco-Prussian war won him the entry to the exclusive Jockey Club, of which the only other members of his race were the Rothschilds. Earlier still he had moved in the court society

[1] I, 859

of the Second Empire: we have a glimpse of him in December 1863, playing in private theatricals at the Duc de Mouchy's country house, along with the Galliffets, the Pourtalès's, Gaston de Saint-Maurice, and other persons fashionable in their day. In 1868 Haas appears in Tissot's famous painting of the balcony of the Club in the Rue Royale,[1] with the Prince de Polignac and Saint-Maurice again ('the only two people in the picture, besides Haas, whom I knew personally,' Proust told Paul Brach in 1922), the Marquis's du Lau and de Ganay, General de Galliffet and others. He is tall and svelte, wise, sad and arrogant; he cocks his walking-cane on his right shoulder; he lolls astride in the french window of the balcony, ineffably elegant in grey top-hat and striped trousers. His hair was frizzled and reddish, and later as it receded turned pepper-and-salt colour. He had arched, amused but puzzled eyebrows, an upturned moustache into which he faintly smiled, and his nose, people would say, was hardly curved at all; but in his last days, when his skin stretched over it like parchment and his ancestry reappeared, it was found, like Swann's in his last illness, to be enormously hooked. He died in July 1902.

Haas frequented Mme Straus's salon during the late 1880s and early '90s, and Proust probably met him there. But he must also have seen him as the guest of several other hostesses: the Princesse Mathilde in the early '90s, and later, when Proust had succeeded in penetrating to the Faubourg Saint-Germain, the Princesse de Polignac, Comtesse Rosa de FitzJames, and Comtesse Greffulhe. Haas had met Mme Greffulhe's cousin Robert de Montesquiou as early as 1871, and was, we are told 'the darling of her coterie in the Rue d'Astorg'. Correspondingly in Proust's novel Swann is the intimate friend of the Duchesse de Guermantes, and one of the earliest friends of her cousin, the Baron de Charlus. Like Swann, Haas was also a favourite companion of Edward VII as Prince of Wales and of the Orleanist pretender to the throne of France, the Comte de Paris, who lived in exile at Twickenham. Apart from social life, his chief interests were woman-chasing and Italian painting, on both of which subjects he was regarded

---

[1] This club, although Saint-Loup (I, 772) thought Bloch senior might possibly belong to it ('his family considered it "lowering", and he knew several Israelites had been admitted'), was second only to the Jockey. The Cercle Agricole and Cercle de l'Union came next, and some of the best people liked to belong to all four, as did Swann (III, 199).

as a connoisseur. Once Saint-Maurice showed him a new acquisi-
tion, a horrible, blackened Italian daub, and proudly asked:
"What do you think it is?" "A joke in rather poor taste," replied
Haas, as did Swann to the Duc de Guermantes when shown his
new 'Velasquez'.[1]

In some respects Swann is to be differentiated from Haas. As
we have seen, Swann at Combray was suggested by a family
friend at Illiers. There is no evidence that Haas was acquainted
with the chief original of Odette, Laure Hayman, who was, however, so popular with his fellow-clubmen. It is doubtful whether
he knew, as Swann knew Uncle Adolphe, Proust's great-uncle
Louis Weil.[2] Haas's Odette was a Spanish lady of noble birth
from whom he had a daughter, who is said to be still living; but
he never married. In the Dreyfus Affair Swann had the loyalty
and courage to turn from those of his old friends who became
anti-Dreyfusards; but Haas, we are told by Jacques Émile Blanche,
joined his nationalist fellow-members of the Jockey Club in
cutting General de Galliffet when he became war minister in the
revisionist government of Waldeck-Rousseau.

In his novel Proust proclaimed Swann's origin in the famous
apostrophe to 'dear Charles Swann, whom I knew when I was
still so young and you were near the grave—it is because he
whom you must have thought a silly young man has made you
the hero of his volumes that people begin to talk of you again,
and that your name will perhaps live,' and in the allusion which
follows to Haas's presence in Tissot's painting.[3] He also characteristically gave the clue to their identity, as he did with so many of
the people in *A la Recherche*, by unobtrusively juxtaposing the
name of the character with that of the original: Swann, he tells us,
wears a grey top-hat of a shape which Delion makes only for him
and Charles Haas.[4] Those who had known Haas immediately
recognised him in Swann, whom Mme Straus insisted on calling
Swann-Haas. 'What, you recognised Haas?' Proust wrote to
Gabriel Astruc. Some, including Montesquiou, thought they

---

[1] II, 580

[2] The prevalent idea that he did seems to rest solely on a general remark
by Robert de Billy, that in his belief Proust learned from Louis Weil 'of the
structure of Jewish society and of the existence of Haas' (*Billy*, 64).

[3] III, 200

[4] II, 579

detected elements in Swann, particularly his erudition in art, which belonged to Charles Ephrussi; though Haas's own knowledge of art was quite sufficient to supply Swann's. Ephrussi edited the *Gazette des Beaux Arts*, an expensive art-magazine which every great lady kept open but unread on her table. He was a Polish Jew whose career was parallel to that of Haas, for he frequented much the same salons, but on a lower plane, for he was sought after less for his personal charm than as a fashionable art-expert. He was stout, bearded and ugly, his manner was ponderous and uncouth, and he was nicknamed 'Matame', not for any discreditable reason, but because he pronounced the word 'Madame' with a Polish accent.[1] It is difficult to think of any feature of Swann to be found in Ephrussi and not in Haas; except that Swann wrote an essay on Vermeer and Ephrussi one on Dürer, while Haas wrote nothing. Neither Haas nor Ephrussi were particularly interested in Vermeer: it was Proust himself who bestowed his own love of the Dutch master, as one of their saving graces, on both Swann and Bergotte.

Proust knew Ephrussi well, but was never intimate with Haas. He saw this mysterious and fascinating figure only from a distance and in his late middle age: in life as in his novel he learned from others of the days of his glory in the Second Empire—before his own birth and the Narrator's—of his great love and his illegitimate daughter, who supplied this feature to Gilberte. There is no trace of Swann-Haas in Proust's work until the beginnings of *A la Recherche* nearly twenty years later. But it may well be, as some have suggested, that he saw Haas even at this early period as a hero and an example, another self. Haas, like himself, was a Jew, a pariah by birth; yet by his own merits of intelligence and charm he had made society a career open to the talents. Whether or not he was aided by the inspiration of Haas, Proust set himself to do the same. Social acceptance was a symbol—though, as he was to discover, an illusory one—of salvation.

Another of Proust's early salons was that of Princesse Mathilde, Napoleon's niece, now in her seventies. Long ago she had been the hostess of Flaubert, Renan, Sainte-Beuve, Taine, Dumas Fils, Mérimée and Edmond de Goncourt, and her friends had called her 'Notre Dame des Arts'. All were now dead, except Goncourt

---

[1] The Prince von Faffenheim addresses Mme de Villeparisis as 'Matame la Marquise', (II 263).

and Taine, and with Taine she had quarrelled in 1887, after his series of hostile articles on her uncle, leaving on him the famous visiting-card marked P.P.C.[1] Her house was at 20 Rue de Berri, and her guests, with a nucleus of old Bonapartists such as Counts Benedetti and Primoli, now included the Straus's, Charles Haas, Ephrussi, Dr Pozzi, Ganderax, Bourget and Porto-Riche. Count Benedetti had been the French ambassador at Berlin in 1870, a post which he shared with M. de Norpois.[2] Count Joseph Primoli, a nephew of the Princess, was a bald-headed gentleman with a white beard, who looked rather like God the Father. He was despised for collecting postage-stamps, until people heard that he had sold his collection for a million francs; and he was addicted to the tiresome form of humour which consists in asking awkward questions with a straight face, and inviting deadly enemies to dinner on the same evening. His nickname was Gégé, which may be compared with the Babals, Grigris and Mamas of the Guermantes set. There was also a sprinkling of society from the Faubourg—the Gramonts, Rohans, Comte Louis de Turenne, a few others; but the majority of the Princess's titled guests were of the Napoleonic creation, with names mostly taken from battles— like the fictitious Iénas, whom Charlus called 'those people who are named after a bridge'[3]—on whom the Faubourg tended to look down: the Wagrams, Albuferas, Elchingens, Esslings, Murats.

The Princess was a portly little lady, with a startling resemblance to her uncle Napoleon. "If it weren't for him, I'd be selling oranges in the streets of Ajaccio," she would say in the gruff, plebeian, soldierly voice of the Bonapartes. She sat, wearing a string of black pearls, in a humble armchair to which her presence somehow gave the air of a throne. She liked to feel that she was no stickler for etiquette, and would allow the ladies only to begin the movement of a curtsey before pulling them up by main force for an embrace; while the gentlemen, once they had shown their intention of kissing her hand, would receive an informal hand-

[1] The newspapers got hold of the story, and various rude interpretations of the initials (which of course stand for '*Pour prendre congé*') were suggested: among the more innocent was '*Princesse pas contente*'. Taine tried to get sympathy from Renan, who only remarked: "My *Vie de Jésus* put me in bad odour with a *much* greater lady!"

[2] III, 637-9

[3] II, 564. Cf. I, 338

shake. If asked by some uninstructed, ultra-polite newcomer: "And how is your Imperial Highness's health?" she would growl: "Not so bad! How's yours?" Her last of several lovers, himself now dismissed for infidelity, had been Claudius Popelin, the artist in enamel to whom Heredia devoted a sonnet.[1] Proust became so affectionately appreciated by her that her disgruntled habitués referred to him, in allusion to the stage dynasty of Coquelin *aîné* and Coquelin *cadet*, as Popelin the Younger. She gave him a piece of silk from one of her dresses for a cravat, and another to Barrès.

In *A la Recherche* the Princess appears in her own person, when the Narrator is introduced to her by Swann and Odette in the Bois de Boulogne.[2] Her conversation on this occasion is a pot-pourri of her authentic sayings over a long period: the anecdote of Alfred de Musset coming to dinner dead-drunk and speechless; the quarrel with Taine in 1887; her remark when her favourite nephew Prince Louis Napoleon joined the Russian army—"just because there's already been a soldier in the family, that's no reason"; and the story of Tsar Nicolas II's visit to Napoleon's tomb at the Invalides, which occurred on 7 October 1896, when she refused an official invitation, saying, "I have my own keys." But she also supplied several traits for the Princesse de Parme, a name which was perhaps suggested to Proust by the connecting-link of imperial violets. The Princesse de Parme, unlike the Princesse Mathilde, traces her noble descent back to A.D. 63, and is a non-intellectual, who listens to the Duchesse de Guermantes's conversation with admiring amazement. But she too is a little dark lady, her mock-simple manner of salutation is Princesse Mathilde's, so is the inferior social level of her salon; and the Princesse de Parme has a comically stupid lady-in-waiting, Mme de Varambon, whose sayings were actually uttered by Princess Mathilde's attendant, the Baronne de Galbois. Mme de Galbois, who knitted and embroidered at the Princess's side for forty years, was the constant joy of her guests, though the Princess would crossly exclaim: "Really, Galbois, you're such a fool!" She claimed that Flaubert had read *Bouvard et Pécuchet* to her, and when everybody seemed incredulous corrected herself: "Well,

---

[1] The *Almanach de Gotha* even stated in 1879 that she had secretly married him, but the Princess immediately issued a denial.
[2] I, 541-4

perhaps he didn't read *Pécuchet*, but I'm quite sure he read *Bouvard*." After a visit to the country she spoke of "a cow that gave so much milk, everyone thought it must be a stallion!" In a season of untimely rain she said: "You'd think the barometer had stopped having any influence on the weather"; and on a cold winter's day she assured the company that "it can't possibly snow, they've spread salt on the pavements." The second and last of these anecdotes are told of the Princesse de Parme's lady-in-waiting Mme de Varambon.[1] Another of Mme de Galbois's absurdities is given to the Comtesse de Monteriender, who says to Swann of the musicians who perform the Vinteuil Sonata at Mme de Sainte-Euverte's reception: "I've never seen anything so amazing—except table-turning, of course."[2]

Of the literary and artistic bourgeois salons those of Mme Aubernon de Nerville and Mme Lemaire, to both of which Proust gained admission in 1892 or a little before, were supreme in their prestige. A great artist is remembered, a great hostess is forgotten when the last of her guests has died; yet each of these ladies contributed to the immortal Mme Verdurin, and lives still in her.

Mme Lydie Aubernon had been blissfully parted from her husband since 1867, and was in the habit of remarking that she was looking forward to her 'golden separation'. M. Georges Aubernon lived with their son Raoul, at Antibes, and his wife was known as 'the Widow'. Until the end of the 1880s she was assisted in the running of her salon by her mother, whose own drawing-room had been famous in the 1840s under Louis Philippe. The two ladies, in allusion to their republican sympathies and to Molière's comedy, were called '*Les Précieuses Radicales*'. But Mme Aubernon showed little positive interest in politics, and used to say: "I'm a republican, but only in sheer desperation." After old Mme de Nerville died she told Edmond de Goncourt: "I miss her often, but only a little at a time"—a remark also uttered by Swann's father after the death of his wife.[3] She received at her house in the Avenue de Messine, later in the Rue d'Astorg, where (incongruous conjunction) the Comtesse Greffulhe also lived, and last at 11 Rue Montchanin. Along with her more brilliant guests she entertained a hard core of mysterious elderly ladies, widows of writers or friends of her dead mother, who sat in the back-

---

[1] II, 547; III, 1009   [2] I, 353
[3] I, 15

ground, like the pianist's aunt or Princesse Sherbatoff at Mme Verdurin's, and were known as 'my sacred monsters'. One of the monsters was once reproached for frivolity by her son, who felt that her name appeared far too frequently in the society columns of the newspapers. "You're quite right, my dear," she said, "tomorrow I'll give up going to funerals."

Mme Aubernon was a fat, lively little woman, with dimpled arms, and wore loud beribboned dresses and shoes with pompoms. "She looked like Queen Pomaré on the lavatory seat," Montesquiou used to say. She was sixty-seven in 1892, and was not unaware that her beauty had vanished: "I realised it," she said, "when men stopped raving about my face and only told me how intelligent I was." Her evening receptions on Wednesdays (Mme Verdurin's day) and Saturdays were preceded by a dinner for twelve persons, neither more nor less, for which the subject of conversation was announced in advance. The guests did not always take the custom as seriously as she wished. "What is your opinion of adultery?" she asked Mme Straus one week, when that happened to be the theme, and Mme Straus replied: "I'm so sorry, I prepared incest by mistake." Labiche, when asked what he thought of Shakespeare, enquired: "Why, is he marrying someone we know?" And d'Annunzio, when asked to talk about love, was even less forthcoming: "Read my books, madam," he said, "and let me get on with my food." Thinking a change of subject might thaw her guest, Mme Aubernon began to ask after his distinguished contemporaries. "Tell me about Fogazzaro," she implored. "Fogazzaro?" echoed the poet, "he's at Vicenza"; and the meal finished in frozen silence. When Mme Laure Baignères was asked the same question: "What do you think about love?" she could only reply, "I make it, often, but I never, never talk about it."[1] If conversation at the other end of the table became general, Mme Aubernon would ring her famous little bell[2] to secure attention for the speaker of the moment. Once, on his very first visit, Labiche was heard to murmur "I ... I ..." The Widow jingled with her bell and shouted: "Monsieur Labiche, you will have your turn in a minute." The speaker finished, and she said

[1] A remark attributed to Mme Leroi in *Le Côté de Guermantes* (II, 195).
[2] It was of silver, the handle was a figure of St Louis, and on the bell was engraved the maxim attributed to that king by Joinville: 'If you have anything worth saying, let everyone hear it; if not, be silent.'

graciously: "You may speak now, Monsieur Labiche." But the unhappy dramatist only mumbled: "I just wanted to ask for another helping of peas."

Mme Aubernon's salon was remarkable, like Mme Verdurin's, for the absence of beautiful women. "I provide conversation," she would say, "not love"; or, "Women are a subject men are too fond of getting on top of." But she was thought once to have been not averse to love in its time and place, and had been heard to announce: "I have a *glorious* body." To attend one's first dinner in the Rue d'Astorg was like sitting for an examination. Afterwards the result would be proclaimed: "Monsieur So-and-so dined very well," or "Monsieur So-and-so didn't dine at all well, he talked to the lady next to him." Proust, however, dined exceedingly well, and Mme Aubernon would say: "Marcel's epigrams are *definitive*." Now and then, like Mme Verdurin, she would hold a public execution of some offender, which would end in an outburst of tears, sometimes the victim's, sometimes the executioner's; for Mme Aubernon's rages were genuine, not cold-blooded like Mme Verdurin's. But she was not vindictive for long, and a few months later a whole series of criminals would be pardoned and reappear at what she called 'a dinner of forgiveness'. Silence, and being a bore, were the only unforgivable sins: after a series of boring visitors, she declared: "I've been outraged nine times this morning." But with her as with Mme Arman the word 'bore' had its ordinary meaning, and was not a euphemism for a person in high society who could not be lured to her salon. The Faubourg never appeared there, and there is no reason to believe that she ever missed it. Unlike Mme Verdurin, again, she did not pretend to be fond of music; but her amateur theatricals, which in *A la Recherche* are transferred to Mme de Villeparisis, were famous, and it is to her credit that the first performances of Ibsen's *A Doll's House* and *John Gabriel Borkman* took place in her drawing-room. It was at this time that a visitor found her engrossed in a volume of Ibsen: "Don't disturb me! I'm acquiring a Norwegian soul!"

In some points of detail, it is clear, Mme Aubernon differed from Mme Verdurin: she was unmusical, non-political, and in the social sense unsnobbish. She was capable, as Mme Verdurin was not, of a kind of wit; though her witticisms, it will be noticed, are remarkable chiefly for their unconscious absurdity, for she could

where Mme Aubernon puts away the dolls, male or female, that don't amuse her any more." Perhaps he could be induced to reform? Brochard was persuaded to give him a good talking to, "so that you can recover all the ground you've lost. People would soon forget your horrible language, and *everything else*, if you took as much trouble to be nice as you do to make enemies." Doasan listened without a word, till Brochard had quite finished, but only said, "It can't be helped, I prefer my vices to my friends." When Proust first attended a Wednesday he became aware that the dreadful Baron's eyes were staring at him, in a fixed, vacant gaze which pretended not to see him. He remembered the incident twenty years later when describing the meeting of Charlus and the Narrator at Balbec. But in 1892 at the Rue d'Astorg its significance must have been a little different: the eyes of Baron Doasan expressed not a questioning desire, but the recognition by one active invert of another. Proust was not a potential conquest, but a possible rival or even betrayer; and Doasan forbade his cousin to receive "that 'little Marcel'", but in vain. Montesquiou, the other original of Charlus, whom Proust was to meet a year later, was also an occasional guest of Mme Aubernon; but these two halves of Charlus were at daggers drawn, and it is said that Montesquiou's faithful secretary Gabriel d'Yturri was stolen by him from Doasan.

The train for Cœur-Volant, on which Doasan's conversation was so embarrassing for Proust and his fellow-guests, left Saint-Lazare at 5 p.m., stopped for several minutes at every local station, and took over an hour for the journey. At Louveciennes the guests disembarked, amid titters and elbow-nudging from bystanders convulsed by their incongruous appearance in full evening-dress, into three decrepit victorias sent by Mme Aubernon. As at La Raspelière, there was a long pull to the crest of the hill, where their hostess awaited them on the terrace. In her park was a lake with ducks, whose keep in bread was said by her cheating servants to cost a fortune—"It couldn't have been more expensive if I'd had illegitimate children," she declared— and a meadow with two pretty little cows. Just before dinner Doasan would say to the men: "Let's go and take a look at the cows"; and on the way each would step discreetly behind a tree, for indoor sanitation at Cœur-Volant was limited, and reserved for the ladies.

Mme Aubernon owned a seaside villa at Trouville, the Manoir de la Cour Brûlée, which helped to suggest Mme Verdurin's La Raspelière and to connect Mme Aubernon with the district of Balbec. It had a magnificent view of the Channel, but the 'three views' of La Raspelière belonged, as we shall see, to Les Frémonts near by. The Cour Brûlée was rented from Mme Aubernon by Mme Straus in 1892, and Proust perhaps saw it only as Mme Straus's guest. No doubt the week-ends at Cœur-Volant, preceded as they were by the journeys with Brochard and Doasan in the little train, contributed more than the summer parties at the Cour Brûlée to La Raspelière. We shall meet later, in their place, three other prototypes of the 'little train' of *Sodome et Gomorrhe*. The name of the villa hired by Mme Verdurin from the Cambremers came from La Rachepelière, a hamlet a mile west of Illiers on the Méréglise way.

To complete the foreshadowing of Mme Verdurin's salon in Mme Aubernon's it only remains to discover representatives of Swann and Odette among her guests. Paul Hervieu, the dramatist, was a little like Haas and Swann in appearance, with his rather frigid elegance, his upturned moustache ("Hervieu has tiny icicles in the corners of his moustache," said Fernand Gregh), his air of weary sadness and irony. The remark made by Swann to a girl in a brothel—"How sweet of you, you're wearing blue eyes to go with your sash"[1]—is modelled on a compliment of Hervieu at Mme Aubernon's to the Baronne de Jouvenel: "I see you're wearing black velvet eyes this evening." The lady on this occasion was not flattered, and replied: "Thanks very much—do you mean that I don't wear them every day?" At Mme Aubernon's Hervieu met and fell in love with the beautiful and talented Baronne Marguerite de Pierrebourg ("Mme de Pierrebourg is so eloquent," Mme Aubernon would say appreciatively). She was then thirty-five, and lived apart from her husband Aimery de Pierrebourg: Odette, it will be remembered, was herself the separated wife of Pierre de Verjus, Comte de Crécy, whom the Narrator met during his second visit to Balbec. The baroness deserted Mme Aubernon, taking Hervieu with her, and began, like Odette, a brilliant salon of her own, which Proust afterwards frequented. They never married, or lived together, and their love was life-long; but otherwise their story has clear analogies with that of

[1] I, 373

Swann and Odette.[1] Madeleine, her daughter by the Baron de Pierrebourg, married in 1910 Comte Georges de Lauris, a member of the group of young noblemen, the collective originals of Saint-Loup, whom Proust was to meet in the early 1900s. Perhaps this union helped to suggest the marriage of Odette's daughter and Saint-Loup.

The last of Proust's chief hostesses at this time was Mme Madeleine Lemaire. She conducted the most brilliant and crowded of the bourgeois salons, the only one where it was possible to meet in large numbers all but the most exclusive of the nobility. She began with a few fellow-artists, Puvis de Chavannes, Bonnat, Detaille, Georges Clairin, and the talented *genre* painter Jean Béraud, whose pictures of social life in clubs, soirées, the Opéra and the Bois are nowadays appreciated anew after fifty years of oblivion, and contributed to the paintings by Elstir on similar themes. But soon the Faubourg Saint-Germain arrived, because it was so delightful to meet artists, and then still more artists, because it was so delightful to meet the Faubourg. On Tuesdays from April to June her exiguous house at 31 Rue de Monceau was crowded to suffocation. The neighbouring streets were obstructed with waiting carriages, and ever more drew up, emitting duchesses and countesses with their consorts, the La Rochefoucaulds, Uzès's, Luynes's, Haussonvilles, Chevignés, Greffuhles. Thanks to some long-forgotten excuse for violating the building laws of Paris, Mme Lemaire's little house encroached upon the pavement far beyond its larger neighbours; but the passer-by, irritated here by being pushed into the gutter, would be consoled by the rural scent of the lilacs in her garden. Her receptions were held in a glass-roofed studio-annexe, which despite its huge size rapidly became overcrowded. A late-coming duchess might not only fail to find a seat, amid her hostess's cries of "A chair for Mme la Duchesse!" but even be forced out into the garden. There, pale in the light of lamps inside and street-lamps outside, hung the clusters of flowering lilac; and over the wall and across the street the dim masses of trees in Prince

---

[1] When Hervieu left, on days when Mme de Pierrebourg had company, she would see him to the door of her drawing-room and say, in the manner of Mme de Villeparisis with M. de Norpois: "You know the way, don't you?" Hervieu indeed knew the way, for she lived at 1 *bis* Avenue du Bois, and his own house was at No. 7.

Joachim Murat's garden made Mme Lemaire's yard seem like a glade in a forest.

She was a tall, energetic woman, with arched eyebrows, hair that was not all her own, a great deal of rouge, a spangled evening-gown that seemed to have been thrown on in a hurry, and the remains of pleasant good looks—though later she is said to have become hideous. All day she had indefatigably painted her flower-pieces, which were reputed to fetch 500 francs apiece, and enormous roses still stood in a corner of the studio posing in their glasses of water. "No one, except God, has created more roses," the younger Dumas had said (her daughter Suzette remarked long afterwards that Dumas was the only one of her mother's lovers she had felt quite certain about, "because she always called him 'Monsieur'"); and Montesquiou nicknamed her 'the Empress of roses'.

As a painter of flowers Madeleine Lemaire helped to suggest Mme de Villeparisis; but the chief original of Mme de Villeparisis, as will be seen later, only made artificial flowers. Mme Lemaire contributed more to Mme Verdurin. She was known as *'la Patronne'*, 'the Mistress',[1] and she used to call the painter Clairin by the nickname given by Mme Verdurin to Brichot, 'Chochotte'. Like Mmes Arman and Aubernon, Mme Lemaire spoke incessantly of her dread of bores, *'les ennuyeux'*; but for her this word had the special sense given to it by Mme Verdurin, of people who felt too distinguished to come to her evenings. But like Mme Verdurin, though far more rapidly, she experienced a rise in social standing which made the numerous race of bores dwindle to the verge of extinction. She, too, was not averse to executions of un-satisfactory guests, which would be heralded in the Verdurin manner by ominous pronouncements of "The fact is, that man has lost his talent", or "that woman is a goose", or "I won't allow that sort of behaviour in my house". She frequently interfered in the private lives of her friends, though not as a rule to their detriment. She owned a magnificent country-house called Réveillon in Seine-et-Marne, where we shall see Proust a few years later, and her system of interior decoration there is said to have resembled Mme Verdurin's at La Raspelière. Alone of the hostesses we have so far met, she provided music as an essential

---

[1] She was also called, like Mme Aubernon and for the same reason, 'the Widow'.

part of her evenings, and saw to it that many a great artist was first launched in Paris by performing to the nobility in her house. She insisted on absolute silence during a recital, and would shout across the studio to suppress any offender; but as no memorialist has thought her own behaviour under the influence of music worthy of special attention, it is perhaps unlikely that she gave way to the pantomime of intense emotion attributed to Mme Verdurin. Indeed, if any incident in *A la Recherche* resembles a musical evening at Madeleine Lemaire's, it is rather the soirée at Mme de Saint-Euverte's in *Du Côté de chez Swann* than any Wednesday of Mme Verdurin's. One of her guests, Frédéric de Madrazo, known as 'Coco' to his friends, was an original of the sculptor Ski, the dabbler in all the arts, at Mme Verdurin's. Coco composed a little and sang a little, both very badly, and painted, rather better, a great deal: "This dear young man is so *artissstic*," Mme Lemaire would coo. He was a lifelong friend of Proust and of many friends of Proust: so the unsympathetic character of Ski seems to have had a more sympathetic original.

If a musical evening at Mme Lemaire's was very like the 'crush' at Mme de Saint-Euverte's, where Swann heard the Vinteuil Sonata for the second time, it is none the less certain that the chief original of that hapless lady was Marquise Diane de Saint-Paul. Like Mme de Saint-Euverte she was of excellent family, being born a Feydeau de Brou, and her company was as aristocratic as she pleased: it must be remembered that Mme de Saint-Euverte's salon was attended by the Duchesse, Bréauté, Swann and the rest of the Guermantes set, and it was only M. de Charlus who pretended, for his own sadistic pleasure, that her house was no better than a privy.[1] Mme de Saint-Paul gave concerts at which the greatest artists of the day performed, and dinners for academicians at which the food was not infrequently provided by the guests: "They bring me flowers, so why shouldn't they bring pheasants?" she said. Her biting tongue and her brilliance as a pianist were expressed in her nickname, the *Serpent à Sonates*, or sonata-snake —a pun which Proust gave to Swann's rival Forcheville, who had to explain it to the baffled Cottard.[2] Proust gave Mme de Saint-Euverte the forename, Diane, of her original, and took her surname from the Rue Saint-Euverte near his lodgings at Orleans

[1] II, 700
[2] I, 263. *Serpent à sonnettes*, of course, means 'rattlesnake'.

in his army year. At the Princesse de Guermantes's soirée M. de Charlus taunts her with her 'mystic name'[1]; and Montesquiou had once loudly exclaimed in Mme de Saint-Paul's hearing: "That she should dare to call herself both Diana and Saint Paul is as monstrous an insult to paganism as it is to Christianity!" In his *Figaro* article of 11 May 1903 on Mme Lemaire's salon Proust was to introduce the Marquise de Saint-Paul angling there for her next week's guests (as Mme de Saint-Euverte did at the Princesse de Guermantes's soirée), and promising the singer Gabrielle Krauss 'a fan painted by her own hands if she would promise to perform at her next Thursday in the Rue Nitot'.

Mme Aubernon, nevertheless, remains the most important model of Mme Verdurin; and the chief significance of Mme Lemaire for Proust was that in her salon was the most accessible entrance to the Guermantes Way. Already, in this spring of 1892, he was beginning to meet the people whose recognition, he obscurely hoped, might palliate the guilt of his Jewish blood, his awakening perversion, and the memory of the moonlit night at Auteuil.

[1] II, 700

Chapter 8

THE DUCHESSE AND ALBERTINE

EITHER at Mme Lemaire's or at Mme Straus's, for she was to be seen, a celestial visitor from the Faubourg Saint-Germain, at both these salons, Proust met Comtesse Laure de Chevigné. He therefore had a perfect right to raise his hat when he met her in the street, a better right than the Narrator's to salute the Duchesse de Guermantes, whom he knew only by sight and as the son of her bourgeois lodgers. On the first occasion their morning meeting must have seemed to the hurrying countess a negligible but natural occurrence, on the next a curious co-incidence, on the third an ill-bred attempt, surprising in so elegant a young man, to presume on a casual acquaintance with a social superior. But when, day after day, she encountered the same lifted straw-hat and dark, infatuated eyes, she realised the dreadful truth. It was worse even than a snobbish persecution: the wretched young man was in love with her.

He had discovered that Mme de Chevigné took her daily walk along the Avenue de Marigny; and there he loitered every March morning of 1892 under the budding chestnuts, until he saw her erect shape gliding in the distance, carrying a case of visiting-cards, with a hat trimmed with blue cornflowers over her radiant blue eyes—'unpickable periwinkles sunlit by an azure smile'. Sometimes, in the vain hope of disguising his subterfuge, he would wait near her house at 34 Rue de Miromesnil—not un-observed by Jeanne Pouquet, who lived at No. 62 in the same street—or in the Avenue Gabriel beside the Champs-Élysées. Once, on a morning when Mme de Chevigné unaccountably failed to pass, he brought Robert de Billy to see her. He varied his routine, walking sometimes on the opposite pavement, some-times on the same side as the countess. One morning he would stare greedily as soon as the blue hat appeared far away, while next day he would notice her, with an ostentatious start of surprise, only as they met and passed. Sometimes he lurked behind the glass door of Émile Paul's bookshop, at the corner of the Rue de Miromesnil and the Rue du Faubourg Saint-Honoré. Each day, when the countess drew near, his love combined with the pangs of guilt and danger which his conduct invited, to produce an agonising palpitation of the heart: as he confessed to her long afterwards, "I had a heart-attack every time I saw you." At last he unwisely ventured to stop and speak; but the embarrassed lady only uttered a furious: "FitzJames is expecting me," and sailed on to her morning call on Comte Robert de FitzJames, leaving him standing. Such was the end of this strange and pathetic love-affair. Next year, when the countess saw that his behaviour was normal, his infatuation ended, and his position in society more assured, she was perfectly charming, like the Duchesse at Mme de Villeparisis's matinée; and they remained on ostensibly friendly terms until twenty-eight years later, when with mixed feelings she found her former beauty and cruelty immortalised in the love of the Narrator for the Duchesse de Guermantes. Meanwhile, in a vain attempt to improve his status in her eyes, or at least to procure her photograph, he scraped acquaintance with Gustave and Jacques de Waru, the sons of her sister who was married to Comte Pierre de Waru—but with no more success than the Narrator when he sought similar help from the Duchesse's nephew Saint-Loup.[1]

In his half-incestuous pursuit of ladies old enough to be his mother Proust had now courted in turn a bourgeois hostess, a courtesan and a society beauty. He can hardly have hoped or wished for success with Mme Straus or Laure Hayman; but from the Comtesse de Chevigné a serious rebuff was even more inevitable, and he made it doubly humiliating by the absurd form he chose for his wooing.[2] He was bitterly and unforgettably hurt, and his rage and despised love remained unaltered in his unconscious mind until they should be called upon. The character of the Duchesse de Guermantes was created not only by aesthetic laws, but by a long memory for love and revenge. In 1920, as we shall see, he made sure that the elderly countess should see this and be duly offended; and to exacerbate and reconcile her he deployed his unfaded adoration and anger as if the incident in the

---

[1] II, 79, 103
[2] Nevertheless, he perhaps had daydreams of success with Mme de Chevigné: in an early version of *A la Recherche* the Comtesse de Guermantes, who later turned into the Duchesse, becomes the mistress of the hero.

Avenue Gabriel had happened only yesterday. But by employing an impossible means in pursuit of an unattainable object he had shown an unconscious desire for failure; and a possible latent motive is revealed by the effect that his failure soon produced. He was now deterred from falling in love with mother-images by the fear of reopening the wound he had goaded the countess into inflicting. He could still fall unsuccessfully in love with a young girl, and did so, for the last time for many years, in the following summer. But his concealed perversion had been using the self-sought failure of his early loves, however sincere they had been, to bar all ways that led from itself; and the process was now nearly complete.

Mme de Chevigné, now in her middle thirties, had married in 1879 Comte Adhéaume de Chevigné, a gentleman-in-waiting of the Comte de Chambord, the dispossessed heir to the throne of France, known to his adherents as Henri V. Count Adhéaume was a tall, bald gentleman with a pink, angular face, and a manner so breezy that when he came into the room people half expected the doors and windows to rattle. For eight months of the year, until his exiled master's death in 1883, he served at the gloomy castle of Frohsdorf in Austria, amid a parody of the frozen etiquette of Versailles. For a few weeks in every year his wife accompanied him, and so became well-acquainted with the ancient courtiers whom the Duchesse de Guermantes called 'the old Frohsdorfs'.[1] One day when driving out with her deaf mistress she remarked to their footman: "Oh, Joseph, how bored I'm going to be to-day," and was horrified when the royal lady, whose hearing happened to be better than usual that morning, replied: "My poor child, how sorry I am to hear it!" But for the rest of the year she was free in Paris. At first she preferred a some-what Bohemian society of artists and singers, but gradually she acquired the friendship of a group of elderly, intelligent clubmen who liked to hear her talk—'she is an eighteenth-century woman, whose emotions turn instantaneously into wit,' wrote Proust's friend Reynaldo Hahn. All were intimate friends of Charles Haas, though we are not told that he was among them. Punctually at two o'clock, immediately after lunch, her butler Gustave would admit the Marquis du Lau, Comte Joseph de Gontaut-Biron, Marquis Henri de Breteuil, Comte Costa de Beauregard and the rest; and all stayed until she turned them out at four, sitting each in his own chair in a circle round the countess. She sat bolt upright, smoking endless cigarettes of coarse 'caporal' tobacco through an amber holder, uttering the witticisms of which one would like to have more and better specimens, since they helped her to become the Duchesse de Guermantes. The clubmen were 'as jealous as tomcats', said her friend Barbara Lister, of any younger recruit to their number: "My old men growl when they smell fresh meat," declared the countess. Every New Year's Day they subscribed to add another string to her pearls, whose festoons grew ever more difficult to count as time went by: "I can number my friends and my years on them," she said. She, too, was jealous, and on first meeting the American heiress who had robbed her of a favourite clubman (the Marquis de Breteuil, who married a Miss Garner) she uttered the simple and deadly words: "Thank you for sparing me the sight of Henri's old age."

Comtesse Laure de Chevigné, although she differed from the Duchesse de Guermantes in being neither wealthy nor of particularly exalted rank, was regarded as one of the most distinguished ladies in Parisian society. She could hardly be said to have a salon, nor could it be denied that her company was 'mixed'; but she was felt to be so pre-eminently desirable either as guest or hostess, that wherever she chose to be was exclusive, and whatever company she chose to invite was fashionable. The Duchesse de Guermantes was descended from Geneviève de Brabant; but Mme de Chevigné, though her family belonged only to the provincial nobility, was of almost equally legendary birth. She was a Sade, and among her ancestors were her namesake Laura, to whom Petrarch wrote his sonnets, and the terrible Marquis de Sade of whom, rather creditably, she was equally proud. Her head displayed the fascinating ornithological qualities which Proust transferred to the Duchesse: her neck was long and birdlike, her nose was beaked, and her wide thin mouth, with its subtle pointed smile, was birdlike too. She had azure eyes and golden hair, worn high at the nape of the neck and with ringlets on the forehead. She wore the two kinds of clothing characteristic of the Duchesse: in her early years she favoured white, spangled, plumage-like satin and muslin, but later she discovered that dark grey tailored costumes, created by Creed, which she was the first to launch at Longchamp races, were more elegant still. Her voice was trenchant and hoarse, with a peasant-like roughness which, as Proust realised, came from her provincial ancestry, and was part of her supreme distinction; though Albert Flament prosaically explained it by her excessive cigarette smoking. Like the Duchesse she had two reputations, an early one for impregnable chastity, and another, which spread mysteriously when she was already ageing, for having had secret lovers. It was at this later period that one day, as she was crossing the street, a workman called out from his scaffolding: "Coo, what a lovely tart"; to which she replied: "Not so fast, young man, you haven't seen the front view!" Like the Duchesse, again, the countess was a friend of Queen Isabella of Spain, of Edward VII as Prince of Wales, and of the Grand-Duchess Wladimir, whom she appropriated each November on her arrival from St Petersburg, and advised on her clothes. "Where did your highness get that dress? It looks as if it came from Ménilmontant!"; and the Grand-Duchess was whisked back into her carriage and off to Worth's for refitting.

In May 1892, when the fatal words "FitzJames is expecting me" had already been spoken, Proust had the melancholy pleasure of reading in a little magazine called *Le Banquet* a sketch of Mme de Chevigné, which he had written a month or two earlier when his pursuit was just beginning. The genesis of the Duchesse is already visible: Mme de Chevigné has become Hippolyta, the beauty of Verona, who has a hooked, birdlike nose, piercing eyes and a sharp angle in her mouth when she laughs. He has seen her, as the Narrator was to see the Duchesse, in a box at the theatre, dressed in white gauze like folded wings, waving a white wing-like fan of feathers. She is a white peacock, a hawk with diamond eyes. Whenever he meets her nephew (Gustave de Waru), who has the same curved nose, thin lips, piercing eyes and too delicate skin, he is disturbed at recognising again this race issued from the union of a goddess and a bird. It is an epitome, using many identical words, of passages on the Duchesse and Saint-Loup which would not appear in *Le Côté de Guermantes* until twenty-eight years later.

Le Banquet was founded, in direct descent from the *Revue Lilas* and *Revue Verte*, the schoolboy magazines of three or four years before, by a group of Proust's former schoolfellows. As a compliment to the beloved M. Darlu, who had taught them all in their respective years of *philosophie* at Condorcet, the title was borrowed from the French name of Plato's *Symposium*. In theory the magazine was to be directed by an editorial committee consisting of Daniel Halévy, Robert Dreyfus and Proust; but the management of the second number by Fernand Gregh, a young poet who had reached Condorcet in the term after Proust left in 1889, was found so successful that Gregh became sole editor. Other contributors, several of whose names are still not unknown to fame, included Jacques Bizet, Robert de Flers, Gaston de Caillavet, Louis de la Salle, Gabriel Trarieux, Henri Barbusse author of *Le Feu*, Henri Rabaud the composer, and Léon Blum the socialist prime minister. Each gave ten francs monthly, and four hundred copies of each number were handsomely printed for a mere hundred francs by Eugène Reiter, son of Jacques Bizet's former wet-nurse, then director of the printing-works of the newspaper *Le Temps*. Even so, Gregh took panic at the sight of the bill for the first number, and ordered only two hundred of the second, which is consequently even more unprocurable to-day than the rest. Thereafter circulation rose to safety-level, and Mme Straus's visitors, hearing of her son Jacques's and nephew Daniel's new venture, would take out a subscription with the same benevolent and fashionable air with which they contributed to her charities. The company met above Rouquette's bookshop at 71 Passage Choiseul, in a room magnificently surrounded by green and crimson rows of rare books in glass-fronted bookcases. Jacques's friend Henri de Rothschild procured them this privilege, and even offered to guarantee the costs of printing if they would promise in return to accept his articles; but they refused for the sake of independence.

Le Banquet ran from March 1892 till March 1893. It did not always succeed in appearing monthly, and during this period of thirteen months only eight numbers appeared. In each except the fourth and eighth Proust contributed sketches and short stories, all but two of which were collected in *Les Plaisirs et les Jours*, and essays and reviews, mostly reprinted in *Chroniques*. Next to the exuberant Gregh, who wrote under several pseudonyms as well as his own name, he was the most assiduous contributor. Yet his companions felt it was they who were writers by vocation, while Proust, who appeared to give only a part of himself to his art, could never be more than a talented amateur. 'He seemed to us far more anxious to find a way into certain drawing-rooms of the nobility than to devote himself to literature,' wrote Robert Dreyfus. This unfortunate tendency could be detected even in his writing: his characters were duchesses and countesses with absurd names, with whom dazzling young heroes of independent means fell in love and were frequently loved in return. His prose style was as faded and artificial as it was graceful and highly finished; and he used it for subtle investigations into the psychology of snobism (was he for or against it?), and love and jealousy in high society. It was alarming to see in one so young so total a disenchantment, so final a disbelief in any values more real than those of the social marionette show he described. Perhaps most distressing of all, his work was already too nearly perfect: it left, as it seemed, almost no room for evolution into something more important; it could only become an ever more brilliant pastiche of Bourget and Anatole France. The judgment of his friends of *Le Banquet* would only be confirmed by his writings during the next ten years, by the remainder of *Les Plaisirs et les Jours* and, if they could have read it, *Jean Santeuil*. They may be pardoned for failing to foresee that he would attain greatness through revelation and metamorphosis.

And yet, *Le Banquet* contains the seeds of *A la Recherche*, however different they may seem, as is natural to seeds, from the future tree. Already Proust is trying to use his own experience of life as a metaphorical representation of universal truths: here is Mme Hayman as the courtesan Heldemone, Mme Straus as 'a lady whose intelligence was revealed only by a subtler grace', Mme de Chevigné as a bird-goddess; there is a glimpse of army-life, a child who jumps out of the window for love of a little girl, a band of girls at the seaside, a seascape in Normandy, with the shadows of the clouds and the 'pale pathways' left by the currents. Both these last reminiscences belong to a holiday in August 1892, when he went to Balbec, stayed at La Raspelière, and met Albertine.

She was the sister of one of his associates on *Le Banquet*, Horace Finaly, a former schoolfellow who was the son of a wealthy Jewish banker. Proust had spent part of September 1889 on a visit to the Finalys at Ostend, and on the following 13 December Horace had travelled down to Orleans to see his friend on military service. He was duly pumped on his return by Mme

Proust: 'but I'm afraid, such is his character,' she wrote, 'he stopped at the façade and never even tried to penetrate your inner condition'. He was a short, stout, melancholy young man, interested in metaphysics and fencing, and an ardent reader of Greek poets in the original. His father, Hugo Finaly, was a fat little man with short legs and side-whiskers. Fernand Gregh compared son and father to Hamlet and Polonius; but we may compare them to Bloch and Bloch senior. Horace Finaly became Director of the Bank of Paris and the Netherlands, and for a short period was even Minister of Finance. Proust rather lost sight of him in later years, and, as we shall see, used other models for the later aspects of Bloch; but he still found Horace useful when he needed advice on stocks and shares or a job for some young protégé. Prince André Poniatowski, who knew Finaly many years later, writes rather snobbishly of another character- istic which he shared with Bloch, 'his utter lack of manners, the uncontrollable ill-breeding characteristic of the millionaire who has never ceased to be a clerk'.

Mme Hugo Finaly's uncle, Baron Horace de Landau (1824- 1903), had been the representative of the Rothschilds in the newly created Kingdom of Italy during the railway boom of the 1860s. He was an imposing, white-bearded old gentleman, who smoked an immense pipe that reached nearly to the floor; and Gregh, with his whim for finding Shakespearean equivalents for members of the Finaly family, compared him to King Lear. The Baron was devoted to his niece, to whom he willed his entire fortune, and had recently made her a present of Mme Baignères's villa at Trouville, Les Frémonts. He had bought the property for 200,000 francs from Arthur Baignères, and rewarded Proust for his services as intermediary in the deal with a superb walking- cane, a cross between a sceptre and a sugar-stick. It was said the Baron had given Les Frémonts to his niece to tease her ('*pour la taquiner*') as the outcome of a bet. "That's what I call *Taquin le Superbe*," exclaimed Arthur Baignères; and Proust treasured the epigram to give it to the Duchesse de Guermantes on the occasion of the Baron de Charlus's presenting the draughty château of Brézé to his sister Mme de Marsantes.[1] If Hugo and Horace

---

[1] II, 465. M. Nissim Bernard likewise paid for the Bloch's villa near Balbec, La Commanderie (I, 774; II, 842), and made Mme Bloch his sole heir (I, 773).

Finaly were Bloch father and son, it would follow (though nothing is known of his morals) that Baron Landau was Nissim Bernard. But Proust took the exquisitely Jewish name of Nissim from one of two banker brothers, Abraham and Nissim Camondo, who had come from Constantinople to live in a magnificent mansion in the Rue de Monceau, near Mme Lemaire, where they were to be seen strolling side by side in the garden, still wearing their fezzes.

Early in August 1892 Proust had passed the first part of his law exam with credit, but failed in the oral ('my family is awfully sick about it,' he wrote to Robert de Billy). On Sunday the 14th he left for Trouville with Louis de la Salle, armed, he told Billy, 'with Liberty ties of all possible shades', to spend a few weeks at Les Frémonts. The villa stood high above the sands of the Trouville bathing-beach, at the top of the hill at whose foot was the Hôtel des Roches Noires, where he had stayed with his grandmother in the summers of his childhood: it was one of the originals of the Grand Hotel at Balbec. But Les Frémonts itself possessed the celebrated three views of La Raspelière. Its wide bay-windows commanded three distinct prospects, the blue waters of the Channel, the coast past Cabourg as far as Lion-sur-Mer, and the inland orchards of Normandy. Other fellow-banqueters, Gregh and Trarieux, were staying near by with Jacques Bizet at the Manoir de la Cour Brûlée, which Mme Straus had hired for the season from Mme Aubernon. The walks and carriage-drives with Albertine and her friends, the flowerless, fruiting hawthorns and apple-trees of the hinterland of Balbec, belong to this summer. The young men visited the ivy-covered churches of Hennequeville and Criqueboeuf (the Carqueville to which Mme de Villeparisis takes the Narrator and his grandmother in her carriage),[1] on the way to Honfleur, and the mile-long avenues of pines and rhododendrons, above the estuary of the Seine, called Les Allées Marguerite; they went to the races at Deauville, where Proust bet and lost; and one of their companions was the first original of Albertine.

Horace Finaly's sister Marie was a pale, pretty girl with sea-green eyes, alternately gay and grave: Fernand Gregh gave her the role, in her Shakespearean family, of Ophelia. 'We were all more or less in love with Marie,' he writes; and for Proust it was

1 I, 715

one of the very few occasions on which his love for a woman was returned, for Gregh says again: 'he and the charming Marie felt for one another a childish and reciprocated love'. It is characteristic of Proust that one of the first signs of their sympathy was a common regard for one of his friends, Robert de Billy: 'She talks about you and the nobility of your mind every day,' Proust wrote to Billy, 'in fact I'm quite amazed at the moral, indeed almost religious preoccupations of this girl.' For the first time his love was associated with music: the strange colour of Marie's eyes, the season of the year, the seascapes of their clifftop walks, seemed fully expressed by Fauré's setting of Baudelaire's *Chant d'Automne*. Fifty years later Gregh could still remember his friend ecstatically and discordantly humming, with half-closed eyes and head thrown back, '*J'aime de vos longs yeux la lumière verdâtre.*'[1] A few years afterwards Marie became the wife of a nobleman of Italian family, Thomas de Barbarin, and the mother of three children; in spite of her Jewish parentage she adopted, as Proust regretfully put it, 'anti-Dreyfusism in the name of good taste'; and she died of Spanish influenza at the end of the First World War.

A curious sketch called 'Moonlight Sonata' in *Les Plaisirs et les Jours*[2] relates to this summer, and was suggested by his brief love for Marie Finaly. After driving all day with the pale 'Assunta', the Narrator asks her to go home in the carriage and leave him to rest; he falls asleep near Honfleur in 'a double avenue of great trees, within sound of the sea'—the Allées Marguerite— dreams of an eery cold sunset, and wakes to find himself flooded in moonlight. Assunta returns, saying: "My brother had gone to bed, I was afraid you might be cold"; she wraps her cloak round him, puts her arm round his neck, and they walk weeping in the moonlight. Perhaps the game of ferret took place on the clifftop, as it does in *A l'Ombre*; but more probably it happened in Paris, as in *Jean Santeuil*,[3] for Proust's letters in the following winter show him playing party-games in a circle which apparently

---

[1] The Narrator (I, 674) associates another line of Baudelaire's poem with Balbec: 'I wondered whether Baudelaire's "ray of sunlight on the sea" was not the same that at this very moment was burning the sea like a topaz, fermenting it till it became as pale and milky as beer, as frothy as milk. . . .'
[2] Pp. 192-7
[3] *Pléiade*, I, 918-21; *Jean Santeuil*, vol. 3, 247-9

includes the Finalys. 'Mlle Finaly,' he told Billy at the year's end, 'looks like a painting by Rossetti, who is thus incongruously linked with Shakespeare, the indisputable creator of Horace!'

Proust's love for Marie Finaly can hardly have been of more than minor importance in his life, or its appearance in his letters and other biographical sources would have been less unobtrusive; but its influence on *A la Recherche* was considerable. In his life her position in time and place correspond to that of Albertine in his novel: his love for Marie came immediately after his successive wooings of originals of Gilberte, Odette and the Duchesse de Guermantes; and it happened during a summer on the Normandy coast and a winter in Paris. It was round the distant, half-obliterated figure of Marie Finaly that Albertine was to crystallise. And in its lasting effect this love was one of the turning-points of his life. After the fiasco of Mme de Chevigné he never again fell in love with an older woman; after Marie Finaly it was many years before he next fell in love with a girl. With relief and joy, in the spring of 1893, he took the only path that now lay open, the path he had been deviously and unconsciously seeking all the way from Marie de Benardaky to Marie Finaly. It led into the deep valley of the Cities of the Plain, still green and fertile, untouched as yet by the fire from heaven.

Chapter 9

FIRST GLIMPSES OF THE CITIES OF THE PLAIN

IN the latter half of 1892 Proust began again the series of ardent but still platonic friendships with young men which three years of apparently normal love for women had interrupted. It is probable that in his teens, like Gide, he had remained unaware of his destiny, perhaps ignorant even of the existence of homosexual love. At the Lycée Condorcet M. Darlu would mildly enquire, when he noticed the symptoms of yet another new attachment: "What number did you give him when he came through the door of your heart?" But his pupil, it seemed, was attracted only by intellectual and moral distinction, real or imagined; his utmost desire was for a declaration of exclusive mutual devotion, to be followed by long conversations about literature. If his advances were rejected, if the sacred fire disappointingly faded in Jacques Bizet or 'little Halévy', he turned with unquenchable optimism elsewhere. In his army year the sequence continued: Horace Finaly was closely followed by Gaston de Caillavet, as was Bloch by Saint-Loup. He appreciated at Orleans the simplicity and originality of his peasant comrades; though he did not follow the path thus suggested till fifteen years later, when his mother's death set him free to make friends among the working classes. Next comes the long interlude during which nothing is heard of male friends, when his heart was occupied in turn with Jeanne Pouquet, Mme Straus, Laure Hayman, the Comtesse de Chevigné and Marie Finaly. But from the autumn of 1892 the charming young men appear in uninterrupted succession for many years, handing on, like Grecian runners, the torch of friendship or love. Proust was nearing the period in his life which corresponds in his novel to the Narrator's detection of the true nature of M. de Charlus. It is probable that in this revelation, and the proliferation of Sodom throughout the novel which is its consequence, he symbolised his discovery of his own inversion. In 1893 he met the chief original of Charlus; in 1894 came his first undoubtedly homosexual love-affair.

His new friendships in 1892 were symptoms, though he could not know it, of the approaching change; and young Robert de Billy was the involuntary cause of their beginning. Billy, his fellow-soldier and fellow-student, was a Protestant from Alsace and a lover of mountaineering. In the summer vacation of 1891 he had visited Geneva, where his religion and noble birth enabled him to move in the aristocratic society of the Rue des Granges and to make friends with a young Swiss named Edgar Aubert. In the winter Aubert returned the visit, and was introduced by Billy and Proust to the salons of Mme Straus and the cousins Charlotte and Laure Baignères. His elegance, sincerity and cosmopolitan culture made him an instant success; but his qualities were appreciated by no one more than by Proust himself. Edgar knew English, the language of Dickens and George Eliot, whom Proust could read only in translation. He spoke it at the Finalys', and when he gave Proust a photograph of his austerely handsome features a few lines of an English poet were written on the back: 'the words seem rather sad to me,' Proust commented.[1] He learned from Aubert, moreover, of the intricate social structure of the Swiss Protestant upper classes: they were a fascinating replica in miniature of the Faubourg Saint-Germain, and yet, since their hierarchy was based not on a titled nobility but on the more abstract conception of 'good family', it resembled also the Jewish caste-system which included the Rothschilds, Charles Haas, the Finalys and Mme Proust's relatives. After cross-examining Aubert, Proust made researches of his own, and was particularly delighted when he could discover some scandalous secret in an otherwise respectable Huguenot family: "I'm telling you this for your own good, *mon petit Robert*," he would say to Billy with an air of innocence, "to save you from making some awful *gaffe*." But perhaps the most impressive characteristic of Edgar Aubert was his religious fervour: in his steady eyes Proust saw, together with irony, affection and disenchantment, the light of faith; he thought of his mother's and dead grandmother's grace and good works, and felt a vague remorse for sins he had not yet committed.

[1] The quotation was very probably from Rossetti's sonnet (*The House of Life*, XCVII):

> '*Look in my face; my name is Might-have-been;
> I am also called No-more, Too-late, Farewell.*'

Cf. *Corr. Gén.*, III, 66

The three young men walked in the Tuileries gardens in the warm air of a new spring, or late at night endlessly saw one another home. Edgar, Proust always remembered, was 'so charming and witty and kind'; and though he would sometimes rebuke Marcel's sentimentality or curiosity with cutting sarcasm, he always made up for it with an affectionate glance or a shake of the hand. All too soon, however, it was time for Aubert's return to Geneva. He hoped for so much from life, and yet some presentiment made him uneasy, dejected, engagingly apprehensive. Of one thing, nevertheless, he was quite certain: "I shall come back next year *whatever happens,*" he said. But he never did.

In August, when Proust was at Trouville with the Finalys, Billy joined Aubert at Saint-Moritz. The weather was delightful, they played tennis with a young Indian Rajah and climbed several mountains; and then, only a few days after their parting, on 18 September 1892, Aubert died of appendicitis. He met his end with extraordinary firmness; he sent Proust a keepsake through their friend Jean Boissonnas; but he never had a reply to the two letters he had written to Proust just before his illness began.

Instead, Proust could only write Billy a letter of condolence which showed regret rather than grief. He was, posthumously, a little jealous: Aubert, after all, had been Billy's friend, not his. Now he must find an Aubert of his own, and make sure that Billy knew about it: perhaps Billy could be made to feel jealous in return? Already at Les Frémonts, after receiving a ten-page letter from an unnamed correspondent, he had teasingly informed Billy, in a letter that Aubert would see: 'At last I've found the tender, letter-writing friend of my dreams. It's true he only puts one stamp on his envelopes, so I always have to pay 30 centimes— but what wouldn't one do when one really likes a person?' Early in 1893, when Billy had become a probationer in the French Embassy at Berlin, Proust had found another friend, 'who is everything to me that I should have been to X——, if he hadn't been so unfeeling. I refer to the young, charming, intelligent, kind, affectionate Robert de Flers.' In February he went with Flers to the Lenten sermons, on '*Living for Others*', of Abbé Pierre Vignot, and greatly admired them, though not perhaps in the sense in which the preacher intended. Afterwards he frequently met the Abbé at the home of his Condorcet friend, Pierre

Lavallée. But in the spring, when 'the return of gentle sunlit days' gave him 'the exact illusion, to the point of hallucination, of the time when we used to see Edgar Aubert home', he met a young man who was very like Aubert indeed. He duly told Billy, who was about to visit Paris on leave; he also sent an oval seating-plan of an enormous dinner-party at 9 Boulevard Malesherbes for a select ten of his very best friends, and the names of seven more who came after dinner—'I'm afraid the list isn't quite complete,' he added apologetically. Willie Heath is in the place of honour on Mme Proust's left, while Proust is separated from them by Comte Charles de Grancey and Robert de Flers. Of the ten dinner-guests, four are counts (Grancey, Flers, Louis de la Salle and Gustave de Waru) and two viscounts; the after-dinner guests are all untitled. 'If only I'd known you were coming I'd have put off the dinner,' he said; but Billy was not allowed to meet Heath on this visit, and there was never to be another opportunity.

It was almost as if Aubert had fulfilled his promise of coming next year, *whatever happens*. Willie Heath was quite alarmingly like Aubert. He not only spoke English, he *was* English; he was deeply religious, like Edgar, though after a Protestant upbringing he had been converted to Catholicism at the tender age of twelve; and in his eyes there was the same look of melancholy premonition and resignation as in Aubert's. Of all their circle he was the most serious, and yet the most childlike, not only in the purity of his heart, but in his bursts of delightful, unselfconscious gaiety. Proust noted with some envy that the secret of making Willie laugh seemed denied to himself, whereas Charles de Grancey, with stories of his schooldays, could always send Willie into fits.

They met in the Bois de Boulogne. The morning sunlight slanted through the new leaves as Proust advanced to their meeting-place: there, under the trees, erect yet reposing in his pensive elegance, stood Willie, his eyes already fixed on his friend; and a strange thought came into Proust's mind. In 1891, the first year of their student life, Robert de Billy had shown him Van Dyck's portraits of young English cavaliers in the Louvre: "you see, Marcel," he had explained, "they're all going to be killed soon in the Civil War, and you can tell it in their faces." How like the doomed Duke of Richmond, standing under dark green foliage, was Willie! 'Their elegance, like yours,' Proust wrote later, 'lies not so much in their clothes as in their bodies, and their bodies seem to have received it, and to continue unceasingly to receive it, from their souls: for it is a moral elegance.' Then, as he watched another characteristic attitude of Willie's, the raised finger pointing to some heavenly enigma, the impenetrably smiling eyes, he thought of another favourite picture in the Louvre, in which spirituality, mystery and sexual ambiguity are even more intensely mingled: Willie was very like Leonardo's John the Baptist. When they began to talk in the green glade, it was of a plan 'to live more and more together, in a chosen group of highminded women and men, somewhere too far away from stupidity, vice and malice for their vulgar arrows ever to reach us'. But before this project could be carried out, on 3 October 1893, still in Paris, Willie Heath died of typhoid. His resemblance to Edgar Aubert was now complete.

Meanwhile the spring of 1893 had brought—along with Abbé Vignot's Lenten sermons, and hallucinatory memories of the dead Aubert, and Willie's friendship, and the new leaves in the Bois— the annual resumption of Mme Lemaire's Tuesdays. On Tuesday, 28 March, the event of the evening was a recital by Mlle Bartet from the Comédie Française of poems from *Les Chauves-Souris*, the first published volume of Comte Robert de Montesquiou-Fezensac.[1] Moved by a mild interest in the verses and an intense curiosity about their author, Proust joined the cooing ladies who queued to congratulate the fluting count; and as Montesquiou's appetite for flattery was only equalled by his predilection for handsome young men, the new admirer was graciously received, and his entreaty for permission to call was affably granted. Proust was to meet many writers of more genuine talent, and a few of genius; but in some ways this pseudo-poet and monster of vanity was the most extraordinary person he ever met. For Count Robert, as Proust perhaps obscurely realised as early as this very Tuesday, had the makings of Palamède, Baron de Charlus.

Montesquiou, as he not infrequently explained, was a member of one of the oldest families in the French nobility: it included a

---

[1] It was most incorrect, however, to call him by his full name. As the Narrator remarks, 'a guest in a drawing-room proves that he is unfamiliar with society if he refers to M. de Montesquiou as M. de Montesquiou-Fezensac'. (II, 934).

comparatively recent ducal branch, whose title dated only from 1815, but now consisted mostly of innumerable counts and countesses with whom he was on terms of permanent enmity. He claimed descent from the Merovingian kings of France; but among his undoubted ancestors were the crusader Raimond-Aimeri de Montesquiou (*circa* 1190), Blaise de Montluc (1502-72), the marshal of France, massacrer of Protestants and author of the famous *Commentaires*, and Charles de Batz (1611-73), the original of D'Artagnan in *The Three Musketeers*. The château of Artagnan in the Hautes-Pyrénées was still in the possession of the family, and Montesquiou used it as his country-seat and occasional refuge from the fatigues of Paris. Various Montesquious of the *grand siècle* move through the memoirs of Saint-Simon; but the family reached its highest prominence in the church and army under Louis XVI. "There's one good thing about the French Revolution," Hervieu had been heard to remark one evening at Mme de Caillavet's, when Montesquiou was reciting his poems and leaning nobly against the mantelpiece: "if it hadn't happened, that man would have had us beating his ponds to keep the frogs quiet." But there were several scores of families of higher absolute position in the French society of Proust's time; and Count Robert's own social eminence was based partly on his snob-value as a titled intellectual, partly on his hypnotic power of imposing himself on the fashionable world, and partly on the gift his hated relatives possessed for intermarriage with the great. He was related by recent marriages to the ducal families of La Rochefoucauld, Bauffremont, Rohan-Chabot, Gramont, Feltre, Descars, Béthune, Maillé de la Tour Landry, Noailles and Rochechouart-Mortemart; to the princes of Caraman-Chimay, Faucigny-Lucinge, Bibesco and Brancovan; and through these to everyone else who mattered in the slightest. Charlus spoke of 'my cousin Clara de Chimay', 'my cousins the La Rochefoucaulds',[1] and so, incessantly, did Robert de Montesquiou. For the 1910 edition of *Qui êtes-vous* he wrote under his name: 'Allied to the greater part of the European aristocracy.' It was the simple truth.

Montesquiou was now thirty-eight, and the soirée at Mme Lemaire's was the first step in a campaign already long overdue, through which he hoped to exchange his notoriety as a beautiful aesthete for fame as a well-preserved poet. He was born in 1855,

[1] I, 764; III, 268

and became an ailing, frightened little boy, bullied by his father, schoolfellows and Jesuit teachers. In 1871, at the age of sixteen, he met Charles Haas, and was impressed by his wit and easy elegance: Proust, exaggerating a little, for Haas was more than twenty years Montesquiou's senior, made Charlus and Swann friends in their schooldays.[1] Desiring to surround himself with beauty, as a fitting mirror of the beauty he so admired in himself, he became a fanatic of interior decoration, a collector of bric-à-brac. He met Mallarmé late in the '70s, and in 1879 brightened the fatal illness of the poet's little son Anatole with the gift of a cockatoo named Semiramis. Mallarmé told Huysmans of this fantastic young aesthete, and the decadent novelist constructed *A Rebours* (1885) and the character of Des Esseintes about him. Mallarmé was perturbed lest the ultra-susceptible Montesquiou should be annoyed: but no, he was delighted. Yes, it was perfectly true that he had a room decorated as a snow-scene, with a polar-bear rug and a sleigh and mica hoar-frost ("when you went into that room you felt f-r-r-rozen!" his dear secretary Yturri would say). And yes, he did inlay the shell of a pet tortoise with turquoises, of which the poor creature died; and he *had* been known to wear a white velvet suit, with a bunch of violets in the neck of his shirt instead of a cravat. If anything aggrieved him, he revealed, it was that Mallarmé should have paid him only a single visit in search of material.

In the 1880s he met Edmond de Goncourt, and there are admiring glimpses of him in the Goncourt *Journal*, of a delicious absurdity only surpassed by the parody of the *Journal* read at Tansonville by the Narrator. There is an accidental meeting on 6 April 1887 with Montesquiou at Passy, 'in all the correctness of one of his supremely *chic* suitings': he was carrying what looked like a sumptuously bound prayer-book, but turned out to be a copy of one of Goncourt's own novels—'which is some slight compensation for all the setbacks I have had lately,' remarks the poor diarist. There is a visit on 7 July 1891 to Montesquiou's house in the Rue Franklin at Passy, where Proust was to visit him in April 1893. It was 'crammed with a hodge-podge of incongruous objects, old family portraits, Empire furniture, Japanese kakemonos and etchings by Whistler'. But the most amazing room of all was the bathroom, decorated with represen-

[1] III, 299

tations of the count's favourite flower, the hortensia, 'in every possible material and every conceivable art-form', and containing two objects which later must have filled Proust with a special *frisson* of amusement and envy: a glass cupboard with 'the tender pastel shades of a hundred cravats', and above it 'a photograph of La Rochefoucauld, the acrobat at the Cirque Mollier, in tights which do full justice to his elegant ephebic figure'.

Montesquiou was tall and thin—"I look like a greyhound in a greatcoat," he would say complacently. He had abandoned his former eccentricities of dress, and favoured dark grey suits whose harmonies and exquisite drapings made him more noticeable than ever. His hair was black, crisp and artificially waved; he had beetling black eyebrows like circumflex accents, and a moustache with upturned pointed ends, like the Kaiser's but larger. His face was white, long, hawk-like and finely drawn; his cheeks were rouged and delicately wrinkled, so that Proust, greatly to his annoyance, compared them to a moss-rose; and his mouth was small and red, with little black teeth which he hurriedly concealed with one hand whenever he laughed—a gesture unnecessarily copied by Proust, whose teeth were beautifully white in his youth. In these early days he used only a little powder and rouge. Everything in his appearance was studied, for the artist, he felt, should be himself a work of art. But as this strange, black and white nobleman chanted, swayed and gesticulated, he acted a whole series of puppet characters, as if manipulated on wires pulled by some other self in the ceiling: he was a Spanish hidalgo, a duellist, his ancestor D'Artagnan, a screeching black macaw, an angry spinster, the greatest living poet. The sobriety of his colour-scheme was mitigated by the coquetry of his lilac perfume and pastel-hued cravats: "I should like admiration for my person to reach the pitch of physical desire," he confessed.

Montesquiou had inherited from his family great wealth and a delight in spending it: it was one of the few traits he shared with his father, Comte Thierry de Montesquiou, who had once remarked when contemplating marriage with a young heiress: "She has 500,000 francs a year—with what I have that will make 50,000." The increasing splendour of his apartments and the receptions he gave in them sometimes involved him in temporary debt; but, as he said, "It's bad enough not to have any money, it would be too much if one had to deprive oneself of anything."

At such times he was capable of economy: he and Yturri might be seen devouring the cheapest lunch at the humble creamery opposite his apartment, or Yturri would go out and sell something. Sometimes the articles of his collection cost very little: Yturri found Mme de Montespan's pink marble bath in the garden of a Versailles convent, and paid for it with his own cast-off slipper which, he assured the nuns, had once belonged to the Pope. Sometimes they cost nothing at all. Worn out by Montesquiou's nagging, his exclamations of "Don't you see, it's *disgusting* to give away anything you can bear to part with," a noble lady would surrender an eighteenth-century drawing, a porcelain figurine, or a manuscript of Baudelaire; and he would carry off the precious object wrapped in tissue-paper.

The conversation of Montesquiou appealed both to the ear and the eye: it was like an aria by a great singer or a speech by a great actor, yet with something of a clown's antics or a madman's raving. He made beautiful gestures with his white-gloved hands; then he would remove the gloves, displaying a simple but curious ring; his gesticulation became ever more impassioned, till suddenly he would point heavenward: his voice rose like a trumpet in an orchestra, and passed into the soprano register of fortissimo violins; he stamped his foot, threw back his head, and emitted peal upon peal of shrill, maniacal laughter. He spoke of poetry and painting, of countesses' hats, of the splendour of his race, and of himself as its crowning glory. "I can't bear that man who's always telling me about his ancestors," Anatole France would complain; and Charles Haas, on request, would imitate Montesquiou saying, in the choicest accent of the *gratin*—it was a kind of incisive, yelping drawl—"My forebears used up all the family intelligence; my father had nothing left but the sense of his own grandeur; my brother hadn't even that, but had the decency to die young; while I—I have added to our ducal coron*et* the glorious coron*al* of a poet!" Very often he would recite his own verses; and when his hostess whispered: "How very beautiful!" he would reply: "Yes, it *is* a beautiful poem, and I will now recite it to you again." Sometimes he would stand on the staircase, like M. de Charlus at the Princesse de Guermantes's, and make distinctly audible comments on the arriving guests: "I see the Chanoinesse de Faudoas is wearing orange—no doubt she wishes to display the number of her quarters." Once he embarrassed an unfortunate maiden whose dress was garnished with imitation cherries: "I had no idea young girls were allowed to bear fruit." There was, indeed, even apart from his insolent delight in the pleasure of making enemies, his readiness to sacrifice his best friends for the sake of making an epigram, a streak of sadism in his nature. He used to visit his little nieces and say, "My dears, to-day we will play at pretending to cry." He would then mimic bitter sobs, his nieces would imitate him just for fun; and when their tears became real he would slip away, leaving them writhing in hysteria.

Montesquiou was by no means insensible to the beauty of women. He had adored Sarah Bernhardt in the days when she was still ravishingly pretty and young-looking: he had even gone to bed with her, an experience which was unhappily followed by a week of uncontrollable vomiting. He kept up a life-long, semi-mystical cult for the Comtesse de Castiglione, who had been the mistress of Napoleon III and many of his courtiers; she still lived on in the Place Vendôme, half-crazed, emerging only at night, lest people should see the ruin of her beauty. Among his most treasured possessions—along with La Gandara's drawing of Comtesse Greffulhe's chin and Boldini's painting of Yturri's legs in cycling breeches—was a plaster-cast of the Castiglione's knees. His *Les Chauves-Souris* was dedicated to the lovely Marquise Flavie de Casa-Fuerte, whose son Illan was to become one of his last young friends fifteen years later. In his middle age he was to be no less devoted to Eleanora Duse, Isadora Duncan and Ida Rubinstein. His sexual abnormality was so inconspicuous that after his death several of the people who had known him best denied its existence: "he was not an invert, but merely an introvert," says André Germain. In fact, Montesquiou's inversion may have been confined largely to his almost conjugal relations with his secretaries, and his attachments to other young men were perhaps often, if not invariably, platonic. Similarly, in *A la Recherche* the Narrator sometimes surprisingly conjectures that Charlus's liaison with Morel may have been entirely innocent. There is no hint in the life of Montesquiou of casual affairs with waiters, cabmen and other underlings: this feature of Charlus, like his burly physique, was derived from Baron Doasan.

The first of Count Robert's secretaries—followed after his death by the second and last—was Gabriel d'Yturri. The surname is a Basque word meaning a spring of fresh water, and the particle was added at Montesquiou's suggestion. Yturri was born on 12 March 1864 at Tucuman in the Argentine, brought up in Buenos Ayres, and emigrated at the age of fifteen to Paris. Baron Doasan found him serving behind a counter at the Magasins du Louvre, and persuaded him to become his secretary, only to have him stolen by Montesquiou—hence the undying enmity between the count and the baron. For twenty years, from 1885 till he died in harness in 1905, Yturri was the loyal friend and factotum (as was Jupien of the Baron de Charlus) of 'Mossou le Connte', as he called him in his indelible *rastaquouère* accent. At first his status and antecedents were difficult to explain. "From which house does M. d'Yturri derive?" asked the blue-blooded Comte Aimery de La Rochefoucauld, Montesquiou's cousin by marriage, only to be told by a malicious informant: "He derives from a 'house' in the Rue de Boccador!"[1] When Count Aimery pursued his enquiries by asking Yturri himself, the reply was even less satisfactory: "Why, I was ze secretary of ze Baron Doasan!" cried the young man with visible pride. But Yturri was so good-natured and faithful, and lasted so long, that in the end he was universally accepted and even liked. He was short, handsome and excitable; he had coffee-coloured eyes, a deathly pale olive face, a conspicuous mole tufted with hair, and a tendency to baldness against which he fought with desperate unsuccess. He exuded a strange odour of chloroform and rotten apples, which no one realised until too late to be a symptom of diabetes. His relationship with Montesquiou was clouded only by occasional tiffs and sulks, and by the fact that it was impossible to discover just where he went on his bicycle. Once there was a more prolonged absence, by train, and the poor count could only reply to an enquiring friend: "Gabriel has gone to Monte Carlo with a young person who seems to have an extremely bad influence on him."

In one respect Montesquiou's character stands in need of no defence. He invented and kept his own astonishing rules of life:

[1] Such was the rumour, all the more illuminating for being apocryphal. The truth of the story, as told by Montesquiou himself, is simply that, on the occasion of Montesquiou's duel with Henri de Regnier, Comte Aimery (anxious lest his cousin should be fighting a mere commoner) asked Yturri: "To what house does M. de Regnier belong?", and Yturri, deliberately misunderstanding, gave him Regnier's address: "No. 6 Rue du Boccador!"

he was, though of lesser calibre than the Baron de Charlus, an eccentric in his own right, and by far the most remarkable and original person in the empty milieu of the Faubourg Saint-Germain; he was witty, and brilliantly though not profoundly intelligent. But with some research it is possible to detect in him moral qualities which mitigate, though they do not redeem, his charlatanism. He was kind and loyal to his friends, during the short period before he quarrelled with them. He was brave and indomitable. But best of all was his selfless devotion to the artists and writers whom he considered his equals or even superiors. They included Mallarmé, Leconte de Lisle, Heredia, Coppée, Goncourt, Huysmans, Villiers de l'Isle Adam, Barbey d'Aurevilly, Verlaine, Regnier, d'Annunzio, Barrès, Gustave Moreau, Degas, Whistler and Forain: though the list shows no insight in advance of his time, it contains only one or two inferior names. He supported them with tireless propaganda; he supplied them with patrons and purchasers, and to the few who needed it he gave his own money. In return they respected his talent, perhaps more than it deserved, and defended him when taxed with their enjoyment of his company. "He says such marvellous things," said Barrès. "He's so foonny . . . and besides, he comes walking with me in the Bois, and there are so few people who can keep oop with me!" Whistler (one of the many originals of Elstir) painted two portraits of the count in 1891; and it is probable that Whistler was a decisive model for the definitive mask which Montesquiou adopted in the early '90s, and for the publicity campaign of readings, lectures and entertainments which had just opened at the time of his meeting with Proust. He borrowed Whistler's coiffure for his waving black hair, Whistler's moustache, his duellist's stance, his baying laugh with head thrown back, his ferocity and his epigrams, his gentle art of making enemies.

Montesquiou showed rather less abnegation and critical taste in his discoveries: they were mostly artists (he took good care never to 'discover' a writer) of little or secondary merit, whom he pushed with one eye on the credit they would do him. Among them were Helleu, an etcher and painter of real talent, La Gandara, who became a fashionable but execrable society-portraitist, Lobre, the painter of Versailles, and Gallé, the engraver of glass and the creator of Montesquiou's hortensia bathroom. The only one of his discoveries whose work still lives was Proust's friend, Jacques

Émile Blanche, a post-impressionist of enduring charm and originality, except for an unfortunate period during the Edwardian era when he imitated Sargent. The story of their final breach is instructive: it shows the pattern of a typical Montesquiou execution, and it has several features in common with the quarrel-scene of Charlus and the Narrator in *Le Côté de Guermantes*.

For a time Montesquiou called Blanche "the Lord's anointed". He commissioned a portrait of "a Beautiful Unknown—nobody must hear about her"—but when Blanche arrived for the sitting, in came the Marquise de Casa-Fuerte, whom one met everywhere. Similarly he had told her that her portraitist was "an unknown genius I've discovered". One morning, however, when Blanche at Montesquiou's earnest request had asked him to lunch to meet the composer Fauré, the unlucky painter encountered the Prince de Sagan, with his white gloves, white hair and white carnation, walking in the Bois, and invited him to come too. The prince and the count were deadly enemies: Montesquiou took one look, turned green with rage, and left, Fauré or no Fauré. They met once more, on the Ile des Cygnes at Passy, to return their correspondence and bid everlasting farewell: Montesquiou gave back Blanche's letters in a scented coffer of sandalwood, whereupon Blanche hurled Montesquiou's into the Seine. It was the opening day of the Universal Exhibition of 1889 and of its chief attraction, the Eiffel Tower. "If you had understood the tutelary importance of the man who hoped to reveal you to yourself," said Montesquiou mournfully, "it would have helped you to avoid the false steps in which you seem to take such pleasure. But as we shall never meet again, I will consecrate one last hour to you. Let us ascend to the first platform of the Eiffel Tower, and gaze upon the panorama of this tentacular Paris, in which I should have liked to show you the places to shun." And after the ascent Montesquiou saw Blanche home in a cab, as Charlus did the Narrator. Henceforth he exerted all his power to exclude the painter from society; he called him 'the Auteuil shaving-brush'; and when he saw one of his paintings in a noble lady's house he would say: "Isn't it high time you put this piece of linoleum under your bath-tub?"

All in all, Montesquiou was a hollow man. The terrifying, impenetrable façade of his vanity, his insolence, his perversity, covered nothing but the frightened small boy with whom he had mental wigging on which the quarrel between Charlus and the Narrator in *Le Côté de Guermantes* is based. It is very possible that Proust detected beneath the count's anger the notes of despised love; but the whole tenor of their subsequent relationship shows that his advances, if they were made, were veiled and unsuccessful. Montesquiou must have realised, like Baron Doasan before him, that his new friend was (or would soon be) like himself an active, not a passive invert, a rival huntsman, not a possible prey. The ostensible grounds of the dispute, both in real life and in the novel, were a report that the disciple had been talking scandal about the master. Montesquiou had good reason to be touchy: in March 1895 the loyal Yturri felt compelled to challenge Blanche to a duel on a charge of gossiping about his relations with the count; though Blanche was soon able to convince Yturri's second, Henri de Regnier, that it was all a trick of the malicious Comtesse Potocka and her friend Georges Legrand. Charlus's speeches in the quarrel-scene, as elsewhere, are a brilliant parody of Montesquiou; but several of the baron's sayings in this episode are known to be favourite tags of the terrible count's: Proust's letters show that they were uttered to him at some time in the early 1890s, and it may well be that it happened on this very occasion. One is: "Words repeated at second-hand are seldom true"; another is "I have submitted you to the supreme test of excessive amiability, the only one which separates the wheat from the tares"; and another is Montesquiou's infuriating quotation from Psalms ii, 10, with which he invariably accompanied a warning or a complaint: "*Et nunc erudimini*"— 'Be ye now instructed.'

The quarrel with Montesquiou did not last long. In August Proust made the best of two very different friendships by visiting Saint-Moritz with Louis de la Salle, his companion at the Finalys' the summer before, and Montesquiou. With the count was one of his adored lady-friends, Mme Meredith Howland, an intimate of Charles Haas and one of the very few Americans then admitted to high society[1]; she and Montesquiou had been there the previous year at the same time as Billy and Aubert, though the

---

[1] In *Le Temps Retrouvé*, when the Narrator reminds the Duchesse of a hostess who had spoken ill of Mme Howland, Oriane bursts out laughing: "Why, of course, Mme Howland had all the men in her salon, and your friend was trying to lure them to her own!" (III, 1026).

two couples had not met. Proust and La Salle ascended the Righi by funicular and the Alp Grüm on foot, seeing from the summit a dim blue vista that led to Italy; and by the lake of Sils-Maria they watched a flight of pink butterflies cross the water and return. Then, after three weeks, the party moved for a last week to the Lake of Geneva, to find a miniature working-model of Parisian society: it was in expectation of this that Proust had defensively told Billy: 'I shall be meeting lots of women.' There was Laure Baignères in her Villa Quatorze at Clarens, after which (in allusion to the Belgian Comtesse Vilain-Quatorze whom Louis XIV ennobled after a delightful visit) she was nicknamed Comtesse Villa-Quatorze. At Amphion, in her Villa Bassaraba, was Princesse Rachel de Brancovan, who played Chopin so beautifully but so reluctantly, with a musical agony that recalls Mme Verdurin's. "Oh, not to-day, Monsieur, I couldn't!" she would cry: "Oh, what torture! No, it would kill me, feel my hands, they're frozen!" She was one of the leaders of musical society in Paris, a patroness of Paderewski, Fauré and Enesco. Perhaps Proust first met at this time her wild and pretty sixteen-year-old daughter Anna, the future poetess and Comtesse de Noailles, who was later to be his friend. But as he travelled from hostess to hostess round the lake he thought of Aubert's sad, ironic eyes, and reproached himself, as he wrote to Billy, for enjoying the beauty that poor Edgar would never see again.

In September he spent a fortnight with Mme Proust at the Hôtel des Roches Noires, Trouville, at the western end of the boarded promenade—an original of that on which the little band of girls walks at Balbec—which the society gossip columns called 'the summer boulevard of Paris'. Summer, however, was nearly over: evening mists rose in the valley behind the hotel, and the fireplaces, it seemed, were not intended to contain fires. There was only one lavatory to each storey, and the partitions between the bedrooms were too thin; but at least this meant that his mother would hear his tapping on the wall, as did his grandmother long ago, and visit him as soon as he woke. Perhaps he saw Marie Finaly again: at least, he nostalgically quoted to his father after his return Baudelaire's line, which he associated with her, about 'le soleil rayonnant sur la mer'. But Dr Proust was in no mood for quotations. Marcel, if all went well, would soon pass his law diploma (in fact he took it on 10 October 1893, a week after Willy Heath's death); and the holiday at Trouville, after supplying a few hints for the second visit to Balbec, ended in an ultimatum, expressed with the well-meaning father's characteristic impatience and finality: Marcel must choose a career; he must show some will-power.

With an outbreak of genuine panic, and a mask of despairing obedience, Marcel showed so much will-power that in the end nothing happened. 'I had hoped, *mon cher petit papa*,' he wrote, 'to persuade you to allow me to continue the literary and philosophical studies for which I believe I am fitted.' But at this time he felt it no less essential that he should be allowed to pursue his social life. In *A la Recherche* the Narrator is determined not to go into the diplomatic service because he would have to live abroad and cease to see Gilberte; and here, no doubt, Proust remembers the year 1891, when it seemed likely that he would in due course enter the Ministry of Foreign Affairs, with his fellow-students Trarieux and Billy, and so be separated from Jeanne Pouquet. But in 1893 Jeanne was married and forgotten, and the danger had changed. 'I'm determined not to go abroad,' he told Billy; for it would mean renouncing not only the bourgeois hostesses he already possessed, but also the noble hostesses for whom he hoped. Nor could he endure a post that might make him socially unacceptable: 'isn't the magistrature too much looked down upon?' he pathetically asked Billy. 'As for going into a lawyer's office, I'd a thousand times rather it were a stockbroker's—you can be quite sure I wouldn't stay there three days,' he told Dr Proust. He did in fact begin training with a lawyer, a certain Maître Brunet, and endured it for a whole fortnight, but no longer; and for a time there was even some talk of buying him a lawyer's practice. He toyed with the grim idea of the Cour des Comptes, the Government accounting office which was traditionally regarded as being socially distinguished (Billy's father was a *conseiller référendaire* there); but 'the boredom would kill me', and mathematics had been his worst subject at Condorcet. At last, although Marcel promised to work seriously for 'the Foreign Affairs exam or the École des Chartes, the choice to be yours', poor Dr Proust realised it would be simpler to shelve the whole matter. It was agreed that Marcel should spend the next academic year studying for the *licence ès lettres*; and Proust was not dissatisfied with this first step towards family acquiescence in his literary career. As he told his father with unconscious foresight: 'anything but literature and philosophy for me would be *temps perdu*'—Time Lost.

His progress as a writer had already reached a new stage. After the demise of *Le Banquet*, in March 1893, several of the homeless banqueters, including Gregh, Léon Blum, Jacques Baignères and Proust himself, had been offered hospitality by the *Revue Blanche*. This was a high-class, mildly *avant-garde* little review, founded in 1891 by the wealthy Polish brothers Thadée and Alexandre Natanson. Verlaine, Mallarmé, Heredia, Barrès, Jean Lorrain, Pierre Louÿs and the young André Gide were among its contributors. Nine sketches by Proust, of the kind that had already appeared in *Le Banquet*, were published in the *Revue Blanche* for July-August 1893; a short story, *Mélancolique Villégiature de Madame de Breyves*, was in the September number; and several of another group of six sketches, which did not appear till December 1893, were written before this September. The greater part of what was to be *Les Plaisirs et les Jours* was therefore already in existence by September 1893; and towards the end of the month, encouraged by his year's reprieve from the horrors of earning a living, Proust began to plan their publication in volume form. He mentioned the idea to Mme Lemaire a few days after Willie Heath's death on 3 October; and to his delight she offered—or consented—to illustrate the book with the execrable drawings and brushwork which would, he hoped, ensure its success in fashionable circles. He immediately approached Heath's family for permission to dedicate his volume to his dead friend: 'they seemed quite pleased with the suggestion,' he wrote to Billy early in November, but a further application to Aubert's parents, to ask that Edgar's name might be coupled with Willie's, came to nothing.

Any attempt to distinguish autobiographical elements in the *Revue Blanche* sketches must be made with caution. As a rule they have the impersonal air of literary exercises, and there is little of the special feeling which in Proust marks personal experience. The love incidents—nearly all the sketches are about love—are derivative from the contemporary high-society fiction of France and Bourget, and contain almost nothing which can be linked with Proust's emotional life at this time. Proust sometimes tells

THE CITIES OF THE PLAIN 139

his story from the heroine's point of view; but this well-worn
device, used by so many heterosexual authors, need not necessarily be interpreted here as 'transposition'—the use, that is, of
homosexual material in a heterosexual context. If the heroines
were really Proust himself, they would be more alive; if their
lovers were based on young men loved by Proust, they too would
be less dull and conventional. Three pieces, however, share a
similar and thoroughly Proustian theme, the crystallisation of
love for an absent person. *Présence réelle* is set in the landscapes
of the Engadine which Proust visited with Louis de la Salle, and
is told in the first person; but not even the sex of the vague, faraway loved one is revealed. In *Rêve* the narrator dreams he is
making love at Trouville with a Mme Dorothy B——, to whom
he is indifferent in waking life, and on waking finds he is in love
with her. In *Mélancolique Villégiature de Madame de Breyves*,
which is dedicated to Mme Howland but was written before the
visit to Saint-Moritz, the heroine is consumed with a passion for
an insignificant nobleman whom she has met only once and then
disliked. Perhaps this repetition of subject conceals some real
experience; but perhaps Proust was merely experimenting in
variations on a theme that interested him intellectually and
instinctively.

Another sketch, the brief *Avant la nuit*, which Proust discreetly
refrained from reprinting in *Les Plaisirs et les Jours*, concerns a
situation that reappears in the Françoise episode of *Jean Santeuil*,
in Swann's jealousy of Odette's past, and in the Narrator's life
with Albertine. The heroine confesses to her secretly horrified
lover, who tells the story, that she has had homosexual affairs with
other women. Here, at least, is a possible instance of transposition; though whether the underlying circumstance is real or
imagined, and whether Proust is confessing to a young man or a
young man confessing to Proust, it would be hard to say. But
Avant la nuit is also, with one exception, the first reference to the
theme of Lesbianism which is of such importance in both *Jean
Santeuil* and *A la Recherche*. It is often supposed that in *A la
Recherche* the loves of Gomorrah are nothing but transpositions
of the loves of Sodom. But if, as can be shown, the character of
Albertine is based not only on transposition but also, and
primarily, on Proust's affairs over a period of twenty years
with a number of young women, it may well be that his pain-

ful interest in Lesbianism was likewise founded on real experience.[1]

It was perhaps in the winter of 1893-94 that Proust frequented the Saturdays of the great Parnassian Heredia at 11 *bis* Rue Balzac. Guests had the choice of two rooms: their host's study, full of poets and cigar-smoke, and the drawing-room, which Proust preferred, where Heredia's three lovely daughters, Hélène, Louise and Marie, were surrounded by a group of admiring young men. He met there Pierre Louÿs (who married Louise and ill-treated her), the symbolist Henri de Regnier, thirty years old, with a monocle and long drooping moustaches (who married Marie), and possibly André Gide, whom he might also have met with Paul Valéry and the painter Maurice Denis at the Finalys' in the winter of 1892. In parody of her father's campaign for election to the Académie Française Marie organised a secret society of her friends known as the Académie Canaque, which might be roughly translated as 'the Cannibal Academy'. She was Queen of the Academy, Proust was Perpetual Secretary, with the task of calling the meetings and keeping the minutes, and members included Pierre Louÿs, Regnier, Paul Valéry, Fernand Gregh, Léon Blum, the economist and banker Raphael Georges Lévy, the poet Ferdinand Hérold, and the young politicians Philippe and Daniel Berthelot. The formal speech of thanks for

---

[1] If this is so, then the experience of the confession must be looked for in the years before *Avant la nuit* was written; and indeed there seems to be little later evidence of Proust's acquaintance with Lesbians before an advanced stage in the composition of *A la Recherche*. There are a few slight and dubious indications that this early experience, if it occurred, may have been connected with Marie Finaly. There is a single short reference to female homosexuality in Proust's work before *Avant la nuit*, in the short story *Violante, ou la Mondanité*, in which the heroine is unsuccessfully assaulted by a Lesbian. *Violante* was published in *Le Banquet* in February 1893; and since it is perhaps the most mature of the *Le Banquet* pieces, it can hardly have been written before Proust's visit to the Finalys in August 1892. *Violante* is a young girl who is led astray from the life of the spirit and the imagination by a love of society; and although in this respect the character undoubtedly reflects Proust's own feelings of guilt, we have found him later accusing Marie Finaly of having taken the same wrong path. Perhaps, then, *Violante* resembles Marie Finaly in still other ways. Marie was the first original of Albertine; as her brother Horace was an original of Bloch, she may also have had some resemblance to Bloch's Lesbian sisters; and she may have activated the theme of the Proustian hero's jealousy of Lesbian infidelity which begins in *Avant la nuit* and ends in *Albertine Disparue*.

newly elected members which was a feature of the senior institution was replaced by a silent series of artistic and horrible grimaces; and it was unanimously agreed that the inaugural address of Paul Valéry was the finest ever seen in the Cannibal Academy. The members were bound by a pact of mutual assistance—'I trust I may never have reason to repent that I never joined,' remarked Robert de Billy many years later. The Academy soon dissolved; but Proust continued ever after to address Marie as 'My Queen'.

In November 1893 Proust devised a means of continuing his career in the *Revue Blanche*, of opening a new field in his writing, and of regaining the favour of the ever-ruffled Montesquiou. He would write a series of critical essays, and inaugurate it with an article entitled, with mingled paradox, irony and adulation, *La Simplicité de M. de Montesquiou*. Count Robert thought the plan excellent. No one had ever written a full-dress article on him before, and yes, Marcel was perfectly right: people considered his poetry obscure and excessively refined, but it was, in fact, divinely simple. Besides, if published in time, the article would serve as advance publicity for his new volume, *Le Chef des Odeurs Suaves*, due to appear in January 1894. Proust self-sacrificingly begged Natanson to substitute his essay for the six sketches in the December *Revue Blanche*; but the reluctant editor first refused, then consented, and then refused again. Now there would be no room even in the January number: Montesquiou and his simplicity would have to wait till February. As a last resort Proust approached Mme Straus's friend Louis Ganderax, who was about to revive the conservative *Revue de Paris* as a rival to the still more conservative *Revue des Deux Mondes*; but Ganderax would not bite, and now even the February *Revue Blanche* was full. *La Simplicité de M. de Montesquiou* did not appear till sixty years later, in *Contre Sainte-Beuve*.[1] Its theme, which perhaps explains the equal but opposite intransigences of Natanson and Ganderax, is that of Proust's first flattering letter to the count: Montesquiou, he maintains, is not an 1890s decadent but a seventeenth-century classic, and resembles Corneille (which is absurd) just as Baudelaire resembles Racine (which is very true).

With all his efforts Proust had succeeded only in barring against himself the doors of the *Revue Blanche*—in which he

[1] *Contre Sainte-Beuve*, 430-5.

appeared only once more, in 1896—and in aggrieving Montesquiou, who was never the man to take good intentions for good
deeds. "Your conceptions invariably result in abortions," the
count acidly remarked. Perhaps he was still nettled by a request
which Proust had made in the course of the *Revue Blanche*
negotiations. By December 1893 Proust was receiving invitations
from the Princesse de Wagram and her sister the Duchesse de
Gramont: this was a distinct upward step, though still far from
the top, for both these ladies had only been Rothschilds before
their marriages, and it was felt that their husbands had been a
little declassed by marrying outside the nobility into non-Aryan
money. Relying on these invitations and the credit of his still
unrejected article, he begged Montesquiou with would-be tact
'to be so kind, if you are there too, as to point out to me a few
of the ladies in whose circles your name is most frequently
mentioned—Comtesse Greffulhe, or the Princesse de Léon, for
instance'. In this he made two errors, one of greed and one of
social ignorance. Mme Greffulhe, Montesquiou's beloved cousin,
was perhaps the most distinguished lady in the whole of Parisian
society, and an introduction to her could only be the reward of
far higher merit than dear Marcel had yet shown. As for the
'Princesse de Léon', he should have known that since the death
of her father-in-law on the previous 6 August her correct title
was the Duchesse de Rohan. Proust was duly snubbed, and bided
his time; but he did not fail to note this curious feature in the
natural history of titled persons. Several of the French ducal
families had a repertoire of princely titles available for their heirs,
pending their succession to the dukedom; and when the future
Duchesse de Guermantes first appears in the early years of her
marriage, she is known as the Princesse des Laumes.

Meanwhile Montesquiou was arranging his own publicity. On
the afternoon of 17 January 1894, at the Théâtre de la Bodinière,
he gave a lecture on the poetry of Marceline Desbordes-Valmore,
whom he called 'the Christian Sappho'. He had read her poems
for the first time at twilight on a dusty road near Cannes, when
his adored Pauline de Montesquiou, his brother Gontran's wife,
was dying; and bursting into tears he had vowed to rescue the
poetess from undeserved neglect. 'I venture to assert,' he wrote
with some truth, 'that she owes her posthumous fame—the only
fame that really counts—to the incessant efforts that followed my

vow.' So Montesquiou began the movement which restored her to her rightful position as one of the most interesting lesser poets among the French romantics. Her lines

> *Je veux aller mourir aux lieux où je suis née;*
> *Le tombeau d'Albertine est près de mon berceau . . .*

may well have helped in suggesting to Proust the name of his heroine and part of the subject of his novel. But the lecture was also a move in a campaign to save Montesquiou himself from neglect: 'the auditorium was a mosaic of celebrities,' he boasted. Everyone expected the count to appear in his famous green dress-coat, with one of his pink Liberty cravats. But to the astonishment of all he wore a customary suit of solemn black and looked, Proust thought, like a solicitor's clerk. He discreetly mentioned his surprise. "The feeling I had decided to arouse," Montesquiou magnificently explained, "was a disappointed expectation of the ridiculous."

In February, when his article was finally rejected, Proust invented another plan for recovering favour with Montesquiou. Whether or not the count last year had unsuccessfully tempted Proust, Proust now to his extreme annoyance tempted him. At the house of Comte Henri de Saussine, a dilettante composer and musical critic,[1] he had met a nineteen-year-old pianist named Léon Delafosse. The young virtuoso had given his first recital at the age of seven, had won a first prize at the Conservatoire when he was thirteen, and was now in search of a wealthy patron. Who could be more suitable than Montesquiou? By way of preparing the ground Delafosse set three of the *Chauves-Souris* poems to music[2]; on 10 February Proust notified Montesquiou of the fact; and at last, on 15 March, the two tempters were permitted to bring their homage to the Pavillon Montesquiou at Versailles. "Do let me turn the music while he sings," entreated Proust; but Montesquiou smelt a rat. It so happened, he announced, that only

[1] His salon at 14 Rue Saint-Guillaume is described in the sketch '*Éventail*' in *Les Plaisirs et les Jours*, 87-91

[2] Similarly Morel asks the Narrator if he knows of 'any poet with a big position among the nobs', takes a note of a suitable name, and writes that he is a fanatical admirer of his works, has set one of his sonnets to music, and would like him to arrange a performance at Comtesse——'s. But the outcome is different, for 'the poet took offence and did not answer his letter'. (Cf. II, 265-6).

one kind of music would suit his mood that afternoon, namely, the barrel-organ; and he carried them off to the nearby fair at Viroflay, where they wandered dejectedly among the booths, while the diabolical count listened in pretended ecstasy to the strains of the hurdy-gurdy. Soon the kind-hearted Yturri felt Mossou le Connte had gone far enough: "You're always the same, why don't you try to be nice to people!" he whispered crossly. So they returned, and Montesquiou, finding that the young man 'played with incomparable virtuosity, though he sang with the voice of a cat run over by a cab', decided the recital had been intended not as a practical joke but as a sincere tribute to his genius. He took Delafosse into his favour: "I venture to believe that your settings of my poems will last as long as the poems themselves," he prophesied sublimely and, alas, truly. A few days later he visited Delafosse and his doting mother in their huge, gloomy apartment near the Rue d'Antin, with its dining-room adorned only with a seating-plan of the Salle Érard and a grand-piano, 'like an ebony dolmen,' said Montesquiou, 'gleaming with the blackened blood of a paying public'. On 27 April, when Delafosse gave his opening recital at the Salle Érard, many of Montesquiou's friends were in the audience; and the critic from *Le Ménestrel* wrote: 'Simplicity, charm, elegance and distinction are the chief qualities of this brilliant young virtuoso.'

Léon Delafosse was a thin, vain, ambitious, blond young man, with icy blue eyes and diaphanously pale, supernaturally beautiful features. Proust had nicknamed him 'the Angel'. "How annoying it would be not to be famous," Delafosse would say—"an annoyance which he has frequently experienced since I threw him over," said Montesquiou after their subsequent breach. When he was playing, 'this little face, with its silly laugh, became trans-figured with superhuman beauty, and took on the pallor and remoteness of death'; but once the music stopped, Montesquiou almost disliked him. "Try to ensure," he would warn him, "that my love for your art may always prevail over my distaste for your person." The young pianist was clearly an important original of Charlie Morel. But the model for the suffering and moral ruin brought upon Charlus by Morel came from Baron Doasan and his Polish violinist, not from the relationship between Montes-quiou and Delafosse. Montesquiou loved in his protégés only himself as tyrant, impresario, Maecenas and Svengali; and we shall see him ending his attachment to Delafosse at a time of his own choosing, without regret, with delight in vengeance.

Meanwhile, however, Count Robert was in the first enthusiastic stage of a new friendship. 'For three years,' he afterwards con·fessed, 'Delafosse became part of my life.' Proust waited in vain for his reward: the cunning Montesquiou had swallowed the bait and rejected the hook. By way of a reminder he sent Delafosse to the count on 24 March with yet another angel, a rather battered plaster one from an eighteenth-century crèche. 'For those who have ears I am sure he can sing with the same witty voice as our little musician. His tailcoat reveals his wings by its complete absence. His little nose is damaged, but even if it were all there I'm afraid it wouldn't have the expressive dryness, the passionate thinness, the eloquent concision of the nose of our musician.' But Montesquiou was furious: '*our* little musician', indeed!—and at Mme Lemaire's Tuesday on 27 March he pointedly refrained from speaking to the giver of angels. On 17 April Proust tried again. He went straight from one of his lessons for the *licence ès lettres* to the private view of the Marie Antoinette exhibition at the Sedelmayer Gallery, hoping to see Montesquiou 'with one or two ladies who are themselves works of art'; but he arrived too late, when everyone had left except the proprietors, from whose angry glares he became aware that it was long past closing-time. When he first saw Comtesse Greffulhe, early in May, it was by his own efforts. She was at the Princesse de Wagram's, wearing a coiffure of mauve cattleyas, which gave her 'a somehow Polynesian grace'; but he did not dare ask to be presented to her. She was the most beautiful woman he had ever seen; he asked Montesquiou to tell her so; and the count realised that if he did not give this determined young man the introduction he craved for, someone or other soon would.

He was now preparing at the Pavillon Montesquiou the first of the magnificent fêtes which for the next two decades were to be considered among the most brilliant events of the social year. In theory it was in honour of Sarah Bernhardt and her temporary protégé, a Breton sailor named Yann Nibor who was to sing some original verses about storms and albatrosses. But the count saw his chance to support other, even more deserving causes. His own poems and those of Marceline Desbordes-Valmore, recited by Mlles Bartet and Reichenberg from the Comédie Française, figured still more prominently in the programme; and when Delafosse played everyone knew that the real guest of honour was the Angel. As one of the many newspaper accounts put it, whether innocently or not, 'M. Delafosse bore on his forehead the kiss of M. de Montesquiou's Muse.' Round the temporary stage in the garden, the Ephemeral Theatre as Montesquiou called it in the printed programme, Proust now met many of the most exclusive ladies of the Faubourg Saint-Germain: Comtesse Rosa de FitzJames, for whom Mme de Chevigné had left him standing in the Avenue Gabriel two years before, Comtesse Aimery de la Rochefoucauld, Comtesse Potocka, Comtesse Mélanie de Pourtalès, Marquise d' Hervey de Saint-Denis, and Comtesse Greffulhe herself. Mme Greffulhe wore a mauve gown, the colour of her favourite cattleyas (a preference which Proust later, perhaps not without malice, transferred to Odette); and her superb eyes shone, 'like black fireflies,' said Montesquiou, through a veil to match. Proust was made to work for his introductions. All afternoon he feverishly took notes on the ladies' dresses, which he begged each of the lovely wearers to read and correct; and after the party he hurried to the office of *Le Gaulois* with an article ('*A Literary Fête at Versailles*') for next day's gossip column. In the morning, alas, he found his article ruthlessly cut: Mme Potocka was there, but stripped of her dress; Mme Howland was gone altogether; and from the sentence which modestly began 'Among others present', the name of M. Marcel Proust had been deleted.

The fête of 30 May 1894 was one of the crucial events of Proust's youth. At last he had met several of the most brilliant hostesses of the inner Faubourg Saint-Germain, including the lady who was to supply important elements of both the Duchesse and the Princesse de Guermantes. At breakfast next morning they would read his appreciative account of their beauty and their clothes; soon their invitation-cards would be stuck in the dining-room mirror at 9 Boulevard Malesherbes. And he had seen them gathered to do acquiescent homage to the latest homosexual relationship of his powerful friend and sponsor. In the next few months Proust would simultaneously reach the summit of the Guermantes Way, and go down into the valley of the Cities of the Plain.

Chapter 10

THE GUERMANTES WAY

FOR an unbroken period of four years, until he was turned away by growing ill-health, the stresses of the Dreyfus Case, and disillusion with the heartlessness of the Guermantes world, Proust moved with manifold delight in the high society of the Faubourg Saint-Germain. In his novel the social experiences of these years were distilled into three representative functions, the afternoon at Mme de Villeparisis's, the dinner at the Duchesse de Guermantes's, and the Princesse de Guermantes's soirée. The biographer, similarly, must abandon for the space of one chapter the chronological narrative of days and months; and conversely, in the description of the persons and groups Proust then encountered, he must analyse the chemical compounds of Proust's imagination into the human elements from which they were formed.

The agate-eyed Comtesse Élisabeth Greffulhe, when Proust met her at Montesquiou's Delafosse fête, was aged thirty-four. She was the eldest daughter of the Franco-Belgian Prince Joseph de Caraman-Chimay and his wife Marie de Montesquiou, Robert de Montesquiou's aunt: Count Robert was therefore her cousin, just as Charlus was the Duchesse de Guermantes's.[1] Her family was short of money, and had been forced to sell the ancestral Hôtel de Chimay on the Quai Malaquais and to marry into wealth. Her brother, now himself Prince Joseph after their father's death in 1892, had become the husband of an American heiress, Clara Ward, in 1890; but the princess was soon to raise a deplorable scandal by her affair with Jancsi Rigo, the swarthy, pockmarked violinist in Boldi's gipsy orchestra at Maxim's, with whom she eloped in 1896: "my dishonoured cousin Clara de Chimay, who has left her husband," says Charlus.[2] Élisabeth's marriage in 1878 to the fabulously wealthy Comte Henri Greffulhe was considered far more satisfactory.

[1] "I've got furniture that came to Basin from the Montesquious," says the Duchesse de Guermantes (I, 339).   [2] I, 764

Her husband belonged to a Belgian banking family naturalised in France, whose nobility, like the Caraman-Chimays' princedom, dated only from the Restoration. His great-aunt Cordélia Greffulhe, wife of the Maréchal de Castellane, had been a mistress of Chateaubriand; and his father Charles Greffulhe, in collaboration with Charles Laffitte (a relative of Baron Doasan), was one of the original founders of the Jockey Club. Despite the comparative newness of his title, Comte Greffulhe had a leading position in society, and was the chief original of the Duc de Guermantes.

He was a tall, broad-shouldered man, with a yellow beard and an air of majesty and suppressed rage, which made Blanche compare him to a king in a pack of cards, while others likened him to Jove the Thunderer.[1] "He displaces more air than any ordinary mortal," said Barrès. His lordly affability was never more strikingly displayed than when he made the round of his electors, presenting them according to social position with a gold watch or a brace of pheasants from his château at Boisboudran. For many years he represented Melun in the Chamber of Deputies; similarly, the Duc de Guermantes was the member for Méséglise. Like the Duc, Comte Greffulhe was a tyrannical and unfaithful husband, overfond of the society of persons whom the countess disdainfully called 'the little ladies who make such good mattresses'. Once, many years later, an imprudent guest who felt sure that the still-dazzling Mme Greffulhe must be the mistress, and therefore mistook the ugly lady at the far end of the room for the wife, remarked feelingly to the countess: "Ah, Madame, now I've seen you, how I do sympathise with the count!" On another occasion Comte Greffulhe sent his valet to arrange a rendezvous with the beautiful actress Mlle Marsy. "Well, did you see her?" "Yes, Monsieur le Comte, she was sitting with the Prince de Sagan, while he had a footbath." "It's too bad," cried the outraged nobleman, in the words of the Duc de Guermantes complaining of Swann's Dreyfusism, "why, the man dines with us!" But his infidelities did not prevent him being jealous, though entirely without cause; and the brevity of his wife's appearances in society, which was often ascribed to hauteur, was in fact due to his insistence on her being home by eleven-thirty. He did not

[1] The Narrator frequently borrows this comparison for the Duc (e.g. II, 284, 683; III, 42, 1020).

care for Montesquiou and his friends, who descended on his Villa
La Case at Dieppe every September as soon as he left for the
shooting-season at Boisboudran. "They're a lot of Japs," he said,
meaning aesthetes.

Comtesse Greffulhe (the *gratin* pronounced the name
Greffeuille) was considered the supreme society beauty of her
time. As she sailed rapidly through a drawing-room the guests
could be heard murmuring: "Which way did she go? Did you
see her?" She had chestnut hair and dark mineral eyes, like agates
or topazes:

> *'Comtesse Greffulhe*
> *Is two dark glances wrapped in tulle,'*

wrote Montesquiou; but her features, though delicately chiselled,
were somewhat irregular, with a hint of wildness. She was fully
conscious of the uniqueness of her looks, but despaired of finding
an artist to do them justice: "However beautiful one is, there are
days when one looks hideous, and that's when they paint one!"
she exclaimed. She was sculpted by Falguière ("the head wasn't
very good, so I threw it away, but I've kept the shoulders"),
etched and pastelled by Helleu (an original of Elstir), and painted
by Laszlo, Hébert and other society portraitists. But only a poet
or a camera, she thought, could reproduce the loveliness she saw
reflected in her mirror or in the eyes of beholders. She was
particularly gratified, therefore, by a sonnet of Montesquiou
which ended: 'Fair lily, your black pistils are your eyes.' Turning
to her sister (the favourite lady-in-waiting of Queen Elisabeth of
Belgium), she remarked: "Quite a good likeness, Ghislaine, don't
you think?" and added to Montesquiou: "Only you and the sun
really understand me!" "I was glad she put me first," said
Montesquiou afterwards.

The countess and her cousin Count Robert were united by
mutual admiration and genuine affection: "She's the only person
with whom I have never succeeded in quarrelling," he would say.
Montesquiou had a great respect for her intelligence, though in
his belief she never read a book (Edmond de Goncourt thought
her extremely well-read, but that was because she talked to him
about his own novels), and picked up her knowledge through
conversation with learned guests. Like the Duchesse de Guermantes she invited scientists to dinner in her later years; and she

would be heard to remark afterwards: "Did you know that even iron suffers from fatigue?" She took a public interest in the arts, especially in music. She wrote a one-act play for a house-party at Boisboudran, and a book of confessions in which she showed such keen appreciation of her own beauty that Goncourt advised her not to publish.

As we have seen, many features of the Duchesse de Guermantes —her corn-coloured hair and cornflower eyes, her rasping voice. something of her wit, her style of dress, the Narrator's early love for her—derived from Mme de Chevigné. Most of the remainder —including her supreme position in society, her relations with her husband, her cousinship with Charlus-Montesquiou—came from Mme Greffulhe. She had the chiming silvery laugh of the Duchesse: "Mme Greffulhe's laugh sounds like the carillon at Bruges," said Proust, at a later time when he had heard both. Just as the Duc and Duchesse lived in the same house as Mme de Villeparisis—shared also by the Narrator's family and the tailor Jupien—so Comte Greffulhe dwelt in symbiosis at 8 Rue d'Astorg with his widowed mother (born a La Rochefoucauld) and his sisters, the Marquise de l'Aigle and the Princesse d'Arenberg (the wife of Mme Straus's friend, original of the Prince d'Agrigente). Duc Agénor de Gramont playfully called their house Vatican City. Like the Duchesse, Comtesse Greffulhe was famous for the exclusive coterie of her men-friends. Chief of them all was Charles Haas, the original of Swann, now, sixteen years after her marriage, a sick and ageing man. The others, some of whom were among the band of club-men who spent their afternoons with Mme de Chevigné, included the Marquis du Lau, Comte Costa de Beauregard, Comte Albert de Mun, Comte Louis de Turenne and Marquis Henri de Breteuil. The latter pair together made up Hannibal (Babal) de Bréauté. The good-natured but stupid Turenne had blue eyes and a yellow complexion, and wore Bréauté's monocle, 'which carried, glued to the other side, an infinitesimal gaze, swarming with affability, and never ceasing to beam at the height of the ceiling, the magnificence of the reception, the interestingness of the programme and the quality of the refreshments'.[1] Like Bréauté he was thought a connoisseur of objects of art, and loved to give advice with an air of expert knowledge on things he knew nothing whatever about:

[1] I, 327

the marriages he recommended always failed, the interior decora-
tions looked hideous, and the investments immediately slumped.
Breteuil, too, was a would-be connoisseur of art. Like Turenne
and Haas he was an intimate friend of Edward VII as Prince of
Wales; he had married an American heiress, Miss Garner, and
was often to be seen at Sandringham shoots or Windsor Castle
house-parties. He was witty and deformed, and once in *A la
Recherche* Proust maliciously refers to him as Quasimodo de
Breteuil, giving him the name of the Hunchback of Notre Dame.[1]
The Marquis was present at the famous dinner-party given by
Mme Greffulhe in 1910 to Edward VII and Queen Alexandra, at
which the only other guest was the fashionable painter Detaille.
In *Le Côté de Guermantes* this dinner is given by the Duchesse de
Guermantes, and is quoted as a supreme example of her un-
conventionality[2]; but in real life the choice of guests was the
King's, for he had been assured by experts in England that M.
Detaille was the greatest living French painter.

Another member of the Greffulhe coterie, a particular friend of
Charles Haas (with whom he appears in Tissot's painting) and of
the Prince de Sagan, and a probable original of General de
Froberville, was the boastful, loud-voiced and opportunist
General Marquis de Galliffet. He wore a silver plate in his
abdomen, the relic of a wound received at the Battle of Puebla in
the Mexican war of 1863—no doubt Proust was thinking of this
when he compared Froberville's monocle to 'a shell-splinter, a
monstrous wound which it was splendid to have acquired, but
indecent to exhibit'.[3] Curiosity as to the real dimensions of this
silver plate, which some said was no larger than a twenty-franc
piece, while others alleged it was a good six inches across, was
thought to play some part in the General's enormous success with
society ladies. He had married a Laffitte, a relative of Baron
Doasan and Mme Aubernon; and when the priest in his nuptial
address used the unfortunate words "When the inevitable hour of
separation comes", the wedding-guests burst out laughing. Soon,
when that inevitable hour came, Mme de Galliffet was living near
her friend the Princesse de Sagan in the Manoir des Roches at
Trouville, where Proust saw them in 1891, and receiving frequent
visits from the Prince of Wales. Once the Prince de Sagan gave

[1] III, 587   [2] II, 430
[3] I, 326

a dinner to Mme de Chevigné's heroine, the Grand-Duchess Wladimir, and Galliffet. "Your Highness is sitting between the two biggest cuckolds in Europe," announced the Prince; but his remark was coldly received. The General had led the famous cavalry charge at Sedan, and taken part in the savage suppression of the Commune just before Proust's birth. Proust admired him for his wit, of which perhaps the best example is a silent one: when riding one afternoon in the Bois Galliffet met the unfrocked priest Monsignor Bauer, an acquaintance from Second Empire days, when he was the Empress Eugénie's chaplain. Mgr Bauer politely raised his hat; and the General with equal politeness made the sign of priestly benediction.

In several respects, however, Mme Greffulhe resembled not only the Duchesse, but the Duchesse's cousin, the Princesse de Guermantes. Her topaz eyes and statuesque beauty are given to the Princesse; so is her flamboyant style of dress, in which Mme Greffulhe contrasted with the sobriety of Mme de Chevigné as did the Princesse with the Duchesse. A characteristic anecdote of Comtesse Greffulhe is told of the Princesse de Guermantes in a rejected passage of *Sodome et Gomorrhe*.[1] "I shall know I've lost my beauty when people stop turning to stare at me in the street," the Comtesse told Mme Standish; and Mme Standish replied: "Never fear, my dear, so long as you dress as you do, people will always turn and stare!" The famous scene of the Princesse de Guermantes's box at the Opéra in *Le Côté de Guermantes* actually occurred, as we shall see, in May 1912: here the Princesse represents Mme Greffulhe, and the Duchesse Mme Standish. Elstir's portrait of the Princesse with the crescent moon of Diana in her hair[2] was a very bad painting of Mme Greffulhe by Hébert.[3] The Princesse's attitude in the Dreyfus Case was shared, as will be shown later, by Mme Greffulhe; and her chaste but pronounced affection for her cousin Montesquiou no doubt suggested the Princesse's unhappy passion for Charlus.

A later but equally important original of the Princesse was Comtesse Jean (Dolly) de Castellane, a half-sister of Boson de

---

[1] II, 1185   [2] II, 1183

[3] M. de Norpois at Mme de Villeparisis's, when he hears the Narrator declaring his admiration for Elstir's *Bunch of Radishes*, cries: "If you call that clever little sketch a masterpiece, what words will you have left for Hébert's *Virgin?*" (II, 223).

Talleyrand-Périgord, Prince de Sagan. Just as the Princesse de Guermantes was a Bavarian royalty, so Comtesse Dolly had married Karl Egon, Prince von Fürstenberg (the former lover of Laure Hayman), and had spent her youth in a German court. It was not till 1898, after her first husband's death, that she married Comte Jean de Castellane, her cousin and nephew, and became, in rivalry to Mme Greffulhe,. one of the rulers of Parisian society. She was majestic, beautiful and Teutonic, and had retained the grand manner of a German princess. People called her 'Gräfin Jean', and she looked, says André Germain, 'as if she'd always just come back from a visit to Wotan'. The jealous Mme Greffulhe affected to confuse her with her less dazzling sister-in-law, and once, when Montesquiou was lamenting her absence from one of his fêtes ("She said she'd been asked to a shooting-party at Mme Porgès's, so I told her that there was some houses where it was absolutely inexcusable to go shooting, unless it was to shoot one's hostess!"), she enquired devastatingly "*Which* Mme de Castellane?"

For the feudal devotion of the Prince de Guermantes to questions of birth and etiquette, the 'almost fossil rigidity of his aristocratic prejudices' ("His ideas are out of this world," said the Duchesse),[1] Proust thought of Comte Aimery de La Rochefoucauld, whose extreme regard for precedence had caused him to be nicknamed 'Place-at-table'. Of a girl who had married beneath her for love he remarked: "A few nights of passion, and then a whole lifetime at the wrong end of the table." It was exceedingly important not to put Comte Aimery at the wrong end of the table: he was liable, if so insulted, to call for his carriage immediately after dinner; and once he was heard to enquire in a loud voice: "Does one get a helping of *everything* where I'm sitting?" Of the Luynes family, into which his aunt the Duchesse Yolande de Luynes had married, he observed: "They were mere nobodies in the year 1000."[2] When the Comtesse de Chabrillan asked whose was a portrait on his drawing-room wall, he replied: "That is Henry the Fourth, madam." "Really, I should never have recognised him." "I refer, Madam, to Henry, the Fourth

---

[1] II, 570, 523
[2] M. de Charles makes similar remarks about the Luynes family: "I ask you—a mere Alberti, who didn't manage to scrape the mud off his feet until Louis XIII!" (III, 233).

Duc de La Rochefoucauld." And the refusal of the Prince de Guermantes to greet Mme ('Tiny') de Hunolstein at the foot of his stairs[1] may be compared to Comte Aimery's advice to a friend on the correct manner to receive a certain bishop. "When His Grace came to our house my wife saw him out as far as the drawing-room door, and I took him to the front door. So I think *your* wife had better see him as far as the lobby, and *you'd* better take him right out into the street!" He, too, like the Prince de Guermantes, had a Bavarian princely title, though this was not granted till 1909. The incident of the Duc de Guermantes's insistence on attending the fancy-dress ball, in spite of repeated warnings from the Ladies with the Walking-sticks that poor 'Mama' d'Osmond is at death's door, was borrowed by Proust (with the addition of Mme Straus's red shoes) from an anecdote of Montesquiou's about his cousin Aimery. Montesquiou's brother Gontran was dying, but Comte Aimery felt unable to give up his plans for the evening. He was overtaken by a tactless informant, who cried "Gontran's dead!"; whereupon Comte Aimery merely pushed his wife (who was dressed as a queen-bee) up the steps, declared, in the Duc de Guermantes's very words, "People exaggerate!" and fled majestically into the ball.[2] Comte Aimery's son Gabriel, whom Proust met a few years later, was one of the many originals of Saint-Loup.

Other hints for various Guermantes's came from the Talleyrand-Périgord and Castellane families, who were closely related to one another, and more distantly to the Greffulhes. It is clear not only that Proust used individual Talleyrands and Castellanes in the creation of his characters, but that their interrelationships served decisively as a model for the general structure of the Guermantes family. Boson de Talleyrand-Périgord, Prince de Sagan, supplied elements both to the Duc de Guermantes and Charlus; he was half-brother to Comtesse Jean de Castellane, whose affinities with the Princesse de Guermantes have just been noted; he was a cousin of the Comtesse de Beaulaincourt, the chief original of Mme de Villeparisis; and Boni de Castellane, his nephew and heir, was an early original of the Duc de Guermantes's nephew and Mme de Villeparisis's great-nephew, Saint-Loup.

The Prince de Sagan, now in his sixties, was generally considered the most consummate *grand seigneur* and arbiter of

[1] II, 530   [2] Cf. II, 725

elegance of his time. He was unintelligent and devoid of taste except in clothes; but as he had now been separated from his wealthy wife for fifteen years, he could no longer afford the best tailors, and the extraordinary distinction of his appearance came largely from his personal presence. The Prince frequented the foyer of the Comédie-Française, then a fashionable resort, adorned with antique furniture and old prints which made it look like Louis de Turenne's drawing-room. He stood astride in his velvet-collared greatcoat with white rose button-hole, twirling his monocle on a sensationally broad black ribbon, with his friends Robert de FitzJames, General de Galliffet, Charles Haas and Turenne; and after the performance they would depart severally with the actresses of the evening, with Mlle Reichenberg or Mlle Marsy. He lived in bachelor rooms over the Club in the Rue Royale, and with Charles Haas was a favourite of old Isabella, the flower-seller outside the Café Anglais. "You're a real gentleman," she told Boni de Castellane after Haas's death, "there's only you and the Prince de Sagan left of your sort, now Monsieur Haas has gone." His archaic Christian name, Boson, helped by its similar sound to give a contemporary ring to that of the Duc de Guermantes, which was borrowed from Basin, the eleventh-century Count of Illiers. But in his tragic last days the Prince came to resemble the fallen Baron de Charlus. In 1908 he had a paralytic stroke, and was willy-nilly taken back by the wife he had not seen since the 1880s. Looking like an aged, white-maned lion, he was pushed about in a wheel-chair, with bent head and dribbling mouth, as was Charlus by Jupien; he bowed, like Charlus, to all the wrong people, clutched the arms of his chair in a vain effort to rise, and mumbled "Delighted, I'm sure—delighted, I'm sure."

The Princesse de Sagan his wife, born Jeanne-Marguerite Seillière, came of a rich, *parvenu* family of Second Empire barons, related, like Mme de Galliffet, to Mme Aubernon and Baron Doasan. She spent the summer at her Villa Persane at Trouville and was to be seen walking on the front with her negro page, thus serving as a model for the Princesse de Luxembourg at Balbec. She gave a famous ball in 1885 at which all the guests—including Charles Haas, the Chevignés, Turenne, and the rest of the Guermantes set—were dressed as animals, and the whole of the Opéra ballet emerged from an enormous beehive. The Duchesse de Guermantes refers to her as 'my aunt Sagan', and Françoise, with her love of unsafe grammatical analogies, as 'the Sagante'.[1]

The Prince de Sagan's nephew, Boni de Castellane, was now and for the next twelve years the most brilliant young man in Parisian society. He had the golden hair, the dazzling pink complexion, the cold lapis-lazuli eyes, the flying monocle and darting movements, the tall, slim figure of Saint-Loup. His Rachel was Mlle Marsy, the actress, whom he had torn from the embraces of his admiring uncle Sagan and the furious Comte Greffulhe; like Saint-Loup he was blackballed at the Jockey Club, of which his mother's father, the Marquis de Juigné, had been vice-president for many years.

In 1895, when Boni's money was already growing short, he married an American millionaire heiress, Miss Anna Gould. She was short, thin and sallow, with a line of black hair down her spine—'like an Iroquois chieftainess,' people said; but Boni depilated, rouged and dressed her, and taught her to reply, when complimented on her appearance, "Nice of you to say so." Their monumental house in the Avenue du Bois was built to Boni's design, after the Petit Trianon at Versailles. "The staircase will be like the one at the Opéra, only bigger," she told enquirers. Boni went into politics as a royalist and anti-Semite; he gave receptions of a megalomaniac lavishness; but it seemed to some observers that he was riding for a fall. "You need to be used to it, if you're going to handle all that money," remarked Baron Alphonse de Rothschild. Later we shall have further glimpses of Proust's contact with Boni in the periods of his highest glory, his catastrophe and his pathetic, courageous sunset.

Boni de Castellane's great-aunt, Comtesse Sophie de Beaulaincourt, was the original of Mme de Villeparisis, the type of an old lady who has slowly and painfully regained a social position forfeited by the excesses of her youth. She was the daughter, born in 1818, of the Maréchal de Castellane and Comte Greffulhe's great-aunt Cordélia Greffulhe, who was the mistress of Comte Molé and of the great Chateaubriand: well might Mme de Villeparisis say "I remember M. Molé very well," and: "Chateaubriand often came to my father's house"![2] In 1836, under Louis

---

[1] II, 526, 207. Her ball is referred to ironically by Mme de Villeparisis in conversation with Bloch: "Is that what you'd call a great social solemnity?" she asks the Duchesse (II, 244). [2] II, 192; I, 721

Philippe, she married the Marquis de Contades, whose descendant Vicomte Antoine de Contades was to become the husband of Marie de Benardaky's sister Nelly. Of one of her innumerable lovers Mme de Chevigné told Proust: "She ate him up, down to his last farm-rent." During the Second Empire she was the mistress of the Comte de Fleury, the French ambassador at St Petersburg—whose liaison with her suggested that of M. de Norpois with Mme de Villeparisis—and a friend of the Empress Eugénie and of Mérimée, a whole volume of whose letters are addressed to her. From the Comte de Coislin she had a son, whom she acknowledged and kept with her, despite the disapproval of the Faubourg. In 1859 she took her second but short-lived husband, the Comte de Beaulaincourt. Now, two generations after her wild youth, she was an ugly little old lady of seventy-six, with a purple face and big spectacles, like the aged Mme de Villeparisis seen at Venice by Mme Sazerat, whose father she had ruined; but she had succeeded, almost too late, in reconquering her position in society, and was visited by Princesse Mathilde, the ex-Empress Eugénie, and all the Faubourg. She lived in the Rue de Miromesnil, near Mme Straus, Mme de Chevigné and the Pouquets, and sat, wearing a black silk gown, a peasant-woman's bonnet and a white lace-edged apron, at a little desk piled high with paper petals and saucers of paint, making artificial flowers: "when you're no longer young, you have to find a hobby to keep you company," she told Edmond de Goncourt. The flowers were copies from nature, and bunches of roses and violets were sent for the purpose daily from her Château d'Acosta, near Princesse Mathilde's at Saint-Gratien. Proust made Mme de Villeparisis paint flowers, like Mme Lemaire: 'so that she wouldn't be *too* like Mme de Beaulaincourt,' he told Montesquiou in 1921. She watched her great-nephew Boni's career with a sardonic eye: "It's like dining in a red marble aquarium, with goldfish for footmen," she remarked after a visit to his Palais Rose at 45 Avenue du Bois; "and you should see Boni and his wife strutting up that staircase of theirs, with peacock-feathers stuck up their behinds!" She took a fancy to Proust and gave him valuable instruction, from her own unique knowledge, in the state of politics and society under Louis Philippe, Napoleon III and the young Third Republic.

In his account of a visit to Mme de Beaulaincourt (*Journal*, vol. 7, 155-7, 7 September 1887), Edmond de Goncourt wishes 'this witty old woman with her inexhaustible flow of talk' would write her memoirs. She never did; and the Memoirs of Mme de Villeparisis, and those of her equally fictitious sister Mme de Beausergent, who was the Narrator's grandmother's favourite author next to Mme de Sévigné, were both suggested by the voluminous and rather boring *Mémoires* of the Comtesse de Boigne, whose favourite nephew the Marquis d'Osmond[1] was a friend of Proust's parents, whose great-nephew the Comte de Maillé was his near neighbour in the Boulevard Malesherbes, and whose niece the dowager Duchesse de Maillé, then in her seventies, he often saw at the balls of the 1890s. "Mme de Beausergent, afterwards Mme d'Hazfeld, sister of Mme de Villeparisis," says Swann in the Goncourt *Journal* pastiche (III, 715); and the sister of Mme de Beaulaincourt was, in fact, Comtesse Pauline de Hatzfeldt.

Mme de Villeparisis's rival 'Alix', who attends her afternoon receptions in the hope of stealing her guests, was Mme de Chaponay: Proust characteristically mentions her by name, together with Mme de Beaulaincourt, in juxtaposition with the characters they suggested. Mme de Chaponay, like 'Alix', wore her white hair piled high in Marie-Antoinette style, had the same difficulty as Mme de Beaulaincourt, and for the same cause, in recruiting her salon, and was famous for her social raids. But the Christian name Alix came from Vicomtesse Alix de Janzé, who was born (as the Narrator mentions of 'Alix') a Choiseul. Mme de Janzé wrote a book on Alfred de Musset, and 'Alix' has written one on Lamartine. She and Mme de Chaponay were the originals of two of the 'Three Fates, with white, blue or red hair' who were Mme de Villeparisis's friends and competitors: the third was Mme de Blocqueville.[2]

[1] The Marquis d'Osmond appears in Mme de Cambremer's box at the Opera as the charming young Marquis de Beausergent (II, 55), and again, transformed by old age, at the Princesse de Guermantes's matinée (III, 938). But Proust prefers to make the Narrator discover in *Le Temps Retrouvé* that the favourite nephew for whom Mme de Beausergent wrote her memoirs was none other than the Duc de Guermantes as a boy (III, 715, 717). In *Le Côté de Guermantes* the Marquis d'Osmond (nicknamed 'Mama') is the cousin of the Duc de Guermantes whose death, announced by the Ladies with the Walking-sticks, does not prevent the Duc from taking the Duchesse to the fancy-dress ball (II, 575).

[2] For the references in the foregoing paragraph cf. II, 202, 198, 197.

In real life Mme Blanche Leroi, who bows so coldly to poor
Mme de Villeparisis and refuses to attend her salon,[1] was Mme
Gaston (Clothilde) Legrand, née Fournes, known as 'Cloton' to
the Faubourg. She was married to a wealthy owner of coal-mines
—similarly Mme Leroi was the daughter of a timber-merchant.[2]
Montesquiou owned her portrait, 'Mme Legrand returning from
the races', by Mme Romaine Brooks. "Notice those romantic
eyes glowing under her veil," he would say, "and how they are
belied by the wryness of her mouth, embittered by chewing the
cud of the vileness of humanity; in this painting one sees the
fusion of defiant pride and compulsory diffidence!" As we have
seen, the remark attributed to Mme Leroi—"My opinion of love?
I make it, often, but never, never talk about it"[3]—was uttered by
Laure Baignères to Mme Aubernon.

The *gratin* included persons who, without disgracing themselves openly like the poor Princesse Clara de Chimay, contrived
to live a life as wild as Mme de Beaulaincourt's in a previous
generation. One of the late arrivals at the Princesse de Guermantes's soirée is the Princesse d'Orvillers, in whom the Narrator
recognises the lady with gentle blue eyes and opulent bosom who
had made advances to him while pretending to look in a shop-
window near his home. She appears many years later at the final
matinée of the Princesse de Guermantes in *Le Temps Retrouvé*,
still tender and magnificent, but 'hurrying to the grave', though
here Proust forgetfully calls her the Princesse de Nassau. She was
the Marquise d'Hervey de Saint-Denis, one of the guests at
Montesquiou's fête in honour of Delafosse: she was invited at
Proust's earnest request, so she may well have made eyes at him
in real life. Her husband, the much-betrayed Marquis (1823-92),
was an eminent Chinese scholar, and is mentioned under his own
name as having given a Chinese vase to Charlus in his boyhood.
Like the Princesse d'Orvillers, Mme d'Hervey was a natural
daughter of the last reigning Duke of Parma.[4] She was rich, fair-
haired and ever-youthful: people called her the Demi-Chevreul,
in allusion to the long-lived chemist Michel Chevreul, whose
hundredth birthday was celebrated in 1886. After her husband's
death she became younger than ever, and married Mme de
Chevigné's nephew Jacques de Waru, who was fifteen years her

---

[1] II, 186   [2] II, 273
[3] II, 195   [4] II, 373, 720, 721; III, 979-80; II, 718

junior, and one of the two brothers Proust had pursued because they had their aunt's blue eyes and beaked nose. Mme de Chevigné was not altogether pleased to acquire a niece several years older than herself, but was thought to console herself by the thought of the money it brought into the family.

Another salon in which Charles Haas, Breteuil, Turenne and the rest of Comtesse Greffulhe's set were to be met—together with Princesse Mathilde, the Grand-Duchess Wladimir and Comte Robert de FitzJames—was the Duchesse de la Trémoïlle's. "I don't say she's 'profound'," Swann tells Mme Verdurin, "but she's intelligent, and her husband is really cultured." The Duchesse looked like the White Queen in *Alice*, we are told by an English observer, and wouldn't have a mirror in the house. Mme de Chevigné stayed several months in every year at her Château de Serrant in Anjou. Her scholarly husband, who was the premier duke of France, senior even to the La Rochefoucaulds, was tall, bearded, refined and deaf. Charlus, greeting the arriving guests at the Princesse de Guermantes's, calls out: "Good evening, Mme de la Trémoïlle."[1]

When Charlus also says: "Good evening, my dear Herminie," he is addressing the Duchesse Herminie de Rohan-Chabot, the same who before her husband's succession was Princesse de Léon. It was she who gave, in the 1880s, the celebrated 'ball of the Princesse de Léon', which Swann mentions at Combray.[2] Boni de Castellane, still in his teens, had appeared there as the Maréchal de Saxe, in powdered wig, plumed hat and a purple cloak bordered with sables borrowed from Mlle Marsy. The company in her salon was mixed: her daughter, Princesse Marie Murat, was once forced to leave a message with the butler: "Tell Mother I couldn't get to her through all those poets." Even Verlaine might have appeared there, had not the absent-minded duchess invited him for the first time several years after his death. She was exceedingly kind-hearted, and when warned that one of her guests had been in prison, replied only: "Oh, poor dear, no wonder he looks so sad!" Once she helped a peasant-woman in the train to change her baby's napkins. "What is your name, kind lady?" asked the grateful mother. "The Duchesse de Rohan." "Well, I'm the Queen of Sheba." She worked for charities, presided on literary juries, and published several volumes of verses. "She's managed to persuade herself, in a well-meaning sort of way, that she's the muse Polyhymnia," said Montesquiou, who when presented with one of her books had simply returned his card, inscribed 'Yours in spite of everything.' Her husband, Duc Alain, would stop in front of any pretty face not previously known to him and say, "I bet you don't know who *I* am"; but the pretty face invariably replied, "You're the Duc de Rohan." He was particularly fond of foreign lady visitors. "After a month he gets tired of them," said his wife, "and then I have them on my hands for the rest of my life"—a remark which is also given to the Duchesse de Guermantes.[1]

Another Guermantes hostess was Comtesse Rosa de FitzJames, for whose sake (if not for her husband's, of whom she was supposed to be still fonder) Mme de Chevigné had left Proust standing in the Avenue Gabriel. Proust was presented to her by the old Marquise de Brantes; and the Comtesse de Pourtalès remembered him on this very occasion, 'extraordinarily pale, with a fringe of black hair over his huge black eyes'. Comtesse Rosa was a Jewess from Vienna, *née* Gutmann, and at first the Faubourg was inclined to find her unacceptable; but her husband was so unkind and unfaithful that they nicknamed her 'Rosa Malheur' (after the animal-painter Rosa Bonheur) and (except for the inflexible Comte Aimery de La Rochefoucauld, who said: "She wanted a salon, and all she's got is a dining-room") took her to their hearts. The German philosopher Count Keyserling, Bourget and the Abbé Mugnier were to be met in her house, together with the inevitable Charles Haas, Turenne and Marquis du Lau. Comtesse Rosa was plain, melancholy and not very intelligent: "Everyone says you're silly, my dear Rosa," said her best friend, "but I always tell them they exaggerate." She was said to keep a secret weapon in her desk: a list of all the Jewish marriages in the noble families of Europe. Her husband, Comte Robert de FitzJames, when she began "In Vienna, where I was bred," would interrupt with "You mean, born." But he had no respect for anyone's feelings, and to a duchess who said, when her last daughter was engaged, "At last my girls are all placed," he retorted: "Yes, but not in the first three."

Comtesse Mélanie de Pourtalès was a surviving beauty of the Second Empire and had appeared in Winterhalter's famous

[1] III, 1006

painting of the Empress Eugénie's ladies-in-waiting. She was notorious for talking throughout the performance whenever she went to the opera; and Charles Haas, when invited to her box, had murmured: "Yes, I'd love to come, I've never heard you in *Faust*." She still wore imperial violets, and refused to allow her golden hair to turn white; and from force of habit she eyed young men, we are told, with 'matriarchal coquetry'. To an old priest who expressed his gratitude at meeting 'the beautiful Comtesse de Pourtalès of whom I've heard so much', she sighed: "Ah, M. le Curé, if you'd seen me forty years ago you would have said the Almighty created his masterpiece when He made me!" But she stood on her dignity, and when Reynaldo Hahn unfortunately used his friend Proust's favourite adjective of her she retorted: "My dear Reynaldo, you can say the Comtesse de Pourtalès is kind; you can say she is no ordinary woman; but you can't possibly call her *nice!*" Her guests comprised not only the Faubourg, but also Central European dignitaries—her friendship with Princesse Metternich was legendary—Protestants, such as Proust's *bête noire*, the Byzantine historian Gustave Schlumberger, and Bonapartist nobles—the Prince de Borodino at Doncières naturally dines with her whenever he visits Paris.[1] But she wisely refrained from mingling all these with the Faubourg; and the Duchesse de Guermantes says, complaining of the mixed company at her cousin the Princesse's soirée: "It's much better arranged at Mélanie Pourtalès's—she can invite the Holy Synod and the Oratoire chapel if she likes, but she doesn't ask us on the same day."[2]

One of the great ladies to whom Montesquiou was particularly devoted was Mme Greffulhe's friend and his own second cousin, Mme Standish (his cousin Bertrand had married her sister Émilie). Despite her foreign name (the Faubourg called her 'Missis'), she eminently belonged to the *gratin*, being a niece of the Duc des Cars, while her husband was the son of a Noailles. 'It would take a whole lecture,' says the Narrator, 'to explain to certain foolish young men why Mme Standish is at least as great a lady as the Duchesse de Doudeauville.'[3] She had been the mistress of General Galliffet and of Edward VII as Prince of Wales, and dressed (though people could never decide which imitated the other) exactly like the Princess of Wales, later Queen Alexandra, with

[1] II, 132   [2] II, 672   [3] II, 66i

stringed bonnets, wasp-waist, curled fringe and high dog-collar. But when asked by admiring rivals where some amazingly elegant dress came from, she would say: "My maid ran it up for me." She was still beautiful, with a frigid, bolt-upright English manner. Next to the La Trémoïlles and the La Rochefoucaulds the premier dukes of France were the Uzès's, the pronunciation of whose name by the *gratin* ('Uzai', without the final 's') so astonishes and enraptures Legrandin's sister, the Marquise de Cambremer.[1] A former Duc d'Uzès, when the king expressed surprise that no Uzès had ever been Marshal of France, had replied: "Sire, we are always killed in battle too soon." The Dowager Duchesse Anne d'Uzès was a remote cousin of Adhéaume de Chevigné and granddaughter of the Veuve Clicquot of champagne fame; but first and foremost she was a Mortemart, of the family whose wit was so famous under Louis XIV. "I was so exasperated by Saint-Simon's incessant talk about the 'Mortemart wit', without once telling us in what it consisted," Proust says, "that I resolved to go one better and invent the Guermantes wit." The duchesse liked to be told, however untruthfully, that she had the Mortemart wit. She was a dumpy, formidable, horsy woman, a poetess, novelist, sculptress, yachtswoman, feminist, huntress and motorist: by the time of her death in 1933 at the age of 86 the grisly antlers of more than two thousand stags which she had slain in person had been nailed to the walls of her hunting-lodge in the Forest of Rambouillet; and in 1897 she became the first woman in France to hold a driving-licence for one of the new-fangled motor-carriages. She was thought to have been the mistress of General Boulanger (and of the old Prince Joseph de Caraman-Chimay and the Duc de La Trémoïlle), though she always denied it; but it was certain that she had contributed three million francs to the shifty general's lost cause. On another occasion she was more thrifty, to her lasting sorrow. Her son Jacques became infatuated with the cocotte Émilienne d'Alençon, who was exhibiting a troupe of performing white rabbits—though nobody had eyes for the rabbits—to enthusiastic crowds at the Cirque d'Été in the Champs-Élysées. Soon she was to be seen wearing the Uzès family jewels. With the best intentions the Duchesse packed her son off to the Congo; but the poor young man died of enteric

[1] II, 819

fever at Kabinda in the Sudan in 1893, in the fourteenth month of his journey across Africa. This suggested Saint-Loup's exile to Morocco as a punishment for his extravagant gifts to Rachel.

One of the companions of Charles Haas in Tissot's painting is Prince Edmond de Polignac; some say it was he who introduced Proust to Haas. He was the son of Charles X's reactionary minister, a kind, witty, rapidly ageing man, with the bearing of a great nobleman and the face of a scholar: "He looked like a castle-tower converted into a library," said Proust. The prince was devoted to music, and was himself a composer of some distinction, but lacked the money to have his works performed. Montesquiou and Comtesse Greffulhe arranged his wedding in December 1893 to Winnaretta Singer, the heiress to the Singer sewing-machine millions, whose sister Isabelle had married the Duc Decaze in 1888. Jacques Émile Blanche remembered the prince jumping over a chair at the Blanches' Dieppe villa, by way of proving he was still young enough to marry, and old Mme Blanche saying: "So the lute is going to marry the sewing-machine." However, their union was extremely happy, and the prince's compositions were now performed in their studio in the Rue Cortambert by full orchestras and choirs. Proust heard there Fauré's sonata, one of the models for the Vinteuil Sonata. He also recalled with delight the unexpected arrival of his Condorcet tyrant M. Cucheval, and the butler saying to the prince: "This gentleman says his name is Cucheval, ought I to announce him all the same?"; and indeed, when one thought of it, the school-master's name was hardly fit to be pronounced before ladies. In the studio hung the prince's favourite picture, a study by Monet of tulips in a field near Haarlem, snatched from him at a sale a few years before by Miss Singer and now providentially returned. A single point of difference marred their union: the princess loved fresh air, and the prince hated draughts. When his friends teased him for sitting in a corner of the studio, smothered with travelling-rugs as if in a railway-carriage, he would murmur with a smile: "Ah well, as Anaxagoras says, this life is a journey"; and Proust gave the remark to the dying Bergotte.[1]

Another salon which Proust entered about this time was that of Comtesse Pauline d'Haussonville, a daughter of the Duc d'Harcourt. She was tall, haughty and statuesque, was said to

[1] III, 184

have the smallest ears in Paris, and wore red to set off her dark hair and her celebrated blue eyes. We have already seen her husband, Comte Othenin, with his ironic smile, bright, inquisitive eyes and dangling monocle, at Mme Straus's. He was a member of the Académie Française, and their salon became the headquarters of the clique of nobly-born academicians, the so-called 'party of the dukes'. Although his was said to have been the voice that had voted the survival of the Third Republic in 1876 by a majority of one, M. d'Haussonville was a leader of the liberal Orleanists, with whom he united the legitimists after the death of the Comte de Chambord in 1883. He was the grandson of Mme de Staël's daughter Albertine, whose Proustian Christian name was shared by two other ladies known to Proust, Princesse Albertine de Broglie and Comtesse Albertine de Montebello. Both husband and wife were exceedingly courteous and kind-hearted, but none the less conscious of the importance of their position; and the new guest would be gratified by the depth of their bow, only to be snubbed by the 'gymnastic harmony' (as Proust called it) with which, after regaining the perpendicular, they leaned as far backwards as they had bowed forwards. Proust attributed the Haussonville bow to the Guermantes ladies, who had borrowed it, he tells us, from the Courvoisiers, and to the Duchesse de Réveillon in *Jean Santeuil*.[1] In the Haussonvilles' drawing-room in the Rue Saint-Dominique hung the portrait of M. d'Haussonville's ancestress, Béatrix de Lillebonne, abbess under Louis XIV of the exclusive convent of Remiremont. Proust gives this painting to Mme de Villeparisis, who stupefies Bloch by maintaining, a little exaggeratedly, that even the King's own daughter would not have been admitted to this nunnery, "because after its misalliance with the Medicis the House of France hadn't enough quarters".[2] It was an incident in the memoirs of the Count's father, which Proust read only in 1920—in his youth the elder M. d'Haussonville had stood in doubt outside Mme Delessert's house, wondering if he had really been invited to her reception— that suggested the Narrator's anxieties at the Princesse de Guermantes's soirée.[3] In 1907 we shall see Mme d'Haussonville

---

[1] II, 445; *Jean Santeuil*, vol. 1, 285. For Albertine de Staël, afterwards Duchesse de Broglie, and the Haussonvilles, cf. II, 275, and III, 968.
[2] II, 199
[3] II, 633, etc.

contributing for a moment to the character of Mme de Cambremer, and in 1920 her husband prefiguring the old age of the
Duc de Guermantes.

One of the salons in which the *gratin* could meet the arts was
that of the beautiful and cruel Comtesse Emmanuela Potocka,
with whom Jacques Émile Blanche had had a heart-breaking love-
affair in the early 1880s. Her riotous circle, which included
Bourget, Dr Pozzi, Maupassant (one of her lovers), Béraud and
Gervex (yet another original of Elstir), was known as the
Maccabees (meaning Ghouls), and called her sometimes the Siren,
sometimes, like Mme Verdurin, the Mistress. One of Proust's
favourite anecdotes was Mme Potocka's belated reply to a theo-
logical argument of the philosopher Caro: as he was leaving she
leaned over the banisters and spat downstairs on his bald head,
shouting: "Take that for your Idea of God!" One evening at the
Duchesse de La Trémoïlle's, when Mme Potocka graciously rose
to greet the scholar Vaufreland, Mme de Chevigné uttered words
adapted in one of the Duchesse de Guermantes's epigrams: "She's
like the sun, she rises for one man just before going to bed for
another."[1] On one of his visits to Mme Potocka Proust saw the
Duchesse de Luynes's carriage and the Comtesse de Guerne's
motor-car waiting outside, and had the extreme pleasure of
hearing the hall-porter saying "Mme la Comtesse is out," to an
unwanted caller and "Mme la Comtesse is expecting you," to
himself. Towards the end of the 1890s the Siren moved to Auteuil
in order to devote more time to the only creatures she ever really
loved, her greyhounds. "Take care," said Reynaldo Hahn,
"You're too malicious to live so far out." At first the *gratin*
followed her, though with some grumbling: "It's charming out
here," said Proust's friend Gabriel de La Rochefoucauld, "Is
there anything one oughtn't to miss seeing in the vicinity?" She
was to be seen in the morning mists of the Bois, her beauty
fading, with a yelling pack of dogs around her and a huge collie
straining on the leash. But in the end Reynaldo's warning was
justified: during the Occupation, after forty years of isolation,
the deserted countess and her last greyhound died of old age and
hunger in the house at Auteuil. When their bodies were discovered at last, the rats had been at them.

The tale of the salons of the Faubourg Saint-Germain is com-

[1] II, 410

plete. We shall encounter most of them again, in their place and time, and see what further use Proust made of them in his novel. It remains to ask why he entered them, and why, indeed, this obscure, half-Jewish, bourgeois young man was ever allowed in.

We needs must love the highest when we see it. Unfortunately, it is not easy for the idealist young to discern which of the things they see—nature, art, love, friendship, the noble mind of the nobly born—is the highest. Proust pursued all these together, and thought for a long time to find some of them on the Guermantes Way. Perhaps, however they choose, the young are right; for the highest, whatever it be, is not of this earth, and it matters little in which of its earthly symbols they may seek it in vain. A drawing-room, it seemed to Proust, was itself a work of art, of which its habitués were both the performers and the creators, devising the formal movements of the mysterious ballet they danced, inventing the words of the frivolous but portentous drama they played. Then, too, there was the poetic glamour of meeting the modern equivalents of characters in Balzac, or the descendants and namesakes of noble personages of whom he had read in Saint-Simon's memoirs and Mme de Sévigné's letters. There was the intellectual fascination of unravelling the mechanisms of a world in which the interplay of human passions and conventions was so peculiarly intense and so exceptionally disguised. There was the need for enchantment and disenchantment, for the experiences which would go to make his unconceived novel. Perhaps deeper still (if an impulse from the Freudian unconscious can be said to be deeper than an impulse from the creative unconscious) was his need to prove that he was not a pariah, the anxious prompting of his inner guilt. He must be accepted where acceptance would be most difficult and failure most humiliating, in the company of the elect, in the Faubourg which was on earth the image, whether real or merely blasphemous, of the blessed saints in heaven. And he pursued the welcoming smile of a noble hostess as at Auteuil he had pursued his mother's kiss, and for the same reasons.

The influence of Montesquiou in introducing Proust to society has often been exaggerated. Count Robert acted, as we have seen, with the least possible energy and at the last possible moment, when Proust was on the point of attaining the highest levels of the Faubourg (having already reached the lower) by his own devices. Proust reproduced the situation accurately in his novel. The Narrator visits Mme de Villeparisis and dines at the Duchesse's unknown to Charlus, who still hopes, like Mephistopheles tempting Faust, to exact a mysterious and awful price for his services; and the baron has the supreme mortification of meeting him at the Princesse de Guermantes's, where, he had announced, "they never invite *anyone* unless I intervene".[1] Moreover, Montesquiou was not altogether a desirable sponsor. It would not be pleasant to be asked merely because a hostess was terrified of annoying the Count, and in the invidious capacity of his latest young man. Besides, if in a fit of enthusiasm Montesquiou compelled everyone to invite a protégé, he would soon in a fit of rage forbid anyone ever to invite him again. The evidence suggests that after the Delafosse fête, at which Proust met nearly all the ladies mentioned in this chapter, he went everywhere unaided, kept Montesquiou at a safe distance, and employed all his diplomacy in ensuring that the Count should *not* intervene. The uneasy knowledge that he had not, after all, been indispensable, was an important element in the mingled antipathy and admiration with which Montesquiou ever after regarded his 'dear Marcel'.

[1] II, 565

Chapter 11

DESCENT INTO THE CITIES OF THE PLAIN

DURING the summer of 1894, the period of his ascent to the heights of the Faubourg Saint-Germain, Proust continued simultaneously his descent towards Sodom. His uneasy friendship with Montesquiou, however, ceased to be a preponderant motive force, and the Count's honeymoon with Delafosse seemed a model to be avoided. Only politeness was maintained. In July he tried, unsuccessfully, to arrange a 'musical dinner' for the happy couple at the fashionable restaurant of Armenonville in the Bois de Boulogne. No doubt all three had been there before; for it was at Armenonville that the Verdurin's pianist used to play the Vinteuil Sonata to Odette and the 'faithful', so that ever afterwards, when Swann heard the 'little phrase', he could see 'the moonlight preventing the leaves from moving', and hear someone murmuring, "You can almost see to read the newspaper!"[1] Proust learned, too late, that Delafosse had left for London, where he gave a piano-recital on 12 July, while Montesquiou had been ill with laryngitis ('I should so have loved to bring you hot drinks and smoothe your pillow!'). He would be going to Saint-Moritz again in August—could Marcel come too? But Proust had more attractive plans.

Before these plans are revealed, a strange meeting in the previous spring must be mentioned. During the April of 1894, Oscar Wilde paid his last visit to Paris before his self-sought doom of the following year. It was the period of his most triumphant pride, when he felt himself to be, as he said, 'the King of Life', and only disaster could offer him a new experience. His bloated, gloriously insolent features were to be seen at Mme Straus's; and Proust dined with him one evening at Mme Arman de Caillavet's, where the two men eyed one another, as Fernand Gregh noticed, 'with a complex curiosity'. "You know," said Mme Arman afterwards, "Monsieur Wilde looks like a cross between the Apollo Belvedere and Albert Wolff." Everyone knew

[1] I, 533, 534

what she meant; for Albert Wolff, the art and theatre critic of *Le Figaro*—'a creature of no religion, no country, and no sex', the anti-Semite Drumont had written in *La France Juive*—was a fat, fluting, corseted, rouged caricature of Wilde the pervert. Robert de Billy, now back in Paris at the Foreign Ministry, remembered Wilde confessing: "I find an ever-growing difficulty in expressing my originality through my choice of waistcoats and cravats"; and Billy was not sure that Oscar had not had some part, during a previous visit, in the selection of a dove-grey cravat for the well-known portrait which J. E. Blanche had painted of Proust two years before. Wilde even visited 9 Boulevard Malesherbes, where, like the Baron de Charlus,[1] he commented adversely on the furniture, much to Proust's annoyance: "I don't think M. Wilde has been well brought-up," he said afterwards. On the young André Gide, Proust's elder by two years, the influence of Wilde's conversation in preparing him for moral and spiritual liberation had been crucial; for Wilde is Ménalque, the genius of heroic hedonism, in *Les Nourritures Terrestres* and *L'Immoraliste*. He failed to impress Proust: yet perhaps Wilde's glorying in his vice may have taken some effect in that spring of 1894. Possibly there is a little of Wilde in Charlus; and there is, more probably, something of the dangerous, beautiful Lord Alfred Douglas, who accompanied Wilde, and was sometimes to be seen at the *Revue Blanche* office in the Rue Laffitte, in Charlie Morel.

In August Montesquiou was at Saint-Moritz, which he appreciated less than in the two previous years. "Switzerland is a hideous country," he told the young Élisabeth de Gramont, Duc Agénor's daughter and a future friend of Proust, who was staying at the same hotel; "on the rare occasions when one does come across a possible view, it's invariably blocked by an enormous notice-board that says 'Hôtel Belle-Vue'!" But Proust was staying at Mme Lemaire's château in the Marne, Réveillon, with Reynaldo Hahn.

Hahn was a young man of nineteen, the favourite pupil of Massenet at the Conservatoire, and already a singer, pianist and composer of some distinction. He was a Jew, born at Caracas in Venezuela, and now lived in Paris with his parents and several sisters; he had brown eyes, pale brown skin, austerely handsome features and a little dark moustache. Proust met him early this

[1] III, 387

summer at Mme Lemaire's Tuesdays in the Rue Monceau, where Hahn's singing of his own song-cycle from poems of Verlaine, *Les Chansons Grises*, immediately became the rage: he was to be one of the chief performing stars of her musical evenings for the next two decades. His voice was a light but rich tenor; he leaned far back, playing his own accompaniment to his own songs, with half-closed eyes and a convincing air of inspiration. A malicious observer would notice that his singing head cocked from side to side, like a bird's, as he darted keen glances through his long eyelashes at each member of his audience, to make sure that all were properly mesmerised. But he possessed the serious charm, the intelligence and moral distinction that Proust sought in the ideal friend. Their friendship was passionate for the next two years, and temperate but unclouded for the rest of Proust's life.

Réveillon was a rambling seventeenth-century country-house, turreted and moated, with large formal flower-gardens surrounded by dense forest. The interior decoration, in which real flowers from the gardens alternated with painted flowers from Mme Lemaire's brush, resembled that of La Raspelière under the reign of Mme Verdurin.[1] On the first day Proust and Hahn took a walk in the gardens, talking as they went, until they passed a crimson border of Bengal roses, when Proust suddenly became silent. "Would you be annoyed if I stayed behind a minute?" he asked, in the sad, gentle, childish voice which was so characteristic of him. "I want to have another look at those roses." When Reynaldo returned, after walking all round the house, he found his friend standing motionless, frowning and oblivious, biting one end of his long moustache which he held between his teeth with his left hand, still staring at the roses. Reynaldo passed by once more, till he heard Marcel calling and running after him; with a feeling of amused respect he divined that it would be better to ask no questions about his friend's state of trance, and they resumed their conversation as though nothing had happened.[2] Proust can hardly have forgotten that there were Bengal roses in the Pré Catelan at Illiers, so this curious episode cannot have been an onset of unconscious memory, like the eating of the madeleine; it was, rather, the kindred effort to wrest the secret of a natural object,

[1] II, 917, etc.
[2] Andrée shows similar tact when the Narrator wishes to contemplate the hawthorns in the country near Balbec (I, 922); so does Saint-Loup (II, 157).

like the incident of the three trees near Balbec, or the spires on the horizon of the Méséglise Way.

Proust's stay at Réveillon lasted from 18 August to the middle of September, and was followed by ten days with his mother at the Hôtel des Roches Noires at Trouville, where he wrote a short story, *La Mort de Baldassare Silvande*, for *Les Plaisirs et les Jours*. He saw a great deal of Mme Straus at her villa, the Clos des Mûriers, but failed to persuade Reynaldo to visit him and continue his musical education. 'You will find me a much altered Marcel, musically speaking,' he wrote to Pierre Lavallée, 'in fact I'm Romeo-and-Julietising rather to excess, perhaps.' A tiresome event of this holiday was that his brother Robert, while staying at Rueil (a village on the Seine a few miles north of Paris), fell from his tandem-bicycle under a five-ton coal-wagon, which passed over his thigh without causing serious injury. Mme Proust hurried away to nurse him, and found his lower-class girl-friend already installed at his bedside, a situation which she accepted with supreme tact. Proust remembered the incident in *La Prisonnière*: the Narrator's mother, when the captive Albertine accompanied them on the train from Balbec to Paris, 'spoke kindly to my friend, like a mother whose son is gravely injured, and who is grateful to the young mistress who tends him with devoted care'.[1] Nevertheless, Mme Proust had Robert packed off to Uncle Louis's house at Auteuil as soon as he was fit to be moved. Proust returned to Paris on 25 September.

Proust's mention of *Romeo and Juliet* (in which the double meaning, if any, is certainly unconscious) no doubt refers to the opera by Gounod, to whose lineage Reynaldo belonged via his master Saint-Saëns. The musical preferences which Hahn hoped to inculcate in his friend were, by an odd coincidence, those which Proust had already held at the age of fifteen, under the influence of his mother and Mme Catusse, when he wrote in Antoinette Faure's confession-album: 'Favourite composers, Gounod and Mozart.' For Hahn was a Mozartian classicist, and in the delicate, traditional refinement of his own music he showed, by no means discreditably, his indifference to innovators such as Fauré and Debussy, and his antipathy to Wagner. Proust, on the other hand, was by now an ardent Wagnerian, devoted to Fauré and intrigued by Debussy, whose music, now just beginning to

[1] III, 13

be known, he was to admire intensely a decade later. 'Monsieur,' he wrote to Fauré about this time, 'I not only admire and venerate your music, I am in love with it. Long before you met me you used to thank me with a smile when, at a concert or an evening-party, the clamour of my enthusiasm obliged your disdainful in-difference to success to bow a fifth or sixth time to your audience!' It was probably at Comte Henri de Saussine's, in 1893, that he met Fauré, as he had also met Delafosse, for in real life Vinteuil and Morel frequented one and the same salon. But the guest Saussine admired even above Fauré was the Wagnerian pupil of César Franck, Vincent d'Indy, whose name is echoed in the name of Vinteuil. Under Saussine's influence Proust acquired the enthusiasm for Wagner to which he was in any case born: it was on 14 January 1894, at the Sunday Colonne concert, that he first heard the Flower Maiden scene from *Parsifal*, which he recalled in the episode in *Le Côté de Guermantes* where the lady guests of the Duchesse ('their flesh appeared on either side of a sinuous spray of mimosa or the petals of a full-blown rose') are compared to the Flower Maidens.[1]

Hahn's attempt at re-education came, very fortunately, too late to distract Proust from the musical aesthetic which suited his nature and was to inform his novel. Reynaldo's traditionalism was no doubt salutary for himself, but would only have been disastrous for Proust: it could never have led to the invention of Vinteuil. To please Reynaldo he did his best to like Saint-Saëns: he wrote two articles in *Le Gaulois* of 14 January and 11 December 1895, in which, however, his attempts at praise only succeeded in displaying his reservations. 'Saint-Saëns uses archaism to legitimise modernity; he bestows upon a common-place, step by step, through the ingenious, personal, sublime appropriateness of his style, the value of an original creation . . . he is a musical humanist,' says Proust very truly. And yet, it was from Reynaldo's tuition and from the charming, meritorious but secondary music of Saint-Saëns, that the 'little phrase' of the Vinteuil Sonata took its beginning.

It was perhaps at Mme Lemaire's, and played by Ysaye ('his rendering is splendid, majestic and luminous, with admirable form,' wrote Reynaldo in his diary), that Proust first heard the Saint-Saëns Sonata in D Minor for violin and piano. His imagina-

[1] II, 423

tion was captured by the chief theme of the first movement, a
mediocre but haunting melody whose only musical merit is its
simplicity, and whose fascination comes from its very banality, like
that of a popular song or dance-tune, and its incessant repetition.

Afterwards, in Reynaldo's room at 6 Rue du Cirque, with its
enormous stone fireplace, or in the dining-room at 9 Boulevard
Malesherbes, Proust would say: "Play me that bit I like, Reynaldo
—you know, the 'little phrase'." So the little phrase of Saint-
Saëns became the 'national anthem' of his love for Reynaldo, as
Vinteuil's became that of Swann's love for Odette.[1]

[1] I, 218. In *Jean Santeuil* the hero's mistress, Françoise S., plays the Saint-
Saëns sonata under its own name, during an episode of jealous cross-
examination about her Lesbian loves which is retold in *A la Recherche* both
of Swann and Odette, and of the Narrator and Albertine. So it may be
conjectured that there is something of Proust's friendship for Reynaldo in
both Françoise and Albertine. Perhaps, too (though here the transposition
would be particularly devious and dubious), since Albertine and the Sonata
are associated through Mlle Vinteuil and her friend with homosexual
jealousy, it may be guessed that Proust quarrelled with Reynaldo over his
loyal attachment to his master Saint-Saëns, who, as was notorious, was
himself an invert. Another probable relic of Reynaldo in Françoise S. is the
episode of her musician friends, Vésale, Saint-Géron and Griffon, who
perform chamber-music in her apartment, with Françoise at the piano. But
at this point in their friendship no more than the possibility of some relation
between Françoise and Reynaldo can be inferred, and no definite conclusions
about events in real life between Hahn and Proust can be drawn from such
uncertain material. Indeed, the evidence against the connection is more
convincing. The scene of jealousy had already appeared in *Avant la nuit*,
written a year before Proust met Hahn. Françoise is much less closely allied
to Albertine than to Odette in *Un Amour de Swann*, who derives from a
very different region of Proust's life, from his flirtation with Mme Hayman,
his discoveries about the early life of Charles Haas, and most of all from his
imagination, for *Un Amour de Swann* is the only episode of *A la Recherche*
in which there is a large element of fiction. Proust's early association with
Hahn seems to have been free from quarrels, or any unhappiness except his
intermittent feelings of guilt towards his unsuspecting mother. Its passionate
stage ended two years later, when Proust found another young friend, and
a brief period of tension was followed by a loyal and lifelong comradeship.
Except for the few angry months in 1896 which ended their love, nothing
could be further from this most satisfactory and lasting of all Proust's
friendships than the torments inflicted by Françoise and Albertine.

Meanwhile the preparation of *Les Plaisirs et les Jours* was advancing rapidly. The long dedicatory foreword to Willie Heath was written in July 1894; Mme Lemaire was busy with her gracefully repellent brush-drawings; Anatole France used his personal influence to find a publisher; and Montesquiou generously consented to the quotation of his still unpublished verses to Mme Lemaire (*'the goddess and Vigée-Lebrun of flowers'*), 'which display,' wrote the grateful Proust, 'the sententious and subtle elegance, the vigorous sense of form, that so often in his work remind one of the seventeenth century'. But Count Robert refused to allow one of the stories to be dedicated to him, even with the inducement that France and Heredia would be among his fellow-dedicatees, and that his *bête noire* Blanche would be excluded; and in the end it was decided there should be no dedications of individual stories at all. The manuscript—although a few pieces were written and inserted later—was in the hands of the publisher Calmann Lévy by September. And when the year ended Proust found he no longer dreaded New Year's Day—that recurrent point in the spiral of time which in the long-past winter of Marie de Benardaky seemed the beginning of a new life, but afterwards became a mocking admonition that life could not be altered by the calendar alone. 'I used to feel,' he wrote to Montesquiou, 'that however the years change, our character remains the same; and that the future we dream and desire is merely the product of the very past from which we would like it to be so different, and only echoes all the bells of good and evil we have previously set ringing. But now it is with a keener consciousness of divine grace and human liberty, with faith in at least an inner Providence, that I begin the year.' For now the joy of Reynaldo's friendship reached out into an endless future, and the possibility of fame from writing seemed within his grasp.

His new love, however, happy and virtuous as it seemed, had its darker implications. Whether or not his previous friendships had been entirely platonic, they had been transitory, and had never touched his deepest emotions; he had often been in love with women; he could still regard himself as fundamentally normal. Now, once and for all, he must admit to himself that he was a homosexual, one of the exiled, scattered, outlawed inhabitants of Sodom, a race more tragic and despised even than the Jews. He was a criminal, and Reynaldo was his accomplice; they belonged to the kin of Doasan and his Polish violinist, of Montesquiou and Delafosse, Wilde and Lord Alfred. His previous innocent friendships, from 'little Halévy' to Willie Heath, were retrospectively debased into sublimations of a vicious desire. Worst of all, he must now devote his life to an interminable effort to conceal his real nature from his mother. If he succeeded, would he not crucify her daily with his deceit? If he failed, would he not, quite literally, kill her? He wrote a story in which he killed first his mother, and then himself, almost as if this was the only possible solution of his dilemma.

La Confession d'une Jeune Fille is the only certain case of 'transposition' in Proust's early short stories: it is abundantly clear that the heroine is Proust himself. She spends the summers of her childhood in the garden of Les Oublis, which is one and the same as the Pré Catelan at Illiers, the garden at Étreuilles in *Jean Santeuil* (which is likewise called Les Oublis), and Swann's park at Tansonville. There is the incident of the mother's good-night kiss, 'an old habit which she had abandoned, because it gave me too much pleasure and too much pain'. The girl is seduced at the age of fifteen by a boy cousin—did this, too, happen to Proust, and is such an incident alluded to when the Narrator presents the proprietress of Bloch's brothel with Aunt Léonie's sofa, 'on which I first tasted the pleasures of love with a little girl cousin'?[1] She is tortured by indolence, procrastination and 'lack of will-power'. 'I gave myself time, and often felt wretched when I saw time pass, but after all, there was so much of it still before me! . . . Wishing to have will-power was not enough. What I ought to have done was precisely what I could not do without will-power —to will it.' She becomes addicted to 'the desiccating pleasures of society'—'I went into society to calm myself after sinning, and the moment I was calmed I sinned again.' She acquires a brutally sensual fiancé, with her parents' consent, and is seduced once more. Her mother, looking through the window, finds her in the act and dies of a stroke; and the girl shoots herself, like the Lesbian heroine of *Avant la nuit*.

It is surely improbable, though several of Proust's biographers have suggested it, that the melodramatic discovery occurred in real life. The brutal fiancé is very far from the gentle Reynaldo; and though Proust no doubt often ran the horrifying risk of

[1] I, 578

detection in his own home, the event could not have occurred without leaving a permanent scar—of which there is not the least trace—in the relations of mother and son. It is still more inconceivable, even granting his latent sadism towards his mother, that he could have recorded such an incident openly in the book in which he expected her to take pride and pleasure. His remorse, and his fear that the story might come true, were no doubt real enough, but the story itself shows that he succeeded in repressing them. Like the rest of *Les Plaisirs et les Jours* it has the sterile tone of a literary exercise: he had confessed to the world and to his mother as a sop to his conscience, and with no intention of being taken at his word. Nevertheless, *Confession d'une Jeune Fille* is the first clear sign of Proust's recognition of his own inversion. It is also, though he could scarcely have foreseen it, a first embryonic draft of *Jean Santeuil* and *A la Recherche*; the garden of Combray, the mother's kiss refused and extorted, the Guermantes Way and the Cities of the Plain, the obsession of Time Lost, his own life told as an allegory, all are there, though with suicide as the only solution. The final incident of the destroyer taken into the parents' house, the desecration of the mother, and the symbolic window, is a distant prefiguration both of Albertine as captive, and of Mlle Vinteuil's profanation of her dead father's portrait, seen by the Narrator through the window at Montjouvain.

By the New Year of 1895, as we have seen, Proust was already feeling 'a keener consciousness of divine grace and human liberty': he had come to terms with his remorse and accepted his destiny. He took Reynaldo to a careful selection of broadminded hostesses, including Mme Aubernon, Mme Straus and the rich, kind, malicious, white-haired old Marquise de Brantes— "She's worth a whole Council of Trent," her nephew Montesquiou would say with vague approbation. From January onwards they visited Count Robert himself, who was most affable, and was repaid with a shower of grateful letters for 'your kindness to my friend'. On 28 May, at Mme Lemaire's Tuesday, Proust's poem sequence *Portraits de Peintres* was recited, to a piano accompaniment composed by Hahn, in the august presence of Montesquiou and Anatole France. Proust's musician friend Édouard Risler was at the piano, having come up specially for the occasion from his military service at Chartres. Risler is presum-

ably the Marquis de Poitiers, the pianist soldier in *Jean Santeuil*[1];
and as a letter of this summer to Pierre Lavallée suggests that
Proust visited Chartres to dine with Risler, it is probable that
Chartres is one of the many garrison-towns which compose
Doncières in *Le Côté de Guermantes*. Proust's poems, on Paul
Potter, Cuyp, Watteau and Van Dyck (this last with a hint of
Willie Heath, 'erect yet reposing' in the green shade of the Bois
de Boulogne) are almost worthless imitations of Montesquiou, with
a few would-be suggestions of Mallarmé, and inferior to Hahn's
delicate accompaniment. But at least they show the sincerity of
Proust's admiration for Montesquiou's work—an admiration
which came not from bad taste, but from an instinctive knowledge
that Count Robert possessed a secret of supreme aesthetic importance, if only he could discover what it was. He also copied
Montesquiou in a way which was less gratifying to that very
susceptible model. His imitations of the Count's monologues,
with the harsh voice rising to an eldritch scream, the head flung
back and the final stamp of the foot, became a popular party-
piece; they were irresistibly comic, and at the same time hallucina-
torily accurate. Proust's pastiches of Montesquiou are still audible,
brought to the level of great art, in the speeches of the Baron de
Charlus. Of course the Count got wind of these performances:
Proust explained that he was merely quoting his marvellous
sayings to an admiring audience, and that quite involuntarily 'the
body was carried away by the soul, my voice and accent took on
the rhythm of the great thoughts I had for the moment borrowed
—if anyone has told you anything else, or mentioned the word
"caricature", I can only invoke your axiom, that words repeated at
second-hand are never true'.[2] Montesquiou pretended to take his
word for it, but: "I don't know why you should set yourself up as
the travelling-salesman of my wit," he persisted in complaining.

Proust spent one afternoon of this spring at the Jardin des
Plantes with his schoolfriend Pierre Lavallée and Reynaldo, and
contemplated the *colombes poignardées*, the doves with a red spot
as of blood on their breasts, in a recurrence of the trance in which

---

[1] *Jean Santeuil*, vol. 2, 293-7. Risler, as the pet pianist of Mme Lemaire's
salon, is also the pianist Dechambre at Mme Verdurin's. The Marquis de
Poitiers, forever cigarette-smoking as he plays, also resembles Reynaldo Hahn.

[2] An axiom uttered by the Baron de Charlus during his quarrel-scene
with the Narrator (II, 560).

he had gazed at the Bengal roses of Réveillon. "They look like nymphs who've stabbed themselves for love," said Reynaldo, "and some god has changed them into birds." At one time, in 1913, Proust thought of calling the second volume of *À la Recherche*, which was later divided into *À l'Ombre des Jeunes Filles en Fleurs* and *Le Côté de Guermantes, Les Colombes Poignardées*. He visited Lavallée at his parents' country-house at Segrez, Seine-et-Oise, when the trees were still in bud, and wrote the sketch '*Promenade*' in *Les Plaisirs et les Jours* in memory of the afternoon of his arrival. They walked among wood-anemones and cuckoo-flowers, watched eels and perch wandering in their green meadows of water-weed under the blue water of the streams, collected eggs in the farmyard and admired the jewelled, regal peacock. But during the night Proust had an attack of asthma, and in the morning, to everyone's amazement, he insisted on returning to Paris. His malady, after exiling him from Illiers and troubling his early schooldays, had spared him for nearly ten years, during which his health had been good, except for occasional stomach-pains and vague rheumatisms, both presumably of the same nervous origin. But now it was on its way back, summoned no doubt by the double guilt of society and Sodom. Already a year before, in the spring of 1894, as he complained in a letter to Montesquiou, he had suffered 'a horrible attack of choking, which lasted twenty-four hours'. Soon asthma would arrive in full force, and stay for ever.

In June 1895 began the pathetically comic episode of Proust's career as a librarian. He had taken his *licence ès lettres* in March, after a year of private lessons from M. Darlu, with the creditable placing of twenty-third in his year; his family, though with waning hope and vigour, still pressed him to choose a regular occupation, and it was probably Dr Proust's friend Gabriel Hanotaux, then Foreign Minister, and one of the originals of M. de Norpois, who suggested that a post at the Mazarine Library might suit this literary young man. The Mazarine was in the left wing of the Institut de France, the seat of the five Academies; and Sainte-Beuve himself had been a librarian there fifty years before.[1]

[1] No doubt he also had in mind the example of Anatole France, assistant at the Senate Library in the Luxembourg Palace from 1876 to 1890, when he resigned at the urgent request of the chief librarian, Charles Edmond, who complained: "Monsieur France hasn't catalogued a single book since 1882!"

Certainly the duties of an honorary unpaid assistant would be unlikely to interfere with his writing: the working day was of five hours, and attendance was required on a minimum of two and a maximum of five days in the week. Proust was interviewed in a competition for three vacancies on 28 May, and on 29 June was chosen third and last. Every now and then during the next four months, when he felt in the mood, and his health seemed equal to the strain, and (though this was seldom indeed) he was not away on holiday, he actually turned up for a chat with his busy but amiable colleagues and a browse among the Cardinal's books. The books, however, were dusty; and when he emerged on the Quai Conti to meet his new young friend Lucien Daudet, he would produce a throat-spray and counteract the ravages of the day with a cloud of vaporised eucalyptus. His colleagues, Paul Marais the incunabulist and Alfred Franklin the Chief Librarian, thought him nice but quite useless.

Early in July, however, Proust was already on holiday with his mother at Kreuznach, a German spa on the River Nahe, which flows into the Rhine at Bingen ten miles farther east. Robert de Billy came to stay a night with his young wife Jeanne, the daughter of Paul Mirabaud, governor of the Bank of France; they had married a month before, on 4 June, and were still on honeymoon. Mme Proust exerted all her charm, Billy talked about his experiences as a budding diplomat in Germany throughout lunch, and Proust said he must write them down immediately— "and your wife can go upstairs to rest". Billy wrote all afternoon: "It's very good, but you oughtn't to use so many adjectives," declared his friend, who was to make a practice, with such superb effect, of using three or four in a row. Then he produced his short story, *La Mort de Baldassare Silvande*, written at Trouville the previous September, to which Billy in turn made certain objections; they corrected it together in the lamplight, and ever afterwards Proust would say to Billy with a plaintive smile: "You never did like anything I write!" Billy remembered the visit to Kreuznach as the occasion of their first conversations on gothic architecture, which a little later was to become Proust's ruling passion for several years.

After Kreuznach Proust spent a fortnight with Reynaldo and his sister Maria in the forest of Saint-Germain-en-Laye at the Pavillon Louis XIV, a villa belonging to Reynaldo's married

sister Clarita, Mme Seminario, where he finished the revision of
La Mort de Baldassare Silvande. The figure of the dying
Baldassare, little Alexis's uncle with the riotous past, was no doubt
suggested (though Baldassare is a young man of thirty-six) by
the now aged and ailing Louis Weil; but he also contains elements
which recall the later years of Jean Santeuil and even Swann
himself; and in his musical career he is based on both Reynaldo
and Prince Edmond de Polignac. It was probably Baldassare's
gift of a pony to little Alexis (who is Proust as a child) which
made Reynaldo nickname his friend 'Pony': at first much to
Proust's distress ('Marcel the Pony sounds as bad as Jack the
Ripper'), though soon he grew to like it. The story was published
in the *Revue Hebdomadaire* of 29 October 1895, with the dedication 'To Reynaldo Hahn, poet, singer and musician', and earned
Proust 150 francs. This not inconsiderable sum was worth six
pounds then, but would to-day represent nearer fifty: it was an
argument to show his parents that even a writer's career might
be more remunerative than that of an honorary, unpaid librarian
on indefinitely prolonged leave.

Soon, from about 8 August to the end of the month, Proust
was staying with Reynaldo at Mme Lemaire's villa on the sea-
front at 32 Rue Aguado,[1] Dieppe. As a little bird, who was not
improbably Proust himself, informed the society columnist of *Le
Gaulois*: 'Everyone is talking about the well-known members of
Parisian society who happen to be at Dieppe just now. All Paris
is there, the Comte and Comtesse Louis de Talleyrand-Périgord,
Duc Josselin de Rohan, Madeleine Lemaire, and MM. Marcel
Proust and Reynaldo Hahn, who are the guests of that eminent
artist!' But Proust was collecting impressions for Balbec, and
composing a sketch called 'Underwood' for *Les Plaisirs et les
Jours*: 'Lying on our backs, with our heads pillowed in dead
leaves,' he wrote, 'we followed the joyous agility of our thoughts
as they climbed, without making a single leaf quiver, to the
highest branches, where they perched on the edge of the hazy sky,
beside a singing bird.' He wrote to Reynaldo's charming elder

---

[1] Through a misunderstanding of the words 'Petit-Abbeville (Dieppe)
August 1895' at the end of Proust's sketch *'Sous-Bois'* in *Les Plaisirs et les
Jours*, 232-4, it has been wrongly supposed that Mme Lemaire's villa
was called Petit-Abbeville. In fact the name is that of a village a mile or two
south-west of Dieppe.

sister Maria in a flirtatious cadenza of marine epithets—'O my
sister Maria, confidant of my inmost thoughts'—she was reading
his *Baldassare Silvande*—'lighthouse of wandering woes, star of
kindness, halcyon of exiles, sea-breeze, song of mighty oarsmen,
terror of little cabin-boys, perfume of friendship, delicious fluting
of winds that bring lost ships to life . . .' and so on. 'Marcel is
rather tight-chested, his father may advise against Brittany,' wrote
Reynaldo to Maria on the 12th; and Mme Lemaire, with an inexorable hospitality worthy of Mme Verdurin at La Raspelière,
reported on the 17th, 'Marcel is much better—if only they would
give up the Brittany idea—at least I make them eat regular meals,
which they wouldn't do at some dreadful little hotel.' But they
refused to give up this 'Brittany idea'; they returned to Paris on
30 August and left almost immediately for Belle-Isle. The railway
journey, like that of the first visit to Balbec, took all night; they
stayed in the Hôtel de Bretagne at Palais, the chief port of the
island.

No doubt the visit to Brittany was, for Proust, like the arrival
at Balbec for the Narrator, the fulfilment of a childhood longing[1]:
he would see Renan's 'land of the virtuous Armoricans, who
dwell by a dark sea jagged with rocks, beaten by everlasting
storms', and perhaps, too, its 'girls with eyes like green wells, in
whose depths of undulating water-plants the blue sky is
mirrored'. But at first they were more conscious of making a
'pilgrimage to the habitations made glorious by Sarah Bernhardt',
as Proust wrote to Yturri; for Belle-Isle, an island ten miles from
the coast opposite Quiberon, was the summer residence of the
divine Sarah, and the home of the poetry-writing sailor whom she
had brought to the Delafosse fête. But when they had made the
customary excursions in a bumpy governess-cart, through the
purple heather and golden gorse of the slate uplands, and the
palm-trees of the warm valleys, and gazed on the Atlantic from
the hair-raising cliffs, there was nothing left to do: the season was
nearly over, and there was a dreadful smell of sardines. They fled
to the mainland on 6 September and settled at Beg-Meil, a fashionable little *plage* across the bay from Concarneau. Proust had
heard of the place from a friend of his parents, a banker and
music-lover named André Bénac, who owned a château near by:

[1] In point of fact, Proust had already visited Brittany as a child, and seen
Mont Saint-Michel when he was too little to appreciate it. (Cf. *Billy*, 115.)

similarly, in *Jean Santeuil*, Jean is recommended to visit Beg-Meil by his mother's friends the Sauvalgues. Their hotel was a converted farmhouse, and M. Fermont the proprietor had the kindly bluffness of a farmer: soon Proust was treated as one of the family, just as he had been in Mme Renvoyzé's lodgings at Orleans. They stayed in the annexe a hundred yards from the main building, and *pension* was a mere two francs a day. Apple orchards descended to the edge of the sea, and the cider-like smell of rotting wind-falls mingled with the scent of seaweed. Proust made friends with a fisher-boy, who took him out into the bay at evening to hear the bells of Concarneau, and carefully avoided the shoals of jelly-fish which Proust hated, and kept a bottle of ink in his boat in case the young gentleman should wish to write. A shout of "Good-night, good fishing," came from a passing smack, and "Good-night, good fishing," Proust would blissfully call back. In the afternoons after their enormous lunch he lay hidden in the sand-dunes with Reynaldo, reading Balzac, and Carlyle's *Heroes and Hero-worship* in Izoulet-Loubatière's translation. They found that the absence of indoor sanitation was made still more serious by the prevalence of nettles.

Among the other guests at the hotel was a minor Franco-American marine painter, Alexander Harrison, whose *Blue Lake* they had already noticed in the Luxembourg Museum. 'He's stayed here for nine months every year for the last seventeen years,' wrote Reynaldo to his sister Maria. Half-serious, half-joking, they sent him a joint letter announcing their intense admiration for his work and begging to be allowed to meet him; and after dinner the amused but flattered painter joined them at their table. From this incident comes the meeting with the novelist C. at 'Kerengrimen' in *Jean Santeuil*, though C. himself is a memory of Maupassant in Normandy; and in *A l'Ombre* Harrison for a moment becomes Elstir, to whom the Narrator and Saint-Loup introduce themselves in the same way in the restaurant at Rivebelle. He recommended a trip to Penmarch—"a sort of mixture of Holland, the East Indies and Florida,"[1] he

---

[1] Similarly, when Elstir urges the Narrator to visit Carquethuit near Balbec in preference to the Pointe du Raz, he says of Carquethuit: "I don't know anything quite analogous to it in the rest of France, it reminds one more of certain aspects of Florida" (I, 854). Elstir at Rivebelle in the time when the restaurant is still a humble farm (I, 826) resembles Harrison at Beg-Meil.

said, referring to its sand-dunes and sub-tropical climate, "and a storm there is the sublimest thing you could see anywhere". When a storm came they duly went, by pony-trap, to the nearest station at Pont l'Abbé, and then on the little local railway to the Pointe de Penmarch. They crawled on hands and knees through the gale to the edge of the cliff; and below him Proust saw, instead of the expected violence and turmoil, a white procession of calm Alpine heights slowly surging and falling into the abyss, and thundering as they fell.

It was Beg-Meil that gave to Balbec—besides one syllable of its name—the Celtic mystery of its position. The mystery resides in the idea, and dissolves in the reality of Balbec, which is found when the Narrator visits it to be a charming but ordinary Normandy resort like Cabourg, Trouville or Dieppe. But when Legrandin speaks of "Balbec, the most ancient bone in the geological skeleton of our soil, the end of the world, the real country of the Cimmerians, that funereal shore famed for its numberless shipwrecks, the eternal realm of the sea-mists," and the Narrator as a child longs to take 'the beautiful, generous one-twenty-two train' which will land him at Balbec after an all-night journey, 'when the grey dawn rises on a raging sea', and then proceed to the Breton towns of Lannion, Pont-Aven and Quimperlé,[1] the yet unvisited Balbec is united with Beg-Meil. Brittany, also, was a land of many 'little trains', of which Proust travelled on at least two, that from Auray to Quiberon, whence he sailed to Belle-Isle, and that from Pont l'Abbé to Penmarch, when he went to meet the gale.

His return to Paris in mid-October was soon followed by a catastrophe. He had been absent from the Mazarine almost continuously since July, and had made delightful plans for still more leave; but now he heard that the third of the new attachés was to be transferred to the Ministry of Public Instruction for routine service in the registration of books deposited under the law of copyright. He informed his superior at the Ministry of his delicate state of health, and M. Franklin was invited to throw one of the two senior attachés to the wolves in his place. 'Monsieur Proust seemed to me to enjoy excellent health,' replied the inexorable Franklin, 'and if he has been concealing infirmities which render him unfit for his very light duties, he has only to resign.' Instead, Proust asked for further leave, invoking the all-powerful

[1] I, 130, 385-6

name of M. Hanotaux, then Foreign Minister; and just in time for his second visit to Réveillon, leave came.

Whether because she believed *Les Plaisirs et les Jours* would float her drawings to still wider fame, or because she liked people who liked Réveillon, Mme Lemaire had taken a temporary fancy to Proust. The invitation in October came because in August, at Dieppe, she could hardly bear to let him leave for Brittany. But on principle she preferred not to give invitations in the 'bad season', when the garden was past its best. Her daughter Suzette was detailed to speed the coming guests. 'It's fine, though cold, now,' she wrote to Maria Hahn on 19 October, 'but if they dawdle much longer winter will be here, this huge house will be full of draughts and gloom, and I'm afraid Mama won't want them to come—do tell Reynaldo to bring lots of warm clothes, just as if he were spending the winter at the North Pole.' The great chestnuts had turned colour, but still kept their leaves; and the branches, as Proust wrote in one of the last sketches for his coming book,[1] 'seemed like a magnificent comb clasping the flowing golden locks of the leaves'. The autumn visit to Réveillon was almost the last of the events in Proust's life which form the fundamental plot of *Jean Santeuil*. It may be assumed that most of the incidents in the 'Second Visit to Réveillon' of *Jean Santeuil* —the moonlight walks in the hills, the bedroom fires, the delicious food provided by the Duchesse ("I've got them to make you a *soufflé*, my dears, the least I can do is to see you eat well"), the storm that makes Jean long to set off immediately for Penmarch—really occurred. But it will no doubt never be known whether a fellow guest, a 'tall young woman of twenty-two, so kind, cheerful and healthy' really shared Proust's bed, or whether she, too, was a case of 'transposition'. On his return he applied to the Ministry for a whole year's leave, which was granted on 24 December 1895, for nothing could be refused to a protégé of M. Hanotaux.

Another event of the closing year was a dinner on 12 December at Alphonse Daudet's, with Edmond de Goncourt, who hardly spoke, the right-wing journalist Henri Rochefort, Montesquiou, who made the most peculiar serpentine gestures with his hands and chattered infuriatingly about ladies' fashions in the Second Empire, and Albert Flament, who tells the story. When they rose

[1] *'Les Marroniers', P. et J.*, 234-5

from table Montesquiou made a beeline for Flament and asked: "Do you like poetry, and have you read mine?" At one a.m. in the cloakroom Proust gave an imitation of Count Robert's piercing screams to the Daudets' cousins, Adeline and Marthe Allard, muffling the noise against the hanging masses of overcoats. 'Before that evening I'd heard nothing but blame of Proust's idleness, his slavish devotion to Mme Lemaire, his uncontrollable passion for high society, his total lack of personality,' wrote Flament in his diary; but as Proust continued his imitations in the cab going home, Flament was impressed by 'the surprising profundity of his adjectives'.

After eighteen months of complete absorption in Reynaldo Hahn, Proust's interest was now turning to another young man. It was a year before, in the winter of 1894, at a dinner given by Charlotte Baignères, that Proust had first met the great Alphonse Daudet, in whose house Reynaldo was already a regular visitor. "Monsieur de Montesquiou was there," Mme Daudet told her sixteen-year-old son Lucien, "and a charming young man called Marcel Proust, extraordinarily well-read and with beautiful manners—and now go to sleep, dear boy, it's terribly late." Soon Proust was asked to one of the Daudets' Thursday at-homes, and Lucien, who was allowed to serve the coffee before being packed off to bed, remembered his moonlike paleness and jet-black hair, his over-large head drooping on his narrow shoulders, and his enormous eyes, which seemed to take in everything at once without actually looking at anything. "Never in all my days," declared Lucien's grandmother next morning, "have I met a young man so well brought up as that little Monsieur Proust." Lucien was a slim, frail youth, with a classic nose of which he was inordinately proud, and a tiny Chaplinesque moustache: 'a handsome boy,' Jules Renard had written in his journal for 2 March 1895, 'curled and pomaded, painted and powdered, with a little squeaky voice which he takes out of his waistcoat pocket'. He was intelligent, capricious and highly-strung, given to hysterical laughter and weeping, and, a little later, to unhappy relationships with young men of the working classes. His talent for painting and writing came to nothing, crushed by the superiority of his celebrated father and his kind but truculent elder brother, the anti-Semitic, protofascist Léon Daudet. Such was the brilliance of Lucien's conversation—'that astonishing windmill of words which was his only feat of creation'—that André Germain, who married his sister Edmée, thought he had a preponderant influence on the prose-style of Proust; but it is much more probable that the influence was in the opposite direction.

In the autumn of 1895 Lucien, now seventeen, and attending art-school with Albert Flament at the famous studio of M. Jullian, became sufficiently grown up to be interesting. He was invited to tea in Proust's bedroom, where Félicie Fitau, an old servant in a white bonnet, one of the originals of Françoise, brought a dish of cakes, and Proust offered for his entertainment an album of photographs of actresses, writers and society ladies, and the treasured copy of *Gladys Harvey* bound in Mme Hayman's petticoat. "Photographs bore me, I'd rather we talked," declared Lucien disconcertingly; they discussed Jullian's studio, their favourite authors, and Proust's health ("I hardly ever manage to get to the Mazarine Library"); and their friendship began. Soon they met every day. They went to the Louvre, where Proust revelled in Fra Angelico ("His yellows and pinks are creamy and comestible") or, as was Swann's habit, found like-nesses to people they knew in portraits by old masters. "Do you see this Ghirlandaio of the little boy and the old man with a polyp on his nose—it's the very image of the Marquis du Lau"[1]; and with a characteristic dilation of the nostrils Proust would add, "Ah, dear boy, it's *so* amusing to look at pictures!" For a New Year's present, on 31 December 1895, he sent Lucien an eighteenth-century ivory casket, carved with a young lady leaning on an urn and the words '*A l'amitié*'.

Lucien became aware of his brilliant friend's extraordinary simplicity of heart. Sometimes his kindness was absurd but touching: he invited the Daudets' aged maid-servant to an evening at the theatre; and when Lucien prevented him from carrying a heavy parcel for Alphonse Daudet's Italian valet Pietro (Proust always shook hands with the old man, and talked about Dante), he was hurt and angry—"You're violent and heartless," he cried. But sometimes his moral nobility took a dreadfully moving form. Lucien told, as a callous joke, an anec-dote of a schoolfriend who was ashamed of a dowdy mother and

[1] Swann is struck by the resemblance between this picture and M. de Palancy (I, 223).

pretended, when she visited him in the school parlour, that she was a family servant. Proust hid his face in his hands, and Lucien thought he was laughing; but then he saw his friend's cheeks were streaming with tears. 'Marcel Proust was nearer to God than certain hard-hearted and haughty persons I know who are Christians,' he wrote long afterwards. But they shared a keen sense of the ridiculous, and collected clichés of the kind dear to M. de Norpois ('the Emerald Isle', 'our brave little soldiers', 'Albion' instead of England)—which they called *louchonneries*, 'because they make you blink, you know'—and also those of two slightly different varieties which are respectively characteristic of Professor Cottard ('raining cats and dogs', 'deaf as a post') and his wife ('my Abigail' for a maid, 'making an expedition' for a visit to Versailles). Their joint appreciation of people's absurdity brought on a distressing affliction: sooner or later, whenever they went out together, they lapsed into a paroxysm of hysterical laughter. Montesquiou invited them for an evening with Dela-fosse, and they saw fit to warn him, on the pretext that 'we might offend Delafosse', of their propensity to 'blind, agonising, irresistible *fou rire*'. They went, *fou rire* seized them, and Montesquiou never forgot or forgave 'this gross breach of decency'. He remembered the occasion when Lucien as a child (for Count Robert was an old friend of the family) had emptied a plate of bonbons into his top-hat—"He did it on purpose!" he had bitterly cried; and now he told everyone: "Lucien Daudet has a pernicious influence on Marcel Proust." And yet, for a time, just as he had wooed Proust himself, and then Reynaldo Hahn who by now was in disgrace, Montesquiou saw in Lucien a possibility of the longed-for disciple. But the mirage receded, and he sent Mme Daudet an exquisite rose with the message: 'You are a rose, your children are the thorns.' Long afterwards he likened Reynaldo and Lucien to the two thieves, the bad and the good, who were crucified on Calvary: Reynaldo was the bad thief, but Lucien, he hoped, would be with him in Paradise. Montesquiou's involvement with Lucien, however, had one permanent result. He introduced him to his admired Marquise de Casa-Fuerte, who in turn made him known to her aunt the Empress Eugénie; and poor Lucien discovered that his vocation was neither painting nor writing, but to attend the exiled Empress at Farnborough and Cap Martin to the end of her very long life.

Meanwhile, however, perhaps at first only by way of retaliation, Reynaldo himself was straying from their friendship. For a few months, in the spring and early summer of 1896, Proust suffered from excruciating jealousy, in which his anguished curiosity characteristically turned from the present to the past. 'I deserve your reproaches, oftener than you imagine,' he wrote, 'but if ever I do not deserve them, it is in those moments of torturing effort, when by watching a face, or linking one name with another, or reconstituting a past event, I endeavour to fill in the gaps in a life which is dearer to me than all else, but which will continue to cause me the most anxious sorrow until, even in its most innocent details, I know it all.' One evening in society Hahn insisted on staying to supper when Proust begged him to come home. "You'll regret this one day," declared the furious Reynaldo, only to be punished next morning by an appalling letter. 'I owe it to our former friendship not to let you commit such acts of stupidity, spite and cowardice without trying to arouse your conscience, and to persuade you—not to admit, for your pride forbids it—but at least to realise what you have done. ... You don't see that when, after we say good-bye in the evening, I carry away with me the image of a Reynaldo who has ceased to care how he hurts me, I shall no longer have any obstacle to put in the way of my desires, and then nothing will stop me. ... Overwhelmed with remorse for so many evil thoughts, so many weak and wicked intentions, I can't claim to be any better than you are'—and so on. This is the pattern of the many scenes of jealousy in *Les Plaisirs et les Jours,* some written before he met Hahn, all before this most serious of their quarrels: they had occurred, therefore, in Proust's earlier friendships, and we shall find them recurring in later attachments. But the situation revealed in these terrible letters leaves no doubt that in the Françoise episode of *Jean Santeuil,* in Swann's jealousy over Odette and the Narrator's over Albertine, Proust was remembering not only his total experience of love, but the rupture of his love for Reynaldo. His agonies, however, lasted only a few months: it was some consolation for his wounded pride to know that he, in the first place, had jilted Reynaldo, not Reynaldo him; and he still had Lucien. In July, as we shall see shortly, the worst was already over.

Only one obstacle now delayed the publication of *Les Plaisirs et les Jours*: the whole book was now in the hands of Calmann Lévy, with the exception of Anatole France's interminably procrastinated preface. At last, with the help of Mme Arman de Caillavet, Monsieur France was bullied into writing it. A distressing rumour, indeed, which has persisted to this day, declared that Mme Arman had perpetrated the whole preface herself—just as Odette was supposed 'by certain gentlemen of the highest society to have collaborated, more or less, in Bergotte's works'.[1] Only the last phrase, so the rumour went, was by France himself. But the rumour-mongers were mistaken with regard to this last phrase, about Mme Lemaire scattering 'roses and the roses' dew;—'*les roses avec leur rosée*'—which is in fact a quotation from Villiers de l'Isle Adam's well-known poem *Les Présents*; and they were probably equally wrong about the whole preface, which has the inimitable rhythm and preciosity of the master, doing his best to praise a book he does not altogether like or understand. His efforts did Proust little good: for nearly a quarter of a century he was thought of as the writer of whom Anatole France had said: 'he lures us into a hot-house atmosphere, among intelligent orchids whose strange and unhealthy beauty has no roots in the soil . . . there is something in him of a depraved Bernardin de Saint-Pierre and an innocent Petronius'.

Les Plaisirs et les Jours was published on 13 June 1896, at what was then the enormous price of 13 francs 50 centimes. Proust gave away copies to most of the friends and acquaintances who might otherwise have bought his book, and little of the remainder of the edition was sold. There were very few reviews of this luxury quarto. It was automatically praised in *Le Figaro*, *Le Gaulois* and *Le Temps*, because the author was a diner-out, and the illustrations were by Mme Lemaire. His former colleagues of *Le Banquet*, regarding him as a talented traitor to literature, mingled sarcasm with reluctant admiration: Léon Blum in the *Revue Blanche* rebuked him for 'affectation and prettiness—his gifts ought not to be wasted'; and Fernand Gregh in the *Revue de Paris* made fun of his reliance on sponsors—'he has invited all the fairies, without forgetting one, to the cradle of his newborn book'. Charles Maurras, the future anti-Semitic nationalist, wrote benevolently in the *Revue Encyclopédique* of his 'diversity of

---

[1] II, 745. It is true, however, that Mme Arman sometimes helped France in his weekly articles for *L'Univers*.

talents', 'harmonious tonality', and 'pure, transparent language'—
'the new generation will have to acquire the habit of regarding
this young writer as one of its leaders'.[1] But Maurras at this time
was using Mme Arman's salon for the benefit of his career, and
could do no less for her protégé and France's preface. *Les Plaisirs
et les Jours* dropped stone-dead. Proust would not be famous till
a quarter of a century had passed.

To us, with our unfair advantage of after-knowledge, it is
possible to recognise an aspect of *Les Plaisirs et les Jours* which
was invisible to the Banqueters. We can observe, as his contemporaries did, that the author is immature, sentimental,
mannered, acquainted with malice and snobism from the inside,
and aged twenty-five. But we can also see, as they could not, that
these stories are reservoirs of Time Lost, a vat from which, after
their long steeping, Mme Frémer, Baldassare Silvande, Hippolyta,
Honoré will emerge utterly transfigured as Mme Verdurin, Uncle
Adolphe, Oriane de Guermantes, the Narrator. Illiers, Trouville
and Orleans tremble on the verge of becoming Combray, Balbec,
Doncières; and the young Proust is already speaking with
authority of Time, Jealousy, Habit, Oblivion, 'the ephemeral
efficacy of sorrow'. Yet his frivolous though melancholy title,
with its ironic allusion to Hesiod's *Works and Days*, expresses
only one of the double meanings of *Temps Perdu:* he is not yet
consciously aware of Time Lost, but he is remorsefully conscious
of Time Wasted.

[1] As Professor Kolb has pointed out, Maurras also accidentally hit upon
one of Proust's future titles: 'M. Marcel Proust,' he wrote, 'will be a new
witness to truth regained' (*'la vérité retrouvée'*).

Chapter 12

THE EARLY YEARS OF *JEAN SANTEUIL*

THE appearance of *Les Plaisirs et les Jours* was overshadowed in the Proust family by the sudden death, on 10 May 1896, of Great-Uncle Louis Weil. The poor old gentleman hardly knew he was ill. A cold turned to pneumonia overnight; he became unconscious, showed no signs of suffering, and at five in the afternoon departed this life of ladies in pink in Paris and leisured summers in the green garden of Auteuil. So the original of Uncle Adolphe lay, watched by his niece Mme Proust and his great-nephew Marcel, in his town house at 102 Boulevard Haussmann which was to be Proust's home ten years later; they guarded his lifeless body in the very bedroom, then with flesh-pink walls and gilded woodwork, where Proust would sleep by day and write *A la Recherche* all night. Meanwhile, by the terms of his will, the house went to his nephew, Mme Proust's brother, Georges Weil the lawyer.

In accordance with Louis Weil's Jewish faith there was no service for the dead, and he had even asked that his funeral should be 'no flowers by request'. It was an embarrassing moment when, just as the procession of hearse and cabs left 102 Boulevard Haussmann, a cyclist rode up to deliver a magnificent wreath from the lady in pink herself, Mme Hayman. She had shown great tact in not coming in person—'*of course* you wouldn't shock anyone, everybody who knows you admires and likes you, and my great-uncle was so fond of you,' Proust had written, 'but I'm afraid it might tire you, and there'll be so few other ladies there'. For a moment, when he saw the cyclist and the flowers, and thought of old times and the old gentleman, Proust burst into tears; then he took the wreath into his cab and followed his mother, who had left before the incident, to Père La Chaise, half hoping to fall into Mme Hayman's arms there after all. Mme Proust, not to be outdone in tact, had the wreath buried with the coffin; and at the year's end Proust sent Mme Hayman a valuable tie-pin ('I thought it might do for your hat') which had belonged

to Great-Uncle Louis. Among the old man's relics he also discovered a collection of photographs of pretty little, forgotten
actresses, each with a fond inscription, and kept them as a
souvenir. One was of a certain Marie van Zandt, a sweetly
innocent-looking young person in male travesty, with frilled,
knee-length pantaloons: an original of Elstir's sketch of Odette
as Miss Sacripant.[1]

Next month, on 30 June, death returned to take Mme Proust's
father, Nathé Weil. He was a square-faced, hook-nosed old man,
with clean-shaven, rat-trap lips, bristles of white beard from ear to
ear, and an expression of hard incorruptibility. It is said—and one
can almost hear the Narrator's great-aunt at Combray calling:
"Bathilde, come and stop your husband drinking cognac!"—that
he showed his good taste in wines by providing inferior stuff for
his family, while he kept a bottle of the best Bordeaux on the
floor at his feet for his own use. His reluctance to spend a night
away from home—which was inherited by his grandson—was
notorious: the only exception was during the siege of Paris in
1870-71, when he took his wife to Étampes for safety. Grandfather Weil liked to be strict towards Marcel in his earlier youth,
but when he saw the boy in any real distress would show an unexpected, rather touching sympathy. We need not doubt that
Nathé Weil, like M. Sandré in *Jean Santeuil* at the end of the
Marie Kossichef episode, shed tears when he saw Marcel in
despair over his parting with Marie de Benardaky. Proust reproached himself bitterly for his feeling of heartless indifference
at his grandfather's death, and was relieved to find himself, when
he entered the old man's empty room after the funeral, bursting
into uncontrollable weeping. But for Proust, despite his genuine
regret, the passing of Nathé Weil had its compensations: he was
able to tell Montesquiou, who was nagging him to attend the
inauguration of a monument to Marceline Desbordes-Valmore
at Douai on 13 July, that his mother would not hear of his 'going
to a celebration' in this time of mourning. He shamelessly begged

[1] Similarly in *A la Recherche* Morel, the son of Uncle Adolphe's valet,
brings the Narrator a bundle of photographs of actresses as a souvenir of the
dead man. They are inscribed 'To my best friend', and among them is a
reproduction of Elstir's portrait of Miss Sacripant (II, 264-5). Mlle van
Zandt was no doubt either a relative of the Amélie van Zandt who sang
Mignon and created the part of Lakmé at the Opéra Comique in 1883, or
the same person using a different Christian name.

her to corroborate his story if Montesquiou and Yturri, as they threatened, should call to ask her to relent; but neither mourning nor a new attack of asthma prevented him from a round of visits to Mme Arman, Mme Lemaire, Reynaldo at Saint-Cloud, and his publisher Calmann-Lévy. His mother, he told Reynaldo, seemed to be taking her bereavements remarkably well: in fact, as he was to realise a few months later, her heart was broken.

In August he spent a few weeks with her at Mont-Dore, a health-resort in the mountains of the Puy-de-Dôme. Both as a complete mental rest, and as an indirect communication with Reynaldo, he read Reynaldo's favourite author, Dumas; he challenged a fellow-guest at the hotel to a duel, without result; and he received from Dr Cazalis, the original of Legrandin, an over-gushing and under-paid telegram of thanks for a copy of *Les Plaisirs et les Jours*, which cost Mme Proust three francs, 'thus offending,' as he wrote to Reynaldo, 'her twin instincts for economy and concision'. But even in that mountain-air asthma awaited him. Hay-making, several months late in the high hills, was in full progress, and a violent attack of hay-fever drove him back to Paris.

On the eve of his departure he wrote to Reynaldo—who was now, after five weeks spent in Hamburg with Proust's blessing, at Villers-sur-Mer near Cabourg—a letter which sounded the knell of their love and marked the beginning of their friendship. They had released one another from all vows of fidelity and chastity: 'it would be noble, perhaps, but it would not be natural at our age to live as Tolstoy demands of us'. Proust had made the condition that Reynaldo should confess any new lapses, while poor Reynaldo, on the contrary, asked only that Proust should keep quiet about his. 'In future you needn't tell me anything,' Proust wrote, 'seeing it upsets you so. But you'll never find a confessor more gentle, more understanding (alas!) and more un-humiliating—since, if it hadn't been you who asked for silence, and I for avowal, the situation would be reversed: your heart would be the confessional, and I the sinner begging for absolu-tion, for I am as weak as you, or weaker.'

In September Mme Proust continued her interrupted holiday at Dieppe, bathing under medical orders, bruising her feet on the pebbles, and walking like her dead mother in the wind and rain. Proust stayed alone with the servants at home, smoking Espic anti-asthma cigarettes, fumigating with Legras powders, and drugging himself to sleep with amyl, valerian and trional. He dreamed he was at a charity fête at Mme Hochon's (another original of Mme Verdurin), with Mme Lemaire on his arm and the actress Mme Pierson somewhere in the room, and awoke tortured with guilt for having gone into society when still in mourning. Old Félicie came to say the gas-man had called and she was alone in the house; but "I think I'll go down," she concluded, Françoise-like, "the man has such an honest face."

Early in October, when the family was united again, came a state occasion which in *A la Recherche*, where it is relegated to a period ten years earlier in the Narrator's life, became the visit of King Theodosius II. The Emperor Nicolas II of Russia came to Paris as the guest of Félix Faure, the father of Antoinette and Lucie, Proust's playmates in the time of Marie de Benardaky, and now President of the Republic. The trees in the Champs-Élysées were hung with coloured globes of celluloid, paper flowers, and garlands of the new electric lights—most of which, it was discovered when dusk fell, refused to work; and the pale, frigid, twenty-eight-year-old Tzar rode in the presidential landau through frenzied crowds, visibly alarmed at the violence of their cheering. The royalist Duc Honoré de Luynes said hopefully: "The Government has dropped a brick, you can see how the French people love monarchy"; but what the people loved was to have their republic treated as an equal by an emperor. The visit was engineered by the French ambassador at St Petersburg, Marquis Gustave de Montebello, the original of M. de Vaugoubert who arranged the visit of King Theodosius; and the noun 'affinities' which so enraptured M. de Norpois was suggested by the Tzar's equally vague reference (for the word 'alliance' was still taboo) to the 'precious links that unite our two nations'. Two originals of M. de Norpois, Armand Nisard, Marie de Benardaky's uncle by marriage, then director of political affairs at the Quai d'Orsay, and the Foreign Minister Gabriel Hanotaux, both friends of Dr Proust, were present at the state banquet at the Élysée Palace on 6 October when these momentous words were spoken; and it is more than likely that one or the other visited 9 Boulevard Malesherbes soon after, like M. de Norpois when he 'came to dinner for the first time', to dine on Félicie's spiced beef jelly and recount his emotions on hearing the Tzar say 'precious links'.

Another episode in the career of the Vaugouberts is taken from the Montebellos. Mme de Vaugoubert ruins her husband's career by insulting the French ministers' wives during a second visit of King Theodosius, when she monopolises the attention of her friend Queen Eudoxie.[1] Similarly, on the occasion of the reception held at Compiègne during Nicolas II's second state visit to France in September 1901, Mme de Montebello neglected to inform the ministers' wives that hats were *de rigueur*. The ladies disgraced themselves by appearing bareheaded; the only hats to be seen were those of the Empress Alexandra and Mme de Montebello; and it was rumoured that her husband's dismissal by the Combes government in 1902 was in retaliation for this unfortunate incident.[2]

On 19 October Proust went to Fontainebleau, with visions of sunlight on brown leaves, for a writing holiday at the Hôtel de France et d'Angleterre with Lucien's elder brother Léon. Léon Daudet remembered that week as a halcyon period of afternoon walks in the forest, evening drives by moonlight ('Proust, that most enchanting, fantastic and unreal of companions, was like a will-o'-the-wisp at my side in the victoria') and conversations by the fire in the deserted hotel lounge; and for Proust, too, it mellowed sufficiently to play its part in the creation of Doncières. But at the time it seemed a damp inferno of real and imaginary woes. The trees were annoyingly green, it never stopped raining, and they grimly took their daily walk, hearing the horns and baying of a distant hunt, under a steady downpour. His bed was a hateful four-poster, with suffocating curtains and a canopy that seemed always about to fall and crush him; it faced the wrong way; he had asthma and could not sleep. Lucien's longed-for visit on the 22nd ended in a tiff. There was nothing to read but a biography of the Du Barry, which seemed still to preserve the odour of railway-carriages and the excruciating melancholy of departure, for he had started it in the train. He sent urgent and intensely complicated orders to Mme Proust for the despatch of his umbrella, a tie-pin, watch, hat, four Balzacs, *Wilhelm Meister*, Shakespeare's *Julius Caesar* and George Eliot's *Middlemarch*, more money. Thirty francs vanished through a hole in his trouser-

[1] III, 246
[2] The true reason was the change of emphasis in relations with Russia necessitated by the new Entente Cordiale with England.

pocket—an accident which happened with such distressing regularity whenever he went on holiday without his parents, that one suspects him of prevarication to conceal extravagance which he dared not confess. 'The thought pursues me like a crime, a crime against you almost. I can quite understand people who commit suicide for nothing at all.' Mme Proust sent reassuring letters with '100 francs and 100,000 kisses', and offered to take a house for him at Versailles, or to send him to Illiers, 'where you were as miraculously well in the cold weather as you were ill in the hot'. And the weather that year, she pointed out, was quite as dreadful everywhere else as at Fontainebleau: indeed, Dr Proust (who shared the Narrator's father's passion for meteorology) had just made her read him a long article in the *Journal des Débats*, 'which sets out to prove that whenever the weather's bad there's always a reason for it!' But a few days later he returned home, defeated. There had been a real cause behind the misery for which he made so many absurd excuses; he had come suddenly, in another person, upon the abyss of irrevocability, of suffering greater than any of his own. He had experienced a first terrible glimpse of Time Lost.

On 20 October, the day after his departure, Mme Proust had crossed the Boulevard Malesherbes to Cerisier's bakery at No. 8 to telephone her son. 'But Cerisier's subscription didn't include calls outside Paris, and despite all my offers to the Ladies of the Telephone to pay extra, they banished me to the public cabin.' When the call at last reached Proust in the hotel at Fontainebleau he was already anxious and hypersensitised by a long wait. In the disembodied voice of his mother he detected for the first time the note of incurable grief for her dead parents, which at home in Paris the familiar sight of her cheerful, self-sacrificing face had made inaudible. 'When her poor voice reached me,' he wrote to Antoine Bibesco six years later, 'it was broken and bruised, for ever changed from the voice I had known, full of cracks and crevices; and it was only when I reconstituted in the telephone-receiver those shattered and bleeding fragments of words, that I had for the first time the horrible feeling of all that was broken inside her.' He had the thrift and presence of mind, however, to write down his experience immediately and send the manuscript, to his mother: 'please *keep* it, and remember where you put it because it will come in my novel'; and Mme Proust kept it, good-humouredly commenting: 'the story of a convict on his way to Devil's Island could hardly be more despairing'. The incident appears in *Jean Santeuil*, when the hero telephones to his mother from Beg-Meil: Proust even forgot to make the transposition from Fontainebleau to Beg-Meil complete, since Jean thinks of returning immediately to Paris and being with his mother in three hours' time, which would only be possible from Fontainebleau. But in *Jean Santeuil*, as is characteristic of that novel, the keynote is not Jean's awareness of his mother's grief, but his pity for himself. When the Narrator telephones his grandmother from Doncières, yet another theme has taken first place. The Ladies of the Telephone (the phrase is not Proust's own, but the usual Parisian expression, which we have just seen his mother using on this very occasion, for the girl operators at the exchange) have become supernatural deities of the underworld, 'the Danaids of the Invisible'. Perhaps Proust felt a hint of this at the time, for the experience of speaking to an absent person, as if to a talking wraith, through a little black trumpet, was still unusual enough to be uncanny. But in *Le Côté de Guermantes* the episode is a preparation for the death of the grandmother, and it was written after his mother's death.

Proust had now been writing *Jean Santeuil* for a year. As Professor Kolb's study of the original manuscript has shown, the whole of Part I[1] (from the mother's kiss to Jean's early schooldays) was written at Beg-Meil in September-October 1895[2]: it was for this, then, that Proust's friend the fisher-boy kept a bottle of ink in his boat. Some, at least, of Part VI (Jean and Henri's holiday at Beg-Meil) dates from the same time,[3] as also does Part

[1] It is convenient here to refer to *Jean Santeuil* by its 'parts', rather than by the volumes as published, except that page-references must of course be made by the volume.

[2] All six chapters are written mostly on the same cheap local paper ('I'm in a place called Beg-Meil, where you can't get paper,' Proust had written to Robert de Billy). Several pages are written on the backs of draft letters to M. Franklin of the Mazarine Library, asking for an extension of leave from 15 October to 15 December 1895—the leave Proust needed for his November visit to Réveillon.

[3] One page is written on the verso of a letter dated 10 October 1895, extending Proust's and Hahn's return-tickets for a further ten days— a concession for which Proust had characteristically applied direct to André Bénac, who was a member of the government railway commission.

VII, Chapter V ('*Une Petite Ville de Province*').[1] The introductory chapter (in which the novelist C. is met in Brittany, and
after his death a few years later leaves the manuscript of the novel
to his young friends) was not composed until March 1896, at the
home of Léon Yeatman, to whom Proust immediately read it:
'Léon said it was typically "pony",' he told Reynaldo. This was
written in a manuscript-book, no doubt the same of which he told
his mother in August, 'I have paginated the first 90 pages.' In
September he wrote the incident of the children's book with the
picture of the moon with a funny face, which occurs in the
Étreuilles section (Part II, Chapter IV); and a little later he had
filled the 110 leaves of this book, 'besides the loose leaves I
worked on before'. The loose leaves are no doubt Part I, written
at Beg-Meil; so we may deduce that the exercise-book contained,
besides the introductory chapter, all or most of Part II (Étreuilles).
At this time—mid-September 1896—he was negotiating with
Calmann-Lévy for the eventual publication of his novel, and
thought that by working four hours a day he might finish it by
1 February 1897. At Fontainebleau in October 1896 he wrote,
besides the telephone scene at Beg-Meil (Part VI, Chapter II), a
part of the Charlotte Clissette episode in Part X. Part III,
Chapter VIII ('*Une Séance à la Chambre*'), in which the Armenian
massacres of August 1896 are mentioned, dates from shortly after
his return to Paris. Since the next chapters which can be dated by

---

[1] It is written on the official notepaper of the yacht-club at Étel, a little
port on the mainland opposite Belle-Isle. The place described in this chapter
is evidently Fontainebleau, and was in fact called Fontainebleau in the
original manuscript, though Proust later substituted the reading of the
published version, 'Provins'. Ought we to assume that the chapter dates
from after Proust's visit to Fontainebleau in October 1896, and that he had
saved the paper from the year before? Probably not; for Jean's cheerful
bedroom in the hotel, which comforts his homesickness and is clearly the
original of the Narrator's room at Doncières, is very different from the
hated room of October 1896; and the group of young officers whom he
meets in the following pages, and who resemble so closely the Narrator's
friends at Doncières, is equally foreign to the stay at Fontainebleau with
Léon Daudet. But these features may well belong to an earlier visit to
Fontainebleau, perhaps in the autumn of 1893, when his friends Louis
de la Salle and Daniel Halévy were conscripts there. If so, there is
no longer any need to doubt that this chapter was written at Beg-Meil;
and, what is more, the mystery of the primary origin of Doncières is
solved.

evidence now available belong mostly to Part VIII and begin in August 1897, we may reasonably assume that the interval between October 1896 and August 1897 was occupied with the composition of Parts IV, VI and VII, which describe the summer at Réveillon, the visit to Beg-Meil, and the second, winter stay at Réveillon. With the exception of the Dreyfus Case episodes in Part V, Chapters V-IX and a few episodes in Parts VIII-X, the plot of *Jean Santeuil* is the story of Proust's own life up to the end of 1895. It is probable, therefore, that he foresaw and planned the greater part of his novel during the first few months of its composition. The material is the same as that used in the first half of *A la Recherche*, up to the end, say, of the Princesse de Guermantes's soirée in *Sodome et Gomorrhe*. But Proust's selection of it is often different: Charlus and Sodom appear only briefly in *Jean Santeuil*, for they were not fit reading for his mother in her lifetime; the Narrator's schooldays are rarely mentioned in *A la Recherche*; and the story of Swann and Odette is told of Jean and Françoise S. Proust had not yet discovered the master-theme of Time, which would enable him to bring creative imagination to bear upon reality. Because the novel is supposed to be the middle-aged novelist C.'s story of his own youth, there is a basic inconsistency in the time-scheme, far more serious than those in *A la Recherche*,[1] which the reader accepts as mysterious but credible loops in the dimension of Time. Jean is born in 1859, Henri meets the Dutch nun in 1866 (at least ten years too early); yet otherwise the time-scale is that of Proust's own life, and when Jean is in his early twenties he takes part in the events of the Dreyfus Case which belong to 1898. But it is more important to note that Proust is already wrestling with Time, than to complain that he does so without success.

The narrative opens, like *Confession d'une jeune fille* and *Du Côté de chez Swann*, with the crucial incident of the moonlit garden at Auteuil[2] and the mother's kiss refused and exacted. Then Grandfather Weil as M. Sandré deplores, one evening at

---

[1] E.g. the Narrator's encounter with the Lady in Pink, who is Odette before she met Swann, although Odette's affair with Swann happened before the Narrator's birth; the immense age of Odette and Mme Verdurin in *Le Temps Retrouvé*, etc.

[2] Here called Saint-Germain, but later (vol. 3, 307) Auteuil.

Dieppe,[1] the possibility that Jean may become a poet—"you might as well give him a rope and tell him to hang himself!" The year is 1866, and Jean is seven years old; but in Proust's own life this discussion belongs rather to 1893, when he was ordered to choose a career; and M. Santeuil's remark that 'the new Minister of Foreign Affairs has quite a good opinion of writers' is an allusion to Gabriel Hanotaux, who became Foreign Minister in May 1894 and gave the judiciously qualified support to Proust's literary career that is attributed in *A l'Ombre* to M. de Norpois. After a gap of seven years Jean falls in love with Marie Kossichef in the Champs-Élysées, and is parted from her not by his own decision (as was the Narrator from Gilberte) but by the cruelty of his parents. He is sent to the Lycée Henri-Quatre, where his schoolmaster Rustinlor speaks the Homeric language of Bloch; and he pays his unsuccessful visit to the brothel in the Rue Boudreau.

The Easter and May-month interlude at Étreuilles,[2] a half-way stage between Illiers and Combray, belongs both in Proust's own life and in *Du Côté de chez Swann* to the period before the Champs-Élysées, but is displaced in *Jean Santeuil* to the middle of the hero's schooldays. The house in which the family stays, which in real life was the property of Uncle Jules Amiot and in *Swann* was to be that of Aunt Léonie, belongs at one moment (for Proust was undecided) to Jean's paternal grandfather, and then to his father's brother-in-law and sister, the Sureaus. M. Sureau, like Jules Amiot, keeps a draper's shop in the market-place. The garden beyond the river, which later became Swann's Tansonville, and was never entered by the Narrator or his family, is here still owned, like the Pré Catelan at Illiers, by the 'early-rising, gardening uncle'. The servant, who like Françoise kills a chicken and ill-treats the kitchen-maid, is given the real Christian-name of her original, Ernestine Gallou. In many ways Étreuilles already resembles Combray: we meet, in turn, the buzzing flies and hammering in the street by which the hero in his darkened bed-room deduces the heat of the summer's day, the corn-poppy nodding in the plain, the strawberries and cream-cheese, the pink

---

[1] Nathé Weil paid at least one visit to Dieppe, but in accordance with his well-known habit left the same day, rather than spend a night away from Paris. (Cf. *Corr. Mme Proust*, 125.)

[2] The name Étreuilles is taken from Épeautrolles, a village five miles east of Illiers.

and white hawthorn-chapels, the orris-roots in the lavatory, the magic-lantern with Golo and Geneviève de Brabant. But Swann, Gilberte and the Duchesse de Guermantes are absent; there is no Eulalie, and the invalid aunt, Mme Sureau, though she is allowed in a brief episode to question Ernestine on the passers-by in the street, is not given the importance of Aunt Léonie. Sunday mass in the church is described, but not the church itself, nor the parish priest. The Two Ways, along which the whole of *A la Recherche* was to be constructed, remain un-thought of; the dancing spires of Martinville-le-Sec remain invisible until Proust repeats the experience at Caen in 1907; and Montjouvain receives only a passing mention as a place where the family sometimes picnics. The river is still named the Loir; and Proust sometimes forgets himself, and calls the village Illiers, and himself not 'Jean' but 'I'.

When the story re-opens in Part III Jean is seventeen, and beginning his year of *philosophie*. He meets his new schoolmaster, M. Beulier,[1] who is modelled closely on Alphonse Darlu, and a new schoolfellow, Henri, son of the Duc and Duchesse de Réveillon. His parents forbid him to dine out with Henri, unjustly suspecting that the two boys mean to spend the evening with prostitutes, and Jean quarrels with them violently. This parental interference may well have occurred in Proust's late teens, and is less likely to belong to the mid-1890s, when his mother and father usually forbore to meddle with his private life; but the other circumstances of the scene are taken, as we shall see, from a quarrel which occurred in or about May 1897. In Chapter VI Henri's name is suddenly changed to Bertrand de Réveillon, and the character described, in particular his walking, like Saint-Loup, along the partition in a restaurant to fetch Jean's greatcoat, is recognisable as Bertrand de Fénelon. Proust perhaps did not meet Fénelon until November 1901, and this chapter is thus the only one in *Jean Santeuil* which seems likely to have been written after he virtually abandoned his novel in the autumn of 1899.

Part IV describes a summer visit to Réveillon, the château of Henri's parents. Réveillon is modelled on Mme Lemaire's country-house of the same name; and the visit corresponds to Proust's

---

[1] The episode in the classroom cannot have been written before 1897, for it is clearly a counterblast to the opening chapter of Barrès's *Les Déracinés*, which appeared in that year.

stay at Mme Lemaire's Réveillon with Reynaldo Hahn in August-September 1894. The story of the rosebush is told; Henri is an accomplished musician for the moment, to suit his identification here with Reynaldo; and a sister of Henri, Mlle de Réveillon, appears in place of Mme Lemaire's daughter Suzette. The visit to the farmyard and the peacock with the Duchesse is taken from Proust's stay with Pierre Lavallée at Segrez in April 1895. Anatole France, who had no business at Mme Lemaire's Réveillon, appears as the novelist Monsieur de Traves, and is severely criticised as 'an adept of materialist and sceptic philosophy' by the idealist Jean. But M. de Traves already prefigures Bergotte in 'the mysterious resemblance of all his books to one another', in the fact that 'neither his appearance, nor his conversation, nor anything that Jean heard of his life were in any way a continuation of the strange enchantment, the unique world into which he transported one from the very first pages of any of his books'. One of his absurdest shortcomings, as it seems to Jean, apparently with Proust's approval, is his habit of explaining the beauty of a great work by some minute, material detail ("Yes, it's beautiful, because Rome is such a very beautiful word, don't you think?" or "A lance, that's pretty fine, isn't it?"). Yet in *A la Recherche* this foible, which also belonged to Anatole France, is one of the symptoms of Bergotte's genius, and culminates in his obsession with the patch of yellow on the wall in Vermeer's View of Delft, which brought to the dying novelist both death and salvation. Another visitor at Réveillon is Jean's former schoolmaster Rustinlor, now more like Bloch than ever: when Jean admires Barrès, Rustinlor says, "A pretty bad egg, and the same goes for his books"; and despite his fierce hatred of the aristocracy he calls the Réveillons, after dining with them, "exquisite creatures, with a faraway mediaeval quality which I for one find intensely poetic".

Part V, a political interlude, consists of the downfall of the imaginary politician Charles Marie, followed by scenes from the Dreyfus Case belonging to 1898. The episode of the Marie scandal is no doubt based on the Panama affair of 1892, in which several prominent statesmen, including Floquet, Clemenceau, Freycinet and Maurice Rouvier (who, like Charles Marie, was Minister of Finance at the time and a bitter opponent of the proposed income tax), were accused of receiving bribes from the Panama Canal Company. The politicians implicated in the scandal were, unfortunately, the same who in 1889 had opposed and destroyed the nationalist and proto-fascist movement of General Boulanger. Panama was the second round in the struggle between right and left, army and anti-militarists, anti-Semites and Jews, Catholics and anti-clericals, royalists and republicans, nobility and bourgeois, of which the Dreyfus Case was to be the third. France was already, several years before the Dreyfus Case, in process of division into two hostile halves, of which Proust was committed, against the majority of his hostesses in the Faubourg Saint-Germain, to that of the Jews and the progressive intellectuals. But the division was not yet clear-cut at the time of Panama, when the nationalists to the right and socialists to the left were banded in unnatural union against the receivers of bribes. In so far as the extreme right and left oppositions were enemies of corruption, any decent bourgeois, including Proust himself, could not but support them. But in so far as their motives were impure, aiming at political revenge rather than justice, it was possible to sympathise with the politicians exposed in 1892, as Jean sympathises with Charles Marie, and to regard them as victims of a hypocritical intrigue. Although the chapters on the Dreyfus Case form a logical pendant to those on the Marie Scandal, it is doubtful whether they would have remained juxtaposed if Proust had completed his novel, since they are separated historically by an interval of nearly six years. The episode of the Affair will be noticed in its chronological place, at the beginning of 1898.

All but three chapters of Part VI are based with little alteration on Proust's holiday at Beg-Meil with Hahn in September-October 1895. But the telephone conversation with his mother in Chapter II is imported from the week with Léon Daudet at Fontainebleau in October 1896; Chapter VII, in which Jean finds himself with his mother a year later 'at a health-resort in a valley surrounded by high mountains', is a reminiscence of August 1896 at Mont-Dore; and Chapter VIII, 'Beg-Meil in Holland', recalls a visit to Holland in October 1898.

Most of the material for Part VII, the winter visit to Réveillon, comes from Proust's stay with Reynaldo Hahn at Mme Lemaire's château in November 1895. But the scenes of garrison life in Chapters IV-VI and IX, which form a preliminary sketch for Doncières, come from other periods in Proust's life, from his own military service at Orleans, and from visits to conscript friends, Risler at Chartres in 1895 and perhaps Louis de la Salle at Fontainebleau in 1893. The garrison-town is called Provins, 'two hours distant from Réveillon'—and in fact Provins was only some forty miles by rail from Mme Lemaire's Réveillon. But in the manuscript Proust first wrote 'Fontainebleau', and at first the town described is indeed Fontainebleau, with its Hôtel d'Angleterre 'in the Place d'Armes opposite the Château', and the cheerful vista of three rooms which reappears at Doncières. Proust has not yet decided precisely how the scenes of army-life are to be introduced into his novel: at one moment Jean is visiting officer friends with Henri de Réveillon, at another Henri himself is an officer, and then again Jean is a volunteer private not at Provins but at Orleans, walking from barracks, like Proust himself, through the Faubourg Bannier to his lodgings at Mme Renvoyzé's. Jean meets the Bonapartist Prince de Borodino, who is based on Captain Walewski at Orleans, and reappears at Doncières. One of the Réveillon episodes is among the last to be written in the whole novel: the young poetess of Chapter VIII, the Vicomtesse Gaspard de Réveillon, is Comtesse Mathieu (Anna) de Noailles, and the verses she has just published in the *Revue des Deux Mondes* are those by Mme de Noailles in the *Revue de Paris* for 1 February 1899.

'I mean you to be ever-present in my novel,' Proust wrote to Reynaldo Hahn in March 1896, 'like a god in disguise whom no mortal can recognise.' The metamorphosis of the Jewish, middle-class Reynaldo Hahn into the blue-blooded Henri de Réveillon, a prefiguration of Saint-Loup, is even more astonishing than that of Mme Lemaire—who produced in the opposite direction merges with Mme Verdurin—into the Duchesse de Réveillon his mother. Proust intended it, no doubt, as an apotheosis for his friend, and a wish-fulfilment for his own longing to love a Reynaldo of noble birth. The same desire, compounded from his twin vices of homosexuality and snobbism, which had caused him at first to invent Henri de Réveillon, led him afterwards to seek him out in real life. But it was not until several years later, in the early 1900s, that he made friends with the group of young aristocrats who were the collective models for Saint-Loup; and it remains paradoxically true of Saint-Loup that Proust created the character before he met the original.

Henri's parents present a similar paradox. From the benevolent but rapacious Mme-Verdurin-like hospitality of Mme Lemaire Proust created the Duchesse de Réveillon, with her "I've asked them to make a *soufflé*, my dears, the least I can do is to see you eat well"; and since the Widow had no husband, he presented her with a consort whose Olympian bonhomie and snobism are drawn from Comte Greffulhe. The Duc and Duchesse de Réveillon are a homely, dowdy couple; yet with their dukedom dating from the year 887, incredibly senior, by many centuries, even to that of the La Trémoïlles, their social prestige, their inexplicable, almost parental regard for the hero, they foreshadow the Duc and Duchesse de Guermantes. But here fate was less kind to Proust, or rather, his desire to provide himself with noble parent-substitutes was less practical than his desire for a noble Reynaldo-substitute. He was never to take the trouble to become the darling of a ducal château.

And so, through the second half of the 1890s, he worked upon a novel which he hoped would reveal the inner, universal meaning of his childhood and early manhood, a novel, that is, that tells the same story and has the same intention as *A la Recherche* itself. He hoped; but the meaning eluded him, buried deep and inaccessible beneath the vague excitement with which he wrote. He was still living in the illusory world of Time, floating on the dead sea of the phenomenal world and trying in vain to drown: he could not regain Time because he had not yet lost it. Between all the lines of *Jean Santeuil* is his effort to believe he is writing a great novel, his unwilling admission that his work is doomed from the beginning to sterility. There is something heroic in his premature endeavour, his four years' persistence, his ultimate abandonment of this marvellous failure. But as early as September 1896 he wrote to his mother: 'I can't see anything in it, and I feel sure the result will be detestable'; and *Jean Santeuil*, providentially, was not to be Proust's masterpiece, any more than it was to be delivered complete to Calmann-Lévy on 1 February 1897.

In December 1896 he met, without recognising her, the Ariadne whose thread was to lead him near to the heart of the labyrinth. The beautiful Marie Nordlinger, a young English cousin of Reynaldo Hahn, had arrived from darkest Manchester to study painting and sculpture in Paris; and one evening, when Proust called for his friend on the way to some soirée, he found her added to the group of Reynaldo and his sisters which he used to call 'Apollo surrounded by the Muses'. The visitor from the land of George Eliot and Willie Heath was short and slender, with delicate Pre-Raphaelite hands, dark eyes, full lips, and a look of warm sincerity and intelligence. For the eighteen months of her stay, although at this time they never ceased to call one another 'Monsieur' and 'Mademoiselle', she belonged to Proust's circle; and often, when he called on Mme Hahn, he came not to take Reynaldo away but to stay the evening. They talked endlessly about *vers libre*, metaphor, symbolism and gothic cathedrals (which Reynaldo, a classicist in everything, could not abide); they chose for one another the artists most fitted to paint their portraits, Titian for Marie, El Greco for Coco de Madrazo, Pisanello or Whistler for Proust; or they played paper-games. One evening each was asked to confess his worst faults. Coco freely admitted that his was laziness, and "Quite right, Coco!" everyone approved. Reynaldo's was jealousy, "jealousy and pride"; and Proust, following his friend on to this dangerous ground, declared with much insight: "I'm inordinately jealous, but if anything I'm too humble." They visited the Italian primitives and the Chardins at the Louvre, and the Monets at Durand-Ruel's gallery. One afternoon in July 1897 they went to tea, like the Narrator and Albertine with Elstir,[1] at Alexander Harrison's studio in the Rue Campagne-Première in Montparnasse, and inspected innumerable seascapes of Beg-Meil at dawn, noon and night. 'I little thought I was having tea with Elstir,' Marie Nordlinger wrote long afterwards. But at this early period in their friendship the true function of Miss Nordlinger as the Muse of England and harbinger of Ruskin remained unrecognised: indeed, Proust started on the wrong foot by asking whether she had seen Verlaine on his last visit to London. She had not, and received a reproachful gaze and a murmur of "Oh dear, what a pity!"

It was an unkind stroke of fate that, when he had already begun to forget the failure of his short stories, and thought only of the future glory of *Jean Santeuil*, he should be subjected to two distressing attacks on *Les Plaisirs et les Jours*. The first was an article in *Le Journal* on 3 February 1897, signed Raitif de la Bretonne, which everyone knew to be a pseudonym of the decadent novelist and infamous columnist Jean Lorrain. The real

[1] I, 870-6

object of Lorrain's malice, however, which only made it the more galling, was not Proust himself but Montesquiou.

Lorrain was a large, flaccid invert, rather in the manner of Baron Doasan, who was a great friend of his. He drugged, painted and powdered, and wore loads of jewelled rings on his fat, white, fish-like fingers. His lips were moist and red, his eyes were as blue as the circles that surrounded them; and over them hung extraordinary, paralytic eyelids, 'like the hoods on the front of an omnibus,' as Jules Renard said. Lorrain belonged to that dangerous type of invert which tries to avert scandal by pretending to be virile and accusing everyone else of perversion. In 1902, the year of *Pelléas and Mélisande*, he attacked the admirers of Debussy in an article shamelessly entitled '*Les Pelléastres*'; and in his volume of poems *Le Sang des Dieux* (1882) an ostentatiously heterosexual sonnet-sequence beginning '*Filles adorables du reve!*' was dedicated to Doasan, while another called 'Les Ephèbes', on the beautiful youths of classical antiquity—Ganymede, Alexis, Hylas, Antinous and others—was addressed with equal inappropriateness to Flaubert. Lorrain had many respectable friends, who forgave everything for his prose-style or pitied his unhappy life, and was received by some easy-going hostesses, though barred by most: "It's terrible," said Mme Germain, the banker's wife, "I hear he gives little dances for young persons in the artillery!" But he was a perilous acquaintance. On one occasion he asked Heredia to come to Mme de Poilly's soirée: "I'd rather not," replied Heredia lightly, "because, like Diana of the Ephesians, she has several rows of breasts, one above the other." Before long the poet was horrified to find his little joke quoted word for word in an article of Lorrain's, but used of poor Mme Aubernon, with whom Lorrain happened to have quarrelled, and of whom it was equally true; and as Lorrain had a genuine admiration for Heredia, he had added: 'as the great poet Heredia has so beautifully put it'.

It was the sonnet on Antinous that established contact between Lorrain and Montesquiou. Count Robert was so favourably impressed by the lines

> '*He has the narrow forehead and broad eyes*
> *Of passive striplings loved by perverse gods*'

that he asked to be allowed to call. The causes of their subsequent

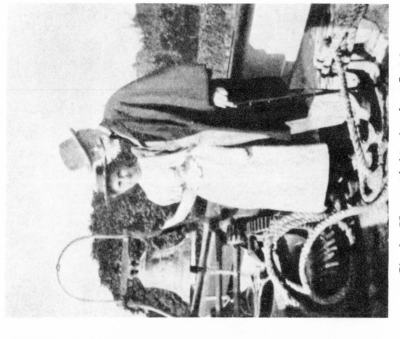

Charles Haas with his daughter Luisita
on the Lake of Thun

Charles Haas, Mme Straus, Albert Cavé
(a friend of Degas) and Émile Straus

Comtesse Laure de Chevigné   Comtesse Élisabeth Greffulhe, 1896

Portrait of Comte Robert de Montesquiou by Boldini, 1897

quarrel are obscure, for we are not compelled to believe the Count's explanation that Lorrain was hurt by his polite refusal to accept the dedication of a new book. Montesquiou soon found he was attacked by Lorrain on every opportunity both in print and in private. One such occasion was the publication in June 1896 of *Les Hortensias bleus*, which earned for Montesquiou from Léon Daudet the nickname of 'Hortensiou' (this was almost more damaging than Forain's 'Grotesquiou'). Proust, unfortunately, was mentioned with approbation in the preface, and Lorrain, leaping to conclusions as to the intimacy of their relationship, had referred to him in his review of 1 July as 'one of those pretty little society boys who've managed to get themselves pregnant with literature'. In *Le Journal* for 3 February 1897 appeared a still more serious libel. Lorrain wrote of the 'elegiac mawkishness' of *Les Plaisirs et les Jours*, 'those elegant, subtle little nothings, thwarted affections, vicarious flirtations, all in a precious and pretentious prose, with Mme Lemaire's flowers strewn by way of symbols all over the margins. All the same, M. Marcel Proust has had his preface from M. Anatole France, who wouldn't have done as much for Marcel Schwob, or Pierre Louys, or Maurice Barrès; but'—and here came the sting in the tail—'such is the way the world wags, and you may be sure that for his next volume M. Proust will extract a preface from the intransigent Alphonse Daudet himself, who won't be able to refuse this service either to Mme Lemaire or to his son Lucien.' Only the most inattentive of *Le Journal's* hundreds of thousands of readers could fail to understand that this was a public accusation of homosexuality, involving both Proust and Lucien Daudet. There was only one way to answer it, and to stop further attacks; and Proust sprang with alacrity to the defence of his friend's honour and his own. Only three days later, on the 6th, he fought a duel with his enemy.

It was a cold, rainy afternoon at the Tour de Villebon in the Bois de Meudon, a traditional duelling-ground for quarrelling Parisians. Lorrain's seconds were Paul Adam, the novelist, who was later on Proust's side in the Dreyfus Affair, and Octave Uzanne, the art-critic, who arrived half an hour late with a grey, drawn face, still under the influence of morphine. Proust's own seconds were a positive social triumph: he had succeeded in persuading Jean Béraud, the painter at Mme Lemaire's, not only to act on his behalf but to bring his great friend, Gustave de Borda, familiarly known as Sword-Thrust Borda. Thus, when the Narrator tells Albertine of a duel he has fought, she remarks: "What very high-class seconds!"[1] Borda had been for many years an unbeatable challenger, and later a much sought-after second in society duels: his assistance was a guarantee of social distinction and, indeed, of virility. This time, however, the weapon was pistols. The combatants exchanged two ineffective shots at a distance of twenty-five yards, probably, as decency demanded except in a life-and-death quarrel, firing into the air. As *Le Figaro* reported on the 7th, 'no one was hurt, and the seconds pronounced that this meeting put an end to the dispute'. "Proust behaved very pluckily, though he wasn't physically strong," Béraud told Robert Dreyfus many years later; Reynaldo, who had come to see his friend through, wrote in his diary: 'Marcel's coolness and firmness during these three days seemed incompatible with his nervous disposition, but did not surprise me in the least'; and Robert de Flers, who was also present, wrote to Gaston de Caillavet: 'Marcel was brave, frail and charming.' Next morning letters of congratulation flowed in, including one from Willy, otherwise Henri Gauthier-Villars, the witty, shifty first husband of the young Colette; but this had to be kept from Mme Arman, who had quarrelled with Willy and had already given Proust a severe wigging for not dropping his acquaintance.

After the duel Lorrain let Proust lie, but assailed Montesquiou with redoubled venom. In the April of 1897 Count Robert was much in view. His verses on Delafosse's piano-playing, entitled *Flower-Quintet*, appeared in *Le Figaro* on the 10th; and on the 23rd his portrait by Boldini—an almost spherical society-painter of whom Mme Straus said "He looks like a toad in a strawberry-bed"—was one of the sensations of the Spring Salon at the Champ de Mars. Boldini had done his utmost to represent the Count, fiercely contemplating a blue-porcelain-handled walking-cane which he clutched like a rapier, as the image of his ancestor d'Artagnan. But the fluidity of the subject's attitude was quite embarrassing, and it was noticeable that his cuff-links, too, were of blue porcelain to match. 'This year,' wrote Lorrain, 'M. Robert de Montesquiou has confided the task of reproducing his elegant silhouette to M. Boldini, that habitual distorter of little women

[1] II, 355

with nervous grimaces, sometimes known as the Paganini of the Peignoir.' On 4 May came the disaster of the Charity Bazaar. A fire started in a cinema booth ('The most amazing invention of the century, admission 50 centimes'); and in ten minutes the temporary building in the Cours la Reine, with its wooden walls, roof of tarred canvas and insufficient exits, was a charred ruin. One hundred and forty-three prominent figures in society, mostly ladies, were burned alive. Montesquiou—who would certainly have behaved with his undoubted courage and nobility if he had been there, but as it happened was not—was maliciously rumoured to have used his famous cane in forcing a way out. Lorrain, in an article on the 14th, gleefully resumed his criticism of the Boldini portrait. 'He seems hypnotised in adoration of his cane, that battle-axe for live ladies and tongs for removal of the corpses of dead ones, henceforth so dismally celebrated in the annals of masculine elegance.' So Montesquiou in turn had to fight a duel, not, strangely enough, with Lorrain but with Henri de Regnier. The Count had arranged on 5 June an afternoon visit to Baroness Adolphe de Rothschild's art-collection, during the course of which Delafosse obliged with a recital. While the guests were collecting their hats and sticks before leaving, Regnier's wife (*née* Marie de Heredia, a friend of Proust in her girlhood) took the opportunity to remark: "That's a splendid cane for a bazaar, you could hit dozens of women without breaking it"; and Regnier, instead of making peace, joined in with: "You'd look still better with a fan!" "I'd feel far more at home with a sword," replied Montesquiou with dignity; and swords it was, a more dangerous weapon in the etiquette of duelling than the pistols chosen by Lorrain.[1] They fought at the Pré aux Clercs in the Bois on 9 June, with Barrès as Montesquiou's second, Béraud, this time on the other side, as Regnier's, and Dr Pozzi in attendance as Montesquiou's doctor. Count Robert's idea of duelling was to whirl his sword like the sails of a windmill. A few moments after joining combat for the third time he received a wound in the thumb, bled profusely, and retired to Touraine to recuperate. The numerous spectators had included more than one priest sent by noble ladies to give 'Quiou-Quiou', in case of need, the last

[1] With pistols it was bad form not to miss your opponent, unless you had an exceptionally serious grievance; but with swords the combatants were in honour bound to go on fighting until one was hurt.

consolations of the Church. "It was one of the best fêtes I've ever given," he exulted. Curiously enough, he found it impossible to dislike Lorrain. Yturri, always glad to act as a dove of peace, was sent to negotiate, and they made it up. Despite a rather unfortunate dinner with Lorrain, during which he was several times called downstairs by blackmailers ("People keep bringing me proofs to correct," he mumbled to Montesquiou), they remained on affable terms until the deplorable Lorrain's death, from multiple anal fistulas, in 1906.

The recital at Mme de Rothschild's was the last given by Delafosse as Montesquiou's protégé. The young pianist had committed the unforgivable treachery of flirting with another patron: 'He threw himself,' said Montesquiou, 'not into the arms, for she can hardly be said to have had any, but at the feet, which were enormous, of an aged spinster of Swiss origin.' Their estrangement was very different from that between Charlus and Morel. Far from being heartbroken, Montesquiou dismissed the unhappy young man with vengeful delight, and when, one day, Delafosse found himself cut in public, the Count's explanation was unanswerable: "One bows when the Cross passes, but one does not expect the Cross to bow back." Visiting friends noted that the Angel's portrait had been transferred from the drawing-room to the lavatory, and that a sure means of giving pleasure to the Count was to speak ill of Delafosse. Mme Howland could call him 'that little "Defosse" girl' with impunity; Montesquiou referred to him no longer as 'the Angel' but as 'the Scrambled Egg'[1]; and during the Dreyfus Affair Proust curried favour by pretending that the famous reference in the 'Alexandrine' letter to 'that swine D——' alluded not to Dreyfus but to Delafosse.[2] The pianist's career, much to Montesquiou's disappointment, was not broken. He played for Countess Metternich at Vienna, in Paris at Princesse Rachel de Brancovan's musical evenings, where Proust continued to see him, and during the 1900s to Edwardian society in London, where he was a friend of Percy Grainger and

[1] L'œuf brouillé, 'brouillé' meaning also 'someone with whom one has quarrelled'.

[2] The true identity of 'D——' in the letter signed Alexandrine from Schwartzkoppen to the Italian military attaché Panizzardi, written at an unknown date in 1891 or 1893, has never been established; but as he was engaged in selling maps of fortifications at a mere 10 fr. apiece, D—— must have been a very small-time spy.

Sargent. After the First World War, however, he declined with the fall of the Guermantes world on which he had lived; and the poverty and obscurity of his death in old age in 1955 were a belated consequence of his first fatal choice sixty-one years before, when instead of relying solely on his art he had sought the patronage of Montesquiou and high society.

Meanwhile the delayed results of *Les Plaisirs et les Jours* had caused Proust further distress, this time from his former comrades of *Le Banquet*. Jacques Bizet, now in his last year as a medical student and living in a bachelor-garret on the Quai Bourbon in the Ile Saint-Louis, had collaborated with Robert Dreyfus in a little revue for shadow-figures, after the manner popularised by the famous Chat-Noir cabaret in Montmartre. The paper figures were cut by distinguished artists, among them Forain and Jacques Émile Blanche; the lighting was provided by a fearsome cylinder of acetylene gas ("if that tube blows up, we'll all be buried in the ruins," Bizet warned); and the revue, which satirised the literary successes of their friends in the previous year, was wittily entitled *'The Laurels all are Cut'*. Fernand Gregh, who nobly accompanied at the piano, was one of the chief victims, for his first volume of poems, *La Maison de l'Enfance*, had just been hailed as a masterpiece. Proust, whose voice was imitated perfectly by Léon Yeatman behind the screen, was seen in grimacing silhouette talking to Ernest La Jeunesse: perhaps this partly accounted for his subsequent annoyance, for La Jeunesse was a malicious, falsetto-voiced, Jewish homosexual, unwashed, deformed, and notorious for his physical resemblance to a body-louse. "I have nothing but contempt for you," he had once declared to the critic Henri Bauer, who replied: "And I have nothing but mercury-ointment for you." So on three evenings, from 18 to 20 March 1897, an appreciative cross-section of literary and social Paris listened to the following:

PROUST. Have you read my book, Monsieur La Jeunesse?
LA JEUNESSE. No, it was too expensive.
PROUST. Oh dear, that's what everybody says. . . . And yet, a
    preface by M. France, 4 francs—pictures by Mme Lemaire,
    4 francs—music by Reynaldo Hahn, 4 francs—prose by me,
    1 franc—verses by me, 50 centimes—surely that's value for
    money?

LA JEUNESSE. Yes, but you get a lot more in the *Almanac Hachette*, and it only costs 2 francs 50.

PROUST (*laughing heartily*). Oh, very good! Oh, how it hurts me to laugh like that! How witty you are, Monsieur La Jeunesse! How delightful it must be, to be as witty as that!

Proust, when it was duly reported to him, was inconsolable. "They have hurt me enormously," he said, weeping, to Gaston de Caillavet at Mme Arman's next Wednesday; "I thought they were so nice—and they're utterly heartless!" But his distress, though disproportionate, was not unreasonable; for the apparently harmless mockery of his former schoolfriends was the anger of Bloch aware of the Narrator's preference for Saint-Loup.

A few weeks later, on 11 April, he paid a visit to two retired servants of the family in an old folks' home at Issy, accompanied by Albert Flament. Again Flament noticed his astonishing gift for mimicry and pastiche, 'like the touch of colour on a pencil-sketch by Forain', as he impersonated the ladies of the Faubourg Saint-Germain, or Mme Arman with her stricken "If only Marcel would work!" They waited in the garden by a bed of pansies— "The only flower I can smell without getting asthma," remarked Proust, and added as he inhaled one cupped in his hand: "It smells like skin." The old couple hurried up, overjoyed to see 'Monsieur Marcel'; he enquired after their wants, insisted on their wanting something, pressed a handful of crumpled banknotes into the old woman's hand, and promised, dancing from one foot to the other, to come again soon and stay longer. On the way back they stopped at a fair on the outskirts of Paris and devoured, under naphtha flares in the cold spring dusk, fried chipped potatoes from paper bags.

On 24 May Proust gave one of the spectacular dinners at 9 Boulevard Malesherbes to which he delighted to invite his best friends, anyone who happened to have done him a good turn recently, stars of the bourgeois salons, and a sprinkling of persons from the Faubourg Saint-Germain whose presence would flatter everyone. The friends were Reynaldo and Gaston; the benefactors were his seconds, Béraud and Borda; Anatole France and the Jewish dramatist Porto-Riche were the *salonnards*; and the flattering company comprised Montesquiou, Marquis Antoine de

Castellane (Boni's father) and Comte Louis de Turenne, original of Babal de Bréauté. The willingness of these distinguished noblemen to dine in Proust's bourgeois home proves two mutually contradictory facts: that the Guermantes set were more human, less exclusive in real life than in *A la Recherche*; and that Proust did not exaggerate his own social position when he portrayed the Narrator's. But the account in next morning's *Le Gaulois* suggests a vague cloud behind the scenes: the Marquis de Castellane left as early as possible for an engagement with his cousin, Boson Prince de Sagan; Mme Proust, still in mourning for her parents, was not to be seen; and 'the famous Dr Proust effaced himself, leaving his son to do the honours of this brilliant dinner-party, during which the most Parisian wit never ceased to sparkle'. Proust thriftily passed on the floral decorations to Mme Straus next morning.

It was about this time, and perhaps in consequence of the trouble and expense of this dinner, that Proust had the quarrel with his parents which in Part III, Chapter VII of *Jean Santeuil* is transposed to his schooldays. Mme Proust, in the humiliating presence of his father's valet Jean Blanc, reproached him for extravagance and ingratitude; Dr Proust, so easy-going by nature, but so violent when roused, joined in; and their son marched furiously out of the dining-room, slamming the door and smashing its panes of coloured glass to smithereens. In his bedroom he was carried away by a further paroxysm of rage and (as he wrote in *Jean Santeuil* and told his housekeeper Céleste many years later) seized from the mantelpiece a vase of Venetian glass given him by his mother and hurled it to the floor. 'We needn't think or speak of it again,' wrote Mme Proust in a letter of forgiveness, 'and we'll let the broken glass be what it is in the synagogue, a symbol of indestructible union.' She alluded to the Jewish ceremony of marriage, which includes the ritual breaking of a glass from which the bridal couple have drunk; and if her words were given their full, terrible meaning they would imply a mystic union with her son more valid than her marriage, in an alien faith, to his father. But their consequences need not be taken too seriously. Psycho-analysis had not yet been invented; and moreover, the malady in Proust's heart fed not on his present relationship with his mother but on the buried, unalterable fixation of his childhood.

Proust was among the three thousand guests at Boni de Castellane's famous ball in the Bois de Boulogne on 2 July. The ball
was to celebrate the twenty-first birthday of Boni's reluctant wife
("I'm just as good as these princesses of yours!"), though the
host and his uncle gave a different reason when they called on
the President of the Municipal Council to extract permission for
the use of the Bois. "What is the purpose of this ball?" asked the
astonished functionary; and the Prince de Sagan replied, adjusting
his monocle with Olympian impertinence: "This ball, Monsieur,
will be given for pleasure . . . simply and solely for *pleasure!*" So
300,000 francs of Mme de Castellane's fortune were spent; the
trees of the Bois were hung with 80,000 green Venetian lanterns,
shining like unripe fruit; and the entire corps de ballet of the
Opéra danced before the guests. The climax of the evening was
when twenty-five swans, brought by Boni's neighbour Camille
Groult, were released to beat their white wings among the
lanterns, revellers and fountains of fire. But the loveliest swan of
all was Mme Greffulhe, swathed in clouds of white tulle.

M. Groult was a millionaire art-collector, of jolly, piratical
appearance, whose wealth came from flour and meat-paste. His
collection was particularly remarkable for its eighteenth-century
drawings and pastels, beneath which were displayed glass cases
of transfixed butterflies. "These are signed Watteau, Nattier,
Fragonard," M. Groult would say, "and these"—pointing to the
butterflies—"are signed: God." Montesquiou, who frequently
called with sight-seeing parties of his friends, was enamoured of a
portrait of a young nobleman by Perroneau. "You can see the
tooth-marks where that exquisite young mouth has been kissed,"
he announced, and the pretty Marquise de Jaucourt, leaning
eagerly forward, cried "Where? Where? Show me!" M. Groult's
most celebrated jest was on the occasion of Edward VII's visit to
Paris in 1907. Henri de Breteuil (the other original of Hannibal
de Bréauté) was asked to arrange lunch for the King at M.
Groult's, to be followed by a tour of his pictures; and to make
sure that no one unsuitable should be invited, he demanded a
complete list of the guests. 'Don't worry,' M. Groult wrote back,
alluding both to the source of his riches and to La Fontaine's fable
of the miller and his son, in which the third party is their ass;
'There'll only be the miller, the miller's son, and you!' The story
is told in *Le Côté de Guermantes* of the Prince de Luxembourg and

his wife's grandfather, 'who had made that enormous fortune out of cereals and meat-pastes'.[1]

Later that month Proust was ill with asthma, his most serious attack as yet. It was at the time of this illness, on 15 July, that Reynaldo lost his father, Carlos Hahn. On one blazing afternoon Marie Nordlinger rode on her bicycle to the Hahns' villa at Saint-Cloud to enquire, and met Marcel just getting out of his closed cab on the same errand. He was grotesquely muffled in overcoat and scarves and writhing in the throes of an appalling attack of hay-fever. She begged him to come inside out of the sun; but "No, I'll wait here," he panted; "you go in and find out how he is, only for heaven's sake don't tell them I've come." As soon as possible she emerged with her report and Proust, gasping, choking and unannounced, drove straight back to Paris. As early as the winter before he had already begun his habit, from which he was never to succeed in curing himself, of working all night and sleeping by day. Henceforth he slept as a rule from eight in the morning till three in the afternoon; and at the time of his duel, as he told Montesquiou in 1905, his only anxiety had been lest he should have to fight in the morning, when he ought to be asleep. 'When they told me it was arranged for the afternoon, all my fears vanished.'

During the same summer, introduced by Reynaldo and accompanied by Marie Nordlinger, Proust frequented the salon of a cocotte who contributed a little to Odette. Méry Laurent, *née* Louviot, was born in 1849, married at the age of fifteen to Claude Laurent, an insolvent grocer, and separated from him seven months later. During the next twelve years or so she first posed in tights and spangles at the Théâtre du Châtelet, then put on more clothes to become an actress, and lastly took everything off to be an artist's model. Towards the end of the 1870s she became the mistress of the famous Dr Thomas Evans, Napoleon III's American dentist. Evans was wealthy, generous and free from jealousy; he installed Méry in an apartment near his own consulting-room in the Rue de Rome, but had no objection to her indulging her passion for painters and poets, so long as they were out of the way when he called, as he did every day, for lunch. She became a model and mistress of Manet, who introduced her to his friend Mallarmé. Manet painted several of his models in

[1] II, 537

male travesty; although Méry does not seem to have been among these, his association with her is doubtless another link with Elstir and his portrait of Odette as Miss Sacripant. A year after Manet's death in 1883, Mallarmé became her lover; she was the delight of his disappointed life until his own death in 1898.

It was to her charming villa, Les Talus, at 9 Boulevard Lannes near the Bois de Boulogne, that Reynaldo took Proust and Marie Nordlinger. Other guests have described Les Talus as a countrified little house with low ceilings and rustic furniture upholstered in flowered cretonne. But by 1897 Mme Laurent had become converted, like Odette, to Japanese art; and it was at Les Talus that Proust saw Odette's staircase with dark painted walls hung with oriental tapestries and Turkish beads, and the huge Japanese lantern suspended from a silken cord and lit, 'to provide her guests with the latest comforts of Western civilisation', Mlle Nordiinger remembered, 'with a gas-jet!' The large and small drawing-rooms, as at Odette's house in the Rue Lapérouse, were entered through a narrow lobby, the wall of which was covered by a gilded trellis, and lined with a long rectangular box from which grew a lofty row of pink, orange and white chrysanthemums.[1] In Mme Laurent's drawing-room was the same portrait of the hostess on a plush-draped easel as in Odette's[2]; though at Les Talus it was 'Manet's enchanting pastel of his beloved, wearing a little toque with a veil, through which emerged her dreamy eyes, her slightly tilted nose and greedy little mouth'.

Mme Laurent was a tall, pink and gold blonde, with regular features and arched eyebrows which made her look always surprised. So ardent and varied was her love of poets that George Moore called her '*Toute la Lyre*'; though it was said that when she led Moore himself to her blue-satin bedroom he failed to take the hint, and stood looking like a gasping carp until she declared: "I don't think there's any point in our staying any longer in my bedroom," and led him out. Mallarmé, who had borne with equanimity her association with Gervex, Coppée, Dr Robin (Proust's father's friend, who owned her portrait as 'Autumn' by Manet) and so many more, was a little distressed by the new circle of Dreyfusist young men who were gathering round her; and in a letter of that summer in which he sent Méry an item of botanical information he added ironically: "This will give you a chance of

[1] I, 220   [2] I, 221

showing off your knowledge in front of Proust." One evening Reynaldo took Proust, whose interest in Ruskin was already awakening, to Méry's to meet Whistler, Ruskin's arch-opponent since the famous libel-suit in 1878. "Ruskin knew nothing whatever about painting," Whistler asserted; but Proust cajoled him into 'saying a few nice things about Ruskin,' and when the painter left his grey kid gloves behind he appropriated them as a souvenir. Dr Evans died in November 1897, and Mallarmé on 9 September 1898; and this late flowering of Méry Laurent's salon had an early withering.

In August Proust stayed with his mother, as in 1895, at the Kurhaus Hôtel, Kreuznach. At first the weather was fine and dry, but he had asthma—it was because their rooms were on the ground floor, he decided. Then it was rainy and cold, yet the perverse malady receded. At Kreuznach he wrote Part VIII, Chapter V, of *Jean Santeuil*, '*Le Salon de la Duchesse de Réveillon*', and no doubt other episodes of his novel, for he told Léon Yeatman: "I haven't been able to write any letters, because I've been working so hard." All through this holiday, and even as late as October, when he went away with Hahn, Mme Lemaire was hoping to see Marcel and Reynaldo at Réveillon again. In vain she sent full instructions and times of trains, or deputed Suzette to beg Maria Hahn 'to *press* them and *hustle* them a bit'. But Réveillon had already yielded all its sweetness two years before, and they never came.

On 16 December 1897 Alphonse Daudet died, struck down after thirty years of respectable married life by the unforgiving *Spirochaeta pallida* caught in his Bohemian youth. For Proust Daudet's place as a writer was with Théophile Gautier and George Sand, whose works, though he had ceased to overvalue them, retained the irrecoverable but indestructible glamour of the dining-room fireside and the shady recesses of the Pré Catelan at Illiers. He continued all his life to quote Tartarin's 'double muscles', or 'hellish dark and smells of cheese' from *Jack*—he did not know that the Master had stolen the latter from *Handley Cross*. But when he came to know the dying writer personally he felt a new gratitude for his kindness, a respect for his heroic endurance of pain and paralysis. Alphonse Daudet, in turn, was charmed and impressed by Lucien's brilliant friend. From the first he kept Proust's letters with the cherished correspondence of great men, which his family called 'the autographs'. "Marcel Proust's the Devil Himself," he would remark with amused awe, when faced with some new example of his psychological insight; and Proust would be welcomed with a smile when he burst into the study at 31 Rue de Bellechasse to enquire: "Do you know when Lucien will be back from Jullian's?" "The great stumbling-block ('écueil') in your life, my dear boy, will be your health," he once told Proust; and the saying supplied a theme for *Jean Santeuil* and a hint for Bergotte's prophecy to the Narrator.

For three days Proust and Reynaldo rallied round the distraught and weeping Lucien. They saw Alphonse Daudet lying in state, like Bergotte, on his flower-strewn bed: La Gandara was sketching his friend for the last time, while Barrès stood in mournful contemplation, and Hervieu in tears kissed the death-cold forehead. In the funeral procession from Sainte-Clotilde to Père la Chaise on the 21st they walked behind Zola, Drumont and Anatole France, enemies united for a moment in their love for the dead writer. From time to time Proust hurried forward to take Lucien's arm; and that evening he called again to beg his friend to try to sleep. An epoch was over; and as the deaths of Calmette and Agostinelli seventeen years later seemed, for Proust, to herald the World War, so the passing of Alphonse Daudet marked the real beginning of the Dreyfus Affair, the end of the cul-de-sac of the Guermantes Way.

Chapter 13

THE DREYFUS CASE

ON 26 September 1894 Mme Bastian, an elderly charwoman at the German Embassy in Paris, had delivered as usual the contents of the German military attaché's waste-paper basket to Major Henry, the second-in-command of the counter-espionage bureau of the French War Office euphemistically known as the Statistical Section. Usually her carrier-bag contained nothing more exciting than Colonel Schwartzkoppen's love-letters from Mme de Weede[1]; but this time Henry found a note, thereafter known as the *bordereau*, giving a list of five secret documents which the anonymous writer was willing to sell to the Germans. Some were about guns, some were about mobilisation: the Statistical Section decided, reasonably enough, that only a staff-officer who had recently served in the artillery could have had access to all the documents in question. Among four or five possible suspects was Captain Alfred Dreyfus, whose handwriting happened to resemble that of the *bordereau*; and besides, the man was a Jew. Dreyfus was arrested on 15 October, tried by court-martial on 19 December, sentenced to public degradation and life-imprisonment on the 22nd, and shipped to Devil's Island on 21 February 1895. He remained there in solitary confinement, hoping and despairing, for more than four years.

The case roused only temporary interest, and with the exception of Dreyfus's wife and brother none of his later supporters was inclined to quarrel with the verdict. The Jews, shocked and ashamed that one of their number should be a traitor, kept scrupulously quiet. The socialists, led by Jaurès, were at that time inclined to anti-Semitism on the assumption that all Jews were capitalists. They therefore attacked the Government, with the support of the opposition radical Clemenceau, for favouritism in

---

[1] She was the wife of the counsellor at the Dutch Embassy in Paris, and occasionally wrote letters to Schwartzkoppen's dictation when he did not wish the handwriting to be recognisable. The most important of these was the *petit bleu*.

not imposing the death-sentence. Even Major Picquart, the future champion of Dreyfus, disliked Jews; he was present at the court-martial and had been unfavourably impressed by the toneless voice in which Dreyfus had protested his innocence. The various army officers involved in the condemnation, including Major Henry, were perfectly sincere in their belief in his guilt. Rather than let a traitor escape, they felt justified in exaggerating the evidence against him; for its thinness, they thought, only showed the cleverness of the criminal. Their chief error had been failure to realise that the secret documents could have been procured by a person not entitled to possess them. In fact, they had been sold, and the *bordereau* written, by Major Esterhazy, an aggrieved and insolvent infantry officer who had never belonged either to the artillery or to the general staff. It was an unfortunate co-incidence that his handwriting had a superficial resemblance to Dreyfus's.

In July 1895 Major Georges Picquart was placed in charge of the so-called Statistical Section and ordered to re-examine the case against Dreyfus with a view to discovering a motive for the crime. Nothing turned up until March 1896, when the invaluable Mme Bastian brought from Schwartzkoppen's waste-paper basket the torn fragments of a *petit bleu*, or special delivery letter. It was addressed to Esterhazy. At first Picquart only suspected a new traitor; but in August he obtained specimens of Esterhazy's hand-writing and immediately recognised its identity with that of the *bordereau*. His superiors were willing to admit that Esterhazy might be guilty, but not that Dreyfus was innocent. In December Picquart was transferred to Tunisia, and knew his career was broken: "I shan't carry this secret with me to my grave," were his parting words. Meanwhile, from September 1896 onwards, Henry began forging new evidence against Dreyfus, some of which was designed to implicate Picquart as an accomplice. He believed he was acting for the best, that Picquart was a blundering meddler or worse, that Dreyfus was guilty; and he knew that his own reputation, not to mention that of his superiors and the whole army, was at stake. Picquart remained silent from a sense of military duty, though he left a confidential account of his discoveries with his lawyer, Leblois, 'in case anything should happen to me'. For yet another year the Dreyfus Case seemed stifled, as if for ever.

Suddenly, in November 1897, the Affair exploded. On the 9th Dreyfus's brother Mathieu published facsimiles of the *bordereau* for sale in the streets; on the 15th he denounced Esterhazy; on the 29th *Le Figaro* published damning photographs of the *bordereau* and of an old letter of Esterhazy to his mistress, in which he declared his ambition to die 'as a captain of Uhlans, sabring the French'. Clemenceau began a long series of articles in *L'Aurore*, demanding revision of the Dreyfus trial; Picquart was recalled from Tunisia under suspicion of conspiracy with the Dreyfusists; and the gallant Esterhazy, confident of War Office support, requested court-martial in order to clear his name. He was tried on 10-11 January 1898 and duly acquitted. On the 13th Picquart was arrested and confined in the Mont-Valérien fortress; and Zola's famous manifesto *I Accuse* appeared in *L'Aurore*. Next morning's issue contained the first instalment of the 'petition of the intellectuals', demanding the revision of the Dreyfus Case.

'I was the first Dreyfusard,' Proust later claimed, with pardonable exaggeration and pride, 'for it was I who went to ask Anatole France for his signature.' Proust and Gregh tackled France at Mme Arman's, in his little study on the third floor, where Mme Arman knitted in an armchair at his side. "Are you trying to get us all put in prison, young man?" he remarked to the ardent Gregh as he signed, while Mme Arman cried: "Don't do it, the Félix Faures will never forgive us!" The two Halévy brothers, Jacques Bizet, Robert de Flers, Léon Yeatman and Louis de la Salle also collected signatures and signed. They had met, along with Marcel and Robert Proust, every evening since the first day of Esterhazy's court-martial, in the upstairs room of the Café des Variétés to plan their campaign. For a whole week Dr Proust refused to speak to his sons: he was a confirmed anti-Dreyfusist, being a personal friend of almost every minister in the Government, and when asked for his own signature by a medical colleague had shown the canvasser to the door. But the 'manifesto of the hundred and four' organised by Proust and his friends was soon followed by half the professors in the Sorbonne, including Proust's schoolmaster Darlu, and Paul Desjardins whose philosophy lectures he had attended when studying for his *licence en droit*. Several artists, such as Montesquiou's friend Gallé, the glass-maker, Mme Lemaire's guest Jules Clairin, and the great

Monet (Elstir himself!) joined in.[1] By the end of the month the petition numbered three thousand names, and was attacked by Barrès in *Le Journal* for 1 February: 'the petition of the intellectuals is signed mostly by half-wits,' he wrote, and went on to call them 'the semi-intellectuals'.

From 7 to 23 February 1898 Zola was tried for defamation of the officers who had acquitted Esterhazy. 'The Dreyfus courtmartial may have been unintelligent, but the Esterhazy courtmartial was criminal,' he had written in *I Accuse*. His protest was not only a moral act of supreme courage and danger: it was also a tactical move of great skill. By forcing the Government to prosecute him on the Esterhazy question he hoped to enable his lawyers to bring out, in cross-examination of the army witnesses, the new evidence on the Dreyfus Case which was the essential need of the revisionists. Despite the judges' efforts, on instructions from above, to exclude all mention of Dreyfus, a few important facts came out: notably, the admission that Dreyfus had been illegally condemned, since part of the evidence had not been shown to the defence.[2]

A few weeks before Picquart's arrest Proust had been taken to the house of Zola's publisher, Gustave Charpentier, to meet Picquart in person. His admiration for the heroic officer was redoubled when he found he was a friend of Monsieur Darlu, interested in philosophy and music, and well-read. With great

---

[1] Among other signatories were Albert Bloch, '*licencié ès lois*, teacher in the Polytechnic school at Buenos Ayres', whose name Proust used for the character in *A la Recherche*, though there is no evidence that he knew him personally; Pierre Quillard, a poet whom Proust had met at Mallarmé's, and who spoke Bloch's Homeric jargon ("warrior of the shining greaves", of Pierre Louÿs in well-varnished shoes, or "thou of the swift chariot" to a friend alighting from an omnibus, and so on); also Jules Renard and André Gide.

[2] A no less vital consequence (and no doubt purpose) of Zola's action was that in the witness-box Picquart would be free at last to make his own discoveries public. He revealed the existence of the *petit bleu* (Schwartzkoppen's letter to Esterhazy), and told the court of his horrified amazement, on examining the Secret File against Dreyfus, at finding it contained not a shadow of proof. He also expressed his opinion that the letter from the Italian military attaché Panizzardi to Schwartzkoppen, asking him to 'say we've had nothing to do with this Jew . . . no one must ever know what happened with him', was spurious. It was in fact forged by Henry and is generally known as the '*faux-Henry*'.

difficulty he managed to smuggle a copy of *Les Plaisirs et les Jours* to Picquart's cell at Mont-Valérien; though whether or not the martyr's confinement was soothed by this gift remains unknown. All through the Zola trial he climbed with Louis de Robert each morning to the public gallery in the Palais de Justice, feeling the same pleasurable apprehension and mental tension as at the time of his examination for the *licence en droit*, and armed, as then, with a flask of coffee and a packet of sandwiches.[1]

Zola showed to less advantage in his trial than in the magnificent protest which had provoked it: alternately sulky and vain, he made unfortunate remarks such as: "I don't know the law, and I don't want to know it," or "I have won with my writings more victories than these generals who insult me." Proust had eyes only for the officers, the mistaken, unjust kindred of the spiritual fathers and elder brothers he had known at Orleans. The honour of the Army, he knew, could be saved only by admission of error, not by perpetuating injustice; yet it was with admiration mingled with his horror that he studied General de Boisdeffre, tall, elderly and handsome, with violet cheeks and a courteous manner, when on the morning of 18 February he swore to the genuineness of the *faux Henry* and threatened his resignation as Chief of General Staff if disbelieved. But the centre of the interminable trial was Picquart himself, the Angel of the Revision, as Dreyfusist hostesses had already begun to call him. In *Jean Santeuil*,[2] advancing in his sky-blue uniform towards the president of the court, 'with the light, rapid movement of a Spahi, as if he had just dismounted from his horse, his head on one side and glancing right and left with vague astonishment', Picquart has the air of Saint-Loup. In his scrupulous way of pausing to think before he answered, in order to discover not the most telling

---

[1] Robert de Billy was told a few years later by an informant in the inner circle of Reinach's assistants that Proust had been 'singled out to take an active part in the movement; but his ill-health prevented him from accepting'. Jean Santeuil attended the Zola trial with a watching-brief for Zola's lawyer: "Call for me in the morning," he says to his friend Durrieux as they leave the Palais de Justice, "I'll have finished the notes I'm taking for Labori by then" (vol. 2, p. 121). Perhaps Proust, too, had an official task to perform at the trial. In *A la Recherche* the Narrator's attitude to the Affair is more neutral, and Proust transferred his own attendance at the Zola trial, including the coffee and sandwiches, to Bloch (II, 234).

[2] Vol. 2, 134

reply but the very truth, he reminded Proust of Darlu; in his habits of reading and meditation he recalled Proust's own immersion in books at the firesides of Illiers and Orleans; and the ethical beauty of his conduct for which he was now in prison was that of the morality of Saint-André-des-Champs.

The intervention of Boisdeffre was decisive: Zola was found guilty and received the maximum penalty of a year's imprisonment and a 3,000 francs fine. He appealed on technical grounds, was retried with the same result on 18 July, and unwillingly, under pressure from his friends, fled to England, where he remained till the general amnesty eighteen months later. Picquart was released from prison and dismissed the service on 16 February. For several months the Affair was once again suppressed; but meanwhile revisionists and anti-revisionists gathered forces to prepare for the next inevitable explosion.

Already the heroic age of the Affair was ending. Revisionism became less and less a matter of justice, more and more a matter of politics. Since the Government had set its face against revision, revision could only be achieved through the fall of the Government. Nationalists, anti-Semites, Church and Army, all who stood to lose by a shift to the left, must explain away every new fragment of truth as part of the conspiracy of their enemies; socialists, Jews, anti-clericals and anti-militarists saw their chance to ride to power on the Dreyfusist bandwagon. The cause was gradually contaminated by opportunists whom Proust, as a foundation-member, contemptuously called 'the Dreyfusards of the eleventh hour'. France was divided into two blocs, for whose enmity the guilt or martyrdom of the man on Devil's Island was a mere pretext. Injustice was now on both sides.

The split in society was also a split in high society. The Faubourg Saint-Germain, being royalist, nationalist and Catholic, was inevitably anti-Dreyfusist. Even the hostesses who remained neutral, whether from genuine doubt or from desire to keep their guests of both parties, were forced to choose one side or the other, for sooner or later their guests would quarrel about the Affair and refuse to meet one another again. A cartoon of Caran d'Ache represented a dining-room full of smashed crockery and diners sprawling in battle on the floor, with the caption: 'Somebody mentioned it.' There is no evidence that Proust's activities cost him a single invitation; but he deserves full credit for his courage, for he could not foresee that his Dreyfusism would not mean social death, any more than he could have foreseen he would come out of his duel with Jean Lorrain alive. In the event he was saved, socially, by the general liking he inspired in hostesses and guests, his ability to accept another person's point of view providing it was sincere, and the fact that, as Dr Proust's son, he was in theory a Catholic and, at most, only half-Jewish. But he made no secret of his convictions, and wrote a stern letter to the formidable Montesquiou warning him to refrain from anti-Semitic remarks in his presence.

The bourgeois salons, however, were either neutral or Dreyfusist. The Affair, it might be claimed, had almost begun at Mme Straus's. The rumour that she had worn black on the day after Dreyfus's condemnation was no doubt baseless; but her friend and former platonic lover, Joseph Reinach, was one of the chief agitators for revision. Reinach was an old boy of Condorcet, and had been one of the suspects in the Panama scandal through his relationship with his uncle, the crooked financier Baron Jacques de Reinach. He was a squat, bearded Jew of simian appearance; 'Reinach had a voice of wood and leather,' wrote his enemy Léon Daudet, 'and used to leap from chair to chair, in pursuit of bare-bosomed lady guests, with the gallantry of a self-satisfied gorilla.' "He was comic but nice," Proust told Jacques Émile Blanche, "although we did have to pretend he was a reincarnation of Cicero." Reinach revealed the truth about Dreyfus to the Straus's at their Trouville villa, the Clos des Mûriers, as early as August 1897. At one of her Saturday at-homes in October Mme Straus announced to her guests: "My friends, M. Reinach has an important announcement to make to you." Reinach then declared his certainty that the *bordereau* was written by Esterhazy, but spoiled his case by maintaining, sincerely but mistakenly, that the War Office had known all along that Dreyfus was innocent. The Byzantine scholar Gustave Schlumberger,[1] a bore with enormous feet, tried to defend the good faith of the Army, and was set upon by Hervieu, Porto-Riche and Émile Straus, who was apt to use unseemly language when crossed. Schlumberger left in a huff and broke with the Straus's, for which Proust never forgave him; and the same evening also cost them the friendship of Jules

---

[1] He is mentioned by M. d'Argencourt at Mme de Villeparisis's as one of the guests of the Duchesse de Guermantes (II, 213).

Lemaître, who henceforth confined himself to the nationalist salon of his mistress the Comtesse de Loynes, and of Forain, who soon afterwards started his anti-Semitic magazine *Psst*.

Mme Straus's salon, under Reinach's influence, became the G.H.Q. of Dreyfusism: it was here that her son Jacques Bizet, her nephews the Halévys and Proust had organised the first *Aurore* petition. Her noble guests, for the most part, remained loyal and continued to attend her Saturdays. But some awkwardness was inevitable, and the Affair marked the beginning of the decline of her salon; for like Zola, Picquart and Proust, Mme Straus was capable of sacrifice in the cause of truth. Princesse Mathilde, who was genuinely fond of the Straus's, made an attempt to convert them in December 1897. "General de Bois-deffre has assured me," she announced, "that the War Office has letters to Dreyfus in the Kaiser's own handwriting!" On 5 February 1898 at Mme Aubernon's—it was the very luncheon at which d'Annunzio exclaimed: "Read my books, madam, and let me get on with my food"—Mme Straus asked the diplomat Maurice Paléologue whether these dreadful letters existed. "If *one* exists, dear lady," he replied with irony, "I'm quite prepared to believe there are several"; and he went on to explain that emperors rarely or never wrote personally to spies.[1] The Haussonvilles, who despite their haughty bow were convinced of the importance of being fair-minded, were shaken by her arguments, and in April they too cross-examined Paléologue. He told them he had the gravest doubts about Dreyfus's guilt, and suspected the document quoted by Boisdeffre at the Zola trial (the *faux Henry*) of being a forgery. "Why, if you're right . . . ," they said, turning pale; but it was noticed that the perfidious M. d'Haussonville began thereafter to pronounce Mme Straus's name as 'Schtraus'.

For Mme Aubernon the Affair was merely an enthralling subject for discussion, like love or adultery, at her Wednesdays. She delighted to hear her pet Dreyfusists, Dr Pozzi, Brochard (the originals of Cottard and Brichot), Hervieu and Porto-Riche at grips with anti-Dreyfusist visitors such as René Bazin or Brunetière; and when asked, "What are you doing about your

---

[1] These letters were frequently appealed to as evidence by the anti-Dreyfusists, but never actually produced. In view of the activities of Major (by that time Colonel) Henry, and the undoubted good faith of Boisdeffre, they may well have existed as forgeries.

Jews?" by a hostess who was gradually eliminating hers, she grandly replied: "I'm keeping them on!" The Affair, however, was destined to be the poor, foolish lady's last pleasure in this world. Mme Aubernon was reduced to silence at last by a cancer of the tongue ("She's punished in the part that sinned," declared one of her enemies), and died on 2 September 1899, aged seventy-four. The faithful Dr Pozzi tended her to the last, and burst into tears as he closed her eyes. There were few people at her funeral, for at that time of year everyone was away on holiday; but when the 'faithful' returned to Paris they said to one another, scarcely knowing whether they spoke in relief or regret: "There'll never be another woman like her!"

For Mme Verdurin as a Dreyfusist, Proust had other hostesses in mind. Mme Ménard-Dorian in the Rue de la Faisanderie conducted a radical socialist salon which became known as the 'Fortress of Dreyfusism'. She had been a friend of Victor Hugo, whose grandson Georges married her daughter Pauline in 1895; and in her drawing-room no opinions were barred, so long as they were progressive and violent. Mme Claire de Saint-Victor, too, had known Hugo, for she was the daughter of his friend, the romantic critic Paul de Saint-Victor, for whose sake she had returned to her maiden name after the disappearance of her un-satisfactory husband. She was a tiny blonde, who made up for her short stature with a foaming, fantastically high coiffure. Mme Aubernon generously said of her salon: "It's just like mine!" Mme de Saint-Victor would burst into the drawing-rooms of her rivals like a lady missionary visiting cannibals, triumphantly brandish-ing an armful of Dreyfusist newspapers; and people called her 'Our Lady of the Revision'. But when Proust says of Mme Verdurin's salon, 'the Dreyfus Affair was over, but she still had Anatole France',[1] he is thinking of Mme Arman de Caillavet. The Affair cost Mme Arman the friendship of Jules Lemaître and Charles Maurras, but brought her the rising political stars of Clemenceau, Briand and Jaurès. Sometimes, indeed, she may have felt that M. France went too far. In July 1898, when Zola was struck off the rolls of the Légion d'Honneur, France quixotically handed in his own rosette; and all through the following winter, led on by Jaurès, he spoke at riotous public meetings of socialists and anarchists—"our voice will be the voice of justice and reason,

[1] III, 236

but it will sound like thunder!"—until hostile journalists began to call him not Monsieur France but Monsieur Prussia.

Mme Lemaire's salon remained neutral. At her reception on 25 May 1898 the long line of carriages waited once more outside 31 Rue de Monceau, while her flowering lilacs contemplated the tall trees of Prince Joachim Murat's garden over the way. Comtesse Aimery de la Rochefoucauld, Princesse Metternich and the Chevignés were there, only too happy to stand, in that amazing crush, with Dreyfusards such as Porto-Riche, Mme Straus, Reynaldo Hahn and Proust himself. Proust arrived, intentionally, after the music was over and Mme Réjane had recited, with his tailcoat several sizes too large, his eyes sparkling from lack of sleep and his voice choked with hay-fever. "What's happened so far?" he asked Albert Flament, and hurried off to Mme de Chevigné, who explained in her raucous voice that she had just dined with the Grand-Duchess Wladimir, "and she was *burning* to come on here with us!" They watched Mme de Chevigné talking with Mme Lemaire, the countess with her rows of pearls, ringletted forehead and bare nape, the hostess painted, wigged and untidy; yet each lady, confident of her supremacy in her own line, 'watched the other', as Flament wrote, 'with the amicable self-assurance which comes from a feeling of absolute equality'. "Mme Straus's Sunday lunches are so interesting," Proust told Flament: "I can't go to the actual lunch, because I'm never up in time, but I go round afterwards and talk about the Affair to Reinach and Dr Pozzi— their cigar-smoke is terribly bad for my asthma, but it's worth it."

At midsummer, as usual, Proust was ill. He had scarcely recovered when he was vouchsafed one of those dreadful warnings in which Providence is so generous, but which human nature, once they turn out to be merely warnings, prefers to forget. On a Wednesday in July Mme Proust was taken to a nursing-home and operated upon for cancer by Dr Proust's colleague Dr Louis Terrier. Only when the operation was under way did Dr Terrier realise the full gravity of her condition; he wrestled for nearly three hours with unpredictable complications, and declared afterwards that he would never have recommended surgical treatment if he had realised the danger it would involve. 'We can't think how poor Mama managed to carry that enormous weight about with her,' Proust wrote to Mme Catusse. For two days, to the distraction of Dr Proust, she lingered between life and death; and on the third day, when she was pronounced out of danger, her first words were a string of stammered witticisms to reassure the anxious Marcel. But the operation had been a success, and by the end of the year Mme Proust seemed completely recovered. She remained for two months in the nursing-home and in October went to Trouville with Dr Proust for convalescence.

Proust himself seems to have made, in the same month, a trip to Holland which is recalled in Jean Santeuil's visit to the seashore at Scheveningen, perhaps also in the mysterious and—so long as we do not know its key—absurd incident of the Dutch nun.[1] Meanwhile, on 21 August at St Petersburg, his childhood sweetheart Marie de Benardaky had married Prince Michel Radziwill, a distant cousin of the Prince Léon Radziwill whom he was to know a few years later. It is probably that, just as Jean Santeuil meets Marie Kossichef in society ("I believe we used to play together in the Champs-Élysées," she says to the now indifferent Jean),[2] so Proust had seen Mlle de Benardaky after her 'coming-out'. The grown-up Marie, as her photograph shows, was dark and pretty; she had the rosy cheeks, and features at once frank and foxy, of Gilberte Swann. The new Princesse Radziwill was to have a daughter, Léontine, born in 1904; but her marriage was not happy, and was dissolved in 1915.

In August 1898 occurred the most astonishing event of the whole Dreyfus Affair. The Army had always assured the Government that it had the really crushing evidence against Dreyfus in reserve; and the new anti-revisionist war-minister, Cavaignac, decided to produce it. He was furnished with three documents, the 'canaille de D——' letter, which in fact did not refer to Dreyfus at all, a letter of 1896 which would have been completely irrelevant if the ingenious Colonel Henry had not altered the date to 1894 and the initial P—— to D——, and the *faux Henry* itself. He revealed these to the Chamber on 7 July. Picquart immediately denounced all three as forgeries and was duly rearrested on 12 July; the *faux Henry* was carefully inspected for the first time and found to be completely bogus; Henry was taken into custody on 30 August, and cut his throat from ear to ear in Mont-Valérien prison next day. Cavaignac and Boisdeffre, whose only fault had

[1] *Jean Santeuil*, Part VI, ch. VIII, and Part X, ch. IV
[2] *Jean Santeuil*, Part VIII, ch. I; cf. *A la Recherche*, III, 574, where the Narrator fails to recognise Gilberte at the Duchesse de Guermantes's.

been belief in what they wished to believe, furiously resigned on the spot. Esterhazy, seeing the game was up, fled the country. At last the Government realised that revision was inevitable, and that the safest course would be, with the utmost possible delay, to permit it. The Dreyfus Case was put in the hands of the Court of Criminal Appeal, who sat from October to December 1898. When it became clear that the Court was coming to believe in Dreyfus's innocence, the proceedings were transferred, with the support of President Faure, to the United Appeal Courts. From March to May 1899 they re-examined the evidence with a meticulous patience which seemed misplaced only to those who remembered that the guiltless Dreyfus had now been on Devil's Island for over four years.

Meanwhile Picquart, too, was in grave danger. The Dreyfusards had been over-optimistic in assuming that, since he was now a civilian, he would be tried by a civil court. The Army was pressing for his case to be put before a court-martial, and it was only too likely, if they succeeded, that there would be two martyrs on Devil's Island. Picquart was denied access to his lawyer, Labori, who decided to try the effect of a new petition, which he organised with the help of the now militant Anatole France. This time it was France who called on Proust for help: he asked dear Marcel to secure from Mme Straus one or more of the biggest names from her salon, preferably that of Comte Othenin d'Haussonville himself. 'Perhaps he won't refuse, he has such a great heart, such an elevated mind,' Proust wrote to her hopefully, 'and yet, M. d'Haussonville would be too good to be true, so perhaps you could fall back on Ganderax or Dr Pozzi.' But poor Mme Straus, who had seen her salon suffer grievously for Dreyfus's sake, and was already approaching the intermittent nervous exhaustion by which she was to be tortured for the remaining twenty-eight years of her life,[1] could not even attempt so desperate an enterprise. Picquart's petition, however, was no less imposing than Dreyfus's at the time of *I Accuse*: among the signatures, amid a vast array of professors, artists, writers and even ambassadors, were those of France, Rostand, Porto-Riche, Brochard, Comte Mathieu de Noailles and the two originals of

---

[1] Mme Straus's facial tic had been particularly noticeable at Mme Lemaire's on 22 May. Her neurasthenia was hereditary, for her mother, sister and aunt had all died insane.

Berma, Réjane and Sarah Bernhardt. Every night from his cell in Cherche-Midi prison Picquart could hear bands of students from the Sorbonne shouting "*Vive* Picquart!" It was decided that his case should await the decision of the Appeal Court on Dreyfus; but the unfortunate consequence was that Picquart remained incarcerated for ten months. When Proust read the newspaper which contained the first list of signatures he found, to his extreme indignation, that his own name had been omitted. 'I know my name will add nothing to the list; but the fact of appearing in the list will add to my name,' he wrote to the editor; '... I believe that to honour Picquart is to honour the Army, since he incarnates its sublime spirit of sacrifice of the self to ends which surpass the individual.' However Proust might loathe the real Army of Henry and Boisdeffre, he never ceased to admire the ideal Army—to which he himself had belonged under Colonel Arvers and Captain Walewski at Orleans—of Picquart and Saint-Loup.

Even Henry's suicide ('the Affair, which used to be sheer Balzac, is now Shakespearean,' Proust had written to Mme Straus) could not convince the anti-revisionists. It was now the nationalist party-line to pretend that Henry's forgeries were a heroic act in defence of the State, and did not in the least affect the certainty of Dreyfus's guilt. Proust's acquaintance Charles Maurras became famous overnight for an article in the *Gazette de France* promising vengeance to the martyred Henry: 'Your ill-fated forgery will be acclaimed as one of your finest deeds of war!' This appeal to the doctrine that the end justifies the means began the resplendent career of propaganda—Catholic, royalist, anti-parliamentary and fascist—which ended, nearly fifty years later, in an extraordinary stroke of Nemesis: the aged Maurras found himself, like Dreyfus, imprisoned for life for betraying his country to the Germans. Now it was the turn of the anti-Dreyfusists to organise a list of names. The anti-Semitic *Libre Parole* opened a subscription, 'for Colonel Henry's widow against the Jew Reinach', which soon reached 130,000 francs. Contributions came not only from Barrès, the young Paul Valéry and Arthur Meyer, but from half the noble Faubourg, including the Ducs de Brissac, Luynes and La Rochefoucauld, the Duchesse d'Uzès, the Marquis's de Lubersac, Ludre and Luppé, and the Comtes de FitzJames, Ganay and Montesquiou (Robert's cousin Léon).

In opposition to the Dreyfusist Ligue des Droits de l'Homme, which was composed mainly of Sorbonne professors with a large proportion of Protestants, Maurras founded the Ligue de la Patrie Française,[1] which soon had fifteen thousand members, and survived long enough to become the foundation of fascism in France. Several of the most prominent, such as Jules Lemaître, the historian Vandal, Barrès, Forain, the poet Heredia and the Comtesse de Martel (the novelist Gyp) had been acquaintances of Proust in happier days. Their unofficial headquarters was the salon of the wealthy Comtesse de Loynes, on which the nationalist salon of Mme Swann at the time of the Affair is modelled. Mme de Loynes resembled Odette in that she had been a Second Empire cocotte, was at home (a most daring innovation) every day of the week at tea-time, and was given to benevolent but enigmatic silence while her guests talked. Jules Lemaître, her lover, was the Bergotte of her salon: "poor Lemaître, for him she'll never seem a day over fifty," someone said; and after her death in 1908 Adrien Hébrard, the editor of Le Temps, unfeelingly remarked: "Never mind, they'll meet again in a better *demimonde*." But the salon of Mme de Loynes was political and literary, rather than aristocratic; and Proust is thinking of Mme Hayman's drawing-room six years before when he makes the Princesse d'Épinay, opening Odette's door in search of a subscription for the 'Patrie Française', find a fairy palace in which Louis de Turenne and the Marquis du Lau are cup-bearers serving orangeade and iced cakes.[2]

In December 1898 Proust was touched to receive a Christmas card from Marie Nordlinger, who had returned to England early in the summer before. He had ceased, like the Narrator, to believe in anniversaries; but now the memory of Christmasses past, 'of candle-light, of snowfalls, melancholy obstacles to some longed-for visitor, the scent of mandarin oranges absorbing the warmth of the room, the gaiety of frosts and fires, the perfumes of tea and mimosa', returned with a rush of emotion. 'All these things reappear, coated with the delicious honey of our inner being, which we have unconsciously deposited on them during years in which we were under the spell of selfish ends; and now, suddenly, it makes our hearts beat.' And in gratitude he told Marie she was 'fresh and

---

[1] Brichot joined it, much to Mme Verdurin's annoyance, taking the opposite line from his original Brochard, who was a Dreyfusist (II, 583).
[2] II, 745

graceful as a branch of hawthorn'. The incident is one of several which show that Proust was now beginning, at last, to return to the secret springs of his early youth, the source of *A la Recherche*.

On the afternoon of 16 February 1899 the Angel of Death, this time in the guise of the lovely Mme Steinheil, called on yet another enemy of Dreyfus. She was admitted to President Faure's study in the Élysée Palace at 5.30. At 6.45 the President's secretary, hearing loud screams from the lady, broke the door in and found his master lying in a coma from a cerebral haemorrhage, still clutching the flowing hair of his stark-naked companion. Even Dr Potain could do nothing, and at 10 p.m. the father of Proust's playmates Antoinette and Lucie expired, without regaining consciousness. The nationalist newspapers decided it was, somehow, all a Jewish plot, and referred darkly to Judith and Delilah. The brutal Clemenceau wrote: 'Felix Faure is dead. There's still not a man the less in France, but there's a good situation vacant—I vote for Loubet.' Loubet, whom the anti-Dreyfusists hated because he had tried to hush up the Baron de Reinach scandal in the Panama crisis, and was known to be pro-English and a revisionist, was duly elected President of the Republic. For a few days the country was on the verge of revolution: on the 19th the new President was mobbed by Déroulède's nationalists and Guérin's anti-Semites, shouting their slogans of "Panama!" and "Aoh, yes!" (a favourite anti-English expression). On the 23rd, the day of Faure's funeral, the troops in the cortège were followed to their barracks by Déroulède, Guérin and Barrès, imploring them to march on the Élysée and impose a military dictatorship. Déroulède was arrested on a charge of high treason and subsequently acquitted; and this fiasco was the last serious threat to the cause of Dreyfusism.

On 25 February at the Vaudeville theatre Proust attended the first night of *Le Lys rouge*, an adaptation by Gaston de Caillavet of Anatole France's novel about love in high society. Both novel and adaptation had been written to Mme Arman's order, and the décor of the first act, as everyone noticed with satisfaction, was copied from her drawing-room. Proust arrived towards the end of the act and hurried to the dress-circle, where Mme Arman, her cheeks rouged carmine, her greying hair dyed copper-colour, and a toque trimmed with stuffed pink bull-finches perched on her vast forehead, took little trouble to conceal her ill-temper at the play's evident failure. "The actors don't seem real enough, don't you agree, Madame?" he murmured, and escaped to Mme Lemaire's box to bow to the rosy and golden Boni de Castellane, and kiss the diamonded hand of Boni's cross little wife. Gaston, who for the last ten years had found it difficult to be polite to Monsieur France, took offence at slighting references to his mother and his play in an article by the anti-Dreyfusard Pierre Véber. They fought with swords on 1 March at the Grande-Jatte, an island in the Seine beyond the Bois de Boulogne, and Gaston was slightly wounded in the arm. Proust passed on the congratulations of Dr and Mme Proust, who admired a good son even more than they deplored duelling, and took the opportunity to add: 'Please give your wife the respectful homage of her old admirer.'

He had already discovered a new social environment whose pleasures, a few years later, would come for him to surpass the splendours of the drawing-room. In a great restaurant he could observe, sit on plush in a corner free from draughts, be treated as a prince, be fantastically generous to young waiters, and talk endlessly in the small hours in a company almost exclusively male. On 4 March at Larue's in the Place de la Madeleine, while the gipsy orchestra played the waltz *Monte-Cristo* at 1 a.m. in a décor of blue, red and gold, he sat with Albert Flament and Robert de Flers in his favourite place at the far right corner, talking theatre: he had solved the problem of how, when an evening in society had ended and the guests departed, not to go straight home.

On 16 April Flament dined at one of Mme Arman's Sundays. When the inevitable discussion of the Affair became too heated— for M. Arman was 'Anti', and was apt to remark to Anatole France: "My dear anarchist, may I press you to a slice of this excellent ham?"—Mme Arman silenced the whole table with a formidable glare, while France changed the subject with a set-piece about Perugino and his pot of lapis-lazuli. At eleven o'clock, when the guests were beginning to leave, Proust arrived and fastened, with an air of affectionate absent-mindedness, on M. France. Mme Arman watched them. "What a pity Marcel won't work," she lamented to Flament, "he could write such a marvellous novel! But he fritters himself away. Don't you think he's a bit *too* fond of society?" And she added, in a tone at once vulgar and tyrannical, the very voice of Mme Verdurin, "but perhaps we could find a way of *making* him work?" Neither of the speakers was aware that Marcel had already written, by any standards but his own, a 'marvellous novel'. Flament objected that *Les Plaisirs et les Jours* was, all the same, a charming book. "It's charming, all right," she retorted, between her teeth; "but that's not enough. Baldassare Silvande, indeed!!"

Proust left with Flament. "I'll take you home," he promised, and chose, with mingled charity and procrastination, the most aged cabman and most decrepit horse in the Avenue Hoche; but instead of climbing in he said: "Follow us, please, while we walk on." The dark circles round his eyes grew larger; his white face wore an expression of appalling fatigue as he cross-examined Flament on the events of the evening and, by comparing his answers with those of M. France, constructed a stereoscopic picture of all that had happened before his arrival. The cabman fell asleep; he pressed a fistful of money into his hand ("don't you think the poor man looks just like that deaf M. de Saint-Hilaire, who always stands next to the door for fear anyone might speak to him?") and chose another. Flament rejected the offer of a drive through the Bois de Boulogne; they walked past the Parc Monceau, and Proust began to choke as the scent of leaves floated by: 'I don't want you to be tired out to-morrow—I know you get up in the morning *like other people*—" he remarked, "but I'm sure you must be hungry." After supping at Weber's in the Rue Royale they talked for an hour or two more at Flament's door, while the cabman snored on his high perch; and as Flament climbed the stairs, tottering with weariness, he saw Proust plunge at last into the darkness of the cab, as if to shelter from the dawn, while above the chimney-tops showed the accusing finger of a first pink cloud.

The next 'grand dinner at 9 Boulevard Malesherbes', as Proust and his mother were accustomed to call those harassing and expensive functions, was designed to give publicity to three poets, and incidentally to reflect notice upon Proust himself. The guests of honour on that 25 April were Montesquiou, Anatole France and Comtesse Anna de Noailles, who occupied the head of the table opposite Proust himself; and the others included Dr and Mme Proust, Mme Arman, Mme Lemaire, Comte Mathieu de Noailles and Léon Bailby, the editor of *La Presse*, in which a glowing account of the dinner was to appear on the 27th. Smaller fry, including Albert Flament, came after dinner to hear the young and lovely actress Cora Laparcerie reciting verses by M.

France, a selection from Montesquiou's *Les Perles Rouges* (a volume of sonnets on Versailles published on the following 6 June) and the first impassioned poems of Mme de Noailles. The poetess's husband Mathieu looked on, tall and thin with a narrow blond moustache, smiling politely but saying not a word. Flament was captivated by the new Muse: greatly daring, he spoke to her, and listened to a flood of enchanting images, like a river of diamonds. Her black hair hung to her eyebrows in a fringe which she alternately parted and smoothed down with a tiny hand decked with an enormous sapphire. Having said her piece, she enquired of each of the obscurer after-dinner guests: "Who's he? Does he write?"; and already she was calling Flament, as she called everybody, 'my dear'. M. France, he noticed, was beaming at the Comtesse, while Mme Arman pulled a grimace. Flament moved towards her to confide his emotions; but Mme Arman was not interested: "I've made M. France copy out the whole manuscript of *Le Lys Rouge*," she announced, "and we're going to give it to the Bibliothèque Nationale!"

Proust had met Anna de Noailles in Mme Arman's salon, where her success was dazzling but brief. "That little girl's a genius," declared Monsieur France; to which the jealous Mme Arman replied, for she felt that one genius was enough for any drawing-room: "When she's about, you don't exist!" She was the daughter of the Roumanian Princesse Rachel de Brancovan, the excitable Chopin-enthusiast, whom Proust had met at her Villa Bassaraba on Lake Geneva in August 1893, and who was the original of the elder Mme de Cambremer. Princesse Rachel, who lived in the Avenue Hoche near Mme Arman, was the widow of the Roumanian Prince Grégoire de Brancovan (1827-86) and daughter of Musurus Pacha, Turkish Ambassador in London in the 1850s and a descendant of a Greek family whose greatness dated from the mediaeval Byzantine Empire. Mme de Noailles had married Comte Mathieu in 1897 and was now twenty-three years old.[1] It was not till several years later, when his sudden

[1] She was a cousin-by-marriage of Montesquiou several times over, for his cousin Henri had married Mathieu de Noailles's sister Marie in 1889; his uncle Odon de Montesquiou was the husband of Princesse Rachel's cousin Princesse Marie Bibesco; and Anna de Noailles's sister Hélène had married in 1898 Prince Alexandre de Chimay, Mme Greffuhle's brother and the son of the late Prince Joseph de Chimay who had been the husband of Montesquiou's aunt Marie.

passion for her poetry played its part in the gradual liberation of his genius, that her friendship became important to Proust. For the time being he preferred her quiet, shy sister, Princesse Hélène de Chimay, with her gentle, short-sighted eyes and chestnut hair, and mistrusted, although she was an ardent Dreyfusard, the frighteningly brilliant Comtesse Anna. Meanwhile, as we have seen, he put her into *Jean Santeuil* as the Vicomtesse Gaspard de Réveillon.

The decision of the United Appeal Court on 3 June in favour of the re-trial of Dreyfus was followed by the release of Picquart (who had spent just under a year of the past seventeen months in gaol), the despatch of a cruiser to bring Dreyfus back from Devil's Island (he had been there for four years and four months), and the fall of the Government. The new Prime Minister was Waldeck-Rousseau, a revisionist and a moderate anti-clerical. He chose as War Minister General de Galliffet (Charles Haas's friend and the General de Froberville of *A la Recherche*), who was hated by the Right for his revisionism[1] and by the Left for his massacre of Communards in 1871. But the more decent elements in the Army respected him for his heroic cavalry charge at Sedan ("Why, sir, we'll charge as often as you like—so long as there's one of us left alive, that is") and his efficiency. During the wild disorder in the Chamber which greeted his first appearance he was observed to be taking names, and explained: "I thought I'd better invite these chaps to dinner." By a narrow majority, the revisionist ministry was allowed to survive, less for Dreyfus's sake than for fear of revolution and civil war; but in the event it lasted for three years, long enough not only for justice but, unfortunately, for revenge.

The new court-martial of Dreyfus began at Rennes in Brittany on 9 August. The wretched man's hair had turned white, and he was racked with malaria; solitary confinement had made it difficult for him to speak or understand the speech of others; and he had never even heard of Picquart or of the existence of Dreyfusism. Once more he created an unfortunate impression by his dejected manner, the toneless voice in which he exclaimed "I am innocent!" His case was mishandled tactically by Labori, and turned into an attack on the Army; and the judges, realising that

---

[1] He was not a Dreyfusist, and said: "I never liked the fellow, and I know damn all about his Case"; but for the sake of Army morale he was determined to put an end to the Affair, even at the price of seeing justice done.

to acquit Dreyfus would be to condemn their own superiors, were divided. On 9 September, by five votes to two, they pronounced the absurd and disgraceful verdict: "Guilty of high treason with extenuating circumstances." Dreyfus was sentenced to ten years' imprisonment and to the hideous ordeal of a second degradation. There was an outcry of savage delight from the nationalists, of grief and anger from the Dreyfusists. The Government were embarrassed: they had hoped for an end to the Affair, and now it could only go on for ever, in an interminable sequence of new appeals and new condemnations. They offered Dreyfus a free pardon, which he accepted under pressure from his brother Mathieu, who realised he would not survive another trial; but he made the proviso that he would not abandon the struggle to establish his innocence. The sensible Reinach concurred; Clemenceau, to whom Dreyfus was only a means to political ends, was furious; and the more idealistic of the young Dreyfusists, for whom Dreyfus was not so much a wronged and suffering human being as a symbol, felt themselves entitled to be bitterly disillusioned. 'We were ready to die for Dreyfus,' wrote Péguy, 'but Dreyfus isn't.'

Meanwhile Proust was at Évian on the Lake of Geneva with his father and mother, staying in the luxurious Splendide Hôtel. His passionate day-to-day interest in the Rennes trial, which was shared by Mme Proust but had to be tactfully kept from his anti-Dreyfusist father, did not prevent him from enjoying the social delights of the Lake. The Villa Bassaraba at Amphion was crammed with Brancovans, Noailles's, Chimays and Polignacs, all rabid Dreyfusards, except the poor Prince de Chimay, who did his best to keep out of the way. With them were the society novelist Abel Hermant, and, of all people, Léon Delafosse, now looking a somewhat ravaged angel. Princesse Rachel lived in the main villa, and the guests were scattered over the park in various annexes and châlets, so that on wet days a carriage was sent round to bring them to meals. After lunch the young people met in Mme de Noailles's room, where she usually received them reclining on a chaise-longue, or even in bed, with an extraordinary mingling of languor and effervescence—"I never knew a girl to toss about in bed so!" said Abel Hermant—and proceeded to read the poem she had invariably written the night before. Sometimes Proust would come to dine, and burn his anti-asthma powders

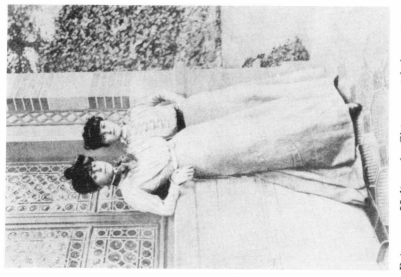

Princesse Hélène de Chimay with her sister
Comtesse Anna de Noailles

Mme Proust with her sons
Marcel and Robert, c. 1897

Left Comte Gabriel de la Rochefoucauld
Right Portrait of Armand, Duc de Guiche, at Vallière, 1902, by Laszlo

Left Prince Léon (Loche) Radziwill at polo
Right Louisa de Mornand, April 1904

beforehand in the châlet of her brother, Prince Constantin de Brancovan; but more often he would come much later. On fine evenings coffee was served on the terrace at the far end of the park, where the long road to Évian could be seen white in the moonlight. About midnight a carriage—Proust called it 'my Brancoach'—would be heard approaching; 'I'll bet anything that's Marcel Proust!" cried the Princesse; and on those evenings the session would be prolonged until three in the morning.

At Coudrée, with its giant plane-trees and box-alleys where Alfieri had wandered with the Countess of Albany a hundred years before, was Mme Bartholoni, a god-daughter of Chateaubriand. "I used to make him go down on all fours to play with me under the table, and I could hear his old knees cracking, but it never occurred to me to feel sorry." She had been a Second Empire beauty, and was still erect and majestic. In memory of her youth she dyed her hair bright red; when her daughters protested, she shouted: "not another word, or I'll dye it green!" Her youngest daughter, Kiki, was a tall, golden-haired, twenty-seven-year old Amazon—'like a heroine in a Scott novel', said the romantic young barrister Henry Bordeaux, who ten years earlier had been accustomed to rush to the schoolroom window with his comrades to see her pass when she rode into Thonon on horseback. All the young men on the lake were either in love with her or, like Proust, pretended to be. In return she took a sisterly interest in Proust's clothing: 'I can't think why you don't dress better, with a tailor like Eppler in the house," she declared.[1] Bordeaux, who was a member of the bar at Thonon and already a well-known novelist, met Proust one day at Coudrée and was delighted to find in him a fellow-enthusiast for Mlle Kiki, Dreyfus and the works of Chateaubriand. He lingered spellbound by Proust's carriage, missing boat after boat home, and remembered ever afterwards the hurt look in Proust's eyes when at last he broke away to catch the last steamer of the day.

Other social possibilities on the lake included the Adolphe de Rothschilds at Prégny near Geneva and the Haussonvilles at Coppet. But at Thonon there were two special friends of Proust, both Dreyfusards afflicted with anti-Dreyfusard fathers, Pierre

---

[1] The tailor Eppler had his shop on the ground floor of the Proust's home at 9 Boulevard Malesherbes, and in this, though perhaps in nothing else, helped to suggest Jupien.

de Chevilly and Vicomte Clément de Maugny. Maugny was staying in his father's ancient and gloomy Château de Lausenette —which reminded Proust of the ruinous castle in Gautier's *Le Capitaine Fracasse*—high on the hills above Thonon. Evening after evening they watched the summit of Mont Blanc turning pink and crimson in the light of the vanished sun, and descended to the lake to take the little train back into Thonon. A curious letter of the previous 13 July, which Proust sent to Maugny with a copy of *Les Plaisirs et les Jours*, shows that they had already been friends and confidants for two years. Maugny has seen 'the beginning and end of sorrows not so very different from those I have tried to define in this book', has been 'intimately associated with the very sources of my joys and griefs during these years', and shows 'unfailing compassion for suffering he can scarcely have understood'. There is an echo here of the emotions Proust mentions in a letter to Reynaldo Hahn, apparently of this same summer. 'I know all the more certainly that my affection for you is a fixed star, when I see it shining still the same after so many other fires have burned away.' Maugny, Chevilly and their friend François d'Oncieu[1] are no doubt the young men whom Proust remembered, in a letter twenty years later to Maugny's wife, as 'my three best friends, long before you knew Clément'.

The weeks at Évian made an important contribution to the Narrator's two visits to Balbec. Mme de Cambremer's country-house at Féterne is based on the Villa Bassaraba and is named after the village of Féternes a few miles inland from Thonon; and the name of Rivebelle, where the Narrator dines with Saint-Loup, is a conflation of Riva-Bella, on the Normandy coast eight miles west of Cabourg, and Belle-Rive, a group of villas on the lake shore a mile east of Geneva. These borrowings are neither accidental nor mechanical: the names are talismans to symbolise the affinities Proust divined in sea-coast and lake-side. Mme Proust and her son made the same mock-serious show as the Narrator and his grandmother of shunning the dangers of un-wanted society, whether noble (the Cambremers or Hausson-villes), bourgeois (there are unwelcome barristers at both Balbec and Évian) or, one regrets to notice, Jewish. Mme Proust even thought of leaving the district for Marcel's sake when they heard

[1] The original link between these three young men was, no doubt, that each had a father who owned a château in Savoy.

that young Chefdebien was 'on the lake'; and after her departure
Proust's letters to her are full of malicious allusions to those
equivalents at Évian of the Blochs at Balbec, the Oulifs, Weisweillers and Biedermanns. He was all the more offended when he
was himself confused with these, as when Chevilly's father
remarked: "I suppose there are a lot of Jews at the Splendide? You
really ought to stay at Thonon next year, the society's much less
cosmopolitan there!" or M. Galard announced with an air of
accusation: "I do believe you're Monsieur Weil's nephew!"
There was a lift-boy, 'who did me a great many services'; and
there was, above all, a little train.

We have seen little trains in Brittany, and on the way to Mme
Aubernon's Cœur Volant near Paris, and shall find another at
Cabourg. But the real 'little train' of his novel, as Proust explained
long afterwards to Maugny's wife, was the one which crawled
from Geneva to Thonon and Évian and back again, stopping at
every village or group of villas, and even sometimes where, as at
Amphion, there was nothing but a château. 'It was a nice, patient,
good-tempered little train,' he wrote, 'which used to wait for late-
comers as long as they liked, and even when it had already started
didn't mind stopping again while, puffing as loudly as it did, they
ran for it at full speed. Their full speed, however, was where the
resemblance ceased; for the little train always moved with
prudent deliberation. At Thonon there was a long wait, while the
passengers shook hands with someone who was seeing his guests
off, or another who'd come to buy newspapers, or a good many
who, I always suspected, came only as an excuse to chat with their
acquaintances. The stop at Thonon station was a form of social
life like any other.'[1]

Dr and Mme Proust returned to Paris on 9 September, after a
lingering embrace on the hotel terrace between Marcel and his
mother, which was eyed with impatience by Dr Proust and with
sentimental approval by M. Gougeon, first president of the court
of appeal at Besançon. He is the original of M. Poncin at Balbec,
who holds the same post at Caen (M. Gougeon himself had
previously served at Rouen), and is addressed as 'Premier' by the
barrister; he took a liking to Proust and on his departure a few
days later gave him a pressing invitation to 'come and see my wife

[1] Proust used many of the actual words of this letter in his description of
the little train at Balbec (II, 1110).

and me at Besançon'. The 9th was the day of the Rennes verdict
and at the Brancovans' that evening, as Proust inhaled his anti-
asthma powders in Constantin's room before dinner, he was
touched to hear Mme de Noailles weeping violently for Dreyfus
and crying "How could they do it? How could they bear to tell
him? What will the foreigners think of us now?" The harassed
Prince de Chimay had left, ostensibly for the opening of the
shooting season ("I don't think he'll find any game as worth
bagging as his wife," remarked Proust), but really to avoid
arguing about the Affair with his Dreyfusard in-laws. The Prince
de Polignac, however, Charles Haas's great friend, was most
affable, and enquired teasingly: "What's the good old syndicate
doing now, eh?"; for he pretended to believe Proust was in close
touch with the mythical secret society of Jews, free-masons and
atheists to which the anti-Dreyfusards were convinced their
opponents belonged. After dinner there were the usual paper-
games, but even here the Affair reared its head and Mme de
Noailles, asked to give circumstantial details about Bertillon (the
handwriting expert who gave preposterous evidence against
Dreyfus), shocked her young friend to the core by writing: 'I
don't know any, it isn't as if I'd ever been to bed with him.'

On the 19th Proust had an inflammation in his wrist, and was
given cold compresses by Dr Cottet, who resembled Dr Cottard
in name only, for he was charming and cultured, and impressed
his patient by showing that he knew Vigny's *La Maison du
Berger* by heart. Perhaps there is some mystery in this wrist.
When Charlotte Clissette is staying the night at Jean Santeuil's
home, he comes to her bedside at midnight and tells her: "My
wrist is hurting me." She takes his hand, saying "Let me massage
it for you"; 'the expression in her eyes gave him the idea that she
was aware of giving him pleasure, and that this was the reason
for her action'; but when he tries to kiss her she threatens to ring
the bell.[1] Clearly this is a prefiguration of the Narrator's attempt

[1] Part of the episode in *Jean Santeuil* is written on the back of an announcement for the wedding of Jeanne Bailby (sister of Léon Bailby, for whose
newspaper *La Presse* Proust was then writing an article) on 21 September
1899. Proust asked his mother about the date of the wedding on 12
September, complained next day of having no news, and thanked her on the
20th for her 'kind trouble'. He must have received the announcement, therefore, at some time after the 13th and before the 20th. See *Jean Santeuil*
vol. 3, 256-62

to kiss Albertine—who does indeed ring the bell—in her bed in the Grand Hôtel at Balbec. Perhaps the incident actually occurred with a guest, whether male or female, of Proust's at Évian; and possibly the guest was Maugny, who stayed the night at the Splendide Hôtel in Dr Proust's old room on 12 September. But probably the fact that Proust does not mention the pain in his wrist until the 19th rules out Maugny, unless he came a second time a week later. There can be no doubt, at least, that Proust's aching wrist is the same as Jean Santeuil's, and that the episode in *Jean Santeuil* was written at Évian.

One of the dilemmas of society on the lake was the necessity of seeing Coppet, with its relics of Mme de Staël, and the danger of meeting its châtelaine. Mme d'Haussonville ('Pauline', as Proust irreverently called her) was particularly formidable at this time of crisis in the Affair. When the Prince de Polignac's American wife (*née* Winnaretta Singer) saw her on the 9th she had, it is true, shown gracious pleasure on hearing Proust was at Évian: "Do tell me where he's staying, we're *such* good friends!"; but the next moment she remarked cuttingly to the Princesse: "I can *quite* understand you foreigners thinking as you do about the Affair!" The only solution was to go on a Thursday, when the house was thrown open to tourists, and Pauline would certainly be lunching out. On the 21st Constantin de Brancovan and Hermant set out from Amphion in one of the new motor-cars, and were joined by Proust, who preferred to travel by the little train for fear of draughts, at Geneva. Coppet was swarming with sightseers and Mme d'Haussonville, sure enough, was lunching in Geneva. They left a card on her, after seeing absolutely everything, and again on Mme de Rothschild at Prégny. When Proust once more insisted on taking the train at Geneva, Constantin was extremely wounding. "Draughts, indeed!" he exclaimed, "it's all your imagination! Why, your father always tells everybody there's nothing whatever the matter with you! He says your asthma's sheer hypochondria!" But Constantin, Proust later discovered, however insensitive he might be to the horrors of asthma, was right about motor-cars. When one felt only just well enough to get out of bed, he found, they would whisk one away to a longed-for place or person; if one felt too ill to get up at all, the friend would be brought to one's bedside; and they were driven by young and charming

chauffeurs. The motor-car, a few years later—such was the indirect consequence of the visit to Coppet—was to become an
indispensable factor in the liberation which enabled him to
conceive *A la Recherche*, and in the web of new habits which
enabled him to write it. Meanwhile Mme d'Haussonville sent a
most amiable letter of disappointment at missing her visitors, with
a whole page devoted to Proust himself and only a single line
for Abel Hermant, who was given to putting his aristocratic
acquaintances into his novels and making them commit the most
appalling crimes in the last chapter. Proust forwarded it to his
mother for safe keeping, remarking: 'Here is a letter from Pauline,
or How to show one's good-breeding gracefully.'

Autumn arrived at the end of September, rain swept the lake,
and the hotel was about to close. Just as at Rivebelle 'one could
be sure of two or three supplementary months of warmth after
the cold weather had reached Balbec',[1] so on the southward-
facing Swiss bank of the lake opposite Évian the sunlight was still
on the hillsides and the season just beginning; but Mme Proust
begged her son in vain to move there. The staff at the Splendide,
like their colleagues at Balbec, began to leave for Nice, headed
by the obliging lift-boy, who was unpopular with the rest, being
a Dreyfusard and a Jew. The omnibus-driver called on Proust to
shake hands and say, with a warmth that was all the more touching
since he had already received his tip: "Ever since I've worked in
hotels, I've never known anyone so kind to the 'employees'.[2]
We're all devoted to you, and I think it's a shame you're so ill,
because if anyone doesn't deserve to be, it's you!"

Proust had a momentary scare when he heard Anatole France
was thinking of him as a possible husband for his daughter
Suzanne. She was now a charming girl of eighteen, but permanently unsettled by the rift between her parents, who alternately
fought for her possession and neglected her.[3] 'I shall never do it,'

---

[1] I, 676

[2] "A charming euphemism," Proust observed to his mother, and used it
for the lift-boy at Balbec (I, 800).

[3] Suzanne ended by marrying Captain Henri Mollin, an assistant to the
Dreyfusist War Minister General André, on 10 December 1901: "the
young man speaks with due admiration of Picquart, and seems a decent
sort, so let us rejoice," said her prodigal father.

Proust wrote in alarm to his mother, adding 'Be very cautious if you talk about any matrimonial desires for me.' It may be inferred that Mme Proust had tried to find him a wife on previous occasions, and that he had made no objection in principle, whether from desire to please her, or to conceal his perversion, or from confidence that he could always refuse any actual candidate for his hand, or because he had not yet entirely renounced the possibility of marriage.

Early in October Maugny left for Paris, tiresomely announcing that he would tell Mme Proust her son would be perfectly well if he didn't take so much medicine. Proust saw more of Chevilly, and thought of moving on with him to Venice, where Coco de Madrazo (whose father Raymond de Madrazo had married Reynaldo's sister Maria in the previous June) had been staying with his aunt Mme Fortuny, the wife of the famous dress-designer. But he abandoned the idea when he heard that Coco had moved to Rome. One evening he drove with Chevilly's sister Marie on the way back from Mme Bartholoni's at Coudrée, and the movement of the carriage on the darkening road recalled Vigny's *Maison du Berger*, already recited by Dr Cottet, in which the poet rides in a shepherd's caravan with his beloved.

> "*Mais toi, ne veux-tu pas, voyageuse indolente,*
> *Rêver sur mon épaule, en y posant ton front?*"

he repeated daringly; for Marie was engaged to be married to the journalist Édouard Trogan, and he felt it safe to flirt with her. In *Sodome et Gomorrhe*[1] it is to Albertine that the Narrator addresses the same lines, as he tears open her raincoat in the little train after their meeting with Saint-Loup at Doncières. 'I don't know which of the two,' Proust wrote to Chevilly, 'those exquisite verses or your sister, seemed more poetic at that moment!' About 7 October he abandoned hope of Italy, broke a dinner-engagement with the Brancovans, and returned precipitately to Paris, where he fell ill and was visited every day by François d'Oncieu.

The Dreyfus Affair was over. On 19 September President Loubet had remitted the remainder of Dreyfus's sentence and

[1] II, 865

cancelled the order for his degradation[1]; on the 21st General de Galliffet announced: 'The incident is closed'; and on 17 November Waldeck-Rousseau tabled an amnesty bill covering all crimes or misdemeanours committed in connection with the Affair.[2] Dreyfus retired to his sister's house at Carpentras near Avignon to recuperate. A year later, in November 1900, he appeared in Paris and was mobbed by hostesses, much to their disappointment and his own disgust. "I hate all this moaning about my sufferings," he remarked to Julien Benda. "I like to talk about my Case *objectively.*" When Mme Straus met him she could not resist a malicious "How d'you do, Captain, I've been hearing such a lot about you!"; and she was heard afterwards to utter the Duchesse de Guermantes's epigram: "What a pity we can't choose someone else for our innocent!"[3] Picquart's dislike of Jews mysteriously returned; he refused to shake hands with Dreyfus, and took to reading Drumont's *La Libre Parole.* The cynical Clemenceau exclaimed: "If Drumont hadn't got in first, what a splendid anti-Semitic newspaper Picquart and I could have run!" Léon Daudet reported two remarks of Dreyfus which were none the less apposite for being totally fictitious: "I've never had a moment's peace since I left Devil's Island," and "Shut up, all of you, or I'll confess."

The enchanting social scene on which Proust had moved for six years was now riven asunder by complex antipathies; he looked back on the Guermantes Way with disillusionment. Two hostile groups confronted one another across a wide limbo of the half-hearted and the indifferent. Not all were as violent as the Marquis de Lubersac, a dreadful miser who thrashed his cabbies and never paid Dr Proust's bills: such was his virulence, after he

[1] A new Dreyfusist petition was organised at this time by *L'Aurore.* A list of signatures with the postmark 20 September 1899, shown at the Proust Exhibition at the Wildenstein Gallery in October 1955 (*Catalogue,* No. 306), has nothing to do with Proust, who was still at Évian, but includes the names of several of his friends—Reynaldo Hahn, René Peter, Édouard Risler, Méry Laurent and Anatole France. Possibly the canvasser was Robert Proust, whose Dreyfusist activity at this time was causing Proust anxiety ('Please advise Robert to keep calm,' he wrote to Mme Proust on 10 September). Dr Robert Le Masle, who lent this list to the Proust exhibition, was a personal friend of Robert Proust in later years.

[2] The bill was not finally carried until 24 December 1900; but in spite of much skirmishing on either side no harm was done in the meantime.

[3] Cf. II, 239

became the lover of the royalist Mme Porgès (although she was born a Wodianer and came from Vienna) that he made each of his sons, one by one, fight duels with the young Rothschilds. Comtesse Potocka lectured Comte Étienne de Lorencez on patriotism, till he retorted: "Surely you, a Neapolitan Pole, aren't going to preach the love of France to the son of a French general?" The lovely Marie Finaly forgot her Jewish birth and adopted ("by way of keeping up with her in-laws," said Proust) the anti-Dreyfusist views of her husband's family, the Barbarins. An ambassador's son remarked to Proust's friend Louis de la Salle : 'Good Lord, are you a Dreyfusist? It won't do your career any good, you know!" Mme Greffulhe became secretly convinced of Dreyfus's innocence, and wrote to her friend the Kaiser begging him to grant her an audience in Berlin, and confide in her whether or not he had employed Dreyfus as a spy; but a large basket of orchids was the only answer Wilhelm II vouchsafed. It is very possible that the story told in *Sodome et Gomorrhe*[1] of the Prince and Princesse de Guermantes—how each unknown to the other asked Abbé Poiré to say a mass for Dreyfus—is true of Mme Greffulhe and her husband; and if so Abbé Poiré may be identified as their friend the Abbé Mugnier, a saintly and delightful high-society priest, whom we shall later find taking an interest in Proust's salvation. But Mme Greffulhe's motives were mixed, for she was becoming interested in politics, moving ever leftward, and had begun to invite those 'Dreyfusards of the eleventh hour', Barthou and Briand, to her dinners. Sometimes, however, as in the dying Charles Haas, Proust saw a genuine conscience in travail. It is probable that Haas, like Swann, risked his social position by proclaiming his belief in Dreyfus's innocence and his support for revision. But it is certain that he resembled Swann (who 'refused to sign, because his name sounded too Hebraic') in refraining from supporting the petition for Picquart. Swann, 'although he approved of revision, would have nothing to do with the campaign against the Army'[2]; and Haas, the veteran of 1870, as Jacques Émile Blanche records, joined the Marquis du Lau and other members of the Jockey Club in 'cutting' their fellow-clubman and former friend General de Galliffet, when he became the revisionist War Minister and undertook the reform of the Army. The Dreyfus Case had broken the spell of the Guermantes

[1] II, 709-11   [2] II, 713

Way. Proust saw his hosts stripped of the poetry with which he himself had clothed them: a duchess was only an ordinary person wearing a tiara, a duke was only a bourgeois with an exaggerated hauteur or affability. He realised that in entering the heartless and empty world of the Guermantes, in searching there for something higher than himself, he had committed an absurdity and a sin. He punished himself. His asthma descended, like a gaoler or a guardian angel, never to leave him again. His face became haggard, anxious and bearded. Exiled in the desert island of his bedroom, a guiltless traitor to society, he must have felt very like Dreyfus. But 'going-out' ceased to be one of his chief preoccupations (though it always remained an occasional mixed pleasure), less because society had banished him, than because, like Coriolanus, he had banished *them*.

He had a further cause for despondency in the apparent failure of *Jean Santeuil*. He had written out his life, hoping that the answer to its mystery would somehow be revealed in the total, but the riddle remained unsolved. He had worked discontinuously, with innumerable fresh starts, as the fitful inspiration came; but the sterile, disjointed incidents did not add up to a novel. Each episode set out hopefully for the country of the imagination, which he knew ought to be always everywhere, and led him into a waste land. Four years of toil, as it seemed, nearly three hundred thousand words, were wasted.

Yet the imperfections of *Jean Santeuil* should not be exaggerated. It is a fragment made of fragments, a jigsaw puzzle with many of the pieces missing or refusing to fit; but another year's labour would have sufficed to join the episodes, to remove superfluous characters and incidents, and to produce a novel fit for publication. A revised *Jean Santeuil* would have been, in its theme and style and freshness, something new and surprising in French literature, yet not too new, not too far ahead of Anatole France and Barrès for the public to assimilate it: it might have made Proust's name, and rendered *A la Recherche* forever impossible. The best of *Jean Santeuil* is not noticeably immature, except to the modern reader, who is aware, with his knowledge of *A la Recherche*, that its maturity of talent is also the immaturity of genius. For such a reader there is in every page, besides the conscious brilliance, unconscious genius, the sense of a miracle about to happen: the overriding impression is of light and music, of endless discoveries always round the next corner, of sun, air and springtime. The bud contains the fruit, and Proust himself must have felt pride as well as disappointment in what he had achieved. Perhaps he also realised, however, that *Jean Santeuil* is disfigured not only by technical lapses but by a moral fault which is inseparable from the main theme. It is a novel of revenges, of resentments felt and gratified, of self-adoration and self-pity. The hero is an ill-used young man, thwarted by unfeeling and philistine parents, insulted by wicked hostesses, self-satisfied snobs and pseudo-artists; a benevolent Providence ensures that he invariably scores off them all; and he is insufferably charming, handsome, intelligent and magnanimous. It is possible to commiserate with Proust's injured susceptibility, but not to admire its literary over-compensation in *Jean Santeuil*.

In no section of the novel is the flaw of hurt vanity so glaring as in the deplorable Part VIII, which consists of a series of incidents in which the hero is first socially outraged, and then has his revenge by being publicly patronised by the social superiors of his enemies. It is probable, however, that in their present form these are merely alternative sketches for what would have been, if Proust had revised his work, not more than two main episodes: a scene in which Jean is insulted by Mme Marmet and befriended by the Duchesse de Réveillon, and another in which he fights a duel and is championed by the Duc de Réveillon. Chapter V ('*Le Salon de Mme de Réveillon*') was written, as we have seen, at Kreuznach in August 1897, and internal evidence suggests that the remainder of Part VIII may have been written about the same time.[1] The whole section is particularly rich in material later used in *A la Recherche*. Mme Marmet is an early form of Mme Verdurin,[2]

---

[1] Datable allusions in Part VIII include the death of Verlaine (8 January 1896), vol. 3, p. 55; the death of Nathé Weil (30 June 1896), p. 125; Proust's duel with Lorrain (6 February 1897) suggests chapters X-XII; Nicolas II first uses the word 'alliance' (August 1897), p. 40.

[2] Mme Marmet has nothing in common with Proust's beloved, intelligent, warm-hearted, unsnobbish Mme Straus, with whom she has been identified merely because her son was Jean's schoolfellow, as Jacques Bizet was Proust's. But Jacques Baignères's mother Laure Baignères would fit equally well. In so far as she has a living original, Mme Marmet is probably Mme Hochon with a little of Mme Lemaire. But in the main Proust has merely borrowed her from the character of the same name in Anatole France's *Le Lys Rouge*.

M. Boissard of M. de Norpois, the Vicomte de Lomperolles of both Charlus (modelled solely on Baron Doasan without, as yet, a trace of Montesquiou) and M. de Vaugoubert. An officer returns Jean's salute in the street, like Saint-Loup, or Lieutenant de Cholet at Orleans, with a hypocritical pretence of not recognising him. And the Duchesse de Réveillon, when Jean is disgraced at Mme Marmet's, offers him her arm precisely as the Queen of Naples was to give hers to the stricken Baron de Charlus at Mme Verdurin's in *La Prisonnière*.[1] Bergotte in *Jean Santeuil* is a painter who talks like Elstir; but a primitive form of the novelist himself appears in Part X, chapter IX as Silvain Bastelle. M. Bastelle is beset by the problem which obsesses the dying Bergotte in *Le Temps Retrouvé*—the difficulty of redeeming his moral evil by the creation of aesthetic good; but his vices turn out, absurdly, to be nothing worse than drink and gluttony.

Jean's love for Mme Françoise S. in Part IX is based, as has already been seen, on several different incidents in Proust's own life: on Mme Hayman, Reynaldo Hahn, and the unidentifiable love-affairs which produced, before he met Reynaldo, the scenes of jealous cross-examination in the earlier stories of *Les Plaisirs et les Jours*. The same material was used in *A la Recherche* for both Odette and Albertine. Jean, like Swann, is tempted to open his mistress's letter to an alleged uncle, knocks on the wrong window and is confronted by two old gentlemen, associates his love with the 'little phrase', and has a dream which marks the end of his jealousy, and therefore of his love. Françoise, Odette and Albertine alike are given to Lesbian love. But other incidents, such as Jean's gift to Françoise of the agate marble, a present from Marie Kossichef in the Champs-Élysées, belong in *A la Recherche* not to Odette but to Albertine. It has been suggested that Françoise, because her Christian name is the same with a feminine ending, is intended for François d'Oncieu; but the identification is quite impossible, for she is already called Françoise in *Les Plaisirs et les Jours*, in stories written several years before Proust met Oncieu.[2] In Part X Charlotte Clissette is another early version of Albertine. Jean plays with her the game of ferret, not at the seaside but in Paris (as he may have done with Marie

[1] *Jean Santeuil*, vol. 3, 93; *Pléïade*, III, 322.
[2] Cf. '*La Fin de la Jalousie*' and '*Mélancolique Villégiature de Mme de Breyves*'.

Finaly), she is jealously guarded by an aunt, as was Albertine by Mme Bontemps, and she thwarts his attempt to kiss her in bed by threatening to ring the bell. Possibly the fact that Jean's love for Charlotte overlaps in time with the end of his love for Françoise is a further hint that the first Albertine was Marie Finaly; for Proust's brief passion for Marie Finaly closely followed his wooing of Mme Hayman.

Towards the end of *Jean Santeuil* appear signs that Proust had made, without realising their full meaning, the discoveries which were to lead to *A la Recherche*. In the last chapters of Part X, written not earlier than the autumn of 1898,[1] Jean shows a new compassion and understanding for his ageing father and mother. Proust had begun to forgive his parents, and the way was now open for the conception in *A la Recherche* of the Narrator's family as a symbol of absolute goodness, a counterbalance to the original sin which corrupts society and sexual love. Through this means the moral disequilibrium of *Jean Santeuil*, in which the unreal virtue of the hero is so unsatisfactory an atonement for the heartless aridity of the other characters, was to be resolved in his great novel.

A second discovery was still more far-reaching. In the Étreuilles section of *Jean Santeuil*, written in the summer of 1896, Jean experiences from time to time, in what is no doubt an un-altered reminiscence of Proust's own boyhood, a rudimentary form of unconscious memory. The apple-blossom at Étreuilles restores the precise sensation of seeing the blossom of the year before, buzzing flies or a noise of hammering heard in Paris bring back the very moment when he heard the same sounds at Étreuilles.[2] But his explanation of the experience ('the sensation of a past moment, in which we saw other such apple-trees, is concealed in it') is not adequate to the delight it causes ('Jean felt a happiness so intense, that he seemed on the point of fainting'). In the very latest parts of the novel, however, the true Proustian concept of unconscious memory is almost complete. Jean hears the little phrase once more, long after the end of his love for Françoise, and feels, even before he recognises it, 'a sensation of

---

[1] In chapter XI (vol. 3, 330) M. Santeuil remarks: "They say Colonel Picquart will get five years' imprisonment," an allusion to the expected court-martial of Picquart in October–November 1898.

[2] *Jean Santeuil*, vol. I, 138, 149, 153, 164

vast freshness, as if he had become young again'.[1] The poems of
the Vicomtesse de Réveillon, which are those of Anna de Noailles
heard in the spring of 1899, show Jean that she, too, has known
'that profound essence of our being, which is restored instantaneously by a perfume, a ray of light falling into our room, and
so intoxicates us that we become indifferent to real life . . . and
are momentarily freed from the tyranny of the present'.[2] But the
mystery is studied most persistently in chapter IX of Part VI,
which describes an incident in Proust's stay at Évian in September
1899, and is therefore among the last passages Proust wrote
before he abandoned his abortive novel. While Jean is driving
back from Mme d'Alériouvres's villa on the Lake of Geneva—
evidently Princesse de Brancovan's Villa Bassaraba—and re-
proaching himself for his wasted life, the tracks of boats on the
lake recall those on the sea at Beg-Meil: 'his heart swelled, and the
life which he had thought so useless and unusable seemed enchanting and beautiful'. Once again he attempts to explain his
feeling, and this time, at least, makes a great advance: he sees that
he has experienced something more than a mere recrudescence of
the past, since his past pleasure at Beg-Meil was much smaller
than his present pleasure by the lake-shore. The meaning of his
experience lies in something incommensurable which has been
added to both past and present. But here Jean, and Proust with
him, lacks the essential clue, and can only enter upon a false path.
The unknown power, he decides, is poetic imagination, 'which
cannot work upon present reality, nor yet upon past reality as
restored to us by memory, but hovers only round the reality of
the past when it is entangled in the reality of the present'. Proust
(for in his excitement he has begun to use the word 'I') presses on,
and once or twice again touches upon the truth: 'what the poet
needs is memory, or not strictly speaking memory at all, but the
transmutation of memory into a reality directly felt'; 'from that
juxtaposition issues a sensation freed from the bonds of the
senses'; 'we are torn loose from the slavery of the present and
flooded with the intuition of an immortal life'. He even divines the
possibility of a work, the future *A la Recherche*, in which he would
write 'nothing of what I saw, or thought, or apprehended by
mere reasoning, or remembered by mere memory, but only of the
past brought to life in an odour or a sight which it causes to

[1] *Jean Santeuil*, vol. 3, 225   [2] *Ibid.*, vol. 2, 305-6

explode'. And the superiority of this pleasure to all other pleasures he has known 'is perhaps the token of the superiority of a state in which we have for our object an eternal essence'; 'our true nature is outside time, born to feed on the eternal'. 'We are justified in giving first place to the imagination, because we now realise that it is the organ that serves the eternal.'

Proust had now experienced, as a first reward for leaving the Guermantes Way, a complete form of 'unconscious memory'; but he was not yet equipped to understand its true nature. Time regained is surpassingly valuable not because it restores a fragment of past sensation—for this, since we were then as blinded by habit as we are now, is worth no more than the present—but because along with that fragment is released, from the unconscious mind in which it was buried and preserved, a vision of the absolute reality which only the unconscious mind can see. And further, in this momentary but endless admission to the world beyond time lies salvation, since there alone is the virtue we lose when we are born, and the joy which earthly love can only take away. Proust would not be granted the final revelation until Time, which so far he had only wasted, was, at last, Time Lost. He names 'le temps perdu' in the last section of his novel, but it still has only the meaning of time misspent: 'he thought unceasingly, with irritation and despair, of the time lost ('temps perdu') in the four years since he left school'.[1] The very last sentence of Jean Santeuil, like that of A la Recherche, contains the word 'time'—'the work of life and death, the work of time, continued unceasingly'—but here it is still only time the destroyer, sapping the life of the parents whom Jean, now that he is strong and they are weak, has at last forgiven. But even Proust's belief in the imagination was still misplaced; for in A la Recherche and perhaps in all great works of art, the true function of the imagination is, paradoxically, not to imagine—in the sense of inventing or transforming—but to see: to see the reality which is concealed by habit and the phenomenal world. He needed, and providentially found, a prophet who would tell him that 'the artist is only a scribe'.

[1] Jean Santeuil, vol. 3, 284

Chapter 14

SALVATION THROUGH RUSKIN

EXCEPT that it brought him joy unspoilt by suffering, Proust's passion for Ruskin took precisely the same course as his love-affairs or ardent friendships. There was a prelude of tepid acquaintance; a crystallisation and a taking fire; and a falling out of love, from which he emerged free, but changed and permanently enriched. The period of mere acquaintance was as protracted as the onset of devotion was sudden. He had learned of Ruskin at second-hand during his student-days at the École des Sciences Politiques from his master Paul Desjardins; and he read the brief translated extracts from Ruskin's works which appeared every year from 1893 to 1903 (with the exception of 1894 and 1901) in a periodical edited by Desjardins, the *Bulletin de l'Union pour l'Action Morale*, to which he was a regular subscriber. But he knew also from Montesquiou, who gave him a sumptuously bound copy of *The Gentle Art of Making Enemies* and was a friend of Whistler, of Ruskin's outrageous attack in 1877 on Whistler's *Nocturnes*; and this enemy of Elstir must have seemed less a prophet than a reactionary, a persecutor rather than an apostle of the religion of beauty. "I will walk with your Majesty," says the Duke of Brittany to the King of Portugal at the Opéra in *Jean Santeuil*; and "No, Brittany," replies the affable monarch, "I'd rather go with my young friend Jean; he can finish telling me about the libel-suit between Ruskin and Whistler, which fascinates me, and besides, it will be one in the eye for Mme Marmet."[1]

In 1897 appeared Robert de La Sizeranne's charmingly written and well-documented study, *Ruskin et la religion de la beauté*, which Proust seems to have read immediately[2]; for in that year[3]

---

[1] *Jean Santeuil*, vol. 3, 70

[2] He may have read La Sizerane's book even before its publication in volume form, for it appeared serially in the *Revue des Deux Mondes* from December 1895 to April 1897.

[3] Ainslie's dating is confirmed by the existence of letters to him from Proust on the occasion of Alphonse Daudet's death in December 1897, after Ainslie's return to England.

Douglas Ainslie, an English friend of Robert de Billy, met Proust at the Daudets' in the Rue de Bellechasse, at 9 Boulevard Malesherbes, and in the Café Weber, where they argued about the relative merits of Ruskin and Pater. Proust arrived late at Weber's with the velvet collar of his greatcoat wrapped about his ears;"I can only stay a minute," he would announce, and then talk, as he did to Albert Flament, till dawn, growing ever more brilliant to stave off the moment of parting: 'to give of his best,' remarks Ainslie, 'he had to feel he was keeping an impatient cabman waiting'. Ainslie quoted a remark made to him by Pater in person: "I can't believe Ruskin could see more in St Mark's at Venice than I do!"; to which Proust retorted, with a despairing shrug of the shoulders: "What's the use! You and I will never see eye to eye about English literature!" Either at this time or a little later Proust read a less authoritative and much earlier study of Ruskin, J. A. Milsand's *L'Ésthétique anglaise*, which appeared in 1864, when only half of Ruskin's work had been written and before his philosophy reached its mature form.

In 1898 two other personal influences converged to join the undercurrent which, beneath the opposing stream of the Dreyfus Case, was directing Proust's thoughts towards Ruskin. In the autumn Robert de Billy visited Paris on leave from the French Embassy in London, where he served from 1896 to 1899. Billy described his recent visit to the romanesque churches of the Auvergne and Poitou, talked of Ruskin, and lent Proust his own copy of Émile Mâle's *L'Art religieux du XIIIe siècle en France*, which had just appeared. The book returned four years later, bereft of its cover and stained with patent medicines: Proust quoted it copiously in his Ruskin studies, and later used it for the iconography of Saint-André-des-Champs and Elstir's explanation of the sculptures in the 'Persian' church of Balbec.

Marie Nordlinger, too, during her stay in Paris from December 1896 to August 1898, was a valuable source of information about Ruskin. She found Proust had read 'everything by Ruskin that had been translated into French'—the extracts in the *Bulletin de l'Union pour l'Action Morale*, that is, and the extensive quotations in La Sizeranne's book. Proust, in turn, was delighted to discover that she came from Rusholme, the very suburb of Manchester in which Ruskin had delivered his lectures of *Sesame and Lilies*; so that henceforth the grey place-name of Manchester incongruously took on a poetic aura hardly inferior to that of the golden Venice or Vézelay. On her way home to England Mlle Nordlinger spent two days at Rouen with Mme Hendlé, wife of the prefect of the town and a relative of her father. She was met at the station by the official landau with a cockaded footman, and drove straight to the cathedral, where she talked to the stone-masons repairing the porch, and to the near-by church of Saint-Ouen, where she met the aged verger, Julien Édouard, who had guided Ruskin and his friends in the autumn of 1880. A still more decisive example was her visit, a little earlier, to Amiens: she had 'examined the cathedral stone by stone, with Ruskin for my guide', and after-wards, in Paris, gave the eager Marcel an impromptu verbal rendering of passages from the 'Separate Travellers' Edition'—which constitutes a complete guide to the sculptures of the cathedral—of Chapter Four of *The Bible of Amiens*.

In the summer of 1899 Proust discussed Ruskin with François d'Oncieu, and lent him La Sizeranne's treatise before he went to Évian. At first, in the lake-level society of the Brancovans and Mlle Kiki, he felt no need of the book; but towards the end of September, when with Clément de Maugny on the hills above Thonon he faced the soaring Alps behind the lake, he was conscious of the discrepancy between his own emotions and the magnificent passage of *Praeterita*, quoted by La Sizeranne in his first chapter, in which Ruskin describes his first sight of the Alps.[1] He begged Mme Proust to rescue and send 'La Sizeranne's book on Ruskin, so that I may see the mountains through the eyes of that great man'. After a few days, before it came, he hurried back to Paris: 'crystallisation' had occurred; his craving had turned from the pinnacles of inaccessible ice to Ruskin himself. During the illness which followed his return the faithful Oncieu called every day to enquire after his health; and when he recovered they went out together on expeditions in quest of Ruskin. 'Oncieu's mind is free of prejudice and full of relish,' Proust wrote to Chevilly, 'and he is so kind as to follow in my footsteps, which lead him, however, only into perfectly respectable and high-

[1] 'There was no thought in any of us for a moment of their being clouds. They were as clear as crystal, sharp on the pure horizon sky, and already tinged with rose by the sinking sun. . . . I went down that evening from the garden-terrace of Schaffhausen with my destiny fixed in all of it that was to be sacred and useful.'

minded places such as the Louvre or the Bibliothèque Nationale.'
In that library he discovered a fragment of *The Seven Lamps of
Architecture* translated in the *Revue Générale* of October 1895,
nestling, as he noticed with amusement, between articles by two
of his summer acquaintances, Henry Bordeaux, and Chevilly's
sister's fiancé Édouard Trogan. Finding that no more translations from Ruskin existed, he began to read him, painfully but
successfully, in the original. A letter of 30 November asks Pierre
Lavallée, then a librarian at the École des Beaux-Arts, whether
his library possesses a copy of *The Queen of the Air* ('please leave
a note with the concierge—I never wake before two in the afternoon'); and whether or not Lavallée could supply the book,
Proust soon had a copy of his own.[1] *The Queen of the Air* was
chosen, no doubt, for the sake of the many superb and brilliantly
translated quotations from it in La Sizeranne: possibly for the
aphorism which fitted so aptly his new fervour and his abandonment of *Jean Santeuil*: 'A truly modest person admires the works
of others with eyes full of wonder, and with a joy that leaves him
no time to deplore his own.' Perhaps he was equally attracted by
the passages on the symbolism of flowers, including the lilies of
Florence, or on the limpid water of the Swiss lakes, which in
La Sizeranne's French astonishingly resemble, with their long
sentences winding in arabesque round the central column of their
meaning, his own prose in *Jean Santeuil*; for the influence of
Ruskin on Proust's later style came not so much from a desire
to write like Ruskin, as from a realisation that Ruskin already
wrote like himself.

On 5 December 1899, encouraged by unexpected praise of *Les
Plaisirs et les Jours* in a letter from Marie Nordlinger, he revealed
his momentous decision. Since they last met, a year and a half
before, he has been unhappy (he means, as always, unhappy in
love), and his creative powers have suffered from the deteriora-
tion in his health; his novel has failed ('*je travaille depuis très
longtemps à un ouvrage de très longue haleine, mais sans rien
achever*'), and he sometimes feels, he confesses, like Mr Casaubon
in *Middlemarch*, who wastes his life on a masterpiece he will never

---

[1] He appealed also to Marie Nordlinger, who sent him her copy of the
Queen of the Air with her own marginal annotations, early in January 1900;
but meanwhile he had acquired one by his own efforts, and gave her it in
exchange.

be able to finish. But for the past fortnight he has been busy 'on a little work, quite different from the sort of thing I usually write, on Ruskin and certain cathedrals.' Meanwhile, a few days before, Mlle Nordlinger's cousin Reynaldo Hahn had written to her what might seem a contradictory report, that Marcel was 'translating the fourth chapter of Ruskin's book on Amiens.' Ought we to deduce that he had already completed the first three chapters? Probably not, for this fourth chapter, to which the preceding three are merely introductory, gives a full guide to the cathedral and is complete in itself. As we have seen, Mlle Nordlinger, after her visit to Amiens eighteen months before, had made him an improvised translation from the 'Separate Travellers' Edition' of this very chapter; he had already begun, partly in emulation of La Sizeranne,[1] a series of pilgrimages to the cathedrals described by Ruskin, of which Amiens was the most accessible for a day-tripper from Paris; so on every account it was natural that he should turn first to this, of all sections of Ruskin's works. His first visit to Amiens had already taken place, in late October or early November, 'in the chill golden air of a French autumn morning',[2] with this same Chapter Four of *The Bible of Amiens* as guide.

Ruskin suggested two possible ways of approaching the cathedral: the first, 'if you are not afraid of an hour's walk', from the citadel on the chalk hill beyond the northernmost of the eleven streams into which the Somme here divides, causing Ruskin to call Amiens 'the Venice of France'; the second, 'if you cannot or will not walk, or if you really must go to Paris this afternoon, and supposing notwithstanding these weaknesses you are still a nice sort of person, for whom it is of some consequence which way you come at a pretty thing', from the Place Gambetta up the busiest street of the town, the Rue des Trois Cailloux. Proust, deciding that he belonged to this latter class, followed the pre-scribed way: past the *pâtisserie* on the left, where he followed Ruskin's advice to 'buy some bonbons or tarts, so as to get into a cheerful temper', and up the Rue Robert de Luzarches to the south façade of the cathedral. To the left of the porch he saw the beggars, and again obeyed Ruskin ('put a sou into every beggar's box who asks it there—it is none of your business whether they

[1] 'In Switzerland, Florence, Amiens, I have worked where Ruskin worked,' wrote La Sizeranne (*R.R.B.*, 9).
[2] *La Bible d'Amiens*, 246, footnote

should be there or not, nor whether they deserve the sou—be sure only whether you yourself deserve to have it to give; and give it prettily, and not as if it burnt your fingers'). The beggars were so ancient, he decided, that they might well be the same Ruskin saw nineteen years before. The master himself seemed to stand beside him and guide his hand; he remembered Frédéric Moreau, in *L'Éducation sentimentale*, tipping the harp-player on the Seine steamer after his first sight of Mme Arnoux, and Flaubert's words: 'it was no mere vanity that urged him to this act of charity, but a feeling of benediction, an almost religious impulse of the heart, in which he associated his companion'.

It was noon: 'the sun was paying his daily call on the Gilded Virgin, nowadays gilded by him alone; and it was to his passing caress that she seemed to address her age-old smile'. He stepped back; the sunshine on the rows of saints gave to one a halo round his forehead, to another a cloak of warm light about his shoulders. Over the transept the slender, immensely tall, slightly leaning spire seemed, as Ruskin suggested, to 'bend to the west wind'. The Virgin was surrounded by flowering sprays of stone hawthorn—like those in the *petit sentier* at Illiers in the Month of Mary—'from whose endless spring the wind of time seemed already to have blown a few petals'. She carried a live jackdaw in the crook of her hand; she smiled, he thought, remembering the ladies of the Faubourg Saint-Germain, like a celestial hostess in her doorway; and as he watched, a few boatmen, hurrying past to meet the high tide on the Somme, raised their eyes to her as the Star of the Sea. He entered the cathedral and wandered among the carved stalls of the choir—'there is nothing else so beautiful cut out of the goodly trees of the world,' wrote Ruskin. Proust had seen casts of them in Paris, which he was not allowed to touch, in the museum at the Trocadéro (where the Narrator saw replicas of the Virgin and Apostles of Balbec[1]); but now, by permission of the verger, he was allowed to tap the long harp-strings of the grain of the wood itself, which gave out 'a sound as of a musical instrument, that seemed to tell how tenuous they were and how indestructible'. He proceeded to the sculptures of the west front, which Ruskin called the Bible of Amiens. Of these he has little to say that is not in Ruskin; but he borrowed for the arms and motto of the Baron de Charlus[2] the figure of Christ trampling on

[1] I, 659   [2] III, 805

the lion and the dragon, and the verse of Psalm lviii, 4, to which Ruskin refers: '*Inculcabis super leonem et aspidem.*' He descended from the cathedral to the river, and looked back at the north front; the sun shone directly through the plain glass of the windows, and the cathedral, which till then had seemed an edifice of stone, seemed to become transparent, 'to hold between its pillars, erect and reaching to the sky, ghostly and immaterial giants of green gold and flame'. He hurried west along the river to the municipal slaughter-houses, to find the precise spot from which Ruskin had made his distant sketch of 'Amiens, All Souls' Day, 1880',[1] and back to catch his train for Paris. After his return he hung in his bedroom, next to the Mona Lisa, a photograph of the Gilded Virgin, whose smile was no less enigmatic than her companion's: 'the one has only the beauty of a masterpiece, but the Gilded Virgin has the melancholy of a memory'.

The visit to Amiens had been preceded by one to Bourges, where he saw the porch carved with hawthorn blossom even more profusely than the lintels round the Gilded Virgin. 'Bourges is the cathedral of hawthorn,' he wrote, and quoted Ruskin: 'never was such hawthorn; you would try to gather it forthwith, but for fear of being pricked.' But Ruskin told him no more about Bourges, or the still prouder cathedral near Illiers, which he also revisited at this time; 'the stones of Chartres and Bourges left unanswered a host of questions which I ponder unceasingly,' he lamented in his *Figaro* article of 13 February 1900.

On 20 January 1900 Ruskin died at Brantwood, his house on the shore of Lake Coniston. He had written his masterpiece *Praeterita* from 1885 to 1889, in the last level light of his declining genius, during the intervals between fits of violent mania; his last journey abroad was to France, Switzerland and Italy in 1888.[2] Thereafter he sank into lethargy and silence. His white prophetic beard grew ever longer, now he had ceased to prophesy; he neither

---

[1] He failed to find it, and no wonder; for there is no point on the banks of the Somme where the cathedral appears to the right of the river (and therefore east of the viewer) and Saint-Leu to the right of the cathedral, as shown in Ruskin's illustration, which in this respect is an imaginary view.

[2] Proust's vivid description in *Contre Sainte-Beuve*, 382-5, of seeing Ruskin at a Rembrandt exhibition at Amsterdam, presumably during his own trip to Holland in October 1898, is totally fictitious. Ruskin was entirely confined to Brantwood at this time; and Proust also seems to have forgotten the Master's lifelong dislike of all Dutch painting.

wrote nor spoke, and refused, like Aunt Léonie, to move, first from his house, at last even from his bedroom. But Proust's sorrow at the passing of his master was short-lived; 'my grief is healthy and full of consolations,' he told Marie Nordlinger, 'for I realise what a trivial thing death is, when I see how intensely this dead man lives, and how I admire and listen to his words, and seek to understand and obey him, more than I would for many who are living'.

He was consoled also by the knowledge that, during the brief wave of publicity that follows the death of a great author, his writings on Ruskin would have news-value; and he acted so promptly that his obituary—signed, however, only with his initials—appeared only a week later, on the 27th, in the *Chronique des arts et de la curiosité*. This periodical was a weekly supplement, containing current art news, to the *Gazette des Beaux-Arts*, edited by Charles Ephrussi, the lesser original of Swann. Ephrussi was eager for more, and Proust took the opportunity to announce in the obituary that 'the *Gazette des Beaux-Arts* will have the honour to give a just idea and impression of Ruskin's work in a forthcoming number'. He also contrived to be introduced, probably by Léon Daudet, to Gaston Calmette, the new editor of *Le Figaro*, in which Daudet was writing at this time. Calmette was exceptionally gifted with the charm and affability which are so unexpected yet so often to be found in editors. "But absolutely, my dear fellow—but certainly, but of course, I shall be only too delighted," he would repeat, in a deep, purring voice, darting a velvet glance under his pince-nez. During the next fourteen years he accepted numerous articles from Proust, who expressed his genuine liking, his overwhelming but uneasy gratitude, by invitations to dine with noble guests, expensive gifts, and finally by the dedication of *Du Côté de chez Swann*. Since *Le Figaro* was the favourite newspaper of the aristocracy, Proust's articles no doubt helped a little to make him known as a writer, but also, still more, to perpetuate his unfortunate reputation as a society amateur. Sometimes, with tongue in cheek, he would write under a pseudonym, and make his articles sly pastiches of the *Figaro* gossip-column clichés[1]; sometimes, as now, under his own name,

---

[1] Several such pastiches appear in *A la Recherche*, notably (though this is supposed to be published in *Le Gaulois*) the obituary on Swann, 'a Parisian whose wit was universally appreciated' (III, 199-200).

he made a successful compromise between the obligatory 'Parisian gaiety' and his own manner, and struck a note which can often be heard in the full orchestra of *A la Recherche*.

He did not have so long to wait as the Narrator for the publication of his first article in *Le Figaro*—'that spiritual bread, still warm and moist from the press and the mists of morning, which we call a newspaper'.[1] *Pèlerinages Ruskiniens en France* appeared on 13 February. He invited his fellow-countrymen to make pilgrimages in honour of Ruskin, not to his grave at Coniston, not even (Proust thinks, with a savour of sour grapes, of his abortive plan to visit Venice from Évian the October before) to Venice, but to Rouen and Amiens, where ('as in the tomb at Rome which contains the heart of Shelley') they will find not his lifeless body, but his soul. He drew attention once more to his forthcoming articles in the *Gazette des Beaux-Arts*, appealed to the friends with whom Ruskin had travelled to tell him what would have been the contents of his unwritten books on Rouen (*Domrémy*) and Chartres (*The Springs of Eure*), and alluded to the Charity of Giotto at Padua, who reminds him at this moment, 'trampling on bags of gold and offering us wheat and flowers', not of the kitchen-maid at Combray but of Ruskin himself.

Early in February, when he was writing his *Figaro* article, he felt unsure of one of the facts he needed; and Léon Yeatman and his wife Madeleine were roused from bed one night by Dr Proust's man-servant with the extraordinary message: "Monsieur Marcel has asked me to ask Monsieur: what became of Shelley's heart?" One evening that spring the Yeatmans returned home and found, to their astonishment, Proust sitting alone in the concierge's lodge: it was he who had pulled the cord to let them in. "Your concierge is ill," he explained, "and her husband had to go to the chemist's for medicine, so I offered to take his place. Don't interrupt me now, I'm busy!" It was with the Yeatmans that, at the same time, he visited Rouen. His purpose was not so much to see the cathedral itself, of which Ruskin, in default of the unwritten *Domrémy*, could tell him little, as to identify a single small sculpture to which Ruskin had once referred in passing. Nothing could show more clearly that at this stage his interest in cathedrals was subsidiary to his passion for Ruskin: if he searched Ruskin's work for all that Ruskin could tell him

[1] III, 568

about cathedrals, it was in order to visit the cathedrals for what they could tell him about Ruskin.

On the very day of Ruskin's death Proust happened to re-read in *The Seven Lamps of Architecture* the description of a little grotesque figure, 'vexed and puzzled in his malice; his hand is pressed hard against his cheek-bone, and the flesh of the cheek is *wrinkled* under the eye by the pressure'.[1] 'I was seized by the desire to see the little man of whom Ruskin speaks,' he wrote, 'and I went to Rouen as if in obedience to a testamentary request, as if he had bequeathed to the care of his readers the insignificant creature whom he had, by speaking of him, restored to life.'

Proust and his friends looked up at the west front. Row upon row of saints warmed themselves in the sunlight of the winter morning, soaring to seemingly uninhabited heights, where, nevertheless, a carved hermit lived in eternal isolation, or a St Christopher glanced back for ever, wry-necked, at the Christ-Child his burden. How, in this thronged city of stone, could they find one tiny mannikin? They walked, with little hope, to his abode in the north porch, the Portail des Libraires, where the mediaeval booksellers had once kept their stalls; and suddenly Yeatman's young wife—who luckily was a trained and talented sculptor—cried: "There's one that looks just like him!" It was the little stone man, not six inches in height, and crumbled by time, but keeping still his angry wrinkled cheek and the minute speck of malice in his eye. Like the surging naked souls in the Last Judgement above him, he seemed resurrected, and Ruskin with him. The party moved to Saint-Maclou near by, where there was another Last Judgement, with roaring flames pursuing souls whose anger and despair had reminded Ruskin of Orcagna and Hogarth; and to Saint-Ouen, where they talked to the verger Julien Édouard who had guided Ruskin in 1880 and Marie Nordlinger in 1898. "Monsieur Ruskin said our church was the finest gothic monument in the world," he told them, much to Proust's bewildered amusement. Armed as he was with *The Seven Lamps of Architecture*, he knew Ruskin had written peevishly of the lantern in the tower: 'it is one of the basest pieces of gothic in Europe . . . resembling, and deserving little more credit than, the burnt sugar ornaments of elaborate confectionery'; and he had called the shafts supporting the piers of the nave 'the

[1] Library Edition, vol. 8, 217

ugliest excrescence I ever saw on a gothic building!'¹ But the success of the day was the stone man regained, a new emblem of the indestructibility of unconscious memory, since the tiny monster had reappeared not from the past of a living man, but from the graves of two dead. 'I was moved to find him still there,' wrote Proust, 'because I realised then that nothing dies that once has lived, neither the sculptor's thought, nor Ruskin's.'

Thanks to his meeting with Ruskin, Proust was not unduly grieved by his parting in March 1900 from the Mazarine Library. It was now four and a half years since, in October 1895 at Beg-Meil, he had requested and received leave till the end of the year for his visit to Réveillon in the 'bad season'. Before 1895 was out he had felt emboldened to ask for additional leave of a whole year, which was granted, like a Christmas present, on 24 December. In 1896 his only visit to the Mazarine was to present *Les Plaisirs et les Jours* to his colleagues. In December he applied again, punctually and punctiliously, for a year's leave. It was, he explained, through the Ministry's fault and from no remissness of his own, that permission did not arrive until January 1897; and he was wounded that M. Franklin, through Paul Marais, had seen fit to send him a sharp letter of rebuke. From a sense of delicacy he even abstained from using the Mazarine for his own studies; and the only library in Paris which he could never enter was the one to whose staff he belonged. Every December he went through the same preposterous formality, the only purpose of which was to preserve in Dr Proust's mind the conviction that his eldest son had, in a manner of speaking, a job. In 1899 a general inspection was held at the Mazarine: it seemed odd that one of the three honorary unpaid attachés should not have set foot in the library for so many years, and on 14 February 1900 Proust was peremptorily ordered to return to work immediately. He refrained; on 1 March he was deemed to have resigned; and so ended his imperceptible career as a librarian.

In *Du Côté de chez Swann* a journey to Venice is one of the dreams of the Narrator's childhood. It is prevented by the sudden illness which causes the family doctor to forbid not only Venice but even a visit to the theatre to see Berma, and to prescribe instead the daily outings in the Champs-Élysées, which alter the

¹ *The Seven Lamps* appeared in 1849. Julian Édouard's honour is saved if we grant that Ruskin might have changed his mind by 1880.

Narrator's life by causing him to fall in love with Gilberte. A second obstacle, after many years during which he longs intermittently for Venice, is his life with Albertine, in spite of which he has decided at last to abandon her and go, only a moment before Françoise announces: "Mademoiselle Albertine has left." His desire is fulfilled only after Albertine is dead and forgotten. In Proust's own life, however, there is little trace of longing for Venice before the summer of 1899,[1] when he thought of going there from Évian, 'supposing I can find a companion', and was prevented partly because Coco de Madrazo happened to be in Rome and could not come, but mostly because of his sudden decision to return to Paris, read Ruskin in the original, and visit cathedrals. The Narrator's thoughts of Italy—of Venice, Florence and Padua—are splendid anachronisms, coloured solely by Proust's experience of Ruskin in the summer and autumn of 1899. The passages which the Narrator as a boy repeats to himself in his enthusiasm, without giving their source—'Venice is the school of Giorgione, the home of Titian', 'a city of marble and gold, embossed with jasper and paved with emerald', 'men majestic and terrible as the sea, wearing armour with glints of bronze beneath the folds of their bloodred mantles', 'rocks of amethyst like a coral reef in Indian seas'—are all quotations from Ruskin.[2] The Narrator's visions of Florence, which Proust was never to visit, were similarly derived from Ruskin, partly through La Sizeranne, partly from his own impressions of *Mornings in Florence* in the original. When he visited Venice it was in continuation of the same plan, less than a year old, which had dictated his winter pilgrimages to the cathedrals of France.

[1] There is only the view of inaccessible Italy from the Alp Grüm in 1893 (but Venice is not mentioned), and the conversation with Douglas Ainslie about Ruskin, Pater and Saint Mark's in 1897. Even at Évian his longing was divided between Venice for Ruskin's sake and the Italian lakes for Stendhal's—'I dream of the journeys I haven't made, which is one way of making them,' he wrote to Chevilly in October 1899 after his return to Paris, 'pending the accomplishment—by the law which always makes the vague hopes of our youth come true in later life, and which brought me to Thonon this summer—of our less unlikely pilgrimages to the shores where Fabrice del Dongo revelled.' He was never to see the Italian lakes.

[2] I, 391-3. The first three come from *Modern Painters*, vol. 5, pt. 9, ch. 9, perhaps borrowed from La Sizeranne, pp. 115-16. The last is from *The Stones of Venice*, vol. 2, ch. 1, §1, presumably read in the original, since La Sizeranne does not quote it.

He had probably intended to go on to Venice from Évian next October ('Constantin de Brancovan assures me it's the best possible time of year from the point of view of health,' he had told Mme Proust the year before). It was mere coincidence that a sudden opportunity allowed him to go in spring, only a little later than the season promised by the Narrator's father. In mid-April Reynaldo Hahn was in Rome with his mother and Coco: could he be persuaded to turn north to Venice? At first Proust hesitated: 'Marcel isn't quite sure whether he's going to Venice —look out, I think we're in for a shower of telegrams,' Reynaldo told his cousin Marie; but when he heard that Marie Nordlinger herself was in Florence (she had left Manchester on 20 April) and would be coming to Venice with Reynaldo, the scale was turned.

'It was on a radiant May morning,'[1] wrote Marie Nordlinger, 'that my aunt, Reynaldo and I saw Marcel and his mother arrive in Venice.' As the train crossed the plain of Lombardy Mme Proust had read aloud from *The Stones of Venice* the cherished passage about 'the coral reef in Indian seas'; and at first, 'because we cannot see things at once through the eyes of the body and the eyes of the mind', Proust was a little disappointed to find the façade of Saint Mark's less like pearls and rubies than Ruskin had given him to expect. But when, after an afternoon nap, he descended to the quays of Venice, imagination and reality had merged. That evening he sat with Mlle Nordlinger at Quadri's café in the square of Saint Mark's, correcting with her help the manuscript of his translation of *The Bible of Amiens*[2]; and next morning at ten o'clock, when his shutters were opened, his eyes were dazzled by the sunlight falling not, as usual, on the iron chimney-cowl of the next-door house in Paris, but on the golden angel over the campanile of Saint Mark's, 'who bore me on his flashing wings a promise of beauty and joy greater than he ever brought to Christian hearts, when he came to announce "glory to God in the highest, and peace on earth to men of good will".'

[1] Perhaps 'May morning' should not be taken literally. Proust sent Mlle Nordlinger a cutting, in which he acknowledged her help, from his article on Ruskin and Amiens in the *Mercure de France* for April. He would surely have sent it well before the end of the month; and as it reached her only the day before his arrival in Venice, this event should perhaps be dated to the last week in April. But she may have received the letter several days late, if it had to be forwarded from Florence.

[2] Chapter Four only, no doubt.

Their hotel was not two hundred yards from the Palace of the Doges, the Piazza, and the golden angel. For wherever Proust or his mother travelled, whether to Trouville, Cabourg, Versailles, Évian or Venice, they were invariably to be found in the very best hotel, the one at the head of Baedeker's list; and at Venice they stayed at the Hôtel Danieli, where Ruskin had been before them, and where Alfred de Musset, delirious with typhoid, had seen George Sand kissing his handsome physician. In front of the hotel was the Riva degli Schiavoni, paved with marble, leading in broad steps, the last of which the tide slowly climbed and descended, to the lagoon and the gondolas. Over the water was the Giudecca, and San Giorgio Maggiore, and on the near horizon the low dunes of the Lido. 'When I went to Venice I found,' Proust wrote some years later to Mme Straus, 'that my dream had become—incredibly but quite simply—my *address!*'

In the mornings, before the greatest heat of the day, he would set out with Reynaldo and Marie in a gondola along the Grand Canal, disembarking at each church or palace described by Ruskin. 'Blessed days,' he wrote in a footnote of *La Bible d'Amiens*, 'when with other disciples of the master I listened at the water's edge to his gospel, alighting at every one of the temples which seemed to rise from the sea expressly to offer us the object of his descriptions and the very image of his thoughts.' When they returned for lunch they could see, from as far off as the Dogana and Santa Maria della Salute, Mme Proust's shawl hung over the hotel balcony, weighed down by her book. For she preferred to stay behind and read, happy and astonished that her son was rising at ten in the morning to wander in the open air, happy too, perhaps, because he was spending the day not only with Reynaldo but with a beautiful girl. Since the deaths of Louis and Nathé Weil she had worn black; but now, when Marcel called up from the quay-side and she smiled back in welcome, she had a coquettish straw hat with a white tulle veil, as if to license his new-found joy in living.

In the afternoon the sun was already too hot for them to go further than the shady side of the Piazza, where they would sit with Mme Proust and Mlle Nordlinger's aunt at Florian's café eating the delicious honeycombed ice known as *granita*, and watching the pigeons with their iridescent breasts: "Pigeons are the lilacs of the animal kingdom,"[1] declared Marcel. Soon he would

[1] A remark reused for the pigeons in the Champs-Élysées (I, 408).

cross the square with Marie to work on Ruskin in the 'dazzling
coolness' of Saint Mark's. Mlle Nordlinger remembered an afternoon when the sky darkened and a storm burst over Venice: she
took shelter with Marcel in the great basilica, and translated for
him the passage of *The Stones of Venice* in which Ruskin explains
the decadence and fall of the Republic. In the mosaics of the
domes of Saint Mark's are represented not only the prophets and
the evangelists, but (for here the Bible of Venice differs from the
Bible of Amiens) the very words of their texts. "The sins of
Venice," repeated Marie, "were done with the Bible at her right
hand. When in her last hours she threw off all shame and all
restraint, be it remembered how much her sin was greater, because
it was done in the face of the house of God, burning with the
letters of His Law. Through century after century of gathering
vanity and festering guilt, that white dome of Saint Mark's had
uttered in the dead ear of Venice: 'Know thou, that for all these
things God will bring thee into judgement.'" Proust took this
tremendous warning, uttered in the oblivious voice of the young
girl, to himself and defied it. When he came to write the last
chapter of his introduction to *La Bible d'Amiens*, he had a logical
answer ready. 'If Ruskin had been quite sincere with himself, he
would not have thought the sins of the Venetians more inexcusable and more severely punished than those of other men, just
because they had a church of many-coloured marble instead of a
cathedral of limestone, or because the Palace of the Doges
happened to be next-door to Saint Mark's instead of being at the
other end of the town,' he ironically objected. But at the moment
he was more serious. 'It was dark, and the mosaics shone only
with their own material light, with an ancient, internal, terrestrial
gold to which the Venetian sun had ceased to contribute. The
emotion I felt on hearing these words, surrounded by all those
angels illumined only by the environing darkness, was very
strong.' And Marie Nordlinger noticed, as had Reynaldo on the
day of the Bengal roses at Réveillon, that her companion was
'strangely moved, and exalted by a kind of ecstasy'.

In the evening it was more necessary than ever to evade the
high moral standards of Mlle Nordlinger's aunt—'that charming
Venetian aunt, fervent and meticulous, devoted to art, kindness
and comfort, and so very full of goodwill towards the person who
signs this letter,' he wrote to Marie Nordlinger some years later.

It was bad enough for a young man to get up so late in the
morning ('She represented for me those *Mornings in Venice*
which Ruskin never wrote and I never saw,' said Proust); but it
was shocking for him to keep a young lady out so late at night.
'Nothing could soften her, nothing could budge the inflexibility
of her principles,' and altogether, he irreverently decided, 'she
was one of the most curious of all the *Stones of Venice*.' Nevertheless, the young people contrived to escape. The sun had set, even
the north side of the Piazza was cool. They sat drinking coffee in
the dusk outside Quadri's, and then took a gondola to the Lagoon.
Reynaldo sang Venetian folk-songs, and Gounod's setting of
Musset's

> *Dans Venise la rouge*
> *Pas un bateau qui bouge,*

while a yellow half-moon high over San Giorgio Maggiore sent
a track of rippling light from the horizon to their trailing hands.

Influenced by a mistaken association of ideas between Florence,
flowers and pollen, Proust had decided that Florence would be
fatal for his hay fever, and the Ponte Vecchio, 'heaped with a
profusion of hyacinths and anemones', remained forever only a
vision of the Narrator. But Padua was only twenty-five miles by
train from Venice, and contained treasures of painting praised by
Ruskin even more highly than the Carpaccios which Proust had
seen at the Accademia di Belle Arti, or, *Saint Mark's Rest* in
hand, after a trip by gondola 'along a calm canal, a little before
one reaches the tremulous infinity of the lagoon', at San Giorgio
degli Schiavoni. Reynaldo was about to rejoin his mother and
Coco in Rome, and consented to break his journey at Padua. So
it was that Proust saw Giotto's frescoes, the Virtues and Vices of
Padua, in the chapel of the Madonna dell'Arena. He knew them
well already, not from childhood, like the Narrator to whom
Swann gave the photographs of them which hung in the schoolroom at Combray, but only since the previous autumn, when he
had found reproductions of Charity, Injustice, Infidelity and
Envy in Ruskin's *Fors Clavigera*. These are the very figures which
Proust introduced into *A la Recherche*: the sturdy, mannish
Charity, with her gown billowing out at the waist, and carrying
what might almost be asparagus in her basket, became an emblem
of the pregnant kitchen-maid at Combray; Envy, with a serpent
issuing from her distended mouth, reminded him of illustrations

of cancer of the tongue in his father's medical books; M. de Palancy's monocle seemed to Swann at Mme de Saint-Euverte's a part intended to symbolise the whole, like the branch carried by Injustice to represent the forests in which he lurks; and Albertine playing diabolo on the promenade at Balbec resembled Infidelity, who carries, attached by a long cord, the idol or 'devil' which is the object of her guilty worship.[1] The Virtues and Vices of Padua, after which he once intended to call a whole section of his novel, were only the lowest rank of four frescoes; in the third row above was a Crucifixion, in which the suffering Christ was attended by diminutive weeping angels, who unlike most of their kind used their wings not as mere emblems, but for actual flying. When he wrote *Albertine Disparue*, late in the World War, and remembered Giotto's angels looping and nose-diving, he compared them to 'the young pupils of Garros'[2]—Roland Garros, the aviator killed in action in 1918, whose aerodrome he had visited with Agostinelli, who, he too, and four years sooner, was destined to die of flying.

Leaving the chapel, and crossing the Piazza dell'Arena under a sky which seemed scarcely brighter than the blue ceiling above the angels, they reached the Eremitani and saw Mantegna's fresco of the life of St James, 'one of the paintings I love best in the world,' Proust wrote to Montesquiou seven years later. One of the soldiers who stands aloof and brooding while St James is martyred is recalled by Swann at Mme de Saint-Euverte's, when he sees the gigantic footman who seemed 'as resolved to ignore the group of his comrades thronging about Swann, although he followed them vaguely with his cruel, grey-green eyes, as if the scene had been a Massacre of the Innocents or a Martyrdom of St James'.[3]

By the third week of May Reynaldo, Mlle Nordlinger and the high-principled aunt had left, and Proust's stay in Venice was nearly over. It is probable that a quarrel with his mother occurred at this time: not so much because it is described in *Albertine Disparue*,[4] for there the episode is aesthetically necessary, in order that the magic of Venice, like that of all other Names and Places, should fade at last; but because, like other incidents in Proust's life, it appears in *Contre Sainte-Beuve* briefly and without apparent purpose, and linked with another memory which is certainly real.[5]

[1] I, 80-2, 327, 886   [2] III, 648   [3] I, 324   [4] III, 651-5
[5] His remorse on his second visit to Venice, described below.

In *Albertine Disparue* the Narrator refuses to leave Venice with his mother, in *Contre Sainte-Beuve*[1] Proust threatens to leave without her: there is nothing to indicate which version is correct. 'I went downstairs,' he wrote in *Contre Sainte-Beuve*, 'I had given up the idea of going, but I wanted to prolong my mother's grief at thinking me gone. I stayed on the quay-side where she could not see me, while a boatman in a gondola sang a serenade to which the sun, about to disappear behind the Salute, had stopped to listen. I could feel the prolongation of my mother's anxiety, the suspense became unbearable, but I could not find the resolution to go and tell her: "I'm staying." It seemed the singer would never finish his song, nor the sun succeed in setting, as if my anguish, the dying light and the metal of the singer's voice had fused forever in a poignant, ambiguous and indissoluble alloy. The time would come when, if I tried to escape the memory of that bronze-like minute, I would not have, as then, my mother near me.' But the remorse in which Venice ended and receded left Proust determined to return, to enjoy pleasures of which the presence of his mother and friends had deprived him, and which were not mentioned anywhere in the works of Ruskin.

A few weeks before his arrival in Venice, on 1 April 1900, the *Gazette des Beaux-Arts* had published the first part of his long essay, *John Ruskin*, which was concluded in the issue of 1 August. This was the study already announced in the *Chronique des Arts et de la Curiosité* in January and in the *Figaro* article in February. Proust had finished it early in February, soon after the visit to Rouen with which it ends, and on the 8th he had written to Mlle Nordlinger: 'All my work on Ruskin is completed.' But it is possible that the first half was written as early as the summer of 1899, before he had begun to read Ruskin in the original. All the quotations from Ruskin in this section, with the exception of one from *The Bible of Amiens* and another from *The Seven Lamps*, which may have been added later, are borrowed with due acknowledgment from Milsand and La Sizeranne, and this suggests that he may have been writing at a time when he had no first-hand knowledge of Ruskin.[2] In the essay as a whole Proust expounds

---

[1] Pp. 123, 124

[2] Here, no doubt, is the article commissioned by Louis Ganderax for the *Revue de Paris*, to which Proust alludes in a letter to J. L. Vaudoyer in 1912. Ganderax, with his pathological inability to publish anything he could not

not only his opinion of the true nature of Ruskin's gospel but, what is still more important, describes the crucial effect of the revelation of Ruskin on his own view of art and human life.

The validity of Proust's opinion of Ruskin rests partly on the extent of his knowledge of English and of his acquaintance with Ruskin's works. His competence in both has been generally underestimated, not only by his critics but by his friends. "How on earth do you manage, Marcel," asked Constantin de Brancovan, "seeing that you don't know English?" 'He would have been hard put to it to order a cutlet in an English restaurant,' wrote Georges de Lauris, though he rightly added: 'he knew no English but Ruskin's, but he understood that in its most subtle shades of meaning.' Proust himself was under no illusions as to

have written himself, kept it, 'torn between the friendship he felt for me personally and the horror inspired in him by my writings', until 'the death of Ruskin made it no less admirable in news-value than it seemed detestable in prose-style'. Even so, Ganderax could not bring himself to use the article, and gave the same 'uniform, affectionate and regretful reason' as he had given for his rejection long ago of the group of sonnets and a short story later included in *Les Plaisirs et les Jours*: that he 'hadn't enough spare time to rewrite it'. In view of the improbability of Proust's having written a long study of Ruskin before the first onset of his enthusiasm in the summer of 1899, his words to Vaudoyer: 'the excellent Ganderax kept my verses, a short story and a study of Ruskin (commissioned!) waiting for years' need not all be taken literally. 'For years' no doubt refers to the sonnets and the story, but not to the Ruskin study, which Ganderax can hardly have kept for more than six months. Proust also expresses himself loosely when he tells Vaudoyer: 'this essay later became the preface to *La Bible d'Amiens*', since of the four sections of the preface the first is a foreword written last of all, the second is the *Mercure de France* article on Amiens written after his visit to the cathedral in October 1899, the latter half of the third describes his visit to Rouen in February 1900, and the fourth is based on his holiday in Venice in May 1900. The article written for Ganderax, therefore, can only be the first half of the third section, that is, the article in the *Gazette des Beaux-Arts* for 1 April 1900, reprinted in *Pastiches et Mélanges*, p. 149, line 17-p. 161, line 3. Even this, however, must have been considerably revised to make it topical, as it contains numerous allusions to the death of Ruskin on 20 January 1900. Perhaps Ganderax's procrastination suggested the Narrator's long wait for the appearance in *Le Figaro* of the article which he submitted soon after his first visit to Balbec, but which was not published until after the death of Albertine. No other article of Proust's was so long delayed; and both his first article in *Le Figaro* (*Pèlerinages Ruskiniens* of 13 February 1900) and the essay which corresponds to the Narrator's on the spires of Martinville (*Impressions de route en automobile* of 19 November 1907) appeared within a few weeks after they were written.

his competence in English: 'I'm so bad at languages,' he wrote to Marie Nordlinger in August 1903; he bitterly lamented, in a letter to Walter Berry in January 1918, his inability to talk English to American soldiers met one night in Paris; 'I read English with great difficulty,' he told Violet Schiff in 1919. He was always prone to the typical mistakes of the beginner. In the *John Ruskin* essay he translated Ruskin's '*a living soul*' by '*une âme aimante*', because in English at least he was unaware of the difference between living and loving; and twenty-two years later, only two months before his death, he was horrified to learn that the title chosen for the English translation of *Du Côté de chez Swann* was *Swann's Way*: he thought the words could only mean 'in the manner of Swann', and died in the pathetic belief that Scott-Moncrieff's great work would be an ignorant travesty of *A la Recherche*. He had no doubt begun English at the Lycée Condorcet[1]; he continued while studying for his *licence ès lettres*, in which he seems to have taken English as his first language[2]; and perhaps he learned a little from Edgar Aubert, and from Willie Heath during their mornings in the Bois. But with the sole exception of Ruskin he seems to have read all the English writers he knew—Dickens, George Eliot, Shakespeare, Carlyle, Pater, and later Stevenson, Kipling, Barrie, Wells and Hardy—in translation. He was exacting in his demands for help from his mother, who knew English well, and from his English-speaking friends, Mlle Nordlinger, Reynaldo Hahn, Robert de Billy, Robert d'Humières (the translator of Kipling), and others. He corresponded with Ruskin's friends, Charles Newton Scott and Alexander Wedderburn. In translating *The Bible of Amiens* he was provided with a crib: according to Mlle Nordlinger, the patient Mme Proust wrote for him a word-for-word translation 'in several red, green and yellow school exercise-books'.

Such are the ascertainable limitations of Proust's knowledge of English: they may seem formidable, but they are, in fact, irrelevant to his knowledge of Ruskin. Even if we assume that

[1] During Proust's first two years at Condorcet Mallarmé was English master there. But Proust was only thirteen years old when Mallarmé left in July 1884, and it is unlikely that he had begun English so early.

[2] It is known that he took German as his second language. He knew enough of it to read and review two German books on Ruskin in 1903 and 1904. As he never shows any considerable knowledge of any others, it seems likely that he took English as his first language.

in the general accuracy of his renderings he was largely indebted to Mme Proust, and that the occasional gross but trivial blunders are all his own, there can still be no doubt that for the elegance of his translation, the deep comprehension and sharing of Ruskin's inmost meaning and feeling, he owed nothing to his helpers. Proust's Ruskin may be compared to another great translation which, although not free from elementary but unimportant errors, is a masterly re-creation of its original: namely, Scott-Moncrieff's Proust. Until Proust's Ruskin manuscripts are published we can only guess at the respective parts played in *La Bible d'Amiens* and *Sésame et les Lys* by his own knowledge and intuition and by the conscripted assistance of his mother and friends. But concerning the extent of his knowledge of Ruskin's other works, as revealed by the hundreds of quotations in his essays and voluminous foot-notes, certainty is possible. The quotations are mostly of his own choice; nearly all are taken from works which had not previously been translated into French; the few which had previously occurred in Milsand or La Sizeranne are mostly retranslated (except in the first section of *John Ruskin*) from the original; and they come from no fewer than twenty-six works, covering virtually the entire range of Ruskin's production. In the *Mercure de France* essay, *Ruskin à Notre-Dame d'Amiens*, he quotes *Praeterita, The Bible of Amiens, The Queen of the Air* and *Val d'Arno*; in the second section of *John Ruskin* he uses passages from *The Pleasures of England, The Seven Lamps of Architecture, Lectures on Architecture and Painting, The Stones of Venice* and *St Mark's Rest*.[1] In his notes to *La Bible d'Amiens* he draws from these and fourteen other works of Ruskin, including *The Two Paths, Unto this Last* and *Modern Painters*; and if only three more are added to the list in *Sésame et les Lys*, it is because the tale of Ruskin's works is by now, except for some half a dozen very minor pieces, complete. Mme Proust can hardly have supplied him with a home-made translation of all Ruskin; and his quotations are made with an ease and appositeness which imply a thorough knowledge of the books from which they are taken. The conclusion is inevitable, that Proust had read and digested

---

[1] This corroborates his claim in the letter to Marie Nordlinger of 8 February 1900, when he had recently finished these essays, to 'know by heart' *The Seven Lamps, The Bible of Amiens, Val d'Arno, Lectures on Architecture and Painting* and *Praeterita.*

in the original most of Ruskin's major works during his first enthusiasm in 1899 and 1900, and the remainder by 1902, when *La Bible d'Amiens* was completed.

The first section of *John Ruskin*, published in the *Gazette des Beaux-Arts* of 1 April 1900 and probably written some eight months before, is a discussion of the views of Milsand and La Sizeranne. The quotations in it, as we have seen, are borrowed with two exceptions from these authors, and it is only in the second section of the essay that Proust shows an independent knowledge of Ruskin's works. Nevertheless, the core of the whole essay is the point at which, in this first section, he parts company with La Sizeranne. He assents to La Sizeranne's concept of the Religion of Beauty, but gives it a special meaning which, although it is true of Ruskin, is henceforth Proust's own, and marks a further advance towards the idea of Time Regained. The true adorer of beauty, he writes, is not the man who 'spends his life in the enjoyment which comes from the voluptuous contemplation of works of art'. 'Beauty cannot be loved fruitfully if it is loved only for the pleasures it gives. Just as the search for happiness for its own sake brings nothing but boredom, because happiness can only be found by seeking something other than happiness, so aesthetic pleasure is a mere by-product which comes to us if we love beauty for itself, as something real which exists outside ourselves and is infinitely more important than the joy it gives us. Very far from being a dilettante or an aesthete, Ruskin was one of those men of whom Carlyle speaks, whose genius warns them of the vanity of all pleasure, and, at the same time, of the presence near at hand of an eternal reality to be perceived intuitively by their inspiration. . . . The Beauty to which he consecrated his life was not conceived by him as an object of enjoyment made for our delight, but as a reality infinitely more important than life, for which he would have sacrificed his own . . . The poet was, for Ruskin as for Carlyle, a kind of scribe writing at the dictation of nature a more or less important part of her secret; and the artist's primary duty is to add nothing of his own to this divine message.' Here is the bridge between Jean Santeuil's meditation by the Lake of Geneva and the final metaphysic of the Narrator. Only two elements are missing: unconscious memory, because Proust had still not solved its mystery, and Time Lost, because he had as yet experienced only Time

Wasted. The meditation by the lake, which was a real event of September 1899, began, as has been seen, with a complete occurrence of unconscious memory; but this, since Proust proceeded to explain it mistakenly as an effect of poetic imagination, was a false start. In *John Ruskin*, however, although by temporarily abandoning the concept of unconscious memory he has retreated, he has also made a vital advance: the duty of the writer, he has decided, is not to imagine, but to perceive reality; the artist is a scribe; and since his task is 'infinitely more important than life', its fulfilment will bring salvation.

In defining the mission of Ruskin, Proust had discovered his own. Temporarily he put the knowledge away; for salvation, perhaps, is a state in which we cannot hope to live, but only, at best, to die. Nine years later he would begin to write the work that would kill and save him: meanwhile he had to live, if not in salvation, then touched, if possible, with grace. During his first worship of Ruskin it seemed sufficient to live as he supposed Ruskin had lived, in a perpetual adoration of gothic churches. This duty, in seeming anticlimax, is the subject of the second section of *John Ruskin*, which describes, as a pendant to the trip to Amiens in *Ruskin à Notre-Dame d'Amiens*, his visit to Rouen and the rediscovery of the stone mannikin. There was another aspect of Ruskin's way of life which attracted him: he learned from Collingwood's *Life and Works of John Ruskin*, published in 1893, of the master's habit of making his tours in the company of a chosen band of young friends; and in his *Figaro* article Proust appealed to these ('whom I have so often envied') for information on Ruskin's opinions of Chartres and Rouen. In the same way the Narrator envies Gilberte when Swann tells him that Bergotte 'is my daughter's great friend—they visit old towns and cathedrals and castles together'; and when he thinks of Gilberte he sees her 'in the porch of a cathedral, explaining to me the meaning of the statues, and introducing me as her friend to Bergotte'.[1] For the next three years Proust's answer to the question: 'What shall I do to be saved?' was: 'Visit cathedrals

---

[1] I, 99-100. Proust is thinking also of another Gilberte and Bergotte: of Jeanne Pouquet's journeys with Anatole France, who with Mme Arman and Gaston de Caillavet accompanied her on her honeymoon in Italy in the summer of 1893, and on other occasions. But the pagan and Grecian France cared little for the art of gothic churches.

with my friends.' Truth and happiness, he felt for a time, could be discovered by seeing the right places with the right persons. His illusion was less absurd and less unfruitful than it might seem: for although reality, in the metaphysic of *A la Recherche*, lies only in the utmost depths of our being which are in contact with eternity, images of reality are wherever we find them. Of the two false quests which for the Narrator were necessary stages in his recovery of Time Lost, and which he calls Names of People and Names of Places, Proust's pursuit of high society corresponded to the first, and his circular journey in the steps of Ruskin to the second.

Ruskin appears occasionally in *A la Recherche* under his own name. The Narrator's mother, seeing her son heartbroken by their parting as he sets out for Balbec with his grandmother, asks: "What would the church at Balbec say? Where's that enraptured tourist we read about in Ruskin?"[1] Bloch exhibits his vulgarity, when the Narrator reveals that the visit to Balbec 'fulfils one of my oldest desires, only less profound than that of going to Venice', by exclaiming: "Yes, you would! You'd like to drink sherbet with the pretty ladies"—as Proust had with Marie Nordlinger—"while you pretend to read *The Stones of Venighce* by Lord John Ruskin, that dreary old fossil, one of the most crashing bores who ever existed!"[2] At Venice the Narrator, like Proust himself, takes 'notes for some work I was doing on Ruskin'.[3] Jupien in his brothel jests upon 'a translation of Ruskin's *Sesame and Lilies* which I had sent to M. de Charlus': "if you see a light in my window you can come in, that's my Open Sesame," he says, "but if it's Lilies you're after, you'd better try elsewhere."[4] These words, as we shall see later, may actually have been spoken to Proust, some eighteen years afterwards, on a dark night in war-time Paris when the bombs were falling.

If Bergotte is in the habit of visiting gothic cathedrals, however, it is not because he has collected in passing—as he takes Renan's snail-shell nose, Bourget's words of advice, Bergson's name, and the magic of Barrès's prose—a trait from Ruskin. Just as much as in his social presence he is Anatole France, in the effect of his works on the Narrator Bergotte *is* Ruskin. 'One of the passages from Bergotte gave me a joy I was aware of feeling in a deeper region of myself,' the Narrator tells us, 'a region vaster

[1] I, 649   [2] I, 739   [3] III, 645   [4] III, 833

and simpler, from which all obstacles and separations seemed to have been removed.'[1] 'The universe suddenly regained an infinite value in my eyes,' wrote Proust in retrospect, at a time when his enthusiasm for Ruskin was cooling, 'and my admiration for Ruskin gave such importance to the things he had made me love that they seemed charged with something more precious than life itself.'[2] The quotations from Bergotte's works read at Combray: 'the inexhaustible torrent of beautiful appearances', 'the moving effigies which forever ennoble the venerable and delightful façades of cathedrals',[3] are like pastiches of Ruskin.

Ruskin also led Proust to one of the most striking aspects of Elstir. Elstir, no doubt, is a generalised Impressionist, just as Vinteuil and Bergotte are generalisations of the great composers and authors of Proust's youth; though each of the three is more supreme in his genius than any one actual artist of the time. In giving to Elstir powers which belonged to so many different painters—the cathedrals and Normandy cliffs of Monet, the race-course subjects of Degas, the gods and centaurs of Gustave Moreau, the firework nocturnes of Whistler, the bathing girls of Renoir—Proust suggested not only the contemporary reality of the imaginary painter, but also his superiority, since his greatness included theirs. But Elstir's salient quality is one in which he differs from the other impressionists. Both they and Elstir make it their task to reproduce the primal freshness of reality as seen in a first glance, before the viewer knows what it is he sees; but whereas Monet, for example, works by decomposing colours and their outlines, without wishing, however, to disguise the fact that it is a tree or a sail that he is showing us, Elstir's art lies in what the Narrator calls 'ambiguities' and 'metaphors': he reproduces the moment in which we are so far from knowing what it is we see, that we think it is something else. The charm of the pictures seen by the Narrator in Elstir's studio at Balbec lay 'in a kind of metamorphosis of the things they represented, analogous to what is called in poetry a metaphor; and if God the Father created

---

[1] I, 94　　　　　[2] Cf. *Pastiches et Mélanges*, 193

[3] I, 94. The phrase *'les belles apparences'*, however, was used more than once by Anatole France, and the whole comes from Leconte de Lisle's lines:

'La vie antique est faite inépuisablement
Du tourbillon sans fin des apparences vaines.'

Nevertheless, the Ruskinian flavour of Proust's adaptations is unmistakable.

things by naming them, it was by taking away their names, or giving them different ones, that Elstir created them anew'.[1] The most frequent metaphor in his seascapes was one which made sea seem land, and land seem sea. In these characteristics Elstir differs from any of the French impressionists, and resembles Turner, to whom Ruskin consecrated *Modern Painters*, the chief work of his youth. Proust knew, as early as 1900, Turner's album *The Rivers of France*, which he mentioned in *John Ruskin*. He borrowed from La Sizeranne in the same essay an anecdote of Turner in Ruskin's *The Eagle's Nest*: to a naval officer who complained that the ships in his view of Plymouth had no port-holes, the painter retorted: "My business is to paint not what I know, but what I see."[2] 'My imagination,' says the Narrator, 'like Elstir reproducing some effect of perspective, painted for me not what I knew, but what I saw.'[3] 'Turner,' wrote Ruskin in *The Harbours of England*, 'was never able to recover the idea of positive distinction between sea and sky, or sea and land.' As Jean Autret has shown, Elstir's *Port of Carquethuit* is a combination of Turner's *Plymouth* and *Scarborough*, which Proust knew from the plates in *The Harbours of England* as published in 1904 in the Library Edition.[4] Turner's and Elstir's aesthetic of meta-phor, the description of one thing in terms of another, is employed by Proust throughout *A la Recherche*. Elstir, indeed, is uniquely blessed, in that he has direct and immediate access to reality, without the intercession and long delay of unconscious memory; he alone can see reality in the present, when it is actually there. On the other hand, this very gift condemns him to perceive reality through one sense only, the vision of the eye; and more-over, he is cut off from the dimension of time, without which the metaphysical significance of reality remains invisible. Thus his art is still inferior to the full revelation of Time Regained: it cannot be more than a symbol of something greater which is out of its reach.

[1] I, 835   [2] *Pastiches et Mélanges*, 169   [3] II, 568
[4] J. Autret, *L'Influence de Ruskin sur Proust*, 130-6. M. Autret has also shown (*ibid.*, 119-24) that Proust was indebted for his knowledge of Botticelli's painting of Jethro's daughter Zipporah, of which Odette so obsessively reminds Swann, to the frontispiece of Ruskin's *Val d'Arno*. The figure reproduced by P. Abraham, *Proust*, pl. XVI, as Zipporah is in fact Moses' wife, whose features are nothing like Odette's. The real Zipporah is reproduced by Autret, *op. cit.*, 119.

At the end of *John Ruskin* Proust applied to Ruskin words which Ruskin had used of Turner: 'It is through those eyes, now closed for ever in the grave, that unborn generations will look upon nature.' Ruskin had given him new eyes, or, rather, restored the sight of his own, on which the years of Time Wasted, the vain pleasures of the Guermantes Way, the sterile sorrows of perverted love, the contamination of justice by politics in the Dreyfus Affair, had cast their temporary scales. But in one work, at least, Ruskin had shown himself aware of Time Regained: it was a book whose very title, *Praeterita*, might be literally translated as 'Things Past', or '*Temps Perdu*'. Ruskin had written the story of his childhood and youth, of the discovery of his vocation, at a time long afterwards when he had realised the meaning of his life; and his method was to re-create each moment, by a deliberate exercise of unconscious memory not unlike Proust's, so that the past should become eternally present. Proust knew *Praeterita* well: it was one of the works of Ruskin which in his letter to Mlle Nordlinger of 8 February 1900 he claimed to know by heart; and a few years later he began a translation of it which he soon abandoned. It is very likely that both the title and the theme of *A la Recherche* owed something to *Praeterita*. There is also at least one particular incident in *Praeterita* which Proust seems to have remembered. In the early summer of 1842 Ruskin set out for Switzerland by the devious way of Rouen, Chartres, Fontainebleau and Auxerre. On the day before he reached Fontainebleau he must have passed through, or very near to Illiers, where Adrien Proust was then a child of eight, and Louis Proust was still selling candles in the Place du Marché. 'The flat country between Chartres and Fontainebleau,' Ruskin recalled, 'with an oppressive sense of Paris to the north, fretted me wickedly.' That night he lay feverishly awake; at noon he 'tottered out, still in an extremely languid and woe-begone condition', into the forest, and lay in anguish on a sandy bank under a group of young trees. He tried in vain to sleep; until gradually 'the branches against the blue sky began to interest me, motionless as the branches of a tree of Jesse on a painted window. . . . Languidly, but not idly, I began to draw the tree; and as I drew the languor passed away: the beautiful lines insisted on being traced—without weariness. More and more beautiful they became, as each rose out of the rest, and took its place in the air.

With wonder increasing every moment, I saw that they "composed" themselves, by finer laws than any known of man. At last the tree was there, and everything that I had thought about trees, nowhere.'[1] This typically Proustian moment of truth surely played its part (though the incidents may none the less have actually occurred in Proust's own life) in the Narrator's questioning of the three trees near Balbec, and again in his sight from a railway-carriage of the trees striped with sunlight and shade, which seemed for ever to forbid, though in fact they preluded, his regaining of Time Lost.

Soon after the publication of the second half of *John Ruskin* on 1 August 1900 Dr and Mme Proust were once more at the Splendide Hôtel, Évian. Taking precautions to avoid what Mme Proust ingenuously called 'the Semitic element', they joined forces with the family of Dr Proust's colleague Dr Simon Duplay (whose son Maurice was to become Proust's friend a year or two later) to form, as Mme Proust put it, 'a miniature independent republican party of our own'. Each morning the now corpulent lady drank three glasses of medicinal water at the Spa; in the evening they attended the theatre at the casino, or played dominoes with the Duplays, to which pursuit Dr Proust brought such fiery energy, and such open joy when he won, as to recall Dr Cottard playing écarté at La Raspelière. He awaited Marcel's telegrams with ill-concealed anxiety, and when they arrived exclaimed: "There! Didn't I tell you everything would be all right!" From time to time distinguished acquaintances sought him out: the left-wing politician Jean Cruppi, a member of the Chamber of Deputies, a future Minister of Commerce, and husband of Mme Proust's cousin Louise Crémieux, was also 'on the lake'; and one Sunday a stout man with a red nose, Charles Dupuy, who had been prime minister in 1899 at the height of the Affair, popped up to slap Dr Proust jovially on the shoulder. Armand Nisard, Marie de Benardaky's uncle by marriage and an original of M. de Norpois, was at Évian on holiday from his post as ambassador at the Vatican. He was most affable, but since he was so deaf as to hear nothing that was said to him, and spoke

---

[1] *Praeterita*, vol. 2, ch. 4. Proust certainly knew this passage even before he read the original, for it is quoted by La Sizeranne, 28-9. Here again, Ruskin's prose in La Sizeranne's French is strikingly like the mature style of Proust.

so quietly as to be inaudible, conversation was difficult. The family thought he had shown far too little zeal a few years before, when Dr Proust had been an unsuccessful candidate for the Académie des Sciences Morales; and in this again he resembled M. de Norpois, who at Mme de Villeparisis's matinée sanctimoniously refuses to vote for the Narrator's father.[1] Marcel was to join them later: Mme Proust advised him to wait, because the hotel was brim-full and noisy; besides, as she would soon have to return to Paris on important business, they would risk crossing one another. Meanwhile he continued his Ruskin pilgrimages: 'when you don't write to me,' she remarked, 'I hope it's because you're off on some interesting, amusing or hygienic excursion'.

He arrived at Évian some time in September, while Dr Proust apparently moved on to Vichy; and in October, presumably about the 7th, when the Splendide Hôtel closed, he fulfilled his plan of the previous autumn and went to Venice from Évian, 'at the best possible time of year'. Of this mysterious second visit to Venice only a single fact is known: on 19 October 1900 Proust signed the visitors' register of the Armenian monastery on the Island of San Lazaro in the Lagoon.[2] But he mentioned it twice in *Contre Sainte-Beuve*[3]: 'the moment I saw Venice for the second time I remembered the evening when, after a quarrel with Mamma, I cruelly told her I was going away'; and: 'if I wept on the day when I again saw the window of her room, it was because it said to me "I remember your mother"'. Perhaps there was some other reason for his return to Venice and for his remorse when he arrived. The palaces, paintings and mosaics of Venice, the blazing sunlight reflected everywhere from cool green water, offered him novel aspects of art and nature which he may well have wished to experience again. But Venice also held less avowable though hardly less tempting charms, which the presence of his mother, Mlle Nordlinger, the strait-laced aunt and the quizzical Reynaldo had prevented him from exploring five months before. For the Narrator the very topography of Venice

[1] II, 225-6

[2] Except for a pleasant trip by *vaporetto* on the Lagoon, and a view of Venice from across the water, no particular motive can be guessed for his visit to San Lazaro. The Monastery was not one of the usual sights of Venice; Ruskin does not mention it; and although Byron spent some time with the Armenian monks there, Proust was not interested in Byron.

[3] p. 123

—the canal on whose yielding waters he seems 'to penetrate further and further into the depths of some secret thing', the moonlit *campo* which he discovers hidden in a labyrinth of narrow streets and can never find again—seems full of symbols of voluptuous desire and possession. He wanders alone, 'through humble *campi* and little abandoned *rii*', in search of the working-class girls whom Albertine might have loved when she was alive and in Venice.[1] Perhaps for Proust, too, Venice was linked with the Cities of the Plain; and perhaps he sought and found there on this second visit the sinister enchantments known to Byron and John Addington Symonds, Henry James, Housman and Baron Corvo, of which Ruskin had nothing to say.

The business on which Mme Proust was recalled to Paris in September was nothing less than the removal of the Proust family to a new home, into which they moved probably about 1 October, the beginning of the new quarter. They had been house-hunting all summer, and thought for a time of taking a second-floor apartment at 127 Boulevard Haussmann. The proprietor of the house, the Marquis des Réaulx, was understood to be unwilling to let to professional men; and Proust asked Pierre Lavallée, who was a friend of the marquis's grandson and tenant, Édouard de Monicault, to explain that Dr Proust had so nearly given up his practice that 'he now has fewer visitors than ordinary persons'. But in the end they decided upon 45 Rue de Courcelles, on the corner of the Rue Monceau, which satisfied their needs for more quiet, and living-space, and a more fashionable address to reflect the eminence Dr Proust had reached during the thirty years since his marriage.

At first sight there is little difference between the architecture of the Boulevard Malesherbes and that of the Rue de Courcelles. Both have the same unbroken line of dignified, seven-storey-high buildings, with iron balconies running along the upper floors. But the Boulevard Malesherbes was Second Empire, put up in the late 1860s and beginning to go down in the world; it was a little too showy, and already far too noisy. The Rue de Courcelles was Third Republic—the foundation-stone of No. 45 is dated 1881; it was solid, narrow, quiet, gloomy and treeless; and although less than half a mile from their old home, it ran, between the Boulevard Haussmann and the Avenue Hoche,

[1] III, 626-7, 650

through the outskirts of the aristocratic Quartier Monceau, a much more suitable district for a distinguished doctor.

This is the change of home which occurs at the beginning of *Le Côté de Guermantes*. Well might Françoise, who at this period of *A la Recherche* is based on the Proust's aged cook, Félicie Fitau, declare in the exile of this noiseless canyon that 'she found the twittering of the birds at daybreak insipid'.[1] But by a typical transposition Proust made the new house of the Narrator, in its most important features, more like his own old home than the new. The house of the Narrator's childhood, it is true, resembled 9 Boulevard Malesherbes in several ways: it was near the Champs-Élysées, had a Morriss column on the pavement opposite, and commanded a distant view of the Piranesi-like dome of Saint-Augustin. The Narrator's new home, like 45 Rue de Courcelles, is quiet, and situated on a steep hill (down which the Ladies with the Walking-Sticks clambered to tell the Duc de Guermantes that poor 'Mama' d'Osmond was dying). The height of the Rue de Courcelles, and its nearness to the Parc Monceau, gave it the better air which in the novel is needed for the Narrator's grandmother ('because, although we did not tell her the reason, she had not been at all well lately')[2] and in real life was desirable for Mme Proust. But it was 9 Boulevard Malesherbes which had a tailor's shop like Jupien's (M. Eppler's, of whom Kiki Bartholoni thought so highly) in the courtyard, and a ducal family as neighbours. At No. 3, only three doors away,[3] lived the Comte and Comtesse François de Maillé, nephew and niece-in-law of the octogenarian Dowager Duchesse de Maillé, whom Proust had so often seen, enthroned with other aged wallflowers, at the balls of his youth: her grey hair piled high over her forehead reminded him of the triple-tiered wig of judges under the *ancien régime*. Mme de Maillé was the niece of the Comtesse de Boigne, who had been dandled on the knees of Louis XVI and Marie Antoinette, and whose memoirs, first published in 1907, suggested those of Mme de Beausergent, the favourite reading of the Narrator's grandmother. The Comtesse de Boigne's nephew, M. d'Osmond,

[1] II, 9   [2] II, 10

[3] 'I was intimidated,' wrote Lucien Daudet of his first invitation to tea at 9 Boulevard Malesherbes, 'because I was under the impression that No. 9 formed part of the Hôtel Maillé, and therefore thought Marcel Proust lived in a house of vast size and extreme magnificence.'

for whose father in the 1850s she had written her memoirs (just as Mme de Villeparisis's sister Mme de Beausergent had written hers for the young Basin de Guermantes), was a frequent dinner-host of Proust's parents; and when Proust went through the family papers after their death he found M. d'Osmond's photograph and a bundle of his letters. One of Montesquiou's innumerable cousins, Madeleine de Montesquiou, had married Françoise de Maillé in 1888. Here then, at 9 Boulevard Malesherbes—just as the Guermantes's as châtelains of Combray were suggested by the Goussencourts at Saint-Éman near Illiers—the Guermantes's as neighbours of the Narrator in Paris were represented by the Maillés. And according to his usual practice Proust left a clue to the relationship, by giving the name Amanien ('Mama') d'Osmond to the Guermantes cousin, whose death does not deter the Duc de Guermantes from going to a fancy-dress ball,[1] and who in earlier days had been one of Odette's lovers, and had fought a duel with the jealous Swann.[2]

Proust returned from Venice towards the end of October 1900 to find the move already completed. His discomfort was none the less extreme: as the Narrator remarks on the occasion, 'I always found it as difficult to assimilate a new environment as I found it easy to abandon an old.' But the next year is a barren period in his biography, though not, it may be, in his life. Only eight letters belonging to this time are available in print, and there is a similar blank in the reminiscences of his friends. But the lacuna may be to some extent real. He probably wrote fewer letters because he was working on *La Bible d'Amiens*: the only other comparable dearth of correspondence occurs in 1911, when his concentration on the first version of *A la Recherche* was at its height. Moreover, this year coincides with a break in his friend-ships: he had abandoned contact with many of his companions of the 1890s, and had not yet found new. Perhaps he was too ill to write: there is evidence of a serious illness in the autumn and early winter of 1901. Whatever the reason, however, his life vanishes into comparative obscurity during his first year in the house where his parents were to die and Time was, at length, to be lost.

[1] II, 575
[2] III, 300. "I had to act as Swann's second," says M. de Charlus, "and Osmond never forgave me."

Chapter 15

SAINT-LOUP

AT 45 Rue de Courcelles Mme Proust continued to allow her son to give 'grand dinners'; and one of the grandest of all was that of 20 June 1901. The guests, among others, were Anatole France and his daughter Suzanne (now no longer dangerous, for she was about to become engaged to the Dreyfusard Captain Mollin); the Comte and Comtesse d'Eyragues (*née* Henriette de Montesquiou, Count Robert's cousin); Mme de Noailles with her husband Mathieu and her sister, Proust's favourite, Princesse Hélène de Caraman-Chimay; the old Comtesse de Brantes (the same whom Count Robert declared 'worth a whole Council of Trent'); Prince Constantin de Brancovan, Léon Daudet, Abel Hermant; and three young counts, Clément de Maugny, the Comte de Briey (whose mother laughed like Mme Verdurin), and Gabriel de La Rochefoucauld, of whom we shall hear more later. Mme de Noailles, whose first volume of poems, *Le Cœur Innombrable*, had appeared with sensational effect in May, was the guest of honour. Proust had already arranged through Reynaldo Hahn, who had just converted Sarah Bernhardt to these poems during a season of *Phèdre* at Brussels, for that great actress to give a reading from them on 30 May at Montesquiou's Pavillon des Muses; he had even persuaded Mme Proust, of all people, to attend, and the *Figaro* gossip-columnist to include her in 'among others recognised'. So the table decoration on 20 June consisted of nosegays culled from wild flowers mentioned in the poetess's verses, which Proust had ordered, at a price far steeper than that of orchids, from Lachaume and Vaillant-Rozier. Mme de Noailles was enraptured by the compliment: possibly, Gabriel de La Rochefoucauld maliciously surmised, she had hitherto known the flowers only by their pretty names; and as she poured out the jewelled river of her conversation, which left her no breath for eating, her eagle's head was turned continually towards 'dear Marcel'. He, too, ate little: it was his practice on these occasions, so that he

Unfortunately, less owing to any personal dislike than to their consciousness of the utter incompatibility of their musical aims, Hahn and Debussy were ineradicably convinced of one another's hatred and contempt; their salutations at the Café Weber became more and more distant, until they ceased altogether. Debussy was therefore inclined to distrust Proust and his group; and although Proust exerted all his charm in conversation ("He's longwinded and precious and a bit of an old woman," said Debussy), and once even saw Debussy home in his cab, their relations remained courteous but distant. Once Proust invited Debussy to dinner at 45 Rue de Courcelles, to meet a mixed company of writers and aristocrats; but Debussy, without ill-feeling, refused: "You see, I'm an absolute bear in company. I'd rather we just went on meeting at Weber's. Don't take it to heart, my dear sir, I was born like this!" So Proust was compelled to revere this Vinteuil from afar.

On 9 August 1901 Prince Edmond de Polignac died. Proust attended his funeral, and was moved by the tears of Princesse Hélène de Caraman-Chimay, and by the symbolism of the black pall with the scarlet princely crown, bearing only the letter 'P': the dead man had resigned all his individuality, and became a simple Polignac.[1] Prince Edmond would never talk again to Charles Haas (himself now near death) of their youth in the Second Empire, or walk across his studio with the splendid Comtesse Greffulhe to hear his own music played by a full orchestra. Proust remembered his kindness at Amphion, the recitals of Fauré's sonata, so like Vinteuil's, at the Rue Cortambert, his love of Venice—"the only city in the world where one can enjoy a conversation with the window open," the Prince would say—and he murmured, quoting *Hamlet*, "Good-night, sweet prince." On the 31st the bereaved Princesse Winnaretta asked Proust to call at tea-time to talk about her husband. One evening at Lady Brooke's he had met Swinburne, who shrilly declared: "I believe our families are related, and I'm flattered to

---

[1] Proust remembered this scene for the burial of Saint-Loup at Combray: 'the church of Saint-Hilaire was hung with black palls on which, below the princely crown, without any other initials to indicate Christian names or titles, stood out the "G" for the Guermantes he had in death once more become' (III, 851). Another image in the same paragraph—'the feudal turret, emptied of its books, had become warlike again'—derives from Proust's comparison of the Prince de Polignac to 'a castle keep converted into a library'.

meet you"; to which the astonished Prince, fully aware that genius takes precedence of noble birth, had gamely replied: "Believe me, I'm the more honoured of the two!"[1] During his last illness he had taken a dislike to his English night-nurse—"I don't want to talk to the Princess of Wales at three in the morning," he would complain; and when the Princesse described how she had sat up reading Mark Twain to her husband (she had retained her love for her native literature and was about to translate Thoreau's *Walden*) Proust thought with nostalgia of the nights of *François le Champi* with his mother at Auteuil.

By this time Mme and Dr Proust were at Zermatt. Proust had taken the opportunity, as he often did when his parents were away, to attempt to reform his lamentable hours: he went to bed at midnight and rose in time for an enormous lunch, 'every day a huge beef-steak without a morsel of waste, whole plates of fried potatoes, cream-cheese, gruyère, peaches and beer'. But as usual asthma intervened. 'I had to walk bent double, and light an anti-asthma cigarette at every tobacconist's I passed.' He consulted his father's colleague Dr Brissaud's *Hygiene for Asthmatics*: Dr Brissaud considered that asthma, in children at least, was often caused by worms; might he not have worms, like M. Homais in *Madame Bovary*? Ought he not to take enemas of mercury, as Dr Brissaud advised? or if that was too drastic, of something milder, such as calomel or glycerine? He had put on weight, but now, dreaming every night that he was holding his corpulence in, 'like a ball', to show his mother on her return, he lost it again. He was well enough, however, to resume his Ruskin pilgrimages. On 7 September he revisited Amiens, and went on to Abbeville to meet Léon Yeatman and see St Wulfram's Church, of which Ruskin had written: 'For cheerful, unalloyed, unwearying pleasure, the getting in sight of Abbeville on a fine summer afternoon, and rushing down the street to see St Wulfram again before the sun was off the towers, are things to cherish the past for—to the end.'[2] This was just such an afternoon: 'I was delighted to see the mines of summer's gold still virgin around me,'

---

[1] Swinburne had a fixed idea that his great-grandmother had been a Polignac, though this was contradicted by the poet's family. Cf. Gosse, *Life of Swinburne*, p. 3.

[2] *Praeterita*, vol. I, ch. 9, section 181, quoted by Proust in his introduction to *La Bible d'Amiens* (cf. *Pastiches et Mélanges*, p. 107).

Proust wrote to his mother. His excursions, however, had taken another trend; he was beginning to visit old churches that Ruskin never mentioned, for their own sake, not for Ruskin's. At this time he planned to go to Mantes and Caen with Robert de Billy, and to Illiers alone. Perhaps, he thought, his Ruskin studies were at last winning recognition: on 13 August an article by André Michel on Amiens Cathedral appeared in the *Journal des Débats*, though he looked in vain for any allusion to his own essay on the cathedral of the year before. Hopefully, he sent Michel a copy of the *Mercure de France* containing his essay; but his only reward was that Michel, in a second article on 10 September, referred sarcastically to 'people who visit Amiens not so much to admire or study the cathedral, as to make a devout Ruskinian pilgrimage', and to Ruskin himself as 'a well-meaning mystical Baedeker'.

During the years in which Proust had travelled the Guermantes Way, from 1892 to 1897, he had made no serious attempt—unless we except his pursuit in 1892 of Mme de Chevigné's nephews, Jacques and Gustave de Waru, because they had their aunt's hair, nose and eyes—to make friends among the young noblemen of the Faubourg Saint-Germain. As if to avert a blow to the heart more cruel than any he feared from titled hostesses, his affections had led him only to intelligent bourgeois youths, Willie Heath, Reynaldo Hahn and Lucien Daudet; and in *Jean Santeuil* he gave his hero, in Henri de Réveillon, a blue-blooded companion whose like he had never known. A new tendency is noticeable from 1898 to 1900, when he had already left the Guermantes Way, in his comradeship with Maugny, Chevilly and Oncieu; though these belonged only to the minor nobility, without any real footing in the Faubourg. But after a year's interval, in 1901, a new and momentous cycle of friendships began, coloured and partly instigated by his enthusiasm for Ruskin. Ruskin had brought him a new conception of art and nature; he now felt the possibility and the need of a corresponding new life of the heart, of companions whose physical and moral beauty would justify them as fit objects of aesthetic passion, and whose race made them living symbols of the cathedrals and castles of old France. By the autumn of 1901 he was already intimate with the first arrivals of the group of young noblemen who in *A la Recherche* merged into the gay, golden figure of Saint-Loup.

The first of these in order of time was Comte Aimery de La

Rochefoucauld's son Gabriel. Shortly before his attendance at the Noailles dinner of 20 June Comte Gabriel had met Proust at a society soirée; and his curiosity was sufficiently aroused to make him ask the friend with whom he left: "What sort of a person is this Proust?" "In my opinion his is the most remarkable literary potentiality that has ever existed," declared the sententious friend. 'I took the remark with friendly scepticism,' wrote Comte Gabriel long afterwards; 'but I was reminded of it the next time I met Proust, and in time I came to regard it as a prophecy.' Proust, he found, seemed to have read everything; his conversation was full of the most piercing psychological observations, and anecdotes of gentle but penetrating irony. Among those treasured by Comte Gabriel was one of a society lady who, when sitting next to Proust at dinner, had asked: "Have you ever heard of a book called *Salammbô*?" Proust stared with childlike astonishment in his eyes, but made no reply. "Come now, you're interested in literature," she prodded, "so you must have heard of it." "I believe it's by Flaubert," he murmured; but the lady, mishearing, and feeling vaguely that she ought to be offended, retorted: "It's beside the point whether it's by Paul Bert or anyone else, all that matters is that I quite liked it!"[1]

Gabriel de La Rochefoucauld was now twenty-six—a few years too old, that is, for Proust to feel more than an ordinary attraction towards him. As a boy he had played, a few years after Proust and Marie de Benardaky, with Duc Agénor de Gramont's daughter Élisabeth in the Tuileries gardens and the Champs-Élysées. He and she had attended the same class for first communion, and exchanged sacred medallions; but when he wrote love-letters to his little playmate she conscientiously showed them to her mother. He resembled Saint-Loup in many ways: he was a would-be intellectual, a Dreyfusard, and a scorner of the aristocracy from which he sprang, particularly of his own father, the overweening Comte Aimery; yet in speaking of persons of birth below his own he was not entirely free from an instinctive sense of his inalienable superiority, and the 'spirit of the Guermantes's seemed to pass over at a great height'.[2] He was tall, and 'bore in his forehead,' Proust wrote of him in 1904, 'like two

---

[1] Paul Bert (1833-86), a physiologist and Minister of Education in 1886, was far from being a prominent literary figure. Proust used the anecdote for Mme d'Arpajon at the Guermantes dinner (II, 489).   [2] II, 694

family jewels, his mother's bright eyes'. He was the only one of Proust's aristocratic young friends whose blood had the supreme nobility claimed by the Guermantes's; for the La Rochefoucaulds were one of the first three ducal families of France, and he would quote with a show of contempt his father's saying: "We're every bit as good as the La Trémoïlles—they've been luckier, that's all!" He was the son (instead of, like Saint-Loup, the nephew) of the originals of the Prince and Princesse de Guermantes; and he was a distant nephew of Comtesse Greffulhe, original of the Duchesse, and of Montesquiou, original of Charlus. He was fond of women and night-life, and was nicknamed, in contradistinction from the *Maximes* of La Rochefoucauld, his ancestor, 'the La Rochefoucauld of Maxim's'. Saint-Loup was banished to Tunisia as a cure for his love of Rachel, and afterwards married Swann's daughter Gilberte. Similarly, we shall find Comte Gabriel in 1904 travelling to Constantinople to recover from a tragic love-affair and in 1905 marrying a girl of half-ducal, half-Jewish birth.

A few hundred yards further up the Rue de Courcelles, at 69, lived Princesse Rachel de Brancovan's cousin Princesse Hélène Bibesco, widow of the Roumanian Prince Alexandre de Bibesco. Like Princesse Rachel she was a virtuoso pianist, and her salon was frequented by a galaxy of musicians, artists, writers and aristocrats. In the past she had known Liszt, Wagner, Gounod, Puvis de Chavannes, the royal Duc d'Aumale; her son Antoine remembered Renan calling to autograph his books, Saint-Saëns and Fauré playing piano duets with her, and the polished cranium of Leconte de Lisle—'I wouldn't have thought it possible for anyone to be so bald.' At the present time her guests included Anatole France, Loti, Jules Lemaître, Maeterlinck, Porto-Riche, Debussy and the painters Bonnard, Vuillard and Odilon Redon. Proust was no doubt invited to her salon through her niece, Mme de Noailles, or her nephew Constantin de Brancovan, who was attending Bergson's lectures at the Sorbonne with his cousins, her sons; and it was there that in 1900 he had met the young Bibesco brothers. Prince Antoine Bibesco was not altogether favourably impressed. He saw a very pale, slightly stooping young man, with unkempt black hair and dark lacquer eyes, who offered and quickly withdrew a drooping, childishly flabby hand. A year later Antoine instructed him in the etiquette of shaking hands: "You must grip powerfully, Marcel, like this," he explained; but "If I followed your example, people would take me for an invert," Marcel objected.

In 1900 Antoine Bibesco was a virilely handsome young man of twenty-three, with stern, chiselled features, implacable eyes, and a slightly cruel twist in his thin lips. Perhaps his cruelty was only apparent, or at worst, not merely gratuitous: he was a loyal friend to the end of Proust's life; but he was inclined to be teasing and revengeful, and when exasperated by Proust's excessive demands or susceptibility he would wait his time and retaliate without scruple. He was studying in Paris for the Roumanian diplomatic service, but soon after their meeting he returned to Roumania for his year's military service.

In the autumn of 1901 Antoine Bibesco returned to Paris, and immediately introduced Proust to his friend Comte Bertrand de Salignac-Fénelon—'the dearest of my friends,' says the Narrator, calling him by name, 'the best, bravest and most intelligent of men, Bertrand de Fénelon, whom no one who ever knew him can forget'.[1] Fénelon, now aged twenty-three, was descended from a brother of the famous bishop of Cambrai, the opponent of Bossuet and author of *Télémaque* under Louis XIV. He shared the blue eyes, the easy, aristocratic manner, the swift movements, and, alas, thirteen years later, the death in battle of the Marquis Robert de Saint-Loup. He was a Dreyfusard, an anti-clerical and an intellectual. 'Bertrand de Fénelon left a glittering wake behind him, and a great emptiness in the minds and hearts of his friends,' wrote Georges de Lauris; 'we have not forgotten the amused and affectionate irony of his gaze, the dauntless impetuosity which we loved, and which he took with him into the battlefield. We expected much of him, and were inclined to be afraid of his verdicts, for he had no use for friendship without plain-speaking. After long absences how enchanting were his returns, his lively eyes, and open arms, and flying coat-tails, in the sunlight before the war!'[2] Soon their group was joined by Comte

[1] II, 771
[2] It is possible (though neither source is quite reliable) that Proust met Fénelon in 1899: Albert Flament mentions him among the habitués of the Café Weber in that year, while Fernand Vandérem names him with Proust as frequenting the salon of Mme Aubernon, who died in 1899. Similarly,

Georges de Lauris, who had met Fénelon in the Bibliothèque Nationale, where Lauris was researching for a doctoral thesis on Benjamin Constant, and Fénelon was studying political history for the diplomatic service. Lauris had already met Proust several times in society, notably amid the glass cupboards and gilded furniture of the salon of Mme Léon Fould, the banker's wife. Proust also made friends this winter with Antoine's brother Emmanuel, who was nicknamed, for his tall, lissom shape and oriental eyes, *l'Almée*, that is, 'the dancing-girl'. Emmanuel, he found, shared his passion for cathedrals, but loved them directly, as did Robert de Billy, without the mediation of Ruskin. Prince Emmanuel Bibesco and Billy, who in May 1899 had returned from the London embassy to work in the Ministry of Foreign Affairs in Paris, helped Proust to win his independence from Ruskin by encouraging a new series of visits to gothic churches, to be enjoyed this time for their own sake. Proust liked and admired Prince Emmanuel; but he did not pursue him, and never reached the point of calling him '*tu*'.

Proust cannot be accused of introducing exalted ideas of friendship into a circle innocent of such ways. The Bibesco brothers and Fénelon already formed a secret society inaccessible to the profane. They had a private language, and called one another by anagrams and palindromes of their real names: the Bibescos were the Ocsebibs, Fénelon was Nonelef, and Marcel, when he arrived, could be none other than Lecram. Antoine, from his addiction to the use of the telephone, was also known as 'Telephas'; and he in turn, when he dared, would call Proust 'the Flatterer'. One of the chief duties of friendship, in their view, lay in a constant exchange of deadly and inviolable confidences: such a secret, therefore, was called a 'tomb'—*tombeau*—and anyone who violated a *tombeau* was, obviously, a 'hyena'. Friendship, however, was not a changeless phenomenon, but subject to the mysterious vicissitudes of the stock-market: when a friend was in a state of mounting prestige, he 'rose' like a share, and when he seemed increasingly tiresome, he 'slumped'. One

Antoine Bibesco (whose memory, however, is often at fault) remembered Proust as making friends with Emmanuel during his (Antoine's) absence on military service in 1900-01. But it is quite clear from Proust's letters to Antoine Bibesco between November 1901 and early March 1902 that at this time Proust was as yet intimate with neither Emmanuel nor Fénelon.

of the most interesting pastimes of friendship was to introduce one friend to another, and see whether they took together, or disliked one another intensely: this was called 'operating a conjunction'. An indispensable element of conversation between friends was gossip, to which Proust was already no stranger: the code-word used as an assurance that one was correctly reporting the words of a third party was '*sic*'; and when a superlative was required one said: '*sicissime*'.

But the comradeship which for the others was a delightful secret game was for Proust a serious and heart-rending passion. Their playful group-friendship was uncongenial to him: he would have preferred an exclusive union with Antoine, or, failing him, with Nonelef. When the others went out together and he was confined to his bedroom, his despair was past bearing: 'I feel the jealousy of a masculine Andromeda chained to his rock,' he wrote to Antoine, 'tortured by the sight of Antoine Bibesco ever receding, ever disappearing and multiplying himself, ever past following.' Another complication, in December 1901, was that Antoine, having written a never-to-be-staged play, *La Lutte*, and made friends with the rising Jewish dramatist Henry Bernstein, was engrossed in an affair with an actress: 'supposing I felt particularly miserable about midnight,' wrote his rock-chained friend, 'I wish you'd tell me where you're likely to be, so long as it isn't in the arms of Salammbo'. Occasionally Antoine would try to console the sufferer with some material bribe; but 'Forgive me,' wrote the unappeasable Marcel, 'if, the day before yesterday, I was too preoccupied by the coil of mythological vipers in your mouth, and the dagger in your right hand, to notice that in your left you were handing me a box of chocolates!' Sometimes he tried to cow the fleeting Bibesco with severity: 'you were perfectly revolting yesterday evening, my dear Telephas, and your shares have slumped'. Soon for the first time Proust announces the paradoxical truth, which is one of the leit-motivs of *A la Recherche*, that friendship, like love, is an illusion: 'friendship is an unreal thing. Renan says we must avoid friendship with individuals, Emerson that we should progressively change every friendship for a better. It's true that equally great writers have said the opposite. But I am growing weary of insincerity and friendship, two things which are practically identical.'

For a time during that winter, perhaps only in the vain hope of provoking Antoine's jealousy, he thought of transferring his devotion to Fénelon. 'With Fénelon, I'm only at the hoping stage; but tell him I have a great deal of affection for him, and I should be delighted if in exchange he would give me a crumb of his own, which he scatters abroad over so many persons.' But the attempt was fruitless: 'soon Nonelef will be no more to me than twenty other people, and there will be no need to wrestle with that classic Siren with the seablue eyes, that direct descendant of Telemachus. . . . But the poor lad, of course, doesn't care a damn for me, and would be amazed if he knew he was the subject of all this heart-searching.' In fact, Proust was still too engrossed in Antoine to woo Nonelef. Nevertheless, it was in this winter of 1901-02 that Fénelon performed two memorable acts of friend-ship. The first was to take Proust, at his own request, to a brothel, where they arrived full of hope. But the girls, Proust complained, were less attractive than he expected, while the central heating left still more to be desired; and the whole establishment had to be turned upside down to provide hot-water bottles and extra bedclothes for this chilly client. Similarly, though the visit never actually occurs, Saint-Loup at the Princesse de Guermantes's soirée promises on his next leave to take the Narrator 'to a place where the women are quite amazing', and where he will meet the mysterious Mlle d'Orgeville.[1] One night at Larue's restaurant in the Place de la Madeleine Proust again complained of the cold; and it was Fénelon who executed Saint-Loup's famous run along the ledge behind the red-plush benches, carrying a greatcoat for his shivering friend. Proust was stirred to record the incident in a new chapter of *Jean Santeuil*, in which he called Fénelon 'Bertrand de Réveillon'.[2] It was the first addition to his novel for two years, and the last he was ever to make; but it was too soon to transfer the new power he had gained through Ruskin to an imaginative work, and the episode is one of the most ill-written (which is saying a great deal) in the whole novel.

[1] II, 694
[2] *Jean Santeuil*, vol. i, pp. 289-98. Here Réveillon performs his feat only to reach his friend more quickly on entering. Perhaps this version is the truer to fact. As we shall see, Proust's overcoat was fetched in this athletic way by Jean Cocteau in or about 1911, and Proust may have combined the two incidents in *A la Recherche* (II, 411).

Early in 1902 Marie Nordlinger returned to Paris, after an absence of three and a half years, to work as a silversmith and enamellist at the Art Nouveau workshops for the jeweller Siegfried Bing. Once more she brought her gentle, unconscious guidance to influence Proust's life: on one of the first days of spring she visited the church of Saint-Loup-de-Naud near Provins, and borrowed from the Abbé Louis Nappe his treatise comparing the sculptures of its porch with those of Chartres. She passed the Abbé's book on to Marcel, and so touched off a new series of visits to gothic churches.

The first of these was to Chartres by rail, on a Sunday, probably 16 March 1902, with Fénelon and unnamed friends of Fénelon; though it was preceded by a still earlier trip by the Bibesco brothers in Emmanuel's motor-car, without Proust, to churches whose names are not revealed. 'I have, alas,' Proust remarked in a letter to Antoine on the Thursday before the journey to Chartres, 'no tempting automobile to offer you, but only a modest first-class railway ticket.' On Friday, to his great disappointment, Antoine declined the proposal; but he tried to make up for this unkindness by inviting Proust, for the first time, to call him '*tu*'. He also promised to see Proust that evening at Larue's, but spoilt even this by a further dig at his sensitive friend. So Proust's reply, the first letter in which he says *tu* to Antoine (thus providentially enabling the biographer to date the earlier letters in which he had written '*vous*') is one of bitter reproach. 'Let this be the last time you say "Don't be afraid, I shall only stay a minute", because my nerves are too much on edge to bear that particular irony again. I'm keeping your letter, and I shall compare it before your very eyes with one of Nonelef's, and I shall have something to say on the subject which you will think neither nice—though it is extremely so—nor just—though it is the truth itself!'

At Chartres that Sunday Proust studied the cathedral with the help of Mâle's book, and then went on alone to Illiers, arranging to rejoin his companions at Chartres the same evening. There may have been family reasons for the visit to Illiers; but there can be little doubt that Proust's own purpose was to see the church of Saint-Jacques with the new eyes given him by Ruskin. Previously he had always taken Saint-Jacques for granted. In the scene of Sunday mass at Étreuilles in *Jean Santeuil* there is no hint that the church might possess a beauty of its own, independent of the hot sunlight in the market-place, the townsfolk in their Sunday clothes, and the sound of the bells. But he now contributed something also of his own vision; for Ruskin would have remained indifferent to the humble merits of the eleventh-century romanesque door which matched that of the long-dead Louis Proust's house in the Rue du Cheval Blanc, or the massive roughstone walls, still encroached upon by the hatter's and other shops, of the market-place front; and the Master would have called down fire from heaven on the modern stained-glass and purple panelling of Abbé Carré, or the floor-tiles and altar 'in fifteenth-century style' of the good Canon Marquis, which seemed natural and kindly to Proust, because they had already been there in his childhood. The visit marks a further stage in Proust's recovery of his past, and his growing ability to perceive in it the truths of which his boyhood eyes had been only unconsciously aware.

On the way back from Chartres Proust had a violent attack of asthma, which prevented him from going to bed that night, but not from lunching, still sleepless, with Antoine at Weber's next morning: 'I've been longing for ages, I don't know why, to see you in that place at midday, when the sun is shining.'

It was after the Chartres visit that he began to take a moderate interest in Emmanuel Bibesco. At first he forbade Antoine to bring him to 45 Rue de Courcelles: 'I've nothing against him, of course, as he's charming, but I couldn't possibly see him, and Mama would never allow it, when I'm in bed undressed and wearing my untidy pullovers.' But soon he was writing: 'If your brother wants to see me we could all three meet in the evening, whenever he likes, or even in the daytime if he wants to visit country churches, but it will have to be before my hay-fever begins, that is, not later than 17 or 18 April.' This plan led to two other memorable journeys, the first of which was a direct consequence of Marie Nordlinger's example, and a logical sequel to the visit to Chartres.

On a Friday, probably 21 March, they set out in a cavalcade of two motor-cars: one of these, belonging to Emmanuel Bibesco, was enclosed, enabling Proust to travel without fear of draughts and asthma, while the other, Lucien Henraux's, was open and suitable for fresh-air fiends. They visited Provins and Saint-

Loup-de-Naud, a partly romanesque and partly gothic church, with the sculptured portal which showed, as Abbé Nappe had pointed out, such striking analogies with Chartres, and which Proust transferred to the imaginary church of Saint-André-des-Champs near Combray. The name of Saint-Loup was already familiar to him from the village near Illiers and the château on the Loire above Orleans; but this visit to the church of Saint-Loup-de-Naud, with the collective originals of the Marquis de Saint-Loup-en-Bray, was no doubt decisive for Proust's choice of his hero's name.

The other journey was the longest and best attended of all. On Good Friday, 28 March 1902, the automobiles set out to the north-east of Paris, bearing Proust, the two Bibescos, Fénelon, Lauris and Robert de Billy—perhaps, also, Lucien Henraux and Marquis François de Pâris. Proust solved the problem of getting up early enough by not going to bed at all; and at every stop on the way he fortified himself with a stiff *café-au-lait*, for which he insisted on giving an enormous tip. Their first call was at Saint-Leu-d'Esserent, a vast church on the Oise not far from Chantilly, mostly of twelfth-century and earlier date, with one romanesque and two gothic towers. Inside the church Antoine disgraced himself in Proust's eyes by singing the noisy Boulangist ditty, *En revenant de la revue*, with appropriate actions. They went on to the twelfth-century cathedral of Senlis, with its two belfries and exquisite spire. Lauris remembered Emmanuel here 'explaining to the attentive Marcel, but refraining from any appearance of giving a lecture, the features which characterise the church-towers of the Ile-de-France'. Proust already knew the spire from a water-colour painted by Marie Nordlinger in 1898, and was to see it two years later, far away over an endless forest, from the Duc de Gramont's château of Vallière: the town was to be sacked and the cathedral damaged, much to his grief, by the German invaders in September 1914. The friends reached their furthest point at Laon, eighty-seven miles from Paris. Laon, ostensibly, was the town at which Gilberte was staying, when the wind, 'the tutelary genius of Combray', seemed to waft her distant presence to the Narrator over the cornfields of the Méséglise Way; though in fact, as we have seen, Proust was thinking secretly of the village of Laons near Illiers, and perhaps of Mme Goupil's niece there. High in the belfries of the twin towers of the cathedral appear the sculptured heads of eight colossal oxen, carved in memory of the beasts who dragged the stones for the building—surely the strangest and most Proustian feature in all the cathedrals of France; and Emmanuel ingeniously arranged that his friends should have their first glimpse of the oxen when he led them suddenly round a street corner. The Narrator compares the proud race of the Guermantes's to 'a carved, mellow tower, rising over France before the cathedral nave had come to rest, like a Noah's Ark, on the hill of Laon, crammed with animals in the act of escaping through the towers, and with oxen grazing on the roof and looking down over the meadows of Champagne'.[1] Proust was delighted with the figures of the Liberal Arts in the porch, which he enumerated three years afterwards to Mme Catusse: 'Philosophy with the ladder of knowledge leaning against her bosom, Astronomy with eyes fixed on the heavens, Geometry with her compass and Arithmetic counting on her fingers, Logic with her wise serpent, but rather a banal Medicine, not as interesting as the one at Rheims who (if you will pardon my saying so) is examining a patient's urine in a vase.' In the same porch was a series of scenes from the life of the Virgin; and he borrowed these for the sculptures in the church at Balbec, which Elstir in his studio expounds to the Narrator.[2]

On the homeward journey that afternoon they stopped at Coucy, ten miles from Laon, to see the thirteenth-century castle, 'whose keep,' Proust had read in Viollet-le-Duc, 'is the finest specimen of mediaeval military architecture in France: beside this giant all others seem the merest spindles'. Here, too, Emmanuel contrived that they should first see the castle from a point at the foot of the hill, whence even its base showed high above the tree-tops. The friends climbed the spiral staircase of the great tower together. Marcel leaned on Fénelon's arm, while Fénelon, to encourage his asthmatic companion, and because the day was indeed Good Friday, sang the Good Friday-Spell motif from *Parsifal*. When they reached the platform at the top, one hundred and eighty feet from the ground, they gazed, in one of the eternal moments of which Time Lost is made, on the flowering apple-trees far below over the Ile-de-France, the last sunlight, the

[1] II, 13
[2] I, 840

endless green landscape of their youth.[1] Then night came, and cold; it was after midnight when they reached Paris, and Proust, utterly exhausted, took to his bed for several days.

By the middle of June his translation of *The Bible of Amiens* was nearly complete. On the 28th he asked Mme de Noailles to persuade her husband to lend him his Bible 'provided it isn't too enormous', for the quotations in the footnotes, at which he had been at work 'for the last few months'. 'At the moment of transscribing them I find they seem quite colourless, owing to the bad translation I've been using, and he told me he had an excellent Bible.' He adds that his 'documentation is now complete'. Perhaps it was at this time, when his erudition in Christian iconography was at its height, that Proust had the conversation recorded by Georges de Lauris with his former playmate of the Champs-Élysées, Lucie Faure, now Mme Goyau, an ardent Catholic and a scholarly student of Dante: 'he revealed a subtle and finely shaded mastery of the most difficult problems of religious philosophy and exegesis; could he have read the whole of the *Golden Legend*, and all the works of the learned Bollandists?'

He now sent his manuscript to the publisher Charles Ollendorff, who kept it for five months without deciding whether to accept or reject it, and then providentially went out of business to become editor of *Gil Blas*, leaving his successor to go bankrupt. 'If this hadn't happened,' Proust told Antoine Bibesco two years later, 'I doubt whether I'd ever have been able to recover my *Bible*, at once so cruelly scorned and so jealously detained.' But his memory was at fault when he told Antoine that Ollendorff 'had my Ruskin in his hands for a whole year before I could extract it from him'; for he had already recovered his manuscript and signed a contract with the *Mercure de France* for its publication as early as mid-December 1902.

On 29 June Proust wrote to Mme de Noailles: 'There's only one person who understands me, and that's Antoine Bibesco: I

[1] The tower of Coucy was blown up by the Germans in their retreat to the Hindenburg Line in March 1917. Perhaps it was the thought of this, among other such incidents, which made Proust allow the church of Saint-Hilaire to be destroyed in the Great War, when, as Gilberte wrote to the Narrator from Tansonville, 'for a year and a half the Germans held one half of Combray, the French the other' (III, 756), and according to the Baron de Charlus, 'the church was demolished by the French and English because the Germans were using it as an observation post' (III, 795).

hope he continues to do so! He is so intelligently kind to me, so
kind, and so intelligent.' But during July he transferred, or rather
extended, his pursuit from Antoine to Fénelon. It was one of the
stormiest and most disappointing of his friendships, the only one
on which he looked back with lasting bitterness, not because
he lost Fénelon, but because he never won him. The long-
accumulated strain on his nerves, added to the dual necessity of
lunching and dining with his friends without ceasing to stay up
all night, not infrequently prevented him from going to bed at
all; and when in total exhaustion at the beginning of August he
took to his bed in the evenings, it was not a return to the human
norm: on the contrary, he realised with horror, his life was a whole
twenty-four hours out of gear. Before leaving for Évian on 12
August Mme Proust took the extreme step of writing to Fénelon
to beg him to see her son regularly; but, Marcel grumbled,
'Fénelon has taken no notice of your requests—still, whatever
you do, don't begin again, because there's absolutely nothing
more to be said; and Bibesco is taken up every evening just now
by his double absorption in ham acting and making love.' 'I
never stop hearing new stories of women you've tried to assault,'
he rebuked Antoine, 'your violence is simply fantastic!' On the
14th, demoralised by lack of sleep, indigestion and a racing pulse,
he visited Dr Vaquez, who advised a régime of bed, trional and
cold tubs, and abstention from alcohol and morphine. "I never
could understand," said the wise doctor, "why invalids can't be
content with their own illnesses, instead of insisting on creating
new ones by making themselves unhappy over people who aren't
worth the trouble!" That night Proust dined at Larue's, alone
except for the waiters, under the glare of sixty electric lights:
Fénelon and Constantin de Brancovan had broken their promise
to join him, and he was again left in the lurch. But his woes were
alleviated by the kindness of old Félicie, of whom he wrote to
his mother in words which recall the Narrator's regard for
Françoise: 'Peace is restored, and a very affectionate one, between
Félicie and me. I'd far rather have her than Marie in a situation
like this. Marie is more educated, but less literary in her language,
and above all, Félicie's affection is so charming and simple.'

However, Proust and Fénelon had their times of laughter and
delight that summer. He recalled afterwards a day on which they
visited Mme Straus at her villa, Le Clos des Mûriers, at Trouville;

she took them over the clifftops in her motor-car to Honfleur, through the landscapes he had roamed with Marie Finaly ten years before. For once he enjoyed without asthma 'the mingled scent of leaves, milk and sea-salt'. And he remembered how every Sunday Bertrand would say: "Do find me the Stock Exchange column in *Le Figaro*, Marcel," and he would search in vain, because on Sundays there was no such column.

Early in September he thought of visiting his parents at Évian for the week-end—'I've been longing to see the beautiful lake again'—but he could not bring himself to leave the pleasures and miseries of Paris. The difficulty of persuading Marcel to take a holiday that year was only solved when Fénelon consented to go with him. After hastily reading up the Dutch and Flemish old masters in Antoine's copy of Fromentin's *Les Maîtres d'autrefois*, and buying another to take with him, he left with Bertrand on 2 October for Bruges. He heard the carillon, which reminded him of Mme Greffulhe's silvery laugh; and he met Harlette Comte, who was to marry his friend Fernand Gregh in March 1903. Soon he went on to Antwerp, where he was on the 9th, while Fénelon went on ahead to Amsterdam to book rooms on the Yeatmans' recommendation at the Hôtel de l'Europe. Even Proust found them fantastically expensive, though they had the advantage of being heated by hot-water pipes, to which he attributed his freedom from asthma during the whole visit; and Fénelon himself took to dining out, rather than pay ten francs for the *table d'hôte* dinner. Proust delighted once more in the seagulls of Amsterdam, of which Albertine says to Mme de Cambremer at Balbec: 'they smell the sea, they come to sniff the salt air even through the paving-stones';[1] and when he returned from the day's excursion he saw, like Albertine, 'the streets and towpaths brimming with a compact and joyful crowd'.[2] He visited Dordrecht on a showery day, and sent Reynaldo a sketch of the ivy-covered church, 'reflected in a network of sleeping canals, and in the tremulous, golden Meuse, in whose water the boats at evening disturb the images of red roofs and blue sky'. At Delft he saw 'an ingenuous little canal, bewildered by the din of seventeenth-century carillons and dazzled by the pale sunlight; it ran between a double row of trees stripped of their leaves by summer's end, and stroking with their branches the mirroring windows of the gabled houses on either bank'. On 15 October he went to Vollendam by barge, 'through flatlands moaning in the wind, while on the banks the reedbeds bowed and raised their heads in endless undulation'. On the 17th, unlike the Narrator, who tells the Duchesse de Guermantes that on his visit to Holland, 'as I didn't want to confuse my impressions, and was short of time, I missed Haarlem', he visited Haarlem to see the paintings of Frans Hals[1]: 'why, even a person who saw them from the top of a tramcar would find them a real eye-opener,' the Duchesse shocks the Narrator by saying. Next day he rejoined Fénelon at The Hague, saw Vermeer's *View of Delft* at the Mauritshuis, and 'recognised it for the most beautiful painting in the world'. The Duc de Guermantes's impression of the picture was less vivid: when the Narrator enquires whether he knows the *View of Delft*, he replies with self-satisfaction: "If it's there to be seen, I certainly saw it!"[2] By now Proust was short of money; he explained to his parents, not for the first time in his life, that his pocket had been picked; and on 20 October he returned to Paris. His relations with Fénelon during these three weeks had been unwontedly serene. He would certainly have seized upon any new opportunity of complaining of him to Mme Proust, but instead he wrote: 'Fénelon was the *only person* with whom I could possibly have gone away . . . he couldn't have been nicer.' His mother would have liked him to go on to Illiers; but in view of the season, for Illiers was at its most melancholy in autumn, and the critical situation of his private life, he refused: 'to stay at Illiers or anywhere else, especially just now, would be absolute madness'.

He returned to find Antoine Bibesco alarmed by the serious illness of his mother, who was in Roumania on the family estate of Corcova. At last, too late, a telegram arrived to call him to her side; she died on 31 October, and Antoine arrived too late to see her alive. Proust rose to the occasion with the peculiar intensity which he always showed when a friend was bereaved: he shared Antoine's grief to the point of making himself ill, he showed exquisite tact, utter unselfishness, an extraordinary insight into the mental processes of the mourner; yet it was as if the idea of a mother's death filled him with a strange, almost pleasurable

[1] At least, he told his mother he intended to do so; but he may have changed his mind.   [2] II, 523-4

excitement. When he saw Antoine's first letter, in which the very handwriting was shrunk by suffering, he was reminded of his own mother's voice on the telephone at Fontainebleau in 1896, after the deaths of Louis and Nathé Weil, 'broken and bruised, cracked and fissured, forever changed from the voice I had always known'. He offered to come to Corcova from February to June, if Antoine could assure him there were no flowers there to give him hay-fever; or to Munich for two days, if Antoine would meet him there half-way; but not till after 2 and 5 January, for the anniversaries of his grandmother's death and burial thirteen years before were still strictly kept in the family; or to Ragusa, Constantinople, or even Egypt. In the end, when all the inextricable web of planning and counter-planning could be spun no further, he stayed in Paris.

Antoine was not his only preoccupation during this November and December. Fénelon had been appointed attaché in the French embassy at Constantinople on 31 October, and was due to leave on 8 December: Proust, knowing his own inability to care long for the absent, did not disguise from himself that this meant the end of their friendship. Another cause for dejection was that his parents, exasperated by the ever-increasing expense of his social life, had insisted on putting him—at the age of thirty-one—on a fixed allowance. The Freudian equation of money and love was particularly strong in Proust: all his life he had expected and taken love and money from his parents, to spend on his friends and give to all who served him. It was as if his parents had decided to give him less love; and he was still more outraged by this betrayal than by what seemed to him the utter inadequacy of the allowance. Perhaps, however, their motive was not mere economy, but their knowledge that they had not long to live, and their desire to discipline the extravagant Marcel at the eleventh hour. His mother, too, who showed almost excessive indulgence when he was ill, was inclined to be jealous of his health, and of the social activities, friendships and freedom from home which it made possible. 'The truth is,' he told her with severity, 'that the moment I'm well, as the way of life which makes me well infuriates you, you demolish every-thing until I'm ill again. . . It's very sad not to be able to have affection and health both at once.' Her jealousy showed itself in all manner of petty restrictions and complaints, which, although

they were no doubt justifiable in themselves, would never have
occurred to her if he had been safely bedridden. He kept the
servants awake, and they in turn kept her awake; they were not
to wait on him at table, but must deposit a tray of food in his
bedroom and go away; they must not light a special fire in the
dining-room when his friends called; and worst of all, the bedside-
table on which he worked must be taken away ('I'd rather do
without chairs!'). Perhaps he was speaking the truth when he
told her that his despair at her unkindness was the sole cause of
his quarrel with Fénelon.

Fénelon and Lauris called one afternoon early in December,
and kept their overcoats on in the unheated dining-room: "I
daren't, Madame would have me dismissed," said Marie, when
asked to light a fire. In this gloomy situation Fénelon was moved
to say 'something extremely disagreeable'; whereupon Marcel
leaped upon him with clenched fists and, when restrained by
Lauris, seized Bertrand's beautiful new hat, stamped upon it, and
tore out the lining. With ludicrous pathos he kept the piece of
lining to show his mother, 'so that you can see I'm not exaggerating; but please don't throw it away, as I want to give it him
back in case it's still of any use to him'. Here is the original of
the incident in which the Narrator desecrates the new top-hat of
the Baron de Charlus.[1] The Baron has insulted him for not
consenting to his veiled overtures: it would be neat and logical
if the offence for which Proust punished Fénelon had been the
exact opposite, namely, an accusation of lack of virility. "Proust
was a Saturnian, and a very difficult friend," Fénelon told Paul
Morand twelve years later.

'Saturnian' was the euphemism in the slang of their group for
'homosexual'; we find Proust using the word on two other
occasions to the Bibesco brothers, but never to anyone else. 'I
have made some rather profound reflections on Saturnism,' he
airily informed Emmanuel Bibesco at about this time, 'which I
shall communicate to you at one of our next metaphysical
discussions. I need hardly add that they are of the utmost severity.
But one clings, all the same, to a philosophical curiosity about
people. Almost the only things worth knowing about a fool are
that he's an anti-Dreyfusard or a Saturnian.' Clearly, Emmanuel
was not supposed to be aware of Proust's own homosexuality;

[1] II, 559

nor was Antoine, when Proust objected to his recommendation of firmness in shaking hands: "but people would take me for an invert!" It is very likely that Proust's relations with all these noble young friends—not only those we have already met, but those, Albufera, Radziwill and Guiche, who are about to arrive—were entirely platonic. They may not have been willingly so; and his ill-success with Antoine and Fénelon may well have been due to his friends' realisation of the true nature of his frustrations. It is probable, too, with two possible exceptions, that all these young men were themselves normal. Marriage and the pursuit of women, it is true, are by no means incompatible with sexual inversion: Wilde and Gide were husbands and fathers, and Proust himself was to portray the woman-chasers and the married men of Sodom. But some weight must be given to the fact that a majority of Proust's friends—Gabriel de La Roche-foucauld, Antoine Bibesco, Lauris, Albufera, Radziwill and Guiche—were engaged in love-affairs with women during the first period of his friendship with them, and later married. Two, however, did not marry. It may or may not be significant that Emmanuel Bibesco was called the Dancing Girl, that there is no trace in the little we know of him of any affairs with women, and that he ultimately committed suicide: on the other hand, it is clear that Proust's feeling for him never went beyond liking. Fénelon, too, remained single: it seems not unlikely that it was to him that Paul Morand so scathingly referred when he alleged that 'the enchanting young man with fair hair and blue eyes, the darling of the ladies in 1900, who served as the model for Saint-Loup, was to end fairly and squarely in heterodoxy, or, as we called it in our jargon of those days, bi-metallism'. Fénelon perhaps suggested the descent into Sodom of Saint-Loup, as he suggested his redemption through death in battle. Did Proust, with his expert intuition in these matters, divine the truth even at this early period? Did their friendship end because Fénelon felt himself on the point of giving way, or because Proust himself made advances for which Fénelon was not yet prepared? However this may be, the swift Fénelon vanished into the East; his keen blue eyes and flying coat-tails were seen by his friends only in brief, yearly glimpses, on his summer leaves, and by Proust still more seldom. He half-forgot Bertrand instantly, and half-remembered him for ever.

Two other complications prevented him from visiting the bereaved Antoine in Roumania. Early in December he signed a contract with Alfred Vallette, editor of the *Mercure de France* and director of the publishing firm attached to that periodical, not only for *La Bible d'Amiens* but for a new translation of *Sesame and Lilies*. On the evening of his quarrel with his mother and Fénelon he had threatened, by way of revenge, to cancel the contract, but soon thought better of it. The manuscript of *La Bible d'Amiens*, which by now he had succeeded in extracting from Ollendorff, had to be revised and handed in on 1 February 1903. Also ('this marriage couldn't have come at a more inconvenient time') his brother Robert had become engaged to Mlle Marthe Dubois-Amiot, of 6 Rue de Messine and Aix-les-Bains; and Proust was faced with the dreadful duty of getting up in the daytime, first 'to make the acquaintance of the young lady, whom I haven't met yet', and then again in order to act as Robert's best man. He was also entrusted with the sending of invitations to the wedding, and was horrified to find, only a week before the great day, that no less than a hundred of these had failed to arrive. Perhaps his jealousy of his brother, repressed and replaced though it was by a genuine and lifelong affection, had risen at this crucial time nearer to the surface. Robert, for once, was the centre of attraction. He had taken his doctorate of medicine in February 1902, and was now in practice; he would soon be a husband and support a family of his own; he had proved his manhood and his normality as Marcel never would. A stay-at-home prodigal, a feeder among the swine of Sodom, Marcel saw with shame and indignation his allowance cut while the fatted calf was slain for his virtuous brother. Inevitably, he was ill for the wedding.

The ceremony took place on 2 February 1903 at noon, in the church of Saint-Augustin. In his capacity as best man Proust took the traditional collection for the poor after the service, assisted by his eighteen-year-old cousin Valentine Thomson. The girl's pleasure in her pretty dress and the bouquet of orchids Mme Proust had given her was spoiled by his distress and lamentable appearance. Marcel's white tie and tails were hidden beneath three overcoats and an indeterminate number of mufflers; his chest was wadded, his collar all too visibly caulked, with swathes of cotton-wool. Thus accoutred he was too bulky to pass along the pews; instead, he stood in the aisle looking like Tweedledum, 'his Lazarus-like face with its melancholy moustache rising like a surprise out of his woolly black cerements. He felt he had to explain himself, and to each row in turn he announced in a loud voice that he was not able to dress otherwise, that he had been ill for months, that he would be still more ill that evening, that it was not his fault.' After the midday reception at 6 Rue de Messine he took to his bed for a fortnight. 'Robert's wedding has been the death of me,' he wrote to Mme Catusse. But the ill wind of Saint-Augustin's brought him two fur coats, one from the good-hearted Robert as the obligatory present to his best man, and one from Antoine Bibesco, which he returned without opening the parcel: he did not wish to hurt Robert's feelings by accepting it, he explained, nor to let his parents think it a stratagem in his campaign against the meagreness of his allowance.

Since Antoine's absence and Fénelon's departure Proust had engaged in a new and even more than usually disappointing friendship with a certain 'M'. Antoine was thinking of a visit to Fénelon at Constantinople—'but if you won't come too, I shan't go'. In a letter of consent so provisional as to be almost a refusal Proust took the opportunity to tell Antoine and Bertrand some home-truths: 'it's curious that each of you has an opposite gift, yours being to dissipate mistrust, his to inspire it; so that you're both likely to make enemies, but yours will be people who don't know you and might well become your friends if you wished it, while Bertrand's enemies will always be his former friends. . . . This doesn't prevent me from being very fond of Bertrand. We're never more unjust than in those affections which we think must be prejudiced just because they're blind, and because for fear of liking him less we shut our eyes to the possible faults of the friend we cherish, and so prevent ourselves from seeing his virtues. I've had proof of this lately with M., whom I respected less the more I liked him, convinced as I was that because I was fond of him I was certain to be over-indulgent. Now I realise he was infinitely superior to the image of him constructed by my consciously indulgent, but therefore depreciatory affection. He would have had everything to gain from a severe, just and clear-sighted friendship.' Proust's biting letter of dismissal to M. survives: 'I don't wish to see you any more, or to write to you, or to know you'; he keeps the inkstand M. has given him for

New Year's Day 1903, but intends to unscrew and return the plaque so ironically engraved with 'Sweetest of blessings is a genuine friend'; he is 'giving several little dinners soon, but if anyone asks why you aren't there I'll explain that you're taken up with your family, your mistress, your country-house and the army' (for M., we are told, was at this time a sub-lieutenant in an infantry regiment); and he signs the letter: 'I was, Your very sincere friend, Marcel Proust.' In a letter to a common friend about M. he quotes Barrès—'yet another lemon squeezed dry'. 'I hope you haven't passed on my kind regards to M., as they would risk resembling those rays from a star which reach us only after the star itself has ceased to shine.'

Spurred on by his mother ('You're quite impossible—instead of admiring my positive resurrection and acquiescing in what made it practicable, you have to insist on my setting to work again'), he entered in December 1902 on a new cycle of literary work. He added still further to his footnotes for *La Bible d'Amiens*: one of his innumerable excuses for not going to Roumania was the necessity of 'bringing thirty volumes of Ruskin with me'. Constantin de Brancovan ('the latest person to call me *tu*') had launched a new literary magazine, *La Renaissance Latine*, and had accepted, as a substitute for the articles he had originally requested, an abridgement of *La Bible d'Amiens* which appeared in the issues for 15 February and 15 March 1903. But Proust had also been commissioned by Gaston Calmette to write a series of articles on prominent hostesses and their salons for *Le Figaro*. This was probably a delayed consequence of a curious incident in the previous August. He had then tried in vain to arrange for Fénelon to write paragraphs for the society gossip-columns of *Le Figaro*, and to persuade Emmanuel Bibesco to supply information on his fellow-guests at dinners and soirées ('of course, if you put in any made-up names or other jokes it would make things so awkward for me that I hope you'll refrain'); but Fénelon had been half-unwilling, Emmanuel had refused outright, and the project fell through. The first article in the series was on Princesse Mathilde (*Un Salon historique: le salon de S.A.I. la Princesse Mathilde*), and appeared on 25 February over the signature 'Dominique', a name Proust had already given himself as the hero of the sketch *'L'Étranger'* in *Les Plaisirs et les Jours*.

In March Proust felt obliged to give a series of dinners of gratitude at 45 Rue de Courcelles, the first for Calmette, another for Vallette, another for Cardane, secretary of *Le Figaro*, and yet others for Mme Lemaire, who was to be the subject of one of his forthcoming salon articles, and Hervieu, whom he had been meeting frequently with Lauris and the Bibescos at Mme de Pierrebourg's. These, no doubt, are the 'little dinners' to which he vengefully refrained from inviting 'M'. He had planned Calmette's dinner ('he would like to meet smart people') in January, but had been persuaded by his mother to postpone it till after Robert's wedding. When March came, however, Mme Proust was no better pleased with what she insultingly called 'this dinner of cocottes'; to Marcel's fury she used it as a menace to enforce a reform of his hours; 'if you don't change your hours, you shan't have your dinner!' He threatened to give it in a restaurant—'when I put myself in your place and imagine myself refusing you not one, but even a hundred dinners!'—but, although the sequel remains unknown, it is likely that he had his way. He did not know how little time the parents he exhausted with these exactions had still to live.

Chapter 16

TIME BEGINS TO BE LOST

BY the spring of 1903 three more young noblemen had joined the little band of Saint-Loups. Armand, Duc de Guiche, was the half-brother of Élisabeth de Gramont (since 1896 wife of Philibert, Marquis de Clermont-Tonnerre), and son of Duc Agénor by his second wife, Marguerite, daughter of Baron Charles de Rothschild: Guiche was therefore, despite his exalted birth on his father's side, half-Jewish. He was a tall, virile young man of twenty-three, with dark, curly hair, pale skin and violet eyes. He rode to hounds, played polo, painted, and already pursued the scientific studies which were to bring him international fame in the fields of optics and aerodynamics. Guiche met Proust early in March at Mme de Noailles's; he remembered how Reynaldo Hahn sang songs by Duparc and Fauré, chain-smoked, and broke into the Marseillaise when Mathieu de Noailles tiptoed in to say good-bye to his guests and leave for army manœuvres. Proust, however, was more interested in the antics of Lucien Daudet, who sat next to Guiche at dinner: demoralised by his noble company 'he chattered with unprecedented volubility and with all the joy of Mme Bovary crying "I've found a lover! I've found a lover!"' There was an awkward moment when Guiche asked, apparently in all innocence, "Have you a brother?" Lucien remained tongue-tied, for his brother, of course, was the now rabidly anti-Semitic Léon. He would have liked, Proust maliciously surmised, to reply: "No, certainly not, and if you should ever hear that someone named Daudet has been saying nasty things about Rothschilds and Jews, he's no relative of mine." But poor Lucien, transfixed by the implacable eyes of his hostess, could only burble a truthful but uninformative "Yes". Guiche had heard of Proust at Mme Straus's in his boyhood: "we invite him when we want someone witty to make up a fourteenth!" Struck by the brilliance of his conversation, he soon wrote to ask him to a party at his parent's house. 'My dear Proust', he began; but Proust answered: 'of course, I realise you can't call me "My dear Marcel", but you might at least put "My dear friend", which commits you to nothing, not even to friendship.' By April, however, their friendship had advanced far enough for Proust already to feel disappointed. He sent Guiche for an Easter present a copy of *Les Plaisirs et les Jours* with a melancholy inscription: 'To the Duc de Guiche, the true one rather than the real one, the one who might have been rather than the one who is. ... I offer this portrait, now so poor a likeness, of a Marcel he has never known.'

Prince Léon Radziwill, nicknamed 'Loche', also aged twenty-three, was the son of Prince Constantin Radziwill,[1] whose remote cousin Prince Michel Radziwill had married Marie de Benardaky in 1897. The other branches of his large and wealthy family were scattered over Russia, Poland and Germany; and although the Constantin Radziwills were by now firmly rooted in France, Loche would complain: "It's very provoking, when I'm in Poland people talk about 'You Frenchmen', and when I'm in France they say 'You Poles'!" His aunt, Princesse Marie Radziwill, was one of the most prominent ladies in the court of the Kaiser, and devoted her life in vain to the promotion of friendship between France and Germany. She was also an aunt of Boni de Castellane, who once delighted and astonished her by taking her to the Ritz: "I'm particularly grateful to you for taking me to that inn, my dear," she said, "because I have never dined at an inn before." Loche was a young man of giant size, 'more like a block than a statue', with 'expressively inexpressive blue eyes', as Proust wrote one evening that autumn at Ermenonville, Prince Constantin Radziwill's château. The others had gone to bed, leaving Proust in the dining-room to write a character-sketch of Loche, and to freeze by the dying stove; he composed a wounded and wounding rigmarole of fifteen hundred words. Loche's voice, 'with its amusing slowness and false affability, seems clotted with foolishness and naïveté'; 'he would do anything for a friend except be his friend, in so far as that word

---

[1] Montesquiou, who might well have claimed to be the inventor of the clerihew, wrote:
> *'It is most uncivil*
> *To mention ladies to Constantin Radziwill.'*

Loche's father, as we shall see, was the original of the Prince de Guermantes in his later aspect as a homosexual.

implies preference, fidelity, security and perseverance'; most horrible of all, he once said of Ruskin that 'his greatest merit was his skill in making even the loftiest ideas agreeable and accessible to all!' 'Only an artist can see Loche's true merits, though women have an inkling of them, because they find him extremely attractive', and 'desire is a kind of sightless comprehension'. Clearly, Loche had sat for Proust's eternal friendship, but failed his examination.

At that time, however, the most important of all the new recruits of 1903 was Marquis (later Duc) Louis d'Albufera, known as 'Albu'. Albu was good-natured, loyal and simple, the only one of Proust's group of young noblemen who was a non-intellectual and an anti-Dreyfusard. He was aged twenty-six, an ardent motorist and traveller, and had made a journey to Tunisia at the time of Proust's winter friendship with M. Like Saint-Loup, he was in love with an actress; he had bought her a horse and buggy, and his delight in this spring was to sit on one of the iron chairs in the Avenue des Acacias and watch her drive up and down. Louisa de Mornand was a tall, willowy young person, with a long nose, arched eyebrows, and features of the most fascinating prettiness. She specialised in light comedy, first in soubrette parts, later in leads, and had a maid, Rachel, from whom Proust took the name of Saint-Loup's mistress. Proust himself immediately succumbed to Mlle de Mornand's charm partly because she was the beloved of a friend, but partly for her own sake; and their amical relationship survived through her subsequent love-affairs until the last years of his life. She made her début at the Théâtre des Mathurins in Tarride's *Coin du feu* on 17 April 1903 as the maid Victorine; and on 24 May at the same theatre she played a rather more important role in a curtain-raiser to the lyrical pantomime '*Rêve d'opium*' which featured the notorious Otéro, *la belle Otéro*, the rival in whoredom and diamonds of Liane de Pougy. On this prominent occasion Proust took it upon himself to organise her publicity: through Antoine Bibesco he asked the dramatist Edmond Sée and Abel Hermant, then dramatic critic of *Gil Blas*, to mention her appreciatively in their criticisms, if it was only to say: 'A friend of mine asks me to mention that Mlle de Mornant is a beauty and a charmer, and I don't mind if I do.' Since Proust here spelled her name wrongly, he can only have met her recently; but soon

he was addressing her as *Chère amie*, which before long became
Ma petite Louisa. Next month she was on holiday at Blois: 'how
I should like to compare the charming embroidery of one of those
blue or pink gowns that suit you so well with the stone lace-
work of the castle!' She must not think he is making love to her;
he knows that if he dared to try, she would only 'send me about
my business'; and besides, he would 'rather die than raise my
eyes to the adored beloved of a friend whose exquisite and noble
heart makes him dearer to me every day'. Nevertheless, he signs
his letter 'with something which would give me intoxicating
pleasure if it were to happen otherwise than by letter, my dear
Louisa—a tender kiss!' His wish was to come true a year later;
meanwhile, 'if Albu is with you, you might ask him to stop
calling me Proust!'

A few days before Antoine Bibesco's return to Paris in the
second week of March Proust met the Princesse de Polignac,
whom he had not seen since August 1901, at Princesse Hélène de
Chimay's. He was pained to learn that she had just completed a
French rendering of Thoreau's *Walden*,[1] which he and Antoine
had planned to translate together in the early days of their
friendship: 'it took me back to the delicious time of our meeting,'
he told Antoine, 'and to hopes which since then have not entirely
been realised'. The delivery of the manuscript of *La Bible
d'Amiens* to the *Mercure de France*, which owing to Robert's
wedding had already been postponed from 1 February to 1
March, probably took place about this time. To greet Antoine's
return Proust had introduced him in an article on the salon of
Mme Greffulhe intended for the Paris edition of the *New York
Herald*, but transferred on Calmette's request to *Le Figaro*. In
an interview at the *Figaro* offices on 15 April Calmette persuaded
him, 'for reasons I cannot fathom', to postpone the article for a
fortnight, and in the end never printed it—most deplorably, for
all too little is known of Proust as Comtesse Greffulhe's guest.
He asked instead for an essay, which Proust had already finished,
on Mme Lemaire's salon; and Proust insisted on transferring to
this the paragraph about Antoine, 'although Ettemlac and
Enadrac [Calmette and Cardane] each separately begged me to do
nothing of the kind, because the Mme Greffuhle article was

[1] Extracts from it appeared in the *Renaissance Latine* of 15 January 1904
over the Princesse's maiden name, W. Singer.

exquisite just as it was'. So on 11 May Antoine had the pleasure of seeing himself in the morning's *Figaro* 'interrogated on the Macedonian question', amid Mme Lemaire's lilacs, by the eminent politician Paul Deschanel. 'Everyone who says "Prince" to this young diplomat with a great future feels like a character in Racine, so inevitably does his mythological appearance remind them of Achilles or Theseus. M. Mézières, who is talking to him now, looks like a high priest asking Apollo to deliver an oracle.... The prince's words, like the bees of Hymettus, are swift on the wing and laden with delicious honey, but do not lack, for all that, a certain sting!' At first, in the Mme Greffuhle article, Proust had made Antoine talk not to Deschanel but to Paul Hervieu, who could not be portrayed in Mme Lemaire's drawing-room because he had quarrelled with the hostess. To make up for this broken promise Proust took Hervieu to the second night of the Caillavet and Flers comedy *Le Sire de Vergy* at the Variétés on 16 April, where in his enthusiasm at his old friends' success he 'narrowly missed blacking Hervieu's eye three times over with my clapping hands'.

Since his outrush of sympathy in the previous autumn Proust's ardour for Antoine had perceptibly cooled; he now pointedly began his letters '*Mon cher Antoine*' instead of '*Mon petit Antoine*'. Antoine was again, or still, in love with an actress; Proust was making himself unhappy over Guiche and the amiable but unforthcoming Albufera. Their friendship had gone full circle and returned to its starting-point; yet, like two former lovers tormenting one another with a meaningless renewal of coquetry, they could not resist beginning again. This time Antoine was the instigator; with his love of mystification and playing with fire, he insisted on a pact that each should tell the other his inmost secrets, and in particular should report any scandal he might hear about his friend. It seemed to each, naturally, that he gave away far too much in return for far too little: 'I've made a thousand revelations to you, and you not the least one to me,' complained Proust. Nevertheless, in his capacity as the perfect friend, Antoine had betrayed at least two sufficiently dangerous secrets. Porto-Riche, he confided, had said to him: "I shouldn't see quite so much of Proust, if I were you, it will only give you a bad reputation." And Léon Daudet had declared: "I can tell you, as a doctor, that Marcel Proust's ill-health is due to

taking morphine.''[1] Soon Proust was racked with misgivings: 'I
see before me the dead, reproachful face of what might have been
but is not,' he wrote, remembering the words of Rossetti's sonnet
written ten years before by Edgar Aubert on the back of his
photograph, 'I mean, of the better person I might have been, if
to satisfy your curiosity at all costs I hadn't sold what no one
ought ever to have bought, and in fact the Devil alone can buy!'
The first move to break the bargain came from him: 'if you agree,
shall we renounce this cruel and impossible pact, which has
already made me so miserable?' But the habit had become too
strong—'the habit of not living for myself alone, of extending
the horizon of my life past the furthest frontiers of another
person, of allowing the stream of my existence to overflow into
this indiscernible prolongation of myself with all the gold and
mud it carried with it day by day, all the sights it had surprised
and reflected, the secrets that had been dropped in its waters'.
But now—he continued his river-metaphor—'just as a river cut
off by a high, impenetrable dike turns its course and fertilises
other lands, so I've been forced to pour into another confidant
what you refuse to accept from me, and to receive from him the
confidences which have become indispensable to me since you
gave me the habit of making them. Let's say no more—what I've
just written makes me blush for shame.' This letter, which marks
the end of the phase, can be dated to the first week in May 1903;
the new friend may be either Albufera or Guiche, or even,
already, 'Loche' Radziwill. But Proust's sufferings during these
two months need not be taken too tragically: in the whole series

---

[1] Léon Daudet had in fact taken his doctor's degree in the late 1880s, but
turned to writing without going into practice. His revelation was no doubt
made with the best intentions, from friendly concern, and without malice or
even untruth; for (a) the dangers of morphine were little understood at that
time. It was prescribed for asthma and other nervous ailments, and to take it
was thought at most an imprudence, certainly not a vice, unless it was taken
for mere pleasure; (b) Daudet of all people was particularly exercised about
the use of morphine, and had written a propaganda novel, *La Lutte*, against
the drug and doctors who prescribed it; (c) Proust undoubtedly took
morphine occasionally at this time, with his parents' knowledge, but disliked
it and never acquired the habit. (Cf. *Mme Proust*, 134 [20 Sept. 1899—but
this is only morphine ointment for his wrist at Évian]; *ibid.*, 190 [15 Aug.
1902—'Dr Vaquez told me not to let myself be carried away by morphine
(he needn't worry!) or alcohol, which he considers equally detrimental in
all forms'].)

of eight letters of pain and alarm there is audible the note of sentimental enjoyment which the French call *marivaudage*, and Proust's friends called Proustification.

During this spring Proust seems to have resumed his trips by motor-car. He asked his mother to invite Robert Proust to lend his own car, promising to have it driven 'by a chauffeur from any firm he cares to name and feels he can trust', or by Albufera, 'who has driven all round France, Belgium, Germany and Switzerland'. It is not impossible that the visit to Saint-Leu-d'Esserent and Senlis took place at this time, rather than on the way to Laon and Coucy on 28 March 1902.[1]

On 9 June the ineffable Mme Lemaire gave a fancy-dress ball on the theme 'Athens in the time of Pericles'. 'Banquet, procession, dancing, *costume strictly Classical Greek*,' enjoined the invitation cards. Montesquiou, a little confused in his chronology, had arranged to come as the poet Anacreon in a purple robe, crowned with ivy, waving a golden lyre, and pelted with roses by a band of youthful disciples in very short white tunics. Could he have had a secret warning that his reception would be less serious than this almost sacred role demanded? He had shown less diffidence at her last ball, when as Haroun al Raschid, in a turban covered with turquoises borrowed from Sarah Bernhardt, he had gone the round of the rival salons before arriving, remarking to every hostess: "Your guests seem unusually ugly this evening!"; but now, purely and simply, he failed to show up. The agonised Empress of Roses sent Proust to telephone the aggrieved Count Robert, once, twice and thrice; but the line was dead. While he was behind the scenes Marie Nordlinger, Reynaldo Hahn and Coco de Madrazo had arrived, flinging themselves into the ball and calling "Have you seen Marcel yet?" every time their paths crossed. Suddenly, as Mlle Nordlinger danced past an alcove, a sepulchral voice exclaimed "Dieu, que vous êtes belle!"; and there, dressed not in 'strictly classical costume' but in white tie, tails and his new furlined overcoat, stood an embarrassed Marcel.

---

[1] Proust mentions Senlis in the letter to Antoine Bibesco quoted above (*Bibesco*, p. 129), and Saint-Leu in the quarrel with Antoine a month or two later (*Mme Proust*, 215), though in such a way as to leave it uncertain whether the visits were recent or a year old. The Laon and Coucy trip, at least, can only have been on Good Friday 1902, because in 1903 Fénelon was in Constantinople.

The Athenian maiden good-naturedly dismissed her partner to sit out with her utterly un-Greek friend; and as was his habit when overcome by the charm of a girl companion, he recited to her the whole of *La Maison du Berger*.

The return of Proust's hay-fever that summer brought a renewal of Mme Proust's indulgence and of the affection which, said her son, 'the contemptuous irony of your many harsh words in these last years had gone far to discourage me from cultivating'. 'It's a long time since I last thought of you with such a paroxysm of effusion,' he wrote one night, when he came home late and longed as of old, but forbore, to enter her room and kiss her in her sleep. One evening in late June, when he was already expecting the first proofs of *La Bible d'Amiens*, she magnanimously gave a little dinner for Antoine Bibesco. Proust primed his friend with a full list of the things he must not say: "No jokes about tipping, for one thing, and none of your stupid questions to Papa!" But the tact he demanded was too one-sided: in the middle of dinner he could not resist telling the dreadful story of Antoine singing '*En revenant de la revue*', with appropriate dance-steps, at Saint-Leu-d'Esserent; and Antoine, in return, began to say everything he had been begged not to say. "Don't you think, sir, that if Marcel wrapped up less? . . ." he began insinuatingly. Dr Proust was in full agreement, but it was not a subject he cared to discuss. Amid an electric silence the relentless Antoine proceeded with an anecdote of their latest night out: "and before I could stop him, Marcel tipped the waiter sixty francs!!" The storm broke; Dr Proust burst into rage, the dinner was spoiled, Marcel wept. Even Antoine was dismayed at the effect of his little revenge; but, as Proust truly told him, "my family affections are dearer to me than the affection of my friends, and I can't help mistrusting anyone who attacks me through them, just as I would someone who, in spite of a noble heart and other remarkable qualities, was liable at times under the influence of drink or for some similar reason to stick a knife into me". He swore never to forgive Antoine, and perhaps he never did. The factitious renewal of their secret game was ended; the bewitching phantom of the ideal friend had moved to other faces, and would never more wear Antoine Bibesco's.

Early in July Bertrand de Fénelon visited Paris for a month's leave. The nightly symposium of the friends at Weber's or

Larue's was now a broken habit, buried for ever in the past by the winter's absence of Antoine and Fénelon. Instead, with Lauris, Guiche, Albu, Gabriel de La Rochefoucauld and Loche Radziwill, they met every evening in Proust's bedroom for an agape of conversation, refreshed by iced cider or the famous beer from Pousset's tavern of which Proust was so fond. Élisabeth de Clermont-Tonnerre was amused and interested on hearing, no doubt from her half-brother Guiche, of these goings-on. She wrote inviting Proust to dinner. But he replied with more annoyance than gratification: 'I'm rather sad to find that someone has unveiled to you the absurd arrangements, the trivial mystery of my existence. I don't know whether it was done maliciously or not; in any case, whether intentionally or otherwise, this "someone" has succeeded in making me ridiculous in your eyes. Your documentation is admirable: everything, the words "nocturnal conversations", the very names of my principal visitors, even the vulgar but undeniable cider, proves the reliability of your information.' He accepted the young marquise's invitation so conditionally that nothing came of it, and their inevitable friendship was delayed for two years.

On 29 July the discussion in Proust's room was heated. For the first time since the Affair he found himself feeling passionately about politics. In June 1902 the Dreyfusist prime minister Waldeck-Rousseau had resigned, after being returned to office with a majority of violent anti-clericals who were too far to his left to accept his own more moderate policies. The new minister, Émile Combes, a militant atheist, who had studied for the priesthood in his youth and was nicknamed the 'Little Father', set himself to destroy the religious orders by a programme of forcible expulsion and confiscation. On that evening the diehard Albufera, devoted to the Church and still convinced of Dreyfus's guilt, was set upon by the progressive sceptics Fénelon and Lauris. "I can't bear the sight of priests reading the *Libre Parole*," declared Lauris; and Fénelon remarked with a snigger: "It's nice to see all these nuns obliged to take a trip for once in their lives!" Proust, when he tried to find common ground for both parties, was trampled in the struggle; and Lauris even accused him of insincerity for praising the conservative Denis Cochin's speeches against the Combes Laws in the Chamber. His friends went home still furious; but late that night Proust made his profession of

faith in a letter to Lauris. Over the ruins of the Church he saw
Saint-Jacques at Illiers; the exiled priests took on the face of the
good Canon Marquis; and the argument about politics led him
back to his childhood at Illiers, further than he had ever yet
penetrated into Time Lost.

Two days before, on 27 July, Dr Proust had visited Illiers, for
what was destined to be the last time, to preside over the prize-
giving at the boys' school. But Canon Marquis was absent: since
the anti-clerical laws of Jules Ferry in 1882 he had never been
invited, and Proust's uncle Jules Amiot, now deputy mayor and
a reader of both the priest-baiting *L'Intransigeant* and the anti-
Semitic *Libre Parole*, refused even to speak to the constant
visitor of his dead wife. Lauris and Fénelon supported the
expulsion of the religious orders in the name of French unity; but
would it forward unity if the Canon was exiled and Saint-Jacques
secularised? 'I remember that little town crouching to the earth,'
he wrote to Lauris, 'that avaricious earth, mother of avarice,
where the only impulse towards the sky—often dappled with
clouds, but often, too, of a heavenly blue, transfigured every
evening in the sunsets of the Beauce—is the exquisite spire of
the church; I remember the priest who taught me Latin and the
names of the flowers in his garden; and I think it unjust that he
should not be invited on prize-day as representing in the town
something harder to define than the social functions symbolised
by the chemist, the retired tax-collector, or the optician, yet none
the less worthy of respect—were it only for the intelligent, de-
materialised spire of his church, which points to the sunset, melts
so lovingly into the pink clouds, and strikes a stranger arriving
in the village as having a nobler air, more disinterestedness, more
intelligence and more love than other buildings,'—such as the
new, secular school—'however recent the laws that have erected
them . . . Supposing the religious orders were expelled, and the
fire of Catholicism quenched in France (if it could be quenched,
whereas in fact it is not by legislation that ideas and faiths perish,
but when the truth or social utility they possessed is corrupted
or diminished), then our clericalist unbelievers would only be
more violently anti-Semitic, anti-Dreyfusard, anti-liberal than
ever; they would be no fewer in number, but a hundred times
worse . . . You can't kill the Christian spirit by closing Christian
schools, and if it is destined to die, it will die even under a

theocracy.' He ended with a warning which history was to justify: 'at the present time the socialists commit the same error by being anti-clerical as the clericals in 1897 by being anti-Dreyfusard. They expiate their fault to-day; but we shall expiate ours to-morrow.' Lauris acknowledged long afterwards that Proust was right; and meanwhile Albufera, astonished that a Dreyfusard could be so fair-minded as to defend the Church in a time of persecution, asked him 'to explain the Affair to me so that I can share your conviction'. 'Only I haven't the heart to,' Proust told Lauris, 'and my one regret in being a Dreyfusard is that it saddens the loyal and noble Albufera.' But the chief consequence of that evening's argument was that Proust had been inspired, in his evocation of the church of Saint-Jacques, to see further into the meaning of Illiers than he could in *Jean Santeuil*. Illiers was now on the verge of becoming Combray, which, 'seen from the railway when we arrived there in the week before Easter, was nothing but a church epitomising the town'.

Early in August Dr and Mme Proust left for their last holiday together. After a few days at St Moritz, a week at Interlaken and a short stay at Ouchy, they arrived by the lake steamer on 18 August at Évian, where Dr Proust was to take a course of treatment. As in any other year the Hellbronners, Weisweillers and Duplays, the barrister Maître Ployel and the judge M. Gougeon were there. But the Splendide Hôtel was so appallingly noisy that Mme Proust recommended her son to go instead to Cabourg, 'because you used to find it suited your health so well'—advice which he only took, like a counsel from beyond the grave, four years later.

Meanwhile Proust was ill with asthma. In an interval between his attacks he dined with Antoine and his friends at Armenonville in the Bois de Boulogne, where Odette, to Swann's despair, listened with the little clan to the Vinteuil Sonata in the moonlight, and where Proust himself nine years before had invited Montesquiou and Delafosse in vain. The painter Vuillard was present and made a sketch of the gathering, 'a unique point of intersection between his admirable talent, which has so often kindled my memory, and one of the most delightful and perfect hours of my life,' as Proust wrote a year later when he asked to be allowed to buy the sketch—where is it now? Fénelon, too, fell ill in the last week of his leave, and was visited daily by Proust, himself choking with asthma and shivering with a high fever. He negotiated busily to prevent a duel between Jacques Bizet and a friend of Antoine and Bertrand, the playwright André Picard, but only at the expense of consenting to be Picard's second, which put him in the bad books of Bizet and the Straus's. Then, on 8 August, after a last supper with the departing and convalescent diplomat, he and Antoine put Bertrand into his train, 'looking as frisky as could be'. Antoine himself left a few days later for a post at the Roumanian Embassy in London, after a new quarrel which they had no time to make up. Proust had recently received his proofs from the *Mercure de France*, made a number of corrections suggested by Marie Nordlinger, and mislaid the whole batch: 'my publisher is annoyed,' he told her, 'and I am not sure whether he will want to publish the work of so un-business-like and boring a translator'. For a time he still hesitated where to go for his holiday. Should he join Lauris in Brittany, and see once more the Pointe du Raz?—'historically, geographically and literally, you know, it's Finisterre, the end of the world, a giant granite cliff round which the sea rages eternally, towering over the Bay of Ghosts, a place of funereal and illustrious malediction!' Or might he visit Mlle Nordlinger in the other half of Balbec, at Varangeville near Dieppe, 'by the exquisite little graveyard, whose quietness is a prelude to the unending silence enjoyed by its dead, which our living ears cannot detect, for they are distracted by this merely relative silence, deepened though it may be by the regular and repeated advance of the waves far below'? Suddenly, in the small hours of a morning in early September, after a farewell dinner with Lauris, Albufera and Louisa de Mornand, he set out by a strangely devious route for Évian.

Feverish, asthmatic and exalted by his solitary journey, he was unable to sleep in the train as it ran in the moonlight past Melun, the Forest of Fontainebleau and Sens. Along the valley of the Yonne towards Auxerre the line threaded between steep, vine-clad hills and little towns, those to the east still silvery-black in the moonlight, those to the west already rose-pink in the rising sun. 'I was seized with a mad desire to ravish little sleeping towns—you notice I say *villes*, not *filles*, towns, not little sleeping girls,' he wrote to Lauris, using the sexual imagery which he so often associated with travel. He transferred this magical ride through hills lit simultaneously by moon and sun to the Narrator's night-journey with his grandmother to Balbec. At eleven in the morning he arrived at Avallon and took a carriage to Vézelay—'a prodigious place in the middle of a kind of Switzerland, solitary on the top of a mountain which dominates the surrounding hills, visible for miles around in a landscape of the most extraordinary harmony; the church is enormous, more like a Turkish bath than Notre-Dame, built in alternating black and white stone, a delicious Christian mosque'. Here at Vézelay, with its union of Norman gothic and almost oriental romanesque, there is something of the 'Persian' church of Balbec. He returned to Avallon for the night, but could not sleep for fever. He walked the streets until it was time for the six a.m. train to Dijon, where he saw in the Hôtel de Ville, once the palace of the Dukes of Burgundy and now the Museum, the polychrome tombs of John the Fearless and Philip the Bold: he already knew the casts of these monuments at the Trocadéro, but 'you can't get any idea of them from the models, because the real thing is painted in so many colours'. Although he had now spent two days and nights without sleep, he continued 'my journey into death; at the stations people asked if they could get me anything, and when I saw my face in a mirror I didn't recognise it'. At dinner-time Maurice Duplay saw his spectral figure tottering from the hotel omnibus at Évian, amid the lightly-clad holiday makers, muffled in his fur-lined winter overcoat.

After a few days in bed Proust was so fully restored that, as he wrote with pride to Lauris and Robert de Billy, 'I'm up every day by two in the afternoon!' He was anxious for Lauris, who was in love with a married woman, and for Fénelon, now back in Constantinople, to whom the Bulgarian rebellion then raging in Macedonia was dangerously near. Mme de Noailles had already left Amphion; but he joined Albufera and Louisa de Mornand at Chamonix for a day's excursion on mule-back to Montanvert, where 'the agile Louisa displayed all her graces on the Mer de Glace'. He thought of the plan he had been discussing with his friends, to form a lay monastery for reading, writing and meditation: an echo of his dream ten years before, in the summer of Willie Heath, of 'living in a chosen circle of noble-minded men and women, far from the arrows of stupidity, vice and malice'. 'If only you could be the admirable abbess, habited all in white!' he wrote to Mme de Noailles; and to Lauris: 'don't tell a soul, because it wouldn't be a monastery if everybody came!' But Proust was destined, though not yet, for a different and even stranger form of solitude. At the end of September, however, on his way home, he visited a rather similar establishment, the fifteenth-century hospital at Beaune, with its nun nurses, all chosen from rich families, wearing their white summer habits and looking like his vision of Mme de Noailles as abbess. He thought of having himself admitted as an emergency case: had not Viollet le Duc said, 'the hospital at Beaune is so beautiful that it makes the tourist long to fall ill there'?; and yet, he wrote to Marie Nordlinger, 'if Viollet le Duc had been in my condition he wouldn't have spoken so lightly'. He dragged himself to Paris and was ill for a month, paying for each evening out with several evenings in bed.

The energetic and distinguished life of Dr Proust was now near its close. It was thirty-three years since the morning in August 1870, a few days before the Battle of Sedan and his marriage to Jeanne Weil, when he received from the Empress Eugénie the cross of chevalier of the Legion of Honour. He had risen through the rank of officer to that of commander; and many years later, when Proust himself received the cross, he remembered his awe as a boy when, on gala evenings, he watched his father putting on the red cravat of his decoration. In 1879 Dr Proust was elected to the seat in the Academy of Medicine left vacant by the death of his master Ambroise Tardieu; in 1884 he succeeded to the post of Fauvel, inventor of the *cordon sanitaire*, as Inspector-General of Sanitary Services; and in 1885 he became Professor of Hygiene in the Faculty of Medicine. Throughout his life he continued his intense activity as a teacher, a writer on medicine,[1] and a practising physician. Marcel was accustomed to invite his friends to consult his father on their ailments: 'would you like Papa to come and see you?' he asked Antoine Bibesco on the occasion of an indisposition in this same summer of 1903. Anatole France, however (perhaps when afflicted with the cyst

[1] His bibliography includes thirty-four items, covering a wide range of interests. Besides international hygiene he wrote on tuberculosis, rabies, deficiency diseases, paralysis, aphasia, various nervous and brain maladies, and occupational ailments, including (as his son must have noticed with a wry smile) 'saturnism', not in the sense familiar to Marcel and the Bibescos but meaning lead-poisoning.

for which he was operated on by Dr Pozzi in September 1899),
was wary: "My dear young friend," he said, "I should never dare
to consult your father; I'm not important enough for him; the
only patients he takes on nowadays are *river-basins*!" But the
sublime task to which Dr Proust had devoted his life was the
exclusion of cholera from the frontiers of Europe. He was the
leading spirit in a series of international conferences for the im-
position, particularly at Suez, of the *cordon sanitaire*; and it must
sadly be confessed that his chief opponent, partly for reasons of
commercial convenience, partly from well-founded suspicion of
French ambitions in Egypt, was the formidable power of
England. At the Rome Sanitary Conference in 1885, thanks to
England, little was accomplished; but at Venice in 1892 and
Dresden in 1893 Dr Proust secured unanimous agreement of the
powers, with the sole exception of England; and in this very year
1903 his life-work was crowned by the adhesion of that refractory
nation and the formation of the International Office of Public
Hygiene in Paris. "In those days," Casimir-Périer, then Minister
of Foreign Affairs, had said in 1894, "the politicians had to
practice a little medicine, and the doctors had to be politicians";
and everyone knew that he was alluding to Dr Proust and M.
Barrère. Western civilisation owes a debt to Proust's father not
only for producing one of its greatest novelists, but for the major
part he played in the banishment of cholera from Europe.

His political colleague during those stirring years was Camille
Barrère, afterwards ambassador at the Quirinal from 1897 to
1925, with his long face, aggressive oblong beard, and keen
Norpois eyes. When *A l'Ombre des Jeunes Filles en Fleurs* was
published in 1919 M. Barrère suspected, with extreme indignation,
that M. de Norpois was meant for himself; 'simply because he
used to dine with us every week when I was a child,' said Proust
mendaciously, 'whereas M. de Norpois is a representative of a
diplomatic type which is the exact opposite of M. Barrère, though
no less utterly detestable!' But Proust also met other originals of
M. de Norpois through his father. Gabriel Hanotaux, Foreign
Minister from 1894 to 1898, had shown in Proust's student days
M. de Norpois's infuriating confidence in the practicability of
combining a diplomatic with a literary career. M. Hanotaux had
every reason to think so; for he became a member of the Académie
Française on 2 April 1897, wrote voluminously and boringly,

though not without talent, on historical subjects, and produced
newspaper articles on foreign affairs under the pseudonym
'Testis'.[1] Armand Nisard, ambassador at the Vatican from 1898
to 1904, had at least two features of M. de Norpois: he was Marie
de Benardaky's uncle by marriage, so that Proust might well
have been on the point of kissing his hand in gratitude for his
promise to put in a word for him with Marie's parents[2]; and he
was felt to have shown lack of zeal in supporting Dr Proust's
candidature for the Academy of Moral Sciences.[3]

   Dr Proust's dining-room was also an ideally situated strategic
point for observing the natural history of doctors, and in particular the originals of Cottard, Du Boulbon, Dieulafoy and
Professor E. Dr Eugène-Louis Doyen (1859-1916), a surgeon of
sensationally original technique, with greying blond hair,
astonished blue eyes and an athletic figure, was a model for many
qualities of Cottard: his icy brutality, naïveté, inspired tactless-
ness, fury when contradicted by a patient, and total, incurable
ignorance in cultural and social matters. "With all her gifts," he
flabbergasted Proust by announcing, "Mme Greffuhle hasn't
managed to make her salon anything like as brilliant as Mme de
Caillavet's!" Dr Doyen regarded himself as Potain's superior—
"Potain's an old fool," he would say—an opinion shared by Mme
Verdurin.[4] The dates of his life fit those of Dr Cottard, who is
young in the 1880s and dies during the war. Professor Guyon,
the urologist and teacher of Robert Proust, was a tall, thin man
with white whiskers, from whose inexhaustible puns and clichés
Proust collected a store of hints for Cottard; and Auguste Broca
was another surgeon who, like Cottard, kept his students in fits
of laughter with puns, chestnuts and oaths. As we have seen,
Cottard, as a foundation-member of Mme Verdurin's 'little

   [1] M. de Norpois at Venice, discussing with Prince Foggi the question of a
successor to the retiring Italian prime minister, remarks: "And has no one
pronounced the name of M. Giolitti?"—'words which supplied the chancel-
leries of Europe with food for conversation throughout the next twenty
years, and when at last forgotten were exhumed by persons signing themselves "One who Knows", "Testis", or "Machiavelli"' (III, 635). Proust is
here at his usual trick of juxtaposing one of his characters with the name of
an original of the character; and the passage is immediately followed (III,
637) by a satirical account of the emotions on this occasion of yet another
model for M. de Norpois, M. Barrère himself.
   [2] Cf. I, 477   [3] Cf. II, 225-6   [4] I, 188

nucleus' and an unfaithful husband, was Dr Pozzi at Mme Aubernon's; his pince-nez and involuntary wink were those of Proust's professor, Albert Vandal; but his name was taken from Dr Proust's fellow-student Cotard and Dr Cottet at Évian. The model for Dr du Boulbon was the favourite physician of the Faubourg Saint-Germain, Dr Le Reboulet; but a guest of Dr Proust, the warty-faced Dr Laboulbène, contributed to his name. Dr Dieulafoy, with his 'charmingly supple figure and face too handsome in itself', who is sent for simply to certify the grand-mother's last agony and, says the Narrator at the time of writing, 'is now no longer with us',[1] was a real person, Professor Georges Dieulafoy (1839-1911). He was Princesse Mathilde's doctor and guest, and Proust's friend Gabriel Astruc took him, no doubt with some good reason, for an original of Cottard. The wife of his brother Marcel, Mme Jane Dieulafoy, was a strange, mannish, emancipated little woman, who wore trousers and smoked cigars, but was much in demand by hostesses in her capacity as an eminent archaeologist and the excavator of Darius's palace at Susa.[2] Once, when she called at the *Revue de Paris* offices, the commissionaire announced her to Ganderax: "there's a gentleman downstairs who says he's a lady!"; and at a society dinner one evening, when she insisted on joining the men in the smoking-room, General de Galliffet took her by the arm and said: "Come along, my dear feller, let's go and have a p—s." Professor E., who automatically quotes poetry before examining the Narrator's grandmother, is Dr Édouard Brissaud, author of *Hygiene for Asthmatics*, 'our dear *médecin malgré lui*, on whom one almost has to use physical force to get him to talk medicine,' wrote Proust after consulting him in 1905.[3] Another friend of the Proust family and guest of Mme Aubernon was Dr Albert Robin, who told Proust: "I might be able to get rid of your asthma, but I wouldn't advise it; in your case it acts as an outlet, and saves you from having other

---

[1] II, 343

[2] 'M. Nissim Bernard's face,' remarks the Narrator on the occasion of his dinner with Bloch's family at Balbec, 'seemed to have been brought back from Darius's palace and restored by Mme Dieulafoy' (I, 774).

[3] Proust told Lucien Daudet in 1921 that there was 'something of Brissaud's type of doctor, more a sceptic and a clever talker than a clinician, in Du Boulbon'. But it was his habit not only to create a single character from several originals, but to distribute elements of a single real person over several characters.

diseases." He was renowned for the mysterious eccentricity of
his prescriptions: for example, to an old lady in whom he wished
to inculcate a certain complicated exercise of muscles and lungs,
he declared: "you must take off all your clothes, and then hop
round a table six feet in circumference, eating an artichoke one
leaf at a time"—'I've exaggerated this only very slightly,' remarks
Léon Daudet, who tells the story. Dr Robin was infatuated with
Liane de Pougy, who was jealous of his family and forbade him
to use the words 'my wife', 'my son'. "What must I say, then?"
"Say 'the monster', and 'the little monster'!" But the form in
which Proust knew this story was very different, whether because
it had been misreported to him, or because it had undergone a
significant transformation in his unconscious: he mistakenly
believed that Dr Robin called his child 'the little monster' not in
jest but in sadistic delight, 'because he couldn't obtain full sexual
pleasure in any other way'; and he told Louis de Robert that he
had used Dr Robin's example, among others, for the scene at
Montjouvain in which Mlle Vinteuil induces her friend to call her
dead father 'that old monkey'.[1] But the mingled admiration and
contempt with which Proust treats the medical profession in *A
la Recherche* is doubtless in part a reflection of his own feelings
towards his father.

Time had played its old, merciless trick on Dr Proust. He was
no longer the handsome, black-bearded man of forty, running in
the early mornings of the 1870s along the Rue La Fontaine to
catch the Auteuil-Madeleine omnibus, or meeting the young
Mme Proust with the infant Marcel and Robert in Louis Weil's
carriage outside the Hôtel-Dieu at the day's end; no longer even
the keen-eyed, pursed-lipped, Holbeinesque figure of Lecomte
du Nouy's portrait in 1885. A photograph of the Doctor outside
St Mark's at Venice, with the pigeons of the Piazza feeding at
his feet, perching in his hands, alighting on his shoulder, or
another in which he stands, morning-paper in hand, with the
fiercely-moustached Robert on the balcony of 45 Rue de
Courcelles, show a fading old gentleman with a short round
grey beard, looking rather like Edward the Seventh. He had
grown corpulent, like his wife; his voice was deep, but slightly
nasal; his habit of wearing his pince-nez far down his nose forced
him to tilt his head far back; his face wore a perspicacious,

[1] I, 162

indulgent smile, an expression of approaching repose. Contrary
to usual report, Marcel had only the sharp-edged, delicately
curved Jewish nose and swimming dark eyes of his mother: the
mould of his face, especially the narrow, thick-lipped mouth, was
startlingly like his father's.

Despite his occasional outbursts of rage, or sudden, arbitrary
vetoes ('my father had a way of refusing to let me do things which
were clearly allowed in the more liberal charters granted me by
my mother and grandmother, because he was careless of
"principles", and had no idea of "international law",' says the
Narrator), Dr Proust had been a touchingly indulgent parent,
more sensibly and equably so than Mme Proust. From sheer
kindness and resignation he had allowed his bewildering son to
lead the life he wished; he never withheld the money for his
clothes, orchids, presents, 'little dinners' of fifteen persons,
Ruskin pilgrimages, or twelve-hour cab-hires. Even the enormous
bills of several hundred francs a month for cotton-wool, and
medicaments for asthma, insomnia, rheumatisms and indiges-
tions, although these hurt his professional conscience as well as
his pocket, were paid with a sigh. He could understand neither
Marcel's passion for society, nor society's passion for Marcel. "Is
he really so charming? Why is he invited out so often?" he asked
one of his son's noble hostesses; but there was no satisfactory
answer. Yet he took pride in Marcel's literary career, such as it
was, and consoled himself for his own failure to enter the
Academy of Moral Sciences with the generous prophecy: "Marcel
will belong to the Académie Française!"

On at least one occasion he made use of Marcel's talent. In his
speech on 7 June 1903 at the unveiling of the monument to
Pasteur at Chartres he compared the discoverer of the bacterial
origin of disease to one of the sculptures in the cathedral. "In
the porch of Chartres you will see a figure whose name is Magas,
the magician of the Encyclopaedia of Chartres. Magas symbolises
alchemy: he is the master of the science which summons from the
domain of mystery so many extraordinary dreams, and trans-
plants them into the real world we know." His audience must
have been astonished by Dr Proust's knowledge of iconography;
but we can hardly doubt that these Ruskinian words were written
for him by his son. Dr Proust himself, however, may be given sole
credit for the moving and eminently Proustian opening of his

speech at the Illiers prize-giving on 27 July. "The emotion I feel on coming to your school sixty years after is something you will perhaps fail to understand," he said, "not because at fifteen one is less intelligent or comprehending than at my age; on the contrary I think one is able to understand a great deal more in boyhood. But there is one thing which is a closed book to the young, or which they can only guess at by a kind of presentiment, and that is the poetry and melancholy of memory." Perhaps father and son were not so different as they believed. Each disappointed his father, and achieved fame long after his father's death; each gave his life for a great aim, and died in the hour of its accomplishment.

On Sunday, 22 November, Dr Proust and Marcel had their last quarrel. 'We had an argument about politics,' Proust told Mme de Noailles a week later, 'and I said things I ought not to have said.[1] I feel as though I'd been hard on someone who could no longer defend himself. I don't know what I wouldn't give to have been more gentle and affectionate that evening. Papa's character was so much nobler than mine. I never stop complaining; but when Papa was ill his only thought was to keep us from knowing it.' And indeed, Dr Proust's last recorded words, probably spoken to Robert Proust a few weeks before, were these: "I've had a happy life. My only wish now is to leave it quietly and without pain."

On Monday, 23 November, Dr Proust took part, with his accustomed energy and lucidity, in a meeting of the Permanent Commission on Tuberculosis. In the afternoon he saw his patients and gave his usual consultations. Next day he called on Robert Proust at his new home, 136 Boulevard Saint-Germain, on his way to preside over an examination at the Faculty of Medicine; and Robert, alarmed at his father's look of harassed exhaustion, insisted on accompanying him to the nearby École de Médecine. Robert, who no doubt would have preferred to be with his pregnant wife, went to his laboratory; but a few minutes later he was summoned by an anxious attendant to the cloakroom, where his father was locked in a water-closet and could

[1] As father and son were in agreement on the injustice of the Combes Laws, and Marcel had moved well to the right of his position during the Affair, it is difficult to see what they can have found to argue about. Perhaps Dr Proust said something like: "Now you see what Dreyfusism leads to!"

not be made to reply. They broke the door in, and found the professor huddled on the floor, paralysed, unconscious and speechless. He was carried on a stretcher to 45 Rue de Courcelles. Marcel, of course, was still asleep; he remembered ever afterwards how his mother tapped on his bedroom door to say: "Forgive me for waking you, my dear, but your father has been taken rather ill at the École de Médecine."[1] Dr Proust died thirty-six hours later, early in the morning of Thursday, 26 November, without regaining consciousness. As she watched by his side, waiting for the end, Mme Proust wrote a journal, as she had done for her own father and mother, of her husband's illness. A few hours before, on the 25th, Robert's only child Suzy had been born.

Dr Proust's funeral procession to Saint-Philippe du Roule on the 28th was an imposing occasion. The mourners were led by Marcel and Robert, followed by the Council of the University and the entire Faculty and Academy of Medicine, the statesmen Méline, Fallières and Barthou, and other colleagues and friends of the doctor. Marcel's group was represented by Antoine Bibesco, Albufera, Baron Henri de Rothschild (who had helped to finance Le Banquet eleven years before) and Mathieu de Noailles. Marie Nordlinger was present, and remembered the frosty morning sunlight, and Marcel in full mourning at Robert's side, tottering with grief and fatigue. The farewell speech over Dr Proust's grave at Père La Chaise was delivered by Professor Debove, doyen of the Faculty of Medicine. "He was sceptic enough to be indulgent to people who left what we like to believe is the path of virtue, epicurean enough to enjoy life without taking the petty miseries of human existence too tragically, and stoic enough to face death without flinching," said Professor Debove rather finely.

Montesquiou, Mme de Noailles, her sister the Princesse de Chimay, Robert Dreyfus and many others wrote charming letters of sympathy. Proust noticed, without surprise, that his mother seemed her usual energetic self, apparently unchanged since the last day, only a week before, when her husband had still appeared strong and well. 'But I know the depth and violence and duration of the drama that is going on inside her,' he told

---

[1] Proust used the circumstances of his father's illness for the Narrator's grandmother's stroke in the public lavatory at the Champs-Élysées, and the words "Forgive me for waking you," for the Narrator's mother when she calls him (II, 335) to witness the grandmother's death-agony.

Mme de Noailles, 'and I can't help being afraid.' He had recently abandoned *La Bible d'Amiens*, perhaps from momentary boredom, or pique at Vallette's impatience, but more probably, as in the December before, to spite his parents. But his mother briskly intervened: "It was your father's one desire," she declared, "he waited from day to day to see it published"; and he wrote once more to Vallette, and resumed the endless task of imposing perfection on his proofs. For the last year or two Mme Proust had slept in a separate room; but she now moved to Dr Proust's bedroom, with its little cabinet from Indo-China and marquetry card-table and bureau, to spend every night with her dead husband for ever. Her time was short; she could not wait to keep, as she did for her parents according to Jewish custom, the 'year's end' of her loss. Every month, at first even every week, the three days of her husband's attack, death and burial were made sacred; and Marcel humoured her by observing them too, partly because it was a useful excuse when Montesquiou or others were pressing and he did not wish to go out.

'Life is beginning again,' he wrote to Mme de Noailles; but the life of every day had somehow become less real. The craving of his childhood, to enjoy his mother's love and be rid of his father, was ironically fulfilled when it was long outgrown. Her mourning presence was an embarrassment: she, not his father, was an unwanted ghost in the house.

The old man was gone; the blowing of his nose, the rustle of his *Journal des Débats* would be heard no more; and it seemed that an indispensable condition of life in the present had been removed. Dr Proust returned, not as a benign, grey-bearded old man, but as a black, ascending shadow on the now demolished staircase at Auteuil. "You can see for yourself the child's unhappy," he declared; "after all, we're not gaolers! You'd better stay with him for the rest of the night." Proust realised with vertigo that only his stricken, weakening mother remained to keep him from falling into the past. He stood at last on the edge of the abyss of Time Lost.

END OF VOLUME ONE

INDEXES

Two separate indexes are provided, the first of real persons and places, the second of fictitious characters and places in Proust's novel, A la Recherche du Temps Perdu. In order to facilitate the tracing of discussions in the text of Proust's models in real life, cross-references from each index to the other have been given, where applicable, in capitals and parentheses; but the reader should remember that these discussions are sometimes necessarily incomplete, and are subject to supplementation in the second and final volume.

I. PERSONS AND PLACES

Heredia, José Maria de, 97, 131, 133, 138, 140, 175, 208, 234
——, Hélène de, 140
——, Louise de, 140
——, Marie de, *see* Regnier
Hermant, Abel, 91, 101, 240, 244-5, 288, 290, 317
Hérold, Ferdinand, 140
Hervey de Saint-Denis, Marquis d', 159
——, Marquise d' (ORVILLERS, Princesse d'), 146, 159-60
Hervieu, Paul (SWANN), 75, 91, 104, 125, 220, 227-8, 289, 314, 319
Hesiod, 191
Hochon, Mme (VERDURIN), 195, 251
Holland, 204, 231, 306-7
Homer, 54-5
Honfleur, 117-18, 306
Housman, A. E., 285
Howland, Mme Meredith, 135, 139, 146, 212
Hugo, Georges, 133, 229
——, Victor, 133, 229
Humières, Vicomte Robert d', 275
Huysmans, Joris Karl, 102, 126, 131

Ibsen, Henrik, 81, 100
Illiers (COMBRAY), 1, 3, 7, 10, 13-39, 52, 191, 197, 282, 293, 300-1, 307, 324-5, 334
——, Basin d', 23, 155
——, Florent d', 21-3
——, Geoffroy d' (GILBERT THE BAD), 23-4
——, Miles d', 23
Indy, Vincent d' (VINTEUIL), 173
Intransigeant, L', 324
Isabella, Queen of Spain, 113
Izoulet-Loubatière, Jean, 183

James, Henry, 285
Jammes, Francis, 38
Janzé, Vicomtesse Alix de (ALIX), 158
Jaucourt, Marquise de, 216
Jaurès, Jean, 221, 229
Jean Santeuil, 3, 6, 7, 10-11, 38, 42, 45, 47, 49, 59, 62, 69, 73, 75, 79, 85, 88, 115, 118, 139, 165, 174-8, 181-5, 189, 193, 197-207, 215, 219-20, 225, 231, 239, 244-5, 250-6, 259, 277-8, 293, 299-301, 325
Joan, of Arc, 23, 42

Joinville d'Artois, Juliette (VINTEUIL, Mlle), 32-3
Journal, Le, 207, 209
—— *des Débats*, 197, 293, 336
Journées de Lecture, 36
Jouvenel, Baronne de, 104
Juigné, Marquis de, 156

Karageorgevitch, 86
Keyserling, Count Hermann, 161
Kipling, Rudyard, 275
Kolb, Philip, xv, 191
Krauss, Gabrielle, 108
Kreuznach, 180, 219, 251

Labiche, Eugène, 99
Labori, Fernand, 225, 232, 239
Laboulbène, Dr (DU BOULBON), 331
Laffitte, Charles, 148
La Fontaine, Jean de, 216
La Gandara, Antoine, 85, 129, 131, 220
Lagrenée, Marquis de, 290
La Jeunesse, Ernest, 213-14
Lamartine, Alphonse de, 44, 46, 158
Landau, Baron Horace de (BERNARD, Nissim), 116-17
Laon, 29, 302-3
Laons, 29, 302
Laparcerie, Cora, 237
Larcher, Mme, 19
——, P. L., xv
Larochefoucauld, acrobat, 127, 134
La Rochefoucauld, family, 125
——, Comte Aimery de (GUERMANTES, Prince de), 130, 153-4, 161, 294-5
——, Comtesse ——, 146, 154, 295
——, Vicomte Charles de, 86
——, Comte Gabriel de (SAINT-LOUP) 154, 166, 288, 294-5, 310, 323
——, Duc Sosthène de, 233
La Salle, Comte Louis de, 43, 75, 114, 117, 123, 135-6, 139, 199, 223, 243, 289-90
La Sizeranne, Robert de, 256-60, 267, 273, 276-7, 281, 283
La Tour, Quentin de, 91
La Trémoille, Duc Charles de, 160, 163
——, Duchesse ——, 160, 166
Lau, Marquis du, 93, 111, 150, 161, 187, 234, 249

II. CHARACTERS AND PLACES

ABOUT THE AUTHOR

GEORGE D. PAINTER was born in Birmingham, England and educated in Classics at Trinity College, Cambridge. From 1938 until his retirement in 1974 he was a curator at the British Museum in London. He is the author of *André Gide: A Critical Biography; William Caxton, A Biography;* a forthcoming three-volume biography of Chateaubriand; and numerous translations, including *Marcel Proust: Letters to His Mother.*